RIDER HAGGARD

His life and works

Rider Haggard in the garden at Ditchingham

*First published in the United States of America
in 1961 by Walker and Company, a division of
Publications Development Corporation.*

RIDER
HAGGARD
His life and work

MORTON N. COHEN

921

WALKER AND COMPANY

NEW YORK

To

P. P. R.

Acknowledgements

MANY persons have helped me in preparing this study of Rider Haggard. I owe an immense debt to Professor Susanne Howe Nobbe. Her lectures stimulated my interest in the nineteenth-century novel, and it was she who, in 1950, helped me embark on this work. Since then she has generously and graciously advised me through the successive stages of research and composition. I am extremely grateful to Professor Jerome Hamilton Buckley for offering me friendly encouragement and valuable criticism. His discerning comments have never failed to give me new insights. For helpful suggestions I should like to thank Professors Chilton Williamson and David A. Robertson, Jr., and for liberal aid and counsel, my colleague and friend, Professor Edgar Johnson. I have also learned much from Professor Bonamy Dobrée, who was a kind and gentle mentor during my year in England.

I am indebted to the United States Department of State and the United Kingdom Fulbright Commission for the opportunity to pursue my research, and I am particularly grateful for the help and hospitality that I found wherever my work led me. Specifically I should like to thank those who shared with me their memories of Rider Haggard and those who gave so freely of their critical judgements: Mr. R. H. Mottram, Dr. Philip Gosse, Sir Harold Nicolson, Mr. R. G. G. Price, Mr. William Longman, Professor C. S. Lewis, Professor and Mrs. F. R. Leavis, Professor C. E. Carrington, Sir James A. Scott Watson, Mr. John Foster White, Mr. W. K. Scudamore, Mr. A. T. Gerard, and Mr. Archibald C. Brown.

Thanks for access to holograph and other material are due the Lockwood Memorial Library, University of Buffalo, and particularly Mr. Charles D. Abbott, Director, and Miss Anna Russell of the Poetry Collection; the Brotherton Library, University of Leeds, Mr. B. S. Page, Librarian; the Huntington Library, San Marino, California, Mr. Tyrus G. Harmson, Cataloguer; the editors of the *New York Post*, the *Boston Herald*, and the *Boston American*; the librarians of the Norwich Castle Museum; the Columbia University Libraries, Mr. Richard H. Logsdon, Associate Director, and Mr. Roland Baughman, Head of Special Collections; Professor Pierre Weil-Nordon, Paris; Mr. Adrian M. Conan Doyle, Geneva; Mr. Michael Gill of the British Broadcasting Corporation; Mr. Gorley Putt, Warden of Harkness House, London; Mr. Alan Maclean of the Macmillan Company, London; Mr. A. B. Cope of the *Eastern Evening News*, Norwich; Myers and Company, Booksellers, London; Maggs Brothers Ltd., London, and especially Miss A. Martin; Mr. P. H. Muir, Takeley; Mr. Crawford E. Cooke, Purley; the James McGregor Stewart Kipling Collection, Dalhousie University, Halifax, Nova Scotia, Mr. Douglas G. Lochhead, Librarian; and Mr. Laurence Urdang, New York.

For permission to print from original documents and copyright works, I am grateful to the Personal Representatives of the Andrew Lang Estate; Macmillan & Co. Ltd., publishers of Rudyard Kipling's *Something of Myself*; and Lloyd's Bank and Miss Irene Cooper Willis, Executors of the Thomas Hardy Estate.

Those who have responded to inquiries and whose help I appreciate include Mr. R. M. Graves, Hon. Librarian, the Savile Club; Mr. J. V. A. Sankey, Assistant Librarian, Lincoln's Inn Library; Mr. Alexander D. Wainwright, Princeton University Library; Sir Newman Flower, Cassell & Company, London; Mr. John S. Mayfield, Bethesda, Maryland; Professor A. C. Partridge, University of Witwatersrand; Mr. Ernest A. Ritter, Umhlanga Rocks, Natal; Colonel Laurens van der Post, London; Professor Richard D. Altick, Ohio State University; Dean Frank Luther Mott, University of Missouri; Mr. P. Hepworth, Librarian, Norwich Public Library; and Mr. John Barkham, Scarsdale, New York. I should like also to acknowledge the editorial assistance of Mr. David Buckley and Dr. Julian B. Kaye.

The owners of Haggardiana who have been obliging and to whom I owe many thanks include Mr. S. Eckman, Jr., London; Sir John Murray, London; and Mr. G. S. Hector, Watlington. Mr. C. O. Clark of Bolton not only permitted me to examine his private collection but also shared with me his vast store of Haggard information.

I could not have hoped to capture the mind and spirit of Rider Haggard without the aid of those who were closest to him. Since I began my research, Miss Lilias Rider Haggard has been exceptionally helpful, answering my specific queries both in writing and in person. Mrs. Thomas Haggard, Admiral V. H. Haggard, Sir Godfrey Haggard, and Lady Joan Buchanan have all put me deep in their debt by their willingness to share their memories with me and to guide me to a better understanding of Sir Rider. Without the friendly help of Mrs.

George Bambridge, this work would contain far less original material and I should have far less insight into Haggard's life and relationship with Rudyard Kipling. And I am especially grateful to Mr. R. P. Watt, who opened many doors to me when I was in England.

Finally, I am particularly indebted to four friends, from whose wise counsel, constant interest, and unsparing assistance I have benefited greatly. They are Roger Lancelyn Green, whom I have come to know through Haggard and whose knowledge and wisdom have been invaluable on many occasions; Cecil Y. Lang, who has generously advised me for many years; Mary Purdie, who gave many hours to typing and proof-reading; and Richard N. Swift, who helped me weigh evidence, organize material, and edit the manuscript.

Contents

NOTE

Superscript numerals in the text
refer to notes beginning on page
287 which indicate the sources
of quoted material and provide
supplementary information.

Illustrations

Preface

ONE afternoon in the spring of 1950, I overheard a customer in the
Columbia University Bookstore ask a salesclerk to recommend 'a
good, clean adventure story' as a birthday present for his twelve-year-
old nephew. 'Would you happen to have any Rider Haggard?' he
asked. 'No, Haggard is completely out of print,' the clerk replied,
and he went on to recommend other authors. Actually the salesclerk
was wrong: there were at least three Haggard issues in print in the
United States that year. His error is understandable, however, because
for twenty-five years after Haggard's death, his popularity declined
sharply and his works were little read. What is more, even though
Haggard wrote fifty-eight volumes of fiction and seven volumes
of political, economic, and social history, took a very active part in
reform movements of his day, and served the British Government
for many years on Royal Commissions, all standard literary, political,
and economic surveys consider him a featherweight, if they consider
him at all.

But although largely ignored by historians, Haggard has enjoyed
high praise from many distinguished men of letters in his own time
and even today. W. E. Henley believed him to have 'the gift of invention to such a point as to be practically a man of genius';[1] Andrew
Lang considered him one of the greatest story-tellers of his time;
and Rudyard Kipling wrote that 'never was a better tale-teller or,
to my mind, a man with a more convincing imagination.'[2] Robert
Louis Stevenson thought Haggard capable of 'pages of eloquence
and poetry';[3] Walter Besant judged him 'at the head – a long way
ahead – of all contemporary imaginative writers';[4] and George
Saintsbury would not say whether he liked '*Treasure Island* better
than *King Solomon's Mines*, or *King Solomon's Mines* better than *Treasure
Island*,' and added, 'I only wish I had drawn the personage of John
Silver or written the fight between Twala and Sir Henry.'[5] Hugh
Walpole, writing after Haggard's death, praised his astonishing

'imaginative vigour' and 'zest in narrative' and claimed that in 'robust-ness' he excelled all his contemporary story-tellers.[6] In our own time Henry Miller has eulogized him and devoted two chapters of his *Books in My Life* to praise of Haggard and his work. Stuart Cloete writes that 'Africa, combined with an inborn quality of creative genius, enabled Haggard to see horizons beyond those available to more ordinary mortals and to produce the books that have in their own particular field of romantic fiction seldom been equalled and never surpassed.'[7] Graham Greene remembers Haggard's books as the most enjoyable in his childhood and admires the 'poetic elements' in his work.[8] And in two essays on books and story-telling, C. S. Lewis has given more than passing approbation to Haggard's ability to tell convincing tales.[9]

That Haggard should receive acclaim through the years from distinguished craftsmen and judicious critics and at the same time be neglected by literary historians is so interesting a circumstance that I have sought the reasons for this strange paradox. I have also tried to understand why Haggard, unlike most of his contemporary story-tellers, A. E. W. Mason, Stanley Weyman, John Buchan, Maurice Hewlett, Arthur Quiller-Couch, Anthony Hope Hawkins, and H. B. Marriott-Watson among them, has in the last six or seven years enjoyed a small revival of interest. For a book buyer would have no difficulty today in purchasing a Rider Haggard adventure story in the Columbia University Bookstore, in most bookstores in England and America – or for that matter in leading bookstores around the world. Since 1951 a number of reprints have come from American presses, and there are today no fewer than eight Haggard titles (some in multiple issues) in print in the United States, among them the Modern Library edition (1957) of *King Solomon's Mines* and *She* in a single volume. In Great Britain, where Haggard has never gone out of vogue, there has also been an increased interest in his works in recent years. The *Reference Catalogue of Current Literature* shows thirty-five Haggard issues in print in 1957, including translations into Swahili and Afrikaans, as compared with nineteen in 1951. Macdonald and Company offers fifteen Haggard titles in uniform bindings and promises soon to bring forth a sixteenth. In 1958, furthermore, Puffin Books added another issue of *King Solomon's Mines*. In both Great Britain and the United States, moreover, there has been a constant flow of tales in the less chartable medium of paperbacks, and hardly a month goes by when the rows of mystery, science, and fantasy magazines, displayed by W. H. Smith & Son in London terminals or hung out by newsdealers on New York sidewalks, fail to produce a Haggard title. And in 1955 alone there were no fewer than nine new translations into foreign languages. In fact, with the single exception of Rudyard Kipling, Haggard outsells all his contemporary story-tellers, including Stevenson and Doyle.

But for an understanding of Rider Haggard one must look beyond his popular appeal and the connoisseurs' approval, and in this study I have tried to make the first critical examination of his life and works. Up to now the relations between Haggard and his literary contemporaries, particularly Andrew Lang, W. E. Henley, and Rudyard Kipling, have not been recorded in sufficient detail; and nowhere has there been any systematic treatment of Haggard's contributions to agriculture, land reform, social work, and colonial affairs. I have tried to fill these gaps, and I have sought to capture the man's complexity and limitations, to evaluate his creative talent, to relate him to the literary and political movements in which he participated, and to suggest his influence. Both Haggard's autobiography and his daughter's reminiscences have been invaluable aids, and I have drawn heavily upon them. But I hope that with the help of new material and the advantage of distance, I have shed more light upon the life and works of Henry Rider Haggard, K.B.E.

Morton N. Cohen
The City College of New York

I

Norfolk Beginnings

'ALL England may be carved out of Norfolk. . . . Here are fens and heaths, and light and deep, and sand and clay-ground, and meadows and pasture, and arable woody, and (generally) woodless land.' These words, written by Thomas Fuller in the seventeenth century, still describe Norfolk. Essentially untouched by industry, this fourth largest of England's shires is the nation's granary; some of the most fertile fields in the land fan away from the narrow roads that run like veins through the countryside. On nearly 100,000 acres grow wheat, barley, oats, beans, potatoes, turnips, and small fruit; and grazing land feeds Norfolk's handsome Red Polled cattle. A few of England's remaining woodlands border the tilled fields, and deep meadow grass still nests pheasant for the shoot. The ninety miles of coast are as varied as the rest of the county, and a harsh sea and brisk wind bite away at the shore-line, as they have for centuries, crumbling cliffs and inundating villages. The south-eastern coast, or the Broads, frames a quiet picture world that has attracted England's greatest painters, Gainsborough and Constable among them. Here are lagoons, windmills, white-sailed yachts, and swaying reeds and rushes that shelter some of the most colourful animal life in western Europe. Up the rivers that lead inland from the sea ply the cargo-laden wherryboats, some still man-powered by broad-chested East Anglians.

The 'north folk' are a leisurely, reserved people born to the land and reared close to nature, with distinct provincial customs, local superstitions, peculiarities of speech, an individual manner, and a strong sense of pride. Because Norfolk through the ages was so vulnerable to sea invasion both from the north and the east, these people look back upon an unusual galaxy of forebears and a romantic history that includes the coming of peaceful Teutonic settlers, incursions by fierce Danes, and periodic arrivals of Romans, Flemings, Dutch, Walloons, and Normans.

The Haggard family believes that it descends from a brave Danish

nobleman, one Andrew Ogard,* who came to England in the fifteenth
century from his native city of Aagard. The College of Heralds,
while begrudging the Haggards the right to the Ogard arms, trace
the family back to Hertfordshire as early as 1561 and confirm that
one of the Hertfordshire Haggards, William Henry Haggard, came
to settle in Norwich in 1760, having wed the daughter of that city's
sheriff. Their son (he bore the same name as his father) was educated
at Emmanuel College, Cambridge, and Lincoln's Inn, but being
'well read in . . . every branch of polite literature,' did not choose to
follow the profession of law. 'Born . . . to the expectations of an
ample fortune, he soon retired into the country and mingled in the
happiness and mutual courtesies of his numerous friends.'[1] Intent
upon a life of leisure, Rider Haggard's great-grandfather acquired
Bradenham Hall and established the Haggard seat in Norfolk.

Bradenham, a small house as manor houses go, is a red brick
Georgian structure in the Adam style that sits on some of the highest
land in the county in an area known as the West Norfolk Hunt.
In its heyday there were three reception rooms, one panelled in oak,
and ten bedrooms; the Hall was bordered by a well-timbered park
and surrounded by the Haggard acres (numbering at different times
from 140 to 400), through which ran the River Wissey. The wood
has since been felled, and the Hall, where for generations the Haggards
thrived as comfortable, landed gentry, served, during World War II,
as an army barracks, and, more recently, as a government bureau.
The only landmarks that recall the Haggard lineage are the headstones
in the churchyard, a portrait of Rider Haggard worked into the design
of a recent village sign erected by the Women's Institute, and a tree
in the garden by the house that still bears the carved-out initials
'R. H.'

But tradition dies hard in Norfolk, and tales of the Haggards
still abound among the villagers of West Bradenham. Many are told
about the Old Squire, William Meybohm Rider Haggard, Rider's
father, who was the last to live and die in the manner of his forebears.

---

* Ogard is variously spelled. Andrew Lang chanced on a possible Haggard ancestor
when he was doing research for his novel *A Monk of Fife*. 'What are your bearings?'
he asked in a letter dated March 12 [1895]. 'I see a chance of getting them into my novel,
as I find one Andrew Oggard, a Danish knight, at the siege of Orleans, 1492. I don't
know if you can trace to an Oggard who may have come over with Anne of Denmark,
but, if so, you probably had a "forebear" (on the English side) at Orleans.' Lang did get
them into his novel. In the last chapter of the serial appearing in the *Monthly Packet*, he
wrote of 'that great Danish knight, who was with us under Orleans, Sir Andrew Oggard
was his name, and his bearings were – ' [the sentence breaks off]. Although the same
wording appears in the American edition of the book, Lang altered the English edition.
Instead of *Oggard* he writes *Haggard* and adds a footnote: 'Substituting "or" for "argent,"
his bearings were those of the distinguished modern novelist of the same name.' Lockwood
Collection; 'A Monk of Fife,' *Monthly Packet*, XC (December 1895), p. 639; *A Monk of Fife*
(New York, 1895), p. 320; *A Monk of Fife* (London, 1896), p. 374.

He was a distinguished personage with a sound education in the law and a clear mind in money matters, whose life spanned the last days of England's squirearchy, when the traditions of the responsible landowner were strongest.

William Haggard was flamboyant, and he ruled Bradenham with a loud voice, an impetuous nature, and a capricious disposition. 'He reigned like a king, blowing everybody up and making rows innumerable.' He lectured, chid, and snapped at his family, strangers, and servants alike. 'He could send back the soup with a request to the cook to drink it all herself, or some other infuriating message. He could pull at the bells until feet of connecting wire hung limply down the wall, and announce when whoever it was he wanted appeared that Thorpe Idiot Asylum was her proper home.' But his explosions merely added colour to the image of the squire and endeared him to the people around him. Local legend recalls, for instance, that Sunday was almost as much the Squire's day as it was God's. When he himself was in time for the church service, he admonished all late-comers by holding up a huge watch for them to see as they entered. If by chance, he had drunk an extra glass of port before coming to church, he was likely, when reading the Lessons, to address the eagle on the dais with his loud and belligerent voice, and command it to stop swaying back and forth. He found the genealogies of the Bible no easier to pronounce than most people, and when he grew dissatisfied with his performance, he read the catalogues aloud a second time.[2]

The villagers also tell of how he seldom allowed enough time for the dogcart to get him to the station when he had to catch a train for Norwich. Often they saw him atop the cart racing through the village, whipping the horse and booming forth in his large voice, 'Hold the train, hold the train!'[3]

Life with father may have been interesting, but it was also a considerable strain, especially for the children. Whatever stability they felt issued not from the impetuous squire, but from their gentle mother. Ella Haggard* was a quiet châtelaine who offered a heart full of love to her husband and children, and whose calm sometimes pervaded even volcanic Bradenham. She made no effort to compete with the loud Haggards, and often simply signalled her messages. When asked how she managed to get any attention at all, she replied, 'My dear, . . . I whisper! When I whisper they all stop talking, because they wonder what is the matter. Then I get my chance.'[4]

* She was the daughter of Bazett Doveton of St. Helena and the Bombay Civil Service. India-reared, she was worldly, well read and sophisticated; and as co-heiress of her father's estate, she brought with her to Bradenham a promise of wealth.

Rider was the eighth of ten children (the sixth of seven sons). He was born on June 22, 1856, not in Bradenham Hall as were all the others, but in the Wood Farm, a small house on the Haggard estate to which his mother had retreated for her confinement. An uncle's suggestion that the child be named Sylvanus out of deference to the house where he was born was rejected, and he was christened Henry Rider, both conventional names within the family. He was a weak, jaundiced child at birth, but under his mother's care and with wholesome nourishment from the Haggard farms, he grew healthy, soon took his place among his brothers and sisters in the Bradenham nursery, and later came to enjoy the pleasures of the open Norfolk fields. As a lad, he was proud to own a gun, and shot everything from rabbits to an excellent egg-laying duck that belonged to a neighbouring farmer. He learned to ride early and often joined his brothers in a day's hunt. On occasion, Rider and his brother Andrew went on expeditions of their own making: accompanied by one of the dogs, they hunted mice in the cellars of Bradenham Hall.

It was an active life the Haggard children led, what with a large house, innumerable farm buildings, stables, sheds, a summer house, open fields, trees, a river, a pond, a maze of narrow lanes for their youthful exploits, and a world full of growing things, dogs, ducks, cattle, sheep, horses, and pigs.

It is not surprising that the atmosphere in which Rider moved as a lad offered little intellectual challenge. True, the squire was himself a respected, educated man, and Rider's mother could even be called 'literary,' for she often wrote verse.* And there were books aplenty in the nursery and round the house. But the table talk was seldom of books. The world at Bradenham, while full of fun, was a world of external and practical reality, not one of metaphysical speculation. It was a world of hunting, shooting, farming, tenanting, and very much a world of pounds, shillings and pence. Men were squires and owned land and knew the law and talked about the price of a prize bull or of making a profit on a crop. It was a life of strong laughter and healthy sport, a life dominated by tangible things.

Rider was taught to read by his eldest sister, Ella,† but although he was exposed to the conventional books for a growing boy, reading did not play a major role in his life. Later, when he was in his thirties, he wrote:

* Some found its way into print. *Myra; or the Rose of the East* (a tale of the Afghan War in nine cantos) appeared in 1857, and in 1890, after her death, Rider arranged for the publication of another volume, *Life and Its Author* (a denunciation of progress and science). In both volumes, strong poetic feeling and vivid imagery compensate somewhat for the unfortunate choice of subject matter.

† He later wrote in the dedication of *The Brethren*: '[She] opened to my childish eyes that gate of ivory and pearl which leads to the blessed kingdom of Romance.'

Now to be frank, I have never been a very great reader . . . and besides, I have always preferred to try to study human character from life rather than in the pages of books. . . . [But] when I was a boy I loved those books that other boys love. . . . I well remember a little scene which took place when I was a child of eight or nine. 'Robinson Crusoe' held me in his golden thrall, and I was expected to go to church. I hid beneath a bed with 'Robinson Crusoe,' and was in due course discovered by an elder sister and a governess, who, on my refusing to come out resorted to force. Then followed a struggle that was quite Homeric. The two ladies tugged as best they might, but I clung to 'Crusoe' and the legs of the bed, and kicked till, perfectly exhausted, they took their departure in no very Christian frame of mind, leaving me panting indeed, but triumphant.[5]

Next to *Robinson Crusoe*, Rider liked *The Arabian Nights* and *The Three Musketeers*, and in time he grew fond of poems by Macaulay and Poe. All in all, his childhood was a vigorous, happy one, and in later years, looking back on it with nostalgia, he told his own children fascinating tales of his young days at Bradenham. But while Rider's body was often put to a test of strength, his imagination was seldom stimulated from without.

Rider's first formal education came at a day school in London, where the family often spent some months of the year at 24 Leinster Square. His initial flight into the world of studies was not, however, very successful and ended abruptly when his father discovered that he had been beaten up by 'a raging usher' at the school. With little delay, the decisive parent sent Rider off to a second day school, one that promised to give the lad a sound business training. But the business day school did not endure either. One day Rider's father asked his future son-in-law, the Reverend Charles Maddison Green, to examine Rider and determine how much he knew. The churchman found the boy's fund of facts sadly deficient, and soon an irate father stormed in upon Rider and 'roared like an angry bull' that he was 'only fit to be a greengrocer.'[6] Some remedy was necessary, and Rider, at the age of ten, was packed off to the Reverend H. J. Graham's at Garsington Rectory, near Oxford, where, probably for the first time, he received disciplined, thoughtful, and kind instruction.

All his life, Rider retained a deep feeling for this period of his childhood, and the little village in the heart of England was one of the few schooltime scenes he later revisited. Garsington was a pleasant country hamlet, and the Reverend Graham, his wife, and the people of the village were amiable. The rector's wife later remembered

Rider as 'the little quiet boy who used to drive with me about the
Garsington lanes.'[7] In later years, Haggard recalled with delight
memories of rolling an iron hoop along the meadow paths, of chasing
pigeons in the garden for pigeon pie; he remembered a Sunday in
church when a donkey stuck its head through the door and interrupted the sermon with violent brays, and an elm beneath which he
used to sit, where he 'and a little fair-haired girl* once taught
each other the rudiments of flirtation.' But perhaps he most significantly revealed his attachment for Garsington and the days he spent
there by taking from one of its villagers a name he made world famous.
The name was Quatermain, and it belonged to an ordinary farmer,
'him as jobbed pigs,' as an innkeeper later described him. But what
Rider remembered was that 'William Quatermain and his wife had
been kind friends. . . . Many a time have I gone with him to feed
his pigs. . . . He used to give me [large walnuts] . . . and I made
boats out of their shells. He was a fine handsome man of about fifty,
with grey hair and aristocratic features . . . and he always wore a
beautiful smock-frock.'[8]

We do not know just how long Rider's one happy experience
with education lasted – perhaps as much as three years – but we
do know that he did not go from Garsington to a public school.
Instead he was led off to the Grammar School at Ipswich, where
during the next two or three years, he fought his bully schoolmates,
achieved the distinction of being nicknamed 'Nosey,' an 'allusion
to the prominence of that organ on my underdeveloped face,' and
became captain of the second football team.[9]

Rider's pillar-to-post education by no means characterized the
kind of training his six brothers received. Five of them went
to public schools (Shrewsbury, Winchester, Haileybury, and Westminster) and universities (Oxford and Cambridge), and the sixth
went into the Navy. Rider alone of all the Haggard sons was sent to
a grammar school. Tightening purse strings is often given as the
excuse for Rider's being denied a public school education, but
if money was the sole reason, it is difficult to explain why Rider's
younger brother went to Shrewsbury and Cambridge, and why of
the seven sons, only Rider was denied a 'proper' schooling. Something
beyond the lack of money seems to have influenced his parents'
decision. We know, for instance, that his father heaped imprecation
after imprecation upon him for his stupidity, and even his mother
conceded that he was 'as heavy as lead in body and mind.' Rider too
seemed convinced that he was blockish, for in later years he looked

---

* Haggard describes Garsington Rectory and Hall in Chapter 1 of *Allan's Wife* (1889),
and the little girl is undoubtedly the model for Stella Carson in the story.

back at himself as 'more or less a dunderhead,'[10] and his daughter tells us that 'he was frankly considered "not to be very bright." '[11] As a boy he could not learn anything by heart, was not good in matters mathematical, and did not care for the Ipswich Grammar School.

Rider's parents obviously thought him unworthy of a public school education. But whether they really understood what set their sixth son off from the others is another matter. Clearly they felt that he was different and that they had to make different provisions for him. But even though they pronounced him stupid, they also indicted him as 'whimsical.'[12] If Victorian parents had been by custom closer to their children, if the nursery (and schoolroom) at Bradenham had been nearer the drawing-room, Rider's mother and father might have realized that stupidity and whimsy make strange bedfellows. Many tales of Rider's childhood bear evidence that, far from being stupid, he was in reality a sensitive youth.

In his nursery days, for instance, he was much moved by a 'disreputable rag doll' which was kept in a deep, dark cupboard. The doll was

> of particularly hideous aspect, with boot-button eyes, hair of black wool and a sinister leer upon its painted face. [It] . . . was something of a fetish, and Rider, as a small child, was terrified by . . . [it], a fact soon discovered by an unscrupulous nurse who made full use of it to frighten him into obedience.[13]

Around the ominous doll, inexplicable in its power, the boy wove a strange mystery which became very much a part of him. He called her She-Who-Must-Be-Obeyed, the name he later gave to the awesome heroine of his famous stories.

Another incident reveals something of the boy's imaginative nature. Rider, who usually shared an attic room with Andrew, had been put to bed one night in the Sandwich, a dark and stuffy dressing-room. He had difficulty falling asleep, and then all at once he seemed to hear the rustling of a silk skirt. He had been told that Lady Hamilton once stayed at Bradenham, and he feared her ghost had returned. He jerked the bedclothes over his head and eventually fell into an uneasy sleep. But suddenly he woke up.

> The moon was shining through the window so brilliantly that he could see every detail in the room. . . . The leaves danced over the bed. He put out his hand and let them flicker over it – how odd it looked in the moonlight, dead – dead. Then it happened. He realized that one day that hand would be limp also, that he could not lift it any more – it would be dead – he would be dead.

The awful, inescapable certainty hung over him like a pall of
misery. He felt it would be better if he died at once – he wished
he were dead, rather than have to live with that in front of him.[14]

Rider's awakening to the irony of life came, it seems, with unusual
force. He always remembered the incident in the Sandwich Room,
and thinking about it or telling of it to those he loved inevitably
brought a brooding melancholy upon him.

Later, when a pupil at Ipswich, Rider showed more evidence of
a strong imagination. He once wrote a set of Latin verses of so high
a quality that a master grew suspicious and accused him of cribbing.
But Rider proved that it was his own work, and the master sportingly
apologized to him in public assembly. Also at Ipswich, Rider won
an essay-writing competition, 'beating all the other essayists hollow.'
The winning essay described a surgical operation – and Rider had
never seen an operation in his life.

Perhaps the best judgement of Rider's ability is his own: 'I think
that on the whole I was rather a quiet youth. . . . Certainly I was very
imaginative, although I kept my thoughts to myself, which I dare
say had a good deal to do with my reputation for stupidity. . . .Without
doubt I was slow at my lessons, chiefly because I was always thinking
of something else . . . [but] I rarely forgot the substance of anything
worth remembering.'[15]

The vagaries of Rider's education continued beyond Ipswich.
When the boy was seventeen, his father suddenly decided he had had
quite enough formal schooling and sent him up to London to be
tutored privately for the Foreign Office examination. Rider was
not lucky in the choice of his tutor; in later years he remembered
only the tutor's family squabbles that raged openly in his presence.
Within the year, however, Rider's father had him removed once
more, this time to Scoones, the crammer. For the first time, Rider,
at eighteen, lived by himself in lodgings and was his own master.
Although we do not have many tales of these young, free days, we
know that he did not shy away from opportunities to taste something
of London life. He recalls that somehow he became a 'frequent visitor
at Lady Paulet's [sic] house at 20 Hanover Square,' where he attended
séances, that his 'acquaintance with Lady Paulet gave me the entrée
to the spiritualistic society of the day,' and that another 'habitué
of the "circle" was Lady Caithness.'

The spiritualist fever was still quite high in London in the 'seventies.
It had swept over England in the mid-'fifties, imported, it seems,
from America, and had become the great fashion. A large distinguished
group of followers collected around Daniel Dunglas Home, the most

remarkable medium of the time, whom Robert Browning later immortalized in 'Mr. Sludge, "The Medium."' Both Lady Poulett (*née* Charlotte Fanny Portman, wife of the fifth Earl of Poulett) and Lady Caithness (*née* Maria Mariatequi, second wife of the fourteenth Earl of Caithness), were great admirers of Home, and he held séances at both their residences. When, in 1866, the Spiritual Athenaeum was formed, with Home as Resident-Secretary, Lady Poulett became a charter member, and when, in 1874, the British National Association of Spiritualists came into being, Lady Caithness was one of the vice-presidents. Furthermore, Lady Poulett, along with William and Mary Howitt, was present, in the early 'sixties, at John Ruskin's first séance.[16]

We do not know whether Haggard was ever present at one of Home's séances or with whom, beyond Ladies Poulett and Caithness, the young Norfolkman associated. But we do know that the séances he attended proved such vivid experiences that he could recall many of the details thirty-five years later.* At one he saw a massive table that skipped like a lamb and a lady spirit with an elongated neck like Alice's in Wonderland. Another account tells of how 'lights floated about the room, and with them a file of *Morning Post*s which normally reposed in a corner. Cold little hands picked at the studs in our shirts, ... feather fans off the mantelpiece floated to and fro, performing their natural office upon our heated brows,' and huge pieces of furniture were piled one atop another.

Haggard clearly implies that these séances disturbed him considerably, and after one of the more ghostly meetings, he decided that he had had quite enough and chucked the whole business. 'Since those days nearly forty years ago,' he later wrote, 'I wonder whether the whole thing was illusion, or, if not, what it can have been. . . . I do not believe that it was a case of trickery; rather am I inclined to think that certain forces . . . were set loose . . . which, perhaps, had their real origin in our minds, but nevertheless were true phenomena.' As he pondered the problem through the years, he came to believe that 'there is an even higher variant of preternatural experience . . . the communion of the individual soul still resident on earth with other souls that have passed from us; this, too, without the intervention of any medium, but as it were face to face in those surrounding solitudes [where] . . . from time to time they find strength to travel.'[17]

The London séances focused Haggard's attention upon the shadowy recesses of the spirit, and they stirred in him thoughts and feelings

---

* Various forms of spiritualist activity occur, furthermore, in his fiction. See especially *Love Eternal* (1918).

that he could neither understand nor explain. And these mysteries undoubtedly intensified a restlessness he had acquired in the rush of life at Bradenham and in his jostling about from school to school.

Nor had Rider met with the last of his father's impetuous decisions. After he had been studying with Scoones for a year and a half, he joined his family for their annual holiday on the Continent, this summer at Tours. Here, for the sixth time, the squire altered Rider's life with characteristic suddenness. William Haggard learned that his Norfolk neighbour and friend, Sir Henry Bulwer (nephew of Bulwer-Lytton, the novelist, and first cousin to 'Owen Meredith,' the poet and Viceroy of India), was leaving England to take up his post as Lieutenant-Governor of Natal, and he saw an opportunity not to be missed. He wrote to Sir Henry, offering him the services of his son Rider, and Bulwer agreed to take the young man along, unseen, as a member of his staff. In a moment the idea of the Foreign Office went up in smoke, and Rider, at age nineteen, sailed off to the Dark Continent, putting Bradenham and England far behind him. But while the squire's decision, in 1875, to send Rider off to Africa was arbitrary, it was also fortunate. Away from his family's close scrutiny and hasty reproof, he was to find a new freedom of mind and spirit, and his young, impressionable senses would be fed with fresh, even incredible, experiences.

2

Africa and Marriage

To the nineteen-year-old Haggard, arriving at the Cape Colony in August 1875, Africa's tumultuous history and contemporary political entanglements could not have meant very much. He could not guess that even as he stepped ashore at Cape Town, Africa stood at a turning-point in history. Neither could he know that in the next few years Africa would write its name deeply into the hearts of men the world over, nor surmise that he himself would play a part in shaping this convulsive continent's future.

As he knew little of Africa's fate, so he knew even less of his own. He must have wondered whether he had come to an obscure British colony, like so many troublesome younger sons of good English families before him, only to fill an obscure bureaucratic niche and be forgotten; whether he would die of the liver sickness; whether he had come to prove just how strong – or weak – his physical and spiritual resources were; whether he would succeed or merely be thrust back in a few months into the unwelcoming arms of his domineering father. Whatever his aspirations and his fears, he was nevertheless filled with the excitement of the fresh experience.

After a week's stay in Government House, Cape Town, the Lieutenant-Governor and his staff sailed on, around the Cape and up the east coast to Durban, and then rode by horse-wagon to Pietermaritzburg, their destination. For some time, Haggard was not entirely clear about what his specific job was to be on Bulwer's staff, and in a letter home from Cape Town he went so far as to assume that he would be Sir Henry's private secretary. He did not immediately become secretary, but his duties did call for him to remain close to the Lieutenant-Governor, even though he was to work more with external, practical details than with official matters. He managed Bulwer's headquarters: he hired servants, ordered food, and arranged all the entertaining. The job carried considerable responsibility, and it suited him, for he had a natural sense of order, which, matched

with his determination to do well, made him in all a very efficient
aide. His letters home showed a grave concern for his work: 'My position is not an easy one. I find myself responsible for everything,
and everybody comes and bothers me.' And again:

> My chief trouble is my housekeeping. I have all this large
> house entirely under me, and being new to it find it difficult work.
> I have often seen with amusement the look of anxiety on a hostess's
> face at a dinner-party, but, by Jove, I find it far from amusing now.
> Dinner days are black Mondays to me. Imagine my dismay the
> other day when the fish did not appear and when, in whispering
> a furious inquiry, I was told the cook had forgotten it![1]

While Haggard took his work seriously, determined as he was
to turn this opportunity to good account, he also plunged into the
activity outside Government House with enthusiasm and vigour.
He was *ipso facto* a member of the most exclusive social caste in South
Africa, the British colonial community, and his affability and good
name won him many friends among the seasoned Maritzburg residents.
With their help, he learned quickly about life in South Africa, about
the dangers of the climate and the various diseases it engendered,
and soon he even acquired the conventional prejudices toward the
Boer. Nor were his duties at Government House so confining that
he could not take an occasional day off for hunting. He bought a
good horse, was willing to listen to and learn from the experienced
hunters whose friendship he now enjoyed, and was quick to profit
from his mistakes. Before long he was a ready match for the best
antelope and gnu on the veld.

The landscape of Natal, its vastness, its brightness, its colour,
stood in vivid contrast to anything he had known in the Norfolk
countryside. But the African natives, the tall, dark, majestic Zulus,
caught his imagination more than anything else, and often he recorded in his notebook the impressions they made on him and the
stories he heard about them. He watched them carefully and admired
their personal dignity, racial pride, their unmatched courage and
profound loyalty. He listened eagerly to the stories of their romantic
past; in fact, the more he learned about them, the more he wished
to know. Soon he understood the Zulu tongue and spoke with the
Africans directly, and then he could capture in his notebooks along
with their stories the rhythms of their speech as well.

He himself may not have known exactly why he was writing so
much down. Perhaps some day he would want to reconstruct his
African life for his family at home; perhaps he would wish, in later
years, to remind himself of his youth spent in the far corners of the

world; perhaps this was merely a means of occupying his idle moments in Natal. We cannot tell; but one thing is certain: these scraps of paper, this cache of impressions would furnish the raw material for his later works. For the Zulus he met and heard about in these early years were to live again and roam through the pages of his romances as they had in their most glorious days over the African veld, shouting their war cries and washing their spears in enemy blood. Through these as-yet-untold tales, the Zulus were to achieve a world-wide renown which ironically would come to them only as the white man invaded their kraals, took their lands, bent their spears, and broke their spirit.

As the months passed, there were numerous reasons for Haggard to leave the relative peace and security of Government House and Maritzburg for the wilder veld and bush country, and for longer periods than a day's buck hunting. The Government had to maintain diplomatic relations with the native chiefs, and frequent journeys to their seats were necessary. These expeditions invariably offered adventure, and Haggard never passed up an opportunity to visit the wilder interior and observe the natives on their home ground. In May 1876 he accompanied Sir Henry Bulwer on a journey up country to witness a mammoth war dance given by Chief Pagate in honour of the Lieutenant-Governor. On this trip, one of his first long journeys, Rider inadvertently lost his way when, without taking his bearings, he left the main party for a bit of shooting. He wandered through the bush for hours, and as day gave way to night, his future looked dim indeed. But his luck turned when he ran into a Kaffir wandering through the bush and the native led him to the area where his party had camped.

The journey up country marked an important milestone in Haggard's development. The war dance he saw at Chief Pagate's kraal so fixed itself in his mind that he decided to write down his own description of it. This on-the-scene report re-created so vividly the native ceremony in all its untamed beauty and read so easily and interestingly that the author met with no difficulty in selling it, and it appeared as 'A Zulu War Dance' in the July 1877 issue of the *Gentleman's Magazine*.

By 1876 Haggard was becoming aware of the political situation in Africa; in a letter home he alludes to the 'stirring news' from the north and to 'skirmishes between the Boers and Secocoeni. . . . War here between white and black is a terrible thing. No quarter is given and none is asked.'[2] Indeed all eyes in Africa and England were then focused on the Transvaal border, where the Basuto chief Secocoeni was gathering his impis, preparing to attack the Boers, his traditional enemy.

The Transvaal territory comprised over a hundred thousand square miles of mostly fertile veld contiguous to the British Crown

Colony of Natal and the Orange Free State. The roots of the Boer republic in the Transvaal reached back to 1835, when their ancestors in the Cape, abhorring the British idea of law and order and refusing to live in a state that had freed the black savage, had packed their ox-wagons, gathered their cattle, and left their homes in the Cape Colony to thread their way north in search of freedom and fertile lands where they might ply their farming skills and live as they had been accustomed. Their advance scouts found the arable lands of what was to become Natal, the Orange Free State, and the Transvaal, and guided the long thin line of trekkers there.

But the Boers bought freedom hard. The native chiefs resented the white man's intrusion, and for years after the Great Trek, they relentlessly harassed the European settlers. The Boers were as determined as the natives, however, and the fearless leaders who emerged from their ranks led them into epic battles. On December 16, 1838, Andreis Pretorius and 430 Boer farmers went out to face a Zulu army of 30,000 and returned successful, the Zulus massacred and scattered. Despite this victory over the natives, the fruits of their struggles were short-lived. In 1843 the British, convinced that they had a responsibility to protect the natives in South Africa, extended England's imperial arm north to annex Natal. The Boers would not remain under alien rule; once again they gathered under the man who had led them in their great victory over the Zulus and struck out to the north, leaving behind the land they had won from the natives at such great odds.

The late eighteen-forties saw the Boers fighting and fleeing, still under Pretorius, always seeking a part of the large continent they could call their own, where they could practise their Calvinist orthodoxy and rule themselves. But the British were always at the rear and on the flanks, and strong resistance from the Kaffirs faced them up ahead. Their doom was almost sealed, when events in Europe came to their rescue. The Irish potato famine and agitation for Irish self-government in the 'forties; the repeal of the Corn Laws in '46; the bank crisis and financial panic following the 'railway mania' of '47; the revolutions of 1848 in France, Germany, Austria, Hungary, Italy, Bohemia; the collapse of Chartism also in '48; and the Great Exhibition of '51 – these events commanded Britain's attention. The colonies would have to fare as best they could; people at 'home' were too occupied with the excitement in their own front gardens. England took the easy way out of the African crisis by recognizing the independence of the Boers beyond the Vaal River (in the Sand River Convention of 1852) and later by doing the same for the Orange Free State (in the Bloemfontein Convention of 1854).

Aged 7

Aged 19

Mrs. Haggard and daughters

Rider Haggard in his conservatory

Rider Haggard in front of
Ditchingham House

Ditchingham House

But this was a policy of convenience rather than conviction, and in the 'sixties, new logs were thrown on the smouldering ashes in South Africa. Overnight the Dark Continent came into new and earth-shaking prominence. For one day in 1867, a Boer lad, playing on the shore of the Orange River, picked out of the earth a *mooi klip* (pretty pebble) that later proved to be a real diamond. Within a year the sub-continent was being raked and dug by hordes of miners, and within four, Cecil Rhodes had come to Africa to fashion a kingdom all his own. In no time at all, African diamonds eclipsed the jewels of India and Brazil, and concession hunters flocked in to make their fortunes. On October 31, 1871, amidst conflicting claims and disorder, Sir Henry Barkly, Governor of the Cape, annexed the diamond fields of Griqualand West. In doing so, he overrode the Boers' claim to the territory and broke the agreement the British had made in the Bloemfontein Convention. After all, the British treasure hunters had poured into the area in large numbers, and they needed British protection. Gladstone had no choice but to ratify Barkly's annexation.

Any reluctance the British may have felt about consolidating South Africa under the Union Jack vanished after the general election of 1874 brought Disraeli back as Prime Minister. His policies were openly imperialistic, and by his side as Colonial Secretary he placed Lord Carnarvon, whose success in confederating Canada in 1867 had only whetted his appetite for unifying and strengthening Britain's colonies. But Disraeli and Carnarvon were twenty-five years too late; the British Imperial Government had done too much to antagonize the Dutch Republic, and all their efforts to unify South Africa were doomed. Carnarvon would not, however, take defeat easily. When negotiations failed, he saw clearly that he would have to use other means. South Africa was in turmoil: the natives threatened war, a bankrupt Transvaal government held on to unexploited mineral fields, and the Germans were considering aggression from the north. The British position was firm, but there was no time to lose if the Empire was to be united.

Carnarvon acted. In October 1876 he appointed as High Commissioner and Governor of the Cape Sir Bartle Frere, a man with a record of brilliant success as an administrator of India and with a strong faith in Britain as a civilizing force. Frere, however, did not know, when he sailed from England to unify the troubled lands, that his mission represented only the right hand of Carnarvon's policy. Actually Carnarvon's left hand worked secretly in a very different way: a week before Carnarvon appointed Frere, he had sent Theophilus Shepstone, secretary of native affairs in Natal, as special commissioner of the Home Government to investigate the causes of friction between the

Transvaal Republic and the natives. But he also gave Shepstone explicit instructions to annex for the Crown any territory he thought should be annexed – and Carnarvon made perfectly clear what his opinion was in the case of the Transvaal – with the singularly vague proviso that 'the inhabitants thereof, or a sufficient number of them, or the Legislature thereof, desire to become Our subjects.'[3] In the same week he sent Shepstone forth, Carnarvon also dispatched a battalion of troops to help Shepstone bring about an orderly annexation.

In December 1876 Shepstone was in Maritzburg making hasty preparations for his journey to the Transvaal; it would be a long and arduous trek through the bush and over the mountains and veld. Shepstone selected some ten men to make up his official party, men whom he knew to be hardy and resourceful. One of them was Rider Haggard. Bulwer had earlier refused to include Haggard among those who would venture forth into the Transvaal – the Lieutenant-Governor knew well the dangers of entering an arena where Zulu and Boer were menacing each other – but Shepstone prevailed. He had two reasons for wanting Haggard to make the journey, the young man told his parents in a letter home about this time: 'First, we are very good friends and he was kind enough to say he wished to have me as companion. Second, I imagine there will be a good deal of what is called the champagne and sherry policy up at Pretoria and he wants somebody to look after the entertaining.'[4]

The party left Maritzburg in late December 1876 and by January 22 had arrived at Pretoria, almost 400 miles away. As the band of Englishmen rode into Pretoria, it was accompanied by a guard of twenty-five mounted police. The battalion which Carnarvon had sent to the Cape to support Shepstone was later brought up to Newcastle and made ready to cross the border into the Transvaal on short notice, but because its mission was not to exert force in the annexation itself and only to maintain order in the Transvaal after the annexation had taken place, it remained in the wings for the time being. The trek had been long, slow, and difficult for Shepstone and his staff, but it was Haggard's first real African travel, and he enjoyed the journey very much.   Monotony was inevitable at times, of course, and on Christmas Day, which happened to be very hot, the young man was quite homesick, as he contrasted his surroundings with those of the traditional English yuletide.

His travelling companions were all interesting people, and he enjoyed the deepening friendship that developed with many of them on this journey. Nor were the more sober implications of the mission lost on him: he sensed full well that he had embarked upon a history-making mission and was entering a lawless land from which he might

never return. But this danger only intensified the experience for him
as he travelled northward through the strange country that impressed
him so. The height of the mountains, the infinity of the veld, the
abrupt and vehement changes in weather, the violence of animal
life, and the unusual beauty of the wilderness – all this struck him with
wonder. At night, after they outspanned their oxen, he often listened
intently to the tales of his companions' experiences in the earlier days
of Africa and other parts of the world. One evening he heard Melmoth
Osborn[5] give an eye-witness account of the battle of Tugela, a savage
encounter between the forces of the famed Cetywayo and his adversary
Umbelazi.[6] Some of these tales he wrote down in his notebook, to
re-create them in later years for the delight of his millions of readers.

But the tales of white men were not all that gripped Haggard's
interest; another member of the party, a special native aide-de-camp
to Shepstone, impressed him greatly and later became a prominent
figure in his Zulu romances. He was a tall, noble fighter, a lithe, black
Achilles, handsome in spite of his sixty years, a Swazi native with a
half-dozen or more unpronounceable names whom the world has
come to know as Umslopogaas. Early in the journey Haggard and
Umslopogaas became friends, and often they would sit together,
Haggard's attention caught as the warrior told stories of his youth
and of his people.

It would be interesting to know how many – if, in fact, any – of
Shepstone's staff on this special mission to the Transvaal knew that
the full purpose of their expedition was to add another name to
Britain's roster of colonies. In any case, Haggard's letters home during
this period and his later reminiscences indicate clearly that he was
not then aware of Shepstone's instructions from the Colonial Office.
It was natural for him to see Shepstone's mission to the north as
something that grew out of the events of the day. There had been
border skirmishes between the Boers and the natives, and both Secocoeni and Cetywayo were threatening to overrun the Transvaal.
The one white man who could speak with confidence and persuasion
to the native chiefs was Shepstone, or 'Sompseu' (Mighty Hunter)
as the natives called him. It was only natural that the Home Government send this man to the Transvaal in a humanitarian effort to avert
war and massacre and reconcile the Zulus and the Boers.

Many factors contributed to the chaos in the Transvaal as Shepstone
crossed its borders with his small band of Englishmen. The traditionally
anarchic 'Dopper' Boers had considerably weakened the central
government in Pretoria. And in the last few years, these orthodox
burghers, who lived on the veld farming and raising cattle, had
come to distrust the President of the Transvaal, T. F. Burgers, a

clergyman in the Dutch Reformed Church, who to the fundamentalist
Boers became the symbol of heretical modernity. He was a brave,
sincere, and energetic man who did all he could to save the Republic
from extinction; but he was not a shrewd politician and lacked judgement in practical matters. His effort to bring immigrant settlers from
the Netherlands was looked upon with suspicion, he bungled a plan
to run a railroad from the Transvaal to Delagoa Bay, and he had failed
to interest European powers in granting financial aid to his government. Suddenly, the very walls of the Transvaal Republic came
crashing down around him, and he was all at once powerless. The
burghers refused to pay taxes, and with the government coffers
empty and the Republic much in debt, government officials could
not be paid. The Postmaster took his salary in postage stamps. Trade
was disrupted. Burgers was unable to enforce law and order, and
he had no means by which to collect taxes – there was no official
police or military force. All he could call upon were the 'filibusters,'
a band of ruthless killers who concentrated on protecting the Transvaal
border territories, and raided native settlements, killing and robbing
mercilessly.

The Boers' hatred of the natives was deep-seated, and they could
not learn to deal with them fairly. Though slavery had been prohibited
in 1852 (the Sand River Convention), many rumours – if very little
evidence – of Boers surreptitiously dealing in slaves, or 'black ivory,'
sped back to Mrs. Jellyby and her army of women fanatically concerned about the natives of Borioboola-Gha. Considerable difficulty
from outside the Transvaal arose to compound the internal disorder.
Threats of foreign intervention continued as European countries
(Germany, Belgium, and Portugal not the least) hammered their
colonial wedges more firmly into the cracks in the Transvaal wall.
The worst fear of all was provoked by the Zulu armies which were
threatening to overrun the country, and although later events proved
the danger to have been far less than was supposed, the word that
came from the Transvaal at this time was that Secocoeni and Cetywayo
were massing their warriors, both eager to settle old grievances. The
prospectors, many of them British, who had swarmed into the
Transvaal from the south in search of quick gold, became suddenly
aware of their weak position and sent out a cry for help. The town
merchants, including many representatives of companies in Natal
and the Cape, added their voices to the alarm. The Dopper Boers
now completely deserted President Burgers and gave their support
to a man of their own ranks, a member of the Volksraad (legislature),
'Oom' Paul Kruger. On the one hand there was talk of civil war,
and on the other, border skirmishes seemed to augur an all-out Zulu

attack. These were the rumblings that had reached Carnarvon's ears in Whitehall, and these were the problems that faced Shepstone as he marched into quiet, bucolic Pretoria.

Carnarvon's old principle that one could not sit by when his neighbour's house was on fire still rang true; no one could argue with it, and certainly not the destitute, bewildered Dutch in Pretoria. When Shepstone's party led their ox-carts into the town on January 22, 1877, they were given a hearty welcome. The English and the Germans looked to Shepstone as a veritable saviour, and the Boers believed him when he said that he had come to help them in their troubled hour and did not intend to interfere with their independence, recognized by England twenty-five years earlier.

Haggard tells us that in spite of the impoverished state of the government, the members of the mission were greeted by an official reception, dinners, and other lavish hospitality, all indicating how high were the hopes that Shepstone would settle the difficulties satisfactorily. Against this backdrop of festivity, Shepstone and his staff discussed the state of affairs with the Boer leaders, and by the middle of March they seemed to have worked out solutions to most of the problems. That the Transvaal would be annexed was by now common knowledge. 'When the [Annexation] Proclamation will go I cannot say, but I think it will be in the course of the next fortnight,' Haggard wrote home on March 13. The same letter reflects the calm that seemed to settle over the Transvaal: 'Matters have been rapidly advancing and drawing to a close. The Raad... has prorogued itself and left matters to take their course. Things are also looking much more peaceable, and I do not think there will be any armed resistance.'[7]

While the British and Boers were working out details of the annexation, word came to Pretoria that Chief Secocoeni had agreed to submit to the will of the Transvaal Republic. In order to determine whether this news was in fact true, Burgers and Shepstone appointed a committee of four, two Boer officials and two members of the special British commission, Melmoth Osborn and Major Marshall Clarke,[8] to journey up country to Secocoeni's kraal. Haggard accompanied the committee of four as a secretary to the British representatives. This journey into the deep interior took them far into Basuto country, where the savage still ruled and the white man was unknown. The little group of men left Pretoria in late March 1877. The scenery was again wild and beautiful, and once more Haggard marvelled at this new world. The committee was received cordially by Secocoeni, whose people flocked to see the strange white men who had come from over the Dark Water. Haggard recorded as best he could the proceedings of a hot morning's *indaba* (discussion), which took place

in the blazing sun according to native custom, and he later wrote
the official report of the meeting, the gist of which was that Secocoeni
was in fact not prepared to become a subject of the Transvaal Republic.

The return journey to Pretoria was marred by more than the
disappointing news of Secocoeni's unwillingness to accept Boer
peace terms. Some of Secocoeni's braves and an unscrupulous Dutch
borderman had set an ambush for the British representatives and
would have killed them outright had the group not, by mere chance,
decided to take a different road back from the one they used on the
journey up. The fortunate decision was a result of Haggard's insistence
that they take the lower road of the two they had to choose from,
because the scenery was bound to be better that way. Osborn 'let
the young donkey have his way,'[9] and thus the contingent returned
safely to Pretoria.

Within a fortnight after Osborn, Clarke, and Haggard returned
from their mission to Chief Secocoeni, the Transvaal was annexed.
On April 11, the day before the annexation, Shepstone sent a message
to Cetywayo telling him he had heard rumours that the Chief intended
to attack the Transvaal. In the dispatch, Shepstone warned him
against the action and notified him that the Republic was now under
the Queen's protection. Haggard, recalling these events later, avers
that Shepstone was the only man who could at that time 'have pre-
vented the Zulus from sweeping the Transvaal.' But some observers
have insisted that there was in fact no real threat at all from the native
forces because the Zulu chiefs did not descend upon the Transvaal
between January and April of that year, when everyone knew that
there was not even a semblance of internal organization or unity
among the Boers, let alone any military force. Others have gone so
far as to suggest that Shepstone's influence with Cetywayo was powerful enough to enable him to stage a mock threat as a backdrop for
his orderly annexation of the Transvaal, but this could hardly have
been the case. Shepstone can be accused of errors in judgement, but
not of dishonesty. Cetywayo's reply to Shepstone, nevertheless,
can be read in support of more than one theory:

> I thank my father Sompseu for his message. I am glad that
> he has sent it because the Dutch have tired me out and I intended
> to fight them once and once only and to drive them over the Vaal.
> Kahana [name of messenger], you see my impis ... gathered.
> It was to fight the Dutch I called them together; now I will send
> them back to their homes.[10]

On April 12, at about eleven in the morning, a small column of
British officials, Haggard among them, marched into Market Square,

Pretoria, to pronounce the annexation. Haggard gives us an eye-witness account of the occasion:

> Osborn stepped forward and read the Proclamation,* which was received with cheers by the crowd that of course was largely composed of English folk or of those who were not unsympathetic. After this ceremony was completed the ex-President Burger's formal protest, of which the draft had already been submitted to the Commissioner and approved by him, was also read, and received respectfully but in silence.[11]

It fell to Haggard to deliver copies of these official documents to the public offices in Pretoria. Under the terms of the Proclamation of 1877, Shepstone annexed the territory to the British Crown, authorized the courts to continue, and proclaimed 'that the Transvaal will remain a separate government, with its own laws and legislature, and . . . the fullest legislative privileges compatible with the circumstances.'[12]

In the weeks following the annexation, a deceptive tranquillity settled over the Transvaal. The last Battalion of the 13th Regiment, the troops that Carnarvon had sent to reinforce Shepstone's decision, entered Pretoria with the band playing; 'it was extremely well received both there and all along the road.' At noon on May 24, the Queen's birthday, an official ceremony was held at which the British flag was raised formally over the Transvaal. Haggard had a key role in this fateful event: 'The band played "God Save the Queen," the artillery boomed a salute, and at midday precisely, amidst the cheers of the crowd, Colonel [T. E.] Brooke, R.E., and I ran up the flag to the head of the lofty staff.'[13]

Shepstone settled down to administer British rule and justice to all. The future looked promising; the natives had been silenced, the Boers had not shown any strong opposition, President Burgers had retired to the Cape Colony, eliminating one of the sources of civil disagreement, and Shepstone had British money and troops to help him set the government back on its feet. He and his staff moved into Government House and put their minds to the business of running the Transvaal. Justice John G. Kotzé gives us an interesting picture of official life during those early days of British rule:

> Government House, in Shepstone's time, was conducted in a simple and homely way. Both Sir Theophilus and his staff . . .

---

* Other observers have supplied additional details: 'The proclamation was read "in a trembling voice" by Melmoth Osborn, Shepstone's secretary, whose "hands trembled so, that his assistant, Mr. . . . Haggard, had to hold the documents for him." ' Don Theod. M. Tromp, *Herinneringen Uit Zuid-Afrika*, p. 269; and Kotzé, *Memoirs*, p. 238; as quoted in Manfred Nathan, *Paul Kruger: His Life and Times* [1942], p. 118.

understood the art of entertaining and welcoming their guests. Sir Theophilus was very popular, especially with the younger generation, on account of his kindly disposition and fatherly manner, and he was much respected. He sometimes did not appear, except of course at dinner, for he was a hard worker and an assiduous writer. His after-dinner anecdotes of frontier life on the Cape Border and of his numerous other native experiences were related with a clearness and impressiveness that made it a real pleasure to listen to him. To young Rider Haggard they were indeed a revelation and delight; and he used often, when retiring to his room, to put down what impressed him, and then weave it into a romantic story, which was sent off to London, and duly appeared in the *Gentleman's Magazine* or the *Cornhill*, for even at that early time Haggard was active with his pen.[14]

But the auspicious signs that greeted Shepstone on his arrival in Pretoria were ephemeral; they lasted only while the Boers savoured the relief from native threats and civil strife. Soon they were to realize that Shepstone himself could not refrain from interfering with Boer autonomy, and they saw that the annexation meant a loss of freedom. Before long they would seek revenge on the battlefield.

Shepstone had erred. Had he waited in Maritzburg perhaps only a fortnight more, the Volksraad might have appealed to him for assistance, and he could have come to Pretoria and annexed the Republic on his own terms. As it was, he had come uninvited, and then he negotiated with the unpopular head of the defunct government, President Burgers. He failed, furthermore, to insist upon popular sanction for the annexation. He should have bargained with the Volksraad itself; sooner or later they would have had to concede to his demands if in fact they had their country's best interests at heart. Shepstone's gravest error, however, was in promising continued autonomy for the Boers and then failing to set up any form of representative government. In spite of his pledges, Shepstone saw fit to govern – but the Boer would not be ruled.

On June 1, 1877, seven weeks after the annexation, Rider wrote his father that he had just received his appointment as English Clerk to Melmoth Osborn, now Colonial Secretary of the Transvaal. This was Haggard's first appointment that carried a salary – £250 per annum – and this happy turn of events evoked in a letter home some rather ambitious speculations about his future. Because of the potential wealth and development of the Transvaal, he expected to settle there, he wrote, rather than in Natal, for if as is probable gold is discovered in large quantities it may take a sudden rush forward, and then one will be borne up with it. However, my aim is of course to rise to the position of a Colonial Governor. . . . At any rate I have now got my foot on the first rung of the Colonial ladder, and D.V. I intend to climb it. . . . [Even though he concluded the letter with a request for £20, there must have been a deep secret pleasure in the young man's heart when he added,] The great thing is I am now independent and shall, I hope, put you to no more expense or trouble, of both of which I am afraid I have given you too much already.[15]

One of Shepstone's early concerns was with the courts in the Transvaal; he was determined to wipe out the neglect and corruption he found when he arrived and to strengthen and dignify the judicial process. What he saw appalled him. All the judges were laymen and some were even illiterate; lawyers were often fugitives who would have faced criminal actions or jail sentences had they returned to their native countries. Prison practices in Pretoria and elsewhere in the Transvaal were thoroughly casual: after the prisoners had had their evening meal, they were often permitted to leave the prison and visit their family and friends in the town; at nine o'clock or so, the prison bell was rung, and any prisoner who did not return by 9.15 was locked out for the night. Shepstone took decisive steps. He set up a high court for the entire Transvaal under the control of a single judge. For this post he chose John G. Kotzé, a man of high character who had made his reputation as a forthright jurist in the service of the Crown in South Africa. On May 22, 1877, Justice Kotzé presided over the ceremonial opening of the new High Court in the hall where the old Republic's Volksraad used to sit.

Haggard had hardly got settled in his post as English Clerk, when in August, the Master and Registrar of the High Court died. Shepstone and Kotzé wanted to fill the vacancy with someone whose reliability and honesty were beyond reproach. Haggard was only twenty-one and had no legal training whatever, but both the shortage of experienced government officials and the favourable impression he had made upon his superiors combined to work in his behalf, and he won the key post.*

* Haggard, at twenty-one, became *ex officio* legal guardian of all the orphans in the Transvaal! He took office formally on August 3, 1877. In late September or early October, Haggard had an amusing encounter with Anthony Trollope:

I had been sent away on some mission, . . . and returned to Government House late one night. On going into the room where I was then sleeping I began to search for matches, and was surprised to hear a gruff voice, proceeding from my bed, asking who the deuce I was. I gave my name and asked who the deuce the speaker might be.

'Anthony Trollope,' replied the gruff voice, 'Anthony Trollope.' Haggard, *Days*, I, pp. 136–137.

The job was an important one, and arduous. Haggard was Kotzé's
right-hand man, reviewing the cases before they came up before the
judge, settling some of them out of court, and writing up decisions.
The young Norfolkman had luck, and where he lacked information
and experience, he pressed courage and nerve into service. He tamed
the wild pleaders of the law, helped impose a strong discipline of
form on the legal proceedings, and instituted a system of stamps
that insured, for the first time, that court taxes were paid before
petitions became valid.

Since there was only one judge, the court of the Transvaal was
peripatetic. Justice Kotzé and his Registrar set out periodically from
Pretoria on a circuit of the larger cities in the colony, trying all
the cases that had arisen. They started on the first of these circuit
journeys soon after Haggard assumed his duties as Magistrate. The
picture of the High Court of the Transvaal travelling across the veld
makes up in colour for what it lacks in judicial dignity. The government had provided Kotzé with a spring-wagon which was to house
and transport the court officials and their provisions, and eight oxen
to tow this heavy burden of the law. The journey was to be a long
one, and Kotzé and Haggard saw to it that they were as well
equipped as possible. Their *maison mobile* was furnished with comfortable beds (they always slept in the wagons when they were not in
a town); folding chairs and table; pots, pans, and cutlery; and the
ever-reliable tea kettle. They went well armed (Haggard used a Martini
Henry carbine and a fowling piece), and having brought along his
horse and his pointer, Ben, Haggard could go after the springbok and
blesbok which covered the veld in tens of thousands. They consequently had ample supplies of fresh meat for roasting, and, Justice
Kotzé tells us that

as Haggard was a better marksman with his shot-gun than his
rifle, we had also for our meals 'of feathered fowl not a few.' . . .
[But, Kotzé goes on to explain,] bagging birds was by no means all
the service that Rider Haggard rendered to his travelling companions. . . . To my pleasant surprise, I may say astonishment and
admiration, this genial, high-spirited and romantic young man
. . . proved himself to be an excellent cook! He prepared for our
evening meal dishes which would have done credit to a first-class
chef. In a baking pot he baked venison, as well as korhaan and
red-wing partridge, in a manner that could not be excelled, and
he steamed the potatoes to perfection. He would also, on occasion,
prepare more dainty dishes, such as roast snipe on toast, which
were simply delicious. All this was done by him with a quiet

ease which appeared to be quite natural. Where he got this useful art from, he himself did not appear to know.[16]

The itinerant judge and registrar were able to replenish their larder with fresh milk, eggs, and homemade bread in the towns they passed through, and they were, of course, well entertained in the cities where the court sat. Because of the climate, they rose early, and they were usually well under way when the sun came over the mountain-tops. The beautiful vistas that lay on both sides of these little-travelled ways compensated for the poor condition of the roads, and the exciting atmosphere of the hunt prevailed and delighted them both. Unexpected incidents were sure to crop up on these circuit jaunts. One day on this first trek, the men stopped to shoot an unusual white bird that looked like an egret. Kotzé's attempt to conceal himself, however, worked out too well, for he suddenly found that he was sinking into quicksand. Fortunately Haggard came to the rescue and by pulling on the muzzle of Kotzé's piece retrieved the honourable Justice from the menacing swamp.

Not very long after this incident, the axle of their wagon broke just as they were taking a short cut across a road that was virtually untravelled. The two men found themselves suddenly surrounded by a thick mist. They could do nothing but sit, wait for the morrow, and hope the mist would clear. 'As however we had our water-cask well filled to keep the kettle going, we waited patiently,' Kotzé tells us. 'We retired into our wagon for the greater part of the time, lit our lanterns, and whiled away the long moments by reading a play or two of Shakespeare, each taking an act in turn.'[17] Help came the next morning, and they arrived in Wakkerstroom safely later that day.

By the end of October they were back in Pretoria, having sworn in civil authorities in the major cities of the new colony, heard innumerable cases, and enjoyed the excitement and endured the hardship of life on the veld. They were now ready for the court's civil term in Pretoria, which was to begin in November. Haggard, writing home just after the return from his trek, shows clearly how well he had taken to frontier life: 'Do you know one quite gets to like this sort of life. It is a savage kind of existence but it certainly has attractions, shooting your own dinner, cooking it – I can hardly sleep in a house now, it seems to stifle one.'

When Kotzé and Haggard returned to Pretoria in October, they learned of fresh threats from native chiefs. It became evident that Shepstone's magic was not potent; the black armies were again brandishing assegais and demanding back their native land. The letter informing Haggard's family that he has grown accustomed to life on the veld goes on to say that 'the Zulus are panting for war,' and quite accurately suggests that 'we are on the eve of a vast native war,' of which, 'if it should happen the results would be terrible beyond words.'[18] As reports of clashes with native tribes and rumours of impending attacks drifted into Pretoria, the small community began to prepare for its defence, and on December 10, 1877, Haggard adds a postscript in a letter to his mother saying that he had just 'taken the shilling' as a cavalry volunteer.[19]

The British dealt neatly with the early native attacks: they repelled the Galekas who swarmed across the Bashee in September 1877, and they routed the Gaikas in the following June. But these early successes gave the British commanders a false sense of confidence – they had not yet felt the onslaught of an organized native attack. The tribal chiefs were communicating with one another, and they all looked to the great warrior Cetywayo to lead them to a new triumph. The Zulus' need for a full-scale war that would permit their young braves to wash their spears in the blood of an enemy (a requirement they had to meet before they could marry) and the British anxiety over their savage neighbours were to plunge the borderland into the Zulu War, one of the bloodiest encounters of the nineteenth century.

By February 1878, Haggard's letters home tell also of increasing Boer discontent with Shepstone's administration of the Transvaal. Paul Kruger's journey to London in May 1877 to demand the repeal of the annexation had not changed Carnarvon's views. In the Annexation Proclamation, Shepstone had promised the Boers that they would virtually remain masters of their own fate, that they would have their own government and make their own laws. But instead of convening a representative assembly, Shepstone conducted 'a narrow and autocratic administration.'[20] He issued proclamation after proclamation in which he made it perfectly clear that he was the single authority in the land and that he felt free to create and alter law and justice. The Boers' freedom had been bought at too high a price for them to relinquish it without a fight, and this is what they were threatening in 1878. The British found themselves besieged on all sides, by natives from without and by Boers from within. On February 11, 1878, Haggard writes,

> We are rather in a state of excitement (as usual), as the Boers are making some decided manifestations against us, and even talking of summoning the Volksraad. They think because we are quiet we are afraid. I should not at all wonder if we had a row, and in many ways it would not be a bad thing.

And on March 4, another letter reflects the grim state of affairs:

> The Zulu business hangs fire, but that cloud will surely burst.
> . . . It is not for a moment to be supposed that Cetewayo will
> be bound by any decree given against him. . . . Our most pressing
> danger now is the Boers. They really seem to mean business this
> time. From every direction we hear of their preparations, etc.
> According to the latest news they are coming in on the 16th . . .
> five thousand strong, to demand back the Government. This
> of course will be refused. Then they are going to try to rush the
> camp and powder magazine and, I suppose, burn the town. I am still
> sceptical about it: not that I doubt that they would like to do it.
> I dare say they will be tempted by the small number of troops
> here (we have only 250 men). . . . I am one of the marked men who
> are to be instantly hung on account of that Secocoeni article I
> wrote. Some spiteful brute translated it into Dutch with comments
> and published it in the local papers. The Boers are furious; there
> are two things they cannot bear – the truth and ridicule. . . . It
> is precious little I care about them and their threats. . . . You
> would not know me again if you could see me as I appear in the
> *Volkstemm* leaders. However, it amuses them and does not hurt us.[21]

But though the clouds gathered and threats continued, neither
the Zulus nor the Boers descended upon the British immediately.
And the longer Haggard remained in Pretoria, the better his fortune
grew. The boy who had not long ago been the scapegoat of a large
family suddenly found he had made a good impression on those around
him, and looking back on his thirty-two months in Africa, he had
every right to be pleased with his success. He was feeling his oats
when he wrote to his father on April 7, 1878:

> I have to tell you what I am sure you will be glad to hear,
> namely, that I have won the day with reference to my appointment
> as Master and Registrar. . . . The last question has also been settled
> in my favour, i.e. whether I was to receive £300 or £400 per
> annum. I believe I am by far the youngest head of Department
> in South Africa.[22]

And by June, Haggard felt sufficiently established to want to settle
down in Pretoria. 'In a place of this sort,' he wrote his father, 'it is
a great thing to have a pleasant home, and it will also be a sound
investment. I have bought two acres at the top end of the town for
this purpose, where land will soon become very valuable.' He asks
his father for a loan of £500 'to build a nice house with Cochrane.'[23]

Arthur H. D. Cochrane, a young man of his own age Haggard had met in Africa, had come to the Transvaal with a Crown Agent to investigate the finances of the Transvaal for the Home Government. Rider and Arthur had hit it off well, and they did build a house together in Pretoria, a three-room bungalow covered by a tin roof. They called it the Palatial,* and they planted blue gums and other flora to beautify it. Haggard's journeys with Kotzé in the ox-wagon kept him away only two or three months in the year, and there was no reason why he should not enjoy the comforts of a *pied à terre* in Pretoria, the major city in the Transvaal, though still hardly more than a rustic frontier village comprising fewer than a hundred thatched-roof houses.

The city was what one would expect of an outpost. Water furrows ran through the streets, tents were pitched haphazardly on the out-skirts of the town, and men on horseback wove in and out among the ox-carts that bumped noisily on the main arteries. But there were many compensations. Life was plain and relaxed, and an atmosphere of friendliness prevailed. The settlers had cultivated gardens around their houses where pink brier and cluster roses added colour to the scene, and in the west one could see the magnificent Magaliesberg range, a beautiful view from almost any part of the city. The climate was superb, and tropical flowers, fruits, and vegetables grew in abundance. There were a number of croquet lawns, where the ladies often gathered for an afternoon game. Both English and Afrikaans were spoken in the town by a very sociable, well-educated group of men and women. In the evening, there were card and chess parties, musical recitals, and dances.

In August 1878 Kotzé and Haggard set out on another circuit tour. They travelled in the same wagon they had used before, but this time they had ten oxen instead of eight. The itinerary was much the same. Both men of course took along their shooting ponies, for they looked forward to the hunt. And they found it: ample springbok, blesbok, black wildebeest, antelope, partridge, korhaan, plover, spur-winged geese, and duck. An Australian named Palmer who had come to Africa to hunt joined the caravan for part of the trip and helped dispel the monotony. On this journey Haggard had the unusual fortune to kill two gnu with a single bullet. Kotzé recalls the trip with pleasure: 'Our friend from the Antipodes proved an agreeable veld companion, and needless to say, Registrar Haggard, as usual, provided a first-rate dish for supper.'[24]

In the meantime, the Zulus, under their great Chief Cetywayo, were gathering and organizing their forces for what they saw as the battle to defend their birthright against the white man and his

* The Palatial became Jess's Cottage in *Jess* (1887).

encroaching civilization. The showdown seemed inevitable. Here were two cultures, as different from each other as the skin colours of their peoples. Their manners, mores, and laws all clashed. The Zulu, thirsting for blood, rattled his raised spear at the British interloper. The Briton, confident after a few isolated victories and secure in the obvious righteousness of his mission to civilize, heard the war cry and responded. On December 11, 1878, Frere sent Cetywayo an ultimatum. Even had the Zulu chief wished to accept it, he could not, for the conditions Frere laid down struck at the very heart of Zulu life. Frere demanded that Cetywayo should disband his army, lift the requirements that his chaste young athletes dip their spears in an enemy's blood before they might marry, make reparations for various local incidents against the British, and accept a British Resident in Zululand who would be the 'eyes, ears and mouth' of the British Government. For Cetywayo to agree to these conditions would have meant surrendering to the white man without a fight when his warriors were standing by eager for the fray. He showed considerable restraint in not using the ultimatum as an excuse for sweeping down upon the challengers. Frere had demanded an answer within thirty days, and when that period expired and none came, he sent his troops across the border into Cetywayo's territory.

On January 11, 1879, the British entered Zululand in four columns, two of which were never to return. One column, consisting of about 800 Natal volunteers and 500 native troops, marched ten miles into Zululand and set up camp. Its commanders, Lieutenant-General F. A. Thesiger and Colonel A. W. Durnford[25] showed little concern for the strategic vulnerability of the camp site they chose for their troops, in the shadow of the beautiful Isandhlwana. As the soldiers pitched their tents near the road, they might have noticed that on three sides of them mountains rose majestically – and only in front of them lay a flat plain. No scouts were sent out to reconnoitre the surrounding area, no precautions were taken against surprise attack – and on the morning of January 22, a black wall of shrieking Zulus rose on the crest of the surrounding mountains. With traditional fanaticism and precision, the Zulus swept down upon the British laagers. Cetywayo and his men had waited a long time to taste war, and they drove with keen ardour at the white intruders. The British soldiers fought bravely and hard, but their moral and physical strength was not enough to set right the bungling of the Home Government and the blind smugness of the general staff in Africa.

The battle continued through the long daylight hours. When English ammunition ran out, the yellow plain was already red with blood. Though the black armies suffered crippling losses – over

3,000 warriors fell – they laid waste the English camp, and virtually every English soldier fell a victim to the Zulu assegai.*

On the morning of January 24, some thirty hours after the battle and 200 miles distant from Isandhlwana, Haggard, working in his garden in Pretoria, heard an old Hottentot washer-woman say that Cetywayo had swept down upon the redcoats in Zululand and killed them by the hundreds. Haggard questioned her carefully, and although he realized it was inconceivable that any news could travel across the veld so rapidly, he went immediately to Government House to report what he had heard. Twenty hours later, a weary messenger on a panting horse shocked all Pretoria by corroborating the old vrouw's forebodings.

Rider's letters home reflect the reaction to the news as the details trickled into Pretoria:

> Osborn's son-in-law dead, and his family wandering in the veldt. We are sending to their assistance. I have just now sent all the money I have in gold to help the people. . . . Sir Theophilus Shepstone has lost probably three, certainly one son. . . . It was the old story of underrating your enemy. . . . Half the women in Newcastle are widows. . . . You and my mother must not be alarmed my dear father when I tell you that I shall very likely go down to the border with a volunteer troop shortly. The emergency is too great, and mounted men are too urgently needed for us to hang back now, especially when one's example may bring others. If I should, and if anything should happen to me, it must be and I am sure will be your consolation that it will be in doing my duty.[26]

The men of Pretoria gathered and formed the Pretoria Horse. Haggard took an active part in raising the corps, was elected Adjutant and served as one of the Corps' two lieutenants.[27] The volunteers were about to leave for Zululand when, because of the threat of a Boer uprising, their orders were suddenly changed; the corps was kept to defend Pretoria. Just as the Zulus had seen their opportunity to rise when the British were occupied with their new responsibilities in the Transvaal, so now when the Zulu War demanded a concentration of British strength in Zululand, the Boers, having chafed long at the

---

* Haggard tells the story of the battle at least four times, in *The Witch's Head* (1885), *The True Story Book* (1893), edited by Lang, *Black Heart and White Heart* (1900), and *Finished* (1917). Haggard writes that the account in *The True Story Book* 'may be taken as accurate, for two reasons: first, I was well acquainted with the circumstances at the time and saw many of those concerned in the matter, and, secondly, I sent the proofs to be checked by my friend Colonel Essex, who was one of the three or four officers in camp who survived the disaster.' Haggard, *Days*, I, p. 120.

bit, saw their appointed hour. Within forty-eight hours after British troops crossed into Zululand, the Boer leaders met at Wonderfontein (January 13, 1879) and rededicated themselves to the cause of regaining their independence. For two years the Transvaalers had been without representative government, and Frere's promises of self-determination did not assuage the freedom-loving Boers now that the British had removed the Zulu threat. The Boers grew bold and demanding; the movement for independence waxed rapidly, and not, ironically, without British help. For a guilt-ridden group had risen in England to denounce the annexation. They took up the Boer cry of 'Transvaal for the Transvaalers,' which, echoing in turn to the Boers in South Africa, drove them to double their own clamour for liberation. The call to arms spread throughout the Transvaal, and from Boer farmhouses everywhere came men with muskets and munitions to await the moment when they could take the steps that would once again make them free.

Some three thousand Boers gathered on a high plateau about thirty miles from Pretoria and here set up an armed laager, where they waited for the appropriate moment to strike. Haggard, in charge of half a dozen picked men, was sent out to an inn near the Boer encampment to spy on the activities of the malcontents. He set agents in the camp who every night crept out with information for him to relay back to Pretoria. There were of course a good many close calls, and rumours of the impending Boer descent from the high veld ran rampant. But the attack did not materialize. The Boers' sense of timing was bad, and by failing to strike immediately after Isandhlwana, when the British forces were weakest, they lost their chance. For the delay allowed time for large reinforcements to arrive. The Boers eventually broke up their camp and returned to their farms. Perhaps they hoped for another clash with the Zulus; but this was not to come. The Zulu force had been dealt an irreparable blow at Isandhlwana, and although a few more encounters followed, by August 1879 the British forces had captured Cetywayo himself and the Zulu nation was subjugated for ever. With the Boers disbanded and the Zulus subdued, the Pretoria Horse demobilized, and its members returned to their civilian occupations.

It comes as something of a surprise to find that, in spite of the success he had already achieved and the promise the future held for him in the government service, Haggard broke all ties with the Government in May 1879, sold his little cottage, and decided to leave Pretoria and turn to ostrich farming with Cochrane. Gone the hopes of a Colonial Governorship, gone the glory of working in the service of the Crown.

But there were reasons – and the most revealing is the story of young Haggard's first love, which had begun back in London in the spring of 1875, when the eighteen-year-old lad was cramming for the Foreign Office examination at Scoones's. At a ball in Richmond he met a very beautiful young lady and immediately fell deeply in love. He saw her frequently in the six or eight weeks he knew her before he left to join his family at Tours for the summer holiday – and thence to Africa. However deep his own feelings were for the girl, her prosperous family undoubtedly would never have considered any overture from this penurious youth. But the couple gave little heed to practical matters, and when Haggard left for Africa, he considered himself as good as engaged. The image of the young beauty – in later years Haggard wrote that she was one of the three really beautiful women he had ever seen* – steadied him, gave him an object in life and someone to work for. No wonder he dreamed of climbing the ladder of success and jotted down in his commonplace book lines from an anonymous poem that read in part:

> My journeyings are long;
> My slumbers short and broken;
> From hill to hill I wander still—
> Kissing thy token.[28]

Nor is it surprising that, when he found he could talk freely to Shepstone, he opened his heart to him, as he might have done to his own father, had the elder Haggard been less erratic. In March 1877, just after Haggard returned from the mission to Secocoeni, he asked Shepstone if he could take a leave of absence and go home to 'bring a certain love affair to a head by a formal engagement, which there was no doubt I could have done at that time.'[29] He suggested to Shepstone that he go as an official messenger to the Colonial Office, bearing dispatches announcing the annexation. But because it was the practise of the day to use the post for official papers, Shepstone could promise only to send him home to the Colonial Office *with* the dispatches and accompanying credentials, identifying him as a 'living dispatch.' Haggard prepared to leave for England, and on March 13, 1877, wrote his father: 'I think I shall come home *via* the Cape. . . . I want if possible to get to London at the same time as the dispatches announcing the Annexation.' But this was not to be. Rider's father had heard, before he received the letter, that his son intended to return home (Rider had confided in his mother and sister Mary), and he exploded. The idea that Rider was about to throw

---

* The other two were the Duchess of Leinster and a 'village girl at Bradenham who was reported to be the daughter of a gentleman.' Haggard, *Days*, I, p. 42.

over a promising post with imminent financial independence was utterly outrageous. He wrote his son a blistering letter. Rider received it a few days after the annexation had been announced and after his trunks had already gone forward to the Cape. He himself was to leave the next day, but the letter was so strongly phrased that he cancelled his plans to return. Unable to break the chains that bound him, even at this great distance, to the impetuous decisions made on the Norfolk hearth, Rider submitted. He regretted his weakness all the rest of his life. He later saw that 'it was a very foolish act on my part. . . . I may say in excuse of this want of judgement,' he continued, 'that I was very young, only twenty, and that I had to make up my mind on the spot, while, as the Zulus say, "my heart was cut in two." '[30]

Rider turned back to his work in Pretoria, and he gave himself to his duties with much energy, trying to forget the pain that resulted from the clash with his father. But before long a great misfortune descended upon him – the end of his love affair: 'One day the mail cart arrived and all was over. It was a crushing blow, so crushing that at the time I should not have been sorry if I could have departed from the world.'[31] 'If all goes ill [in love],' Rider mused in later years, 'it is one of the worst [things that can occur to a young fellow.] . . . It unsteadies him, makes him reckless, and perhaps throws him in the way of undesirable adventures. In my case, in the end all went wrong, or seemed to do so at the time.' During Haggard's latter days in Pretoria, when he was living with Cochrane at the Palatial, he was by his own admission 'restless and reckless,'[32] and Miss Lilias Haggard, writing about this period in her father's life, suggests that he led a somewhat immoderate life. She describes her father and his friend Cochrane as

> both young, healthy and more than a little wild, and in Rider's case [she continues], the shock and bitterness of his disastrous love affair had left him utterly . . . without any anchor or particular goal on which to fix his ambitions. . . . Also there is no doubt 'the accursed Amyand blood'* was having its fling, the inevitable feminine complications ensued, and it became obvious that they would both be better out of Pretoria.[33]

There were other factors that may have influenced Haggard's decision to resign his post and leave the Transvaal, and whether they were in fact contributory motives or not, they certainly could

---

* Rider's paternal great-grandfather, William Henry, who purchased Bradenham Hall in 1781, married Frances Amyand, grand-daughter of George II's surgeon. 'Wayward, wild, excitable and brilliant, with more than a hint of mental instability, the Amyand blood took possession of the Haggard stock,' writes Lilias Haggard. *Cloak*, p. 24.

pass as the public reasons for his decision. Kotzé tells us that Haggard
'rather felt the removal of his former chief, Sir Theophilus Shepstone,*
to whom he was much attached, and whom he loved as a father';
nor did he seem to relish the change that had taken place in the administration. 'I was sorry to part with him,' Kotzé adds, 'for Haggard
was an efficient Master and Registrar, as well as a pleasant and genial
companion.'[34] It is interesting that this time Haggard did not give
his family a chance to influence his decision; he knew his father
would object to his leaving the government service. When he wrote
home, he reported a *fait accompli*.

For a modest sum, Haggard and Cochrane bought a house named
Hilldrop and about three thousand acres of land near Newcastle,
about 200 miles from Pretoria. The property was Melmoth Osborn's,
and they got it from him on credit, without so much as a promissory
note. In May, Haggard sent in his resignation to the Government,
helped Cochrane buy a beginning lot of ostriches, and the two bird
farmers put the dust of Pretoria and the Transvaal behind them.
But Haggard did not join Cochrane in their new home and enterprise
for some eighteen months. While Cochrane went down to Hilldrop
to begin the new life, Haggard boarded a ship, and in August
1879, after an absence of four years, he again set foot on English
soil.

He had missed the physical comforts of Bradenham, the security
he found in the familiar scenes of his childhood and, in spite of everything, the family circle. He had been away a long time for someone
his age, during the crucial years of his development. He had changed.
He had seen history made – had even helped to make some of it
himself – had learned a great deal about a new world, had seen the
brutality and beauty of the veld, had examined at close range the
folklore and customs of the natives, and had grown to dislike the
Boer. He was homesick, lonely, and his mind spun with impressions
and ideas. True, he did not have a fortune to pour on to his father's
hearthrug, but he had experience and authority, and in England he
might find ears willing to listen to his tales, and perhaps a heart that
could love him.

Hard experience had taught Haggard to approach his father
cautiously, and instead of going directly home, he first went to visit
his elder brother Andrew, stationed then with his regiment at Devon-
port. Andrew did not hesitate to tell him that the family thought
him a fool for having thrown up his government post to take up the

---

* Someone had to be blamed for Isandhlwana and the Boer unrest. The Colonial
Office summoned Shepstone to London, made him account for his policies in the Transvaal,
and treated him shabbily thereafter.

precarious business of ostrich farming. But Andrew none the less listened wide-eyed to his brother's tales and aspirations, and then wrote a letter to their father to help cushion Rider's return to Norfolk:

> As far as I can judge his speculation is a thoroughly sound one, and I fancy when you have seen him, and heard what he has to say, that you will agree that he has done well and not thrown up the service for a mere caprice. I do not think he will ever return to Pretoria in an official capacity, and I think it will make his stay at home a much pleasanter one to him and you all if he is not pressed to do so.[35]

But the tenacious squire was not much influenced by Andrew's suggestions (he soon enough crushed Andrew's desire to join Rider in his ostrich business), and many a storm shook old Bradenham's walls in the days following Rider's return. The epithets changed but slightly: Rider had now outgrown the 'greengrocer' sobriquet and had graduated to 'miserable penny-a-liner' (a reference to the few articles of his that had appeared in print). But rant as his father would against ostriches and hack writers, Rider kept his head this time and turned his short stay in England to good account, at least on one front.

A month or two after he arrived home, he met for the first time Louisa Margitson, the only surviving child of Major John Margitson of Ditchingham, Norfolk. A school acquaintance of his sister Mary, Louisa had come to stay at Bradenham for a week, and before the short visit was up, Rider announced to one and all that Louisa and he were engaged. They had known each other so short a time that when, in turn, she announced her engagement to her guardian, she spelled his name *Ryder*.[36]

Rider's display of 'good sense' turned the trick and brought his father over to his side immediately. After all, Louisa came of a respectable Norfolk family and was an orphan who would, in a year's time, inherit her family's estate at Ditchingham. Objections to Rider's madcap schemes suddenly ceased; his decisions were all at once respected and his cause aided.

Rider describes Louisa in a letter written at the time to his eldest brother, William, in government service at Teheran: 'She is good and sensible and true-hearted, and every day I see her I love and respect her more. She is a woman who can be man's friend as well as his lover, and whom I would trust as I would very few.'[37]

But where money and land are at stake, obstacles often arise. Louisa's uncle, William Hartcup, manager of her estate, withdrew his earlier blessing when he discovered that Rider intended to snatch

his niece off to South Africa and support her on an anticipated income
from ostrich farming. Hartcup said flatly that he would not permit
Louisa to marry until she came of age the following October. Rider,
in turn, would not be put off:

> There are evidently rocks ahead of us [he wrote to Louisa],
> it is the dickens and all when one has to deal with lawyers in these
> matters. I am so very glad to see, love, that you are prepared
> to take a line of your own, and to back me up if it should come
> to any difference of opinion. Two things are very clear. 1. That
> I do not see my way clear to stopping in England until next October.
> 2. That I will not leave England without you. So the sooner that
> your respected Uncle makes up his mind to treat the matter on
> that basis the more comfortably we shall get on together. If it
> comes to the worst, we must go to Court, that is all, though I
> should be sorry if we are driven to it. We are not children to be
> played with, as the Kaffirs say.[38]

They did go to court, for Uncle William, wanting none of the
responsibility of this lunatic scheme, made his niece a Ward in
Chancery. The case dragged on and on; not until February (1880)
did it even come before the judge. Louisa, accompanied by her maternal aunt, Mrs. Hildyard, went up to town for the hearing – and came
down with the measles. But she recovered sufficiently to appear on
the appointed day. Her own account of the proceedings, written on
February 14 to Rider's mother, is entertaining:

> Now that all is settled so satisfactorily we can afford to laugh
> at the whole thing and really Rider's interview with V. C. Malins
> was very amusing. From the first V. C. Malins seems to have
> been favourably impressed but Sir Theophilus's letter settled
> the question and old Malins said he thought it was a very 'suitable
> match'. Mr. Rylands (Mr. Hartcup's lawyer) tried to bring in
> something about only four days' acquaintance, but Malins shut
> him up with – 'Have you never heard of love at first sight before?'
> which I thought was a capital answer. Rylands then tried to say
> something about Rider having nursed me through measles, so
> Rider said—
> 'Of course I did – and I should like to know who else had
> so much right.' This seemed to amuse Malins greatly. He then
> said that until a guardian was appointed we had better not see
> too much of each other and limited us to two days a week. At the
> end he shook hands with Rider, asked him about the annexation
> and was quite friendly.[39]

But relatives with a sense of responsibility toward a propertied orphan are not easily swayed, even by a court order. Though the judge ruled in favour of the marriage, he nevertheless appointed Hartcup, along with Louisa's sympathetic aunt, Mrs. Hildyard, as guardian, and the disagreeing uncle found himself still able to make things difficult for the young couple – and he did. He complicated the property settlements that had to be made, and he almost managed to convince the Ditchingham rector, William Edward Scudamore, not to marry the pair unless the Hartcups came amicably to the wedding. He succeeded in getting the marriage postponed from May to June, from June to July, from July to August, and fought all expenditures, even to the £115 for Louisa's wedding wardrobe. But finally on August 11, a bare two months before Louisa would come of age, she and Rider were married, in the little stone church at Ditchingham, albeit the Hartcups and their blessings were absent.

The disagreements had cost much pain for all concerned, primarily Louisa, who had to endure the disapproval of those whom she loved. The legal side had been expensive too – no less than £3,000 – and since Rider was penniless, the costs had to be paid from Louisa's estate.

Naturally, Rider's father did everything he could to lend wings to the courtship and hasten the wedding day. On December 11, 1879, he wrote on behalf of his son to a London acquaintance, Fred John Blake, of Wordsworth, Blake, and Company, asking him to be Rider's solicitor in the difficulty with the Hartcups. In this letter he explained that his son was home from South Africa 'to be married to a lady of some considerable landed property.'* He also kept in close touch with Rider, advising him constantly on how to advance his suit; he was willing to pay some of his son's expenses of the period, and when in March 1880 Rider insured himself for £5,000, William Haggard advanced £135 4s. 2d. to cover the initial premium.[40] When the dispute finally got into the courts, Rider's father seized the opportunity to write to a club friend of his, E. Borton, Secretary to V. C. Malins, the judge who was hearing the case in Chancery:

> I want you to ask Vice Chan' Malins (who has been most kind throughout) to give the Chancery Conveyances who has the making of the settlement a hint that it w^d be a great obligation if he w^d 'polish them off' quick. I am sure the Vice Chancellor

---

* Letter (March 20, 1880), Clark Collection. The full value of the property is difficult to assess, but the gross yearly rental was 'about £1,700.' From an unpublished memorandum (Clark Collection) concerning the terms of settlement of Louisa's property, presented in Chancery Court on December 13, 1879, by Wordsworth, Blake, and Company.

will himself do his part quick. . . . I hope you will give my kind respects to the V.C.*

Rider and Louisa enjoyed a quiet honeymoon in the Lake District, and then rode up to London where they spent a couple of busy months visiting relatives and drawing up wills and other legal documents connected with Louisa's coming of age. They purchased an entire household of furniture for Hilldrop, for although marriage had led Haggard to reconsider his farming plans – he had actually tried unsuccessfully to regain his post as Master of the High Court at Pretoria – Louisa's pluck and the absence of an alternative caused him to reaffirm his intention to farm ostriches with Cochrane. It could not have been a pleasant prospect, for Cochrane's letters were filled with melancholy tales. The ostriches they had bought turned out to be diabolical monsters; some broke their necks and died, and those that lived simply would not grow feathers and worse still beeame fierce and unmanageable. 'The fodder crops failed, the oxen went down with lung sickness and red water, labour was very short . . . the brick kiln that they hoped would bring in a steady income refused to burn the bricks properly,'[41] and the expensive machinery that Haggard had sent from England for a corn-grinding water mill sat idle in Durban, much too heavy to be carted up to Hilldrop by wagon. There were other complications, for Cochrane had left his affections behind in Pretoria (or at least had led various maidens to think so), and he was having a difficult time obliterating the trail of broken hearts.

Political developments were not encouraging either. Although the Zulu armies had been crushed, the Boers were strongly unified and were waiting for a chance to overthrow the British. Haggard had read in the London papers that in December 1879 the Boers again met *en masse* at Wonderfontein – and this time had openly abrogated the annexation agreement. Although there was no violence during the whole year that followed, the Transvaal was fraught with tension. All the same, in November 1880, after Haggard's 'short' holiday had grown eighteen months long, he sailed for Durban. He was accompanied by his wife, a maid, a groom, a small carriage,

---

* Letter (June 14, 1880), Clark Collection. Another letter (April 8, 1880, Clark Collection) reflects further William Haggard's interest in the match and more of the difficulties the young couple faced: '[Rider] is gone down to stay [at the King's Head, Bungay, one mile from Louisa's home in Ditchingham] . . . to see his "Lady Love" there. . . . I hear from my married daughter with whom I have been walking this afternoon that he (& she) have had all sorts of botherings, all sorts of unpleasant remarks being made in that gossiping neighbourhood with regard to her, wch makes me think that the people about there . . . have been "making" free use of her name. I saw there was something on his mind but I asked no questions.'

and a variety of pets. Marriage had made him a man of substance and property.

When the Haggards arrived in Natal, they learned that a few days earlier (December 16, 1880) the Boers had raised the flag of the Republic at their new capital, Heidelberg, and set off the fuse of the Boer Rebellion by firing on the British troops at Potchefstroom. Four days later, the Boers virtually annihilated a detachment of British reinforcements, some 240 strong, on their way to Pretoria.

Christmas in Maritzburg was a sombre affair for the Haggards. Their journey had been rough and uncomfortable, and now the news of the rebellion in the Transvaal created a terrible dilemma for them. To continue up country to their ostrich farm at Hilldrop was to move within one and one-half miles of Newcastle, the headquarters for British troops, dangerously close to the Transvaal border itself. The Boers would consider it a stroke of luck if, on one of their raiding parties across the border into Natal, they stumbled on Rider Haggard, the very chap who had run up the British flag in the annexation cere- monies at Pretoria. To remain in Maritzburg would be equally difficult because of the boom-town prices. On January 2, Louisa wrote their London solicitor: 'We've got this far OK, but we're detained by the Boer outbreak which began as we were about to start up country. We hope it will be safe to venture forth this week.' She goes on to tell that the war has caused inflation – they had to pay £135 to get their furniture up country – and says that they will need money by the next post. She asks to be told what funds they have to draw upon and what their yearly income is likely to be after deducting insurance and law expenses. 'We hope to be able to live very cheaply when once we get settled. . . . I fancy I shall like the life out here very much, though of course now we are in a very unsettled and uncomfortable state as we sent everything . . . up country before this row began so we have hardly more than the clothes we are wearing.'[42] Louisa and Rider resolved to go to Hilldrop, in spite of its proximity to the Boers. The journey promised to be hazardous; they were then in the midst of the wet season and many of the roads would be washed out, troops would be moving over the roads to Newcastle, and vagrants would be wandering down into Natal. Nor was anxiety lessened by Louisa's 'condition' – she would be giving birth to her first child in six months. Nevertheless, on January 10, horses were hitched to their small carriage, and this strange procession of people, dogs, parrots, and various impedimenta set off on the road across which, five years earlier, Haggard the youth had travelled as a member of Shepstone's special commission to the Transvaal. On January 19 the Haggards stopped long enough at Escourt for Louisa to pen a letter to her father-in-law:

'The roads are in a positively fearful state. . . . I walked a good part
of the way, in fact we all did, as it was quite as hard work hanging
on driving as walking.'[43] Finally they arrived at Hilldrop* and were
warmly welcomed by Cochrane, who had arranged the furniture they
had sent ahead and tried to make the house look like home for the
newlyweds. Though the British and Boer guns could be heard in the
distance, Rider and Louisa settled down to enjoy the many pleasures
Hilldrop had to offer. Their home was in a beautiful part of the country,
dotted with tropical plants, and offered a magnificent view of the
snow-capped Drakensberg. Cochrane had made considerable progress
since the Haggards had left England, and he could now hold out the
hope that the farm might prove a paying venture. The Boer uprising
had, moreover, put an end to any romantic connections he thought
he had with Pretoria.

The fighting continued on the borderland during these early
weeks of 1881, always within earshot. Sir George Colley commanded
the handful of British troops, but he too, unfortunately, proved more
courageous than wise. He underestimated the superior marksmanship
of the farming and deer-hunting Boers, and the British paid heavily
in dead and wounded before they learned the true nature of their
enemy, and even then too late to save Colley's life. The news of
successive defeats reached Hilldrop from day to day, and Haggard
grew increasingly anxious about the future.

> We have come out in very troublous times [he wrote his father
> on January 30]. . . . We have got all our things up safely and made
> the place quite pretty, but, somehow, one can take no pleasure
> in anything with blood being shed like water all around. Every
> time one sees a Kaffir runner coming one feels anxious lest he
> should be the announcer of some fresh evil. [And nine days later,
> he wrote his mother:] Last night we slept in our clothes ready
> to make a bolt for it, as there was a report the Boers were coming
> in to Newcastle. . . . We have chosen a bad time to come to Natal.
> Louie is wonderfully plucky about the whole thing, but it is very
> anxious work for me.[44]

The Boers grew bold with repeated success, and soon raiding
parties descended across the border into Natal. The Haggards and
Cochrane maintained a nightly watch with the help of their natives,
kept a team of horses saddled at all times, and slept in their clothes,
firearms by their sides. Then when the Boers raided a neighbouring

---

* A good description of Hilldrop can be found in Haggard's novel *Jess* (1887), where
he calls it Mooifontein.

farm and rumour reached them that Hilldrop would be next, they knew that the time had come to seek shelter in Newcastle. But they lived in their uncomfortable laager in Newcastle only a few days, for on February 17 reinforcements large enough to insure the relative safety of the surrounding country arrived, and the Haggards returned to Hilldrop, where they found everything intact.

Ten days later, a Sunday, was an ill-fated day for the British. Down to Hilldrop from Majuba Hill came the sound of constant firing: clearly a battle of vast dimensions was raging. Haggard and Cochrane, eager for news, went to Newcastle and waited for word to arrive. Slowly the rumours trickled down into the valleys that told of British losses and Boer gains. When the firing had ceased and the truth was known, all were shocked. The British forces had suffered so decisive a defeat that it made the memory of Isandhlwana live freshly again in their hearts. The news stung the Haggards deeply: many of their acquaintances had been wiped out. They sadly realized that of thirteen people at a dinner-party they had attended at Government House in Maritzburg hardly two months earlier, only four now survived. Many of the others lay dead atop Majuba Hill. Actually negotiations for an armistice had been going on for some time before Majuba, but the engagements on the battlefield had gone forward without much regard for diplomatic palaver. Kruger, now acting on behalf of the united Boers, had written accepting an offer of complete self-government under the suzerainty of the Crown, but the dispatch was not received until March 7, more than a week after the battle on Majuba Hill.* By March 23 the armistice was concluded and the Boers went back to their farms. Within the month, Hilldrop, geographically ideal for the purpose, was leased by the British as a headquarters for negotiating peace terms with the Boers. The arrangement brought in fifty pounds a week to the Hilldrop coffers, and though the men had to relinquish their beds and sleep either in tents or at the mill, the compensation made living 'picnic fashion' palatable.[45]

The long and tedious conditions that were to comprise the thirty-two articles of peace were slowly assembled, and finally on August 3, 1881, the Preamble of the Convention of Pretoria was agreed upon. It granted the Transvaalers 'complete self-government, subject to the suzerainty of her Majesty.'[46] Though the Preamble was not actually signed by the representatives of both parties at Hilldrop, the irony

* With Kruger's acceptance of Britain's offer, hostilities ceased, but of course to the fighting Boers, to the saddened British colonials, in fact to the world, it seemed that the armistice agreement, following hard on the heels of the battle of Majuba, was the direct result of a military defeat, when in reality the battle had not influenced British policy at all.

of the case is obvious enough. Haggard had raised the flag signifying British possession of the Transvaal; now the terms for completely wiping away that earlier act and all the labour, personal sacrifice, and national pride it stood for had been devised in his own home. Haggard, by this time an informed and concerned observer of the political scene in South Africa, had no intention of watching the Transvaal slip through British fingers without at least a protest from him. On June 6, even as the negotiators were blueprinting the scheme for giving the Transvaal back to the Boers, Haggard wrote directly to Sir Bartle Frere:

> I do not believe that more than half of those engaged in the late rebellion were free agents, though once forced into committing themselves they fought as hard as the real malcontents. . . . The natives are the real heirs to the soil, and should surely have some protection and consideration, some voice in the settlement of their fate. They outnumber the Boers by twenty-five to one. . . . Leading all these hundreds of thousands of men and women to believe that they were for once and for ever the subjects of Her Majesty, safe from all violence, cruelty, and oppression, we have handed them over without a word of warning to the tender mercies of one, where natives are concerned, of the cruellest white races in the world. . . . Lastly there are the unfortunate English inhabitants, three thousand of whom were gathered during the siege in Pretoria alone, losing their lives in a forsaken cause. I can assure you, sir, that you must see these people to learn how completely is their ruin. They have been pouring through here, many of those who were well-to-do a few months since, hardly knowing how to find food for their families.[47]

But the Transvaal was lost to the British.

While the negotiations were still in progress, Louisa's child was born – a son and heir – whom they named Arthur John Rider, and it was not long after the birth of 'Jock' that Haggard concluded that he and his family had no future in South Africa. If bringing his bride to Africa had been a mistake, there was no logic in letting that mistake rule their lives. He was now a man with a family to support, and it was his responsibility to think clearly and act sensibly. His letters home at the end of July show that he was capable of it. To his father he wrote:

> After thoroughly thinking the matter over I have made up my mind to return to England next month. This will probably seem a rather eccentric announcement, but . . . what brings me

back in such a hurry is the state of the country ... [which is] so unsatisfactory and so dangerous I dare not risk the safety of others – the sooner we go the better. I only hope I have made a wise decision.[48]

And to his mother he wrote:

Every day that passes has only strengthened my conviction that we can look for no peace or security in South Africa. Gladstone's policy has effectually ruined the country. ... We have more or less fixed on Vancouver Island for our next Colonial venture. I dare say you will wonder at this, but there are several reasons, first we both like Colonial life, next it is a satisfaction to earn one's own living, thirdly and chiefly, I am very anxious to form connections with some country in which it is possible for a man of moderate means to start his children in some respectable career in which they can earn their livelihood, and have a fair chance of getting on in the world. This I had hoped to do in Natal – but events have been against us.[49]

Vancouver Island was forgotten, however, when letters from Rider's father and lawyer urged him to come directly home to England for 'reasons both personal and connected with ... [the Ditchingham] property.'[50]

Cochrane decided to return to England with the Haggards, and they all agreed to leave the farm in the hands of two men who had been working at Hilldrop with them, George Blomefield, a young ward of Rider's father who had come out to South Africa to make his way, and a Mr. North, an engineer.*

Parting was difficult. Hilldrop was the Haggards' first home, and in spite of adversity they had spent a few months of happiness there. Leaving was after all an admission of failure, and the future they were going to face was completely uncertain. But more than anything, the political situation discouraged them and made Rider particularly sad, even bitter. By agreeing to an armistice and peace terms in which the Boers exacted practically all their demands immediately following the defeat of Majuba Hill, Downing Street was giving the Boer an exaggerated sense of victory and was placing the British colonial of South Africa in an embarrassing position. All that the loyal colonial had fought for was dissipated in a matter of a few

* On April 29, 1883, almost two years after the Haggards left Africa, a settlement of farm ownership was signed at Ditchingham by Haggard, Cochrane, and Blomefield, dissolving the partnership. Assets, after liabilities, amounted to £250 14s. 7d., and this sum was divided among the three signatories. Clark Collection.

months by unrealistic military strategy and worst of all by singularly
bad timing of the orders from Whitehall. As Haggard had indicated
to Frere, the British in the Transvaal suffered most; they had either
to live side by side with the contemptuous Boers or gather up their
possessions and wander south into Natal. Many years later, Haggard
still felt keenly his disappointment at British policy in South Africa:

> Never shall I forget the scene on the market square of Newcastle
> – it must have been about the 21st or 22nd of March – when it
> became known that peace had been declared as a corollary of our
> defeats, and that the restoration of the Transvaal was practically
> guaranteed within six months. Some thousands of people were
> gathered there, many of them refugees, among whom were a
> number of loyal Boers, and with these soldiers, townsfolk, and
> natives. I saw strong men weeping like children, and heard English-
> born people crying aloud that they were 'b——y Englishmen'
> no more. Soldiers were raging and cursing, and no one tried to
> stop them; natives stood stupefied, staring before them, their
> arms folded on their breasts; women wrung their hands.
> Then an idea struck the crowd; they made a rude effigy of
> Mr. Gladstone and, as was done in most of the other loyal parts
> of South Africa, burnt it with contempt and curses.[51]

At the end of August, having auctioned off their household furniture at a good price, the Haggards left Hilldrop. Haggard found it
most difficult to part from his devoted servant boy, Mazooku, whom
he had acquired in his early days in Africa. Mazooku had been his
constant companion throughout; he had travelled with Haggard
through Natal and the Transvaal, had saved his master's life when
Haggard had lost his way on the veld, had sheltered the little family
group at Hilldrop, and had given his 'Lundanda' (Haggard's Zulu-given
name: the tall and pleasant-natured one) the selfless devotion the
natives were famed for. Rider would have liked to take this true friend
back with him to civilization, but the scheme was obviously impractical – the best he could do would be to bring him back in the
stories he was later to write.*

On August 31, 1881, the small family group sailed for England.
In spite of the sadness and disappointment Haggard must have felt
as he departed, for him the years in Africa had been an inspiration.
He had played the overture of his life through, and the themes he had
sketched there would be enlarged and exhausted in later life, each
in its own time.[52]

* Mazooku appears in person in *The Witch's Head* (1885).

3

Law and Letters

ALTHOUGH it had been their intention to spend four or five years in South Africa, less than a year had passed between the time the Haggards set sail as newlyweds and their return to England. Upon arriving, they went directly to Bradenham, where they spent a few weeks within the family fold. Here Haggard considered the several ways in which he might make a living for his small family, and one day decided that he would read for the bar. No one could accuse him this time of not choosing a practical vocation: he would try to follow in his father's and elder brothers' footsteps. Besides, he had had considerable experience with the law in South Africa and had found his work with Justice Kotzé most agreeable. Certainly with the knowledge he had acquired as a court registrar and magistrate, he would be much better off than a beginning solicitor.

The idea of following the law had actually been planted in Haggard's mind much earlier. Just a year before, while he was waiting to marry Louisa, he had written Justice Kotzé inquiring about the possibilities of returning to his post in the Civil Service, and Kotzé had replied:

Why not read for the Bar? ... It will take you not more than three years, and ... you will have no difficulty in turning out a first-rate man. ... Give it your serious attention. You have a certain prospect of a judgeship, and will without much difficulty get into the Cape Parliament. ... You will have a *fine* and *thoroughly* independent career before you.[1]

Though the decision meant that Haggard would be financially dependent upon his wife's estate for three more years, he made it, and by Christmas, the little family group left Bradenham and settled down in a furnished house in Norwood, south of London. There, following family tradition, Haggard chose to read for Lincoln's Inn and engaged a 'crammer' to help him prepare for the entrance examination, which he passed after a month's study.

Though Haggard, in the subsequent months, concentrated upon his law books and successfully met every challenge of his studies, the law was not the only subject to occupy him. Being back in England was, to be sure, a delight, but the sedentary existence of the law student was not particularly challenging to the young, active mind. The platitudes of daily urban life must have been irritating. He undoubtedly found the narrow quarters of his home in Norwood and the restrictions of English society confining, and he could not help bristling at the ignorance and complacency that characterized the discussions about South African affairs, both in the Press and in private circles. Beside his law books lay his pen, and near at hand were the notebooks and diaries he had filled during those reckless years – and there was time.

Even back in Africa, he had striven to re-create for a reading public part of what he himself was experiencing. He had tried, time and again in the early days in Natal and the Transvaal, to record accurately what he saw and heard, to capture in words a new reality. His eye for detail was good and the pictures he sketched were clear and lifelike. As early as October 6, 1876, Haggard had told, in a letter home from Maritzburg, about 'articles which I am writing,'[2] and in 1877, soon after the annexation of the Transvaal had intensified British interest in South Africa, three essays by 'H.R.H.' appeared in English periodicals. The first, entitled 'The Transvaal,' was published in the May issue of *Macmillan's Magazine*, on the eve of the official announcement of the annexation. In it, Haggard gives a short and fairly accurate historical account of the Dutch in South Africa, and then uses these historical facts as a springboard for launching a diatribe against the Boers, whom he denounces as 'intensely prejudiced against everything modern and civilized.' The message of the article emerges in the last few paragraphs, where Haggard's swelling prose pictures the imminent annexation as a righteous, humane, and beneficent act:

The Dutch have nothing to complain of; they have had their chance, they have been allowed to play at governing themselves and they have failed. . . . Their failure . . . affects us in our feelings as Christians and Englishmen. We can hardly be expected to stand by and see our highest principles as regards the treatment of subject races set utterly at nought. . . . We Englishmen came to this land . . . with 'a high mission of truth and civilization.' . . . We alone of all the nations in the world appear to be able to control coloured races without the exercise of cruelty. . . . It is our mission to conquer and hold in subjection, not from thirst of conquest

Original illustration for *She*

The Ghost Kings

She scores with doctors

Plot outline of Haggard's *Ghost Kings*

but for the sake of law, justice, and order. Decidedly, the day
when the British flag – a flag that has always brought blessings
in its train – is first unfurled there should be a glad day for the
Transvaal, Republic no more – for the South African colonies,
who will welcome a new and beautiful sister, and for England,
who will add another lusty child to her splendid progeny.[3]

This expressed a familiar and welcome notion to an English public
that had been nourished on Disraeli's foreign policy.

The two succeeding articles appeared in the *Gentleman's Magazine*,
'A Zulu War Dance' in the July issue and 'A Visit to the
Chief Secocoeni' in September. These were both expository pieces
in the tradition of travel literature. 'A Zulu War Dance,' the first
article Haggard ever wrote for publication, is an account of his early
visit to Chief Pagate's kraal and describes in breath-taking detail the
war dance that Pagate staged in honour of Sir Henry Bulwer. The
other, 'A Visit to the Chief Secocoeni,' although of a later vintage,
relates with the same clarity and careful observation the journey
Haggard made to Secocoeni's kraal soon after the annexation team
had arrived in Pretoria. What distinguishes these two from the earlier-
published essay is that they take the reader on brief safaris behind
the seemingly impenetrable curtain of African wilderness, and they
succeed. Though Haggard does not harness griffins or uncover the
fountain of youth (not yet, at any rate), the journalistic quality and
the excitement of adventure and discovery they contain are reminiscent
of the tales of Marco Polo and Mandeville. Africa to the British of
the eighteen-seventies was, after all, remote and mysterious. These
two essays were exciting documentary reports from a colonial servant
in the sweltering, savage interior to the people in temperate, civilized
England, those people who had suddenly found themselves owning
and operating a network of colonies they had acquired 'in a fit of
absence of mind.'

Although the two articles describing Haggard's visits to the seats
of native chiefs contain much less flag-waving than his article on the
Transvaal, they too reflect a strong antipathy for the Boers. Haggard
did not bring an anti-Dutch prejudice with him to South Africa;
he acquired it in his early days in Maritzburg, while learning to live
a new life in a new world. The conventional British colonial attitude
towards the Boer was one of disdain, just as the Boer traditionally
looked upon the Briton with loathing. For decades now the British
colonial found his government officially in pursuit of the Boer, who
was continually outwitting British rule and justice. Where the British
could take a paternal interest in the noble savage, and see themselves,

in relation to the black population, as missionary protectors destined to mould the unmoulded, they could not tolerate anything but the British idea of enlightened behaviour from the Boers. The Boers were, after all, whites, and the roots of their civilization lay in Western Europe. There was no excuse for lawlessness, or, for that matter, for behaviour dictated by laws or customs the English settlers could not understand. They would not stand for the Boers' makeshift courts and prisons; they would not endure the coarse personal habits of the Boer farmer; they would not accept Boer Calvinism as a respectable religion; and, most of all, they would under no circumstances stand by and permit the Boer to mistreat the native. Great Britain would not be compromised; her standards of decency and justice would, as long as there was breath in a single British colonial, hold sway. Given continued good fortune, the British would bring to white South Africa the niceties of British civilization and to black South Africa the gift of British protection. The great obstacle that stood in their way was not the native, now subdued, but the Boer, who had to be untaught the wrong before he could be shown the right.

This was the feeling in official circles in which Haggard moved, and he came to share it quite naturally. There was no time to judge everything for himself; he was overwhelmed with the demands the new environment made upon his resources, and the easiest course was to succumb to convention. Later, when he crossed the Transvaal border and came into direct contact with the Boer, much of what he saw corroborated his sentiments. The Boers were a hard-working, hard-living, migratory people. They had not remained in any one part of South Africa long before they found they had to move; their agrarian life did not permit them to cultivate personal grace and gentility; and they were much of the time on the defensive, having incurred the animosity of both the British and the natives. The Dutch were on the whole often crude as well as bold, hot-tempered as well as hard-fighting, unfriendly as well as unwanted. Haggard found ample evidence to support his stereotypes, and the Boer soon became the evil force in his world.

The anti-Boer remarks in Haggard's first published articles unexpectedly found their way back to a Dutch newspaper in South Africa, where they appeared translated for all the Boers to read, and of course damned Haggard's name with them. The young writer also came in for a scolding from Sir Bartle Frere, who feared that the articles might adversely affect his negotiations with the Boers. Justice Kotzé, a man of clear mind and high spirit, was puzzled about Haggard's attitude toward the Boers. Writing of their circuit travels, he said that

wherever possible, the farmers were visited by me ... and
we had many a friendly talk together. ... Haggard could not,
however, be persuaded into visiting the homes of the Boers.
He was strongly prejudiced against them, although they never
offended him in any way. ... This was a pity for Haggard's own
sake, for, had he understood the Boers, he would have written
of them with better knowledge and spirit.[4]

In later years, Haggard himself became aware that the Boers were
an early blind spot in his life: 'I did not like them much at the time
– few Englishmen did. ... Now I know that there is much to admire
in the Boer character, also that among them were many men of real
worth.'[5] But this wisdom he acquired late, only after he had written
a great deal about the Boers with a venomous pen.

A hiatus occurs in the story of Haggard the author after the three
articles about Africa appeared in 1877. His travels with Kotzé, his
duties in the Pretoria Horse, his voyage home, and the nervous activity
attendant upon his courtship and marriage were to keep him from
writing. But once he had put his affairs in order and settled into the
routine life of husband, father, and law student in his Norwood
house, his thoughts turned back to Africa, and his pen lured him
again.

The Zulu War and the Boer Rebellion were still fresh in people's
minds, and England's South African policy was very much a subject
of controversy in gentlemen's clubrooms and in the Press. It was
quite natural that Haggard should be drawn into the discussions.
When an irate letter he sent to *The Times* failed to appear in print,
his indignation flared, and he decided to write a historical account
of the events that had occurred in South Africa during his six-year
stay there. Gladstone had already turned the Transvaal back to the
Dutch, and what England's policy would now be toward this particular
colonial neighbour was not at all clear. Furthermore, though the
native forces had been completely vanquished and Cetywayo was
a British captive, no one, least of all the politicians, knew quite what
to do with the native population, now so tractable. Haggard, along
with other men of experience in colonial affairs, was convinced that
the problem of South Africa should no longer be a political football.
He surrounded himself with blue-books, became engrossed in reminiscences, and set himself to write his first major work. He called
it *Cetywayo and His White Neighbours; or, Remarks on Recent Events
in Zululand, Natal and the Transvaal*, a title with which he hoped to
capture readers of many camps.

But before he could claim readers, he had to find a publisher.

He posted numerous copies of a form letter stating his South African experience as a qualification and assuring prospective publishers that the book was 'written in as interesting a style as I can command.'[6] But no publisher leapt at the opportunity Haggard offered. True, South Africa was an issue of empire-shaking importance. But it had, since Isandhlwana and Majuba, become a very unpleasant subject. It had, furthermore, received much attention in the Press and had been exhausted by professional luminaries such as Trollope and J. A. Froude (his *Two Lectures on South Africa*, delivered before the Philosophical Institute in Edinburgh in 1880, were published later the same year). But in spite of all this, a prospective publisher did appear for Haggard's book, although he required an advance of £50 toward costs. Haggard sent his check, and on June 22, 1882, Trübner and Company placed an edition of 750 copies of *Cetywayo* on sale. Haggard, student of the law, suddenly emerged historian.

Cetywayo and His White Neighbours, Haggard's initial literary effort of sizeable proportions and probably his least professional book–a collection of fact, impression, and opinion – is all the same one of his most important works and a singular contribution to the annals of Empire. It is read today primarily by the specialist – but here precisely is its merit: no scholar writing about South African history can afford to pass by *Cetywayo*. The book itself is really more than a history; it is a historical document, and as such is extremely valuable. It is a lively chronicle that reconstructs for the reader clearly and with considerable detail the events that occurred in Natal, Zululand, and the Transvaal during the crucial years between 1875 and 1881. Haggard's official relationship with British headquarters, the information that his position provided, his knowledge of the people of South Africa and the geography of the country, and his ability to see into the political motives and judge the behaviour of the interested parties – all contribute to the worth of *Cetywayo*.

Haggard knows that colonial affairs are a tiresome subject to most Britons and that an impending catastrophe in one of the colonies would not excite the English public nearly so much as did the 'exodus of Jumbo.' He deplores this complacency and sees it as a great danger to England and her Empire: 'Trade is the life-blood of England,' he writes, and since the fountain-head of English trade is in the colonies, one would think the British, if only for selfish reasons, would take a greater interest in these colonies. For the Mother Country derives many advantages from her Empire. He grows stern and prophetic when he points to the 'odd shuffling of the cards going on now in England,' and augurs – how wisely and how early! – 'that England's future looks by no means sunny,' and that 'Englishmen of . . . two generations hence . . . may not find their country in her present proud position.'

South Africa is one colony that has cried out to England for 'the application to the conduct of its affairs of a firm, considered, and consistent policy,' but that cry has neither touched the heart of the English people nor influenced the minds of the 'amateurs and sentimentalists' whose knowledge comes from a few Foreign Office bluebooks 'superficially got up to enable the reader to indite theoretical articles to the *Nineteenth Century*, or deliver inaccurate speeches in the House of Commons.'[7]

Dealing with first things first, Haggard, in a section called 'Cetywayo and the Zulu Settlement,' devotes himself to the question of the natives. Though England has conquered the natives, she must yet decide what to do with them and their country, Zululand. The Government had still to come upon a satisfactory solution. One very strong register of British opinion deplored, through its ignorance Haggard thought, the deposition of Cetywayo, arguing that Britain had a moral obligation not to dethrone royalty, and especially not Cetywayo, who was a handsome monarch with pearly teeth.

While Haggard was writing, the Home Government decided to bring Cetywayo to England to help determine what to do with Zululand, and the political stage was being set for Cetywayo's visit. Haggard frowns upon all the attention being given to Cetywayo and sets himself the task of recording the historical and political facts for all those concerned with the native problem. He shows a picture of Cetywayo far different from the popular conception of the chieftain and supports this unconventional image with evidence rather than 'feminine sentiment.' Cetywayo, he asserts, is a bloodthirsty tyrant who mercilessly slaughtered his own people without trial. In his dealings with the British, he had been uncompromising and deceitful. In view of the facts, Haggard insists, it would be great folly to trust Cetywayo and outright madness to restore him to the throne. The only just course would be for Britain to follow up its victory over the Zulus by annexing Zululand and ruling the country for the natives. In reinstating Cetywayo, Britain would be relinquishing her victory over the Zulus and restoring the *status quo*. Cetywayo would resort to his old habits of brutality within his country and duplicity in external affairs. Many Zulus, moreover, were by no means eager to see Cetywayo again, and he would certainly inflict punishment on them for their reluctance.

Haggard tells impartially the history of the Zulus in South Africa from the days of Chaka, Cetywayo's great uncle, the first of the great Zulu kings, down to Cetywayo's reign and the Zulu War, and criticizes severely the way the Government handled the settlement of this war.

At the close of hostilities, there were two respectable courses the British might follow: one, to 'take over the country and rule it for the benefit of the Zulus,' and the other, to allow Cetywayo to remain on the throne after he had agreed to reign according to the conditions in Frere's earlier ultimatum. But the Government took neither of these realistic approaches; instead it banished Cetywayo and adopted Sir Garnet Wolseley's 'settlement,' dividing Zululand into thirteen pieces, each under its own petty chief. This arrangement could not and did not work out, for soon the chiefs were warring among themselves. 'Cetywayo's rule, bad as it was, was perhaps preferable to the reign of terror that we have established under the name of the settlement,' Haggard concludes. 'But that we can still remedy if we choose to do so, whereas if we once restore Cetywayo, all power over the Zulus passes out of our hands.'[8]

The climate of opinion and the political atmosphere, however, called for something else. The native question had become a hot coal in Gladstone's palm, and he decided that Britain had to relinquish her power over the Zulus. Nor was Gladstone without popular support: 'Having committed an act of injustice, and made a political mistake,' wrote the *Spectator*, 'our present duty is [not] to persist in the same course.' It is better to 'reverse a mistaken act . . . than knowingly to perpetuate an evil deed.'[9] The *Spectator*'s formula prevailed, and Cetywayo was restored to his throne early in 1883.

Haggard's acerbity in dealing with Cetywayo is honey by comparison with the tone of the large section of the book that deals with the Transvaal. Here, he is not able to sustain the moderation he showed in the earlier part. For the history of the Transvaal is, after all, the story of the Boers – virtually nothing was known of the territory or the people who populated it before 1800 – and the Boers, as we know, were anathema to Haggard. He begins by telling hastily about the early struggles of the Dutch in South Africa and about the Great Trek. He cannot, however, bring himself to tell the heroic story of the early days of the Boer Republic in the Transvaal: 'The history of the Republic between 1852 and 1876 is not very interesting, and is besides too wearisome to enter into here. It consists of an oft-told tale of civil broils, attacks on native tribes, and encroachment on native territories.' He paints a highly opinionated picture, almost a caricature of the Boers, and records his impression of their customs, laws, and government. He calls them a

peculiar people [whose religious zeal] . . . takes its colour from the darkest portions of the Old Testament. . . . [They] delight in stories of wholesale butchery, . . . [and they have no] regard for the truth, especially where land is concerned. . . . Personally Boers are fine men, but as a rule ugly. Their women-folk are good-looking in early life, but get very stout as they grow older. They . . . understand how to use their tongues; indeed it was said that it was the women who caused the rising against the English Government. None of the refinements of civilization enter into the life of an ordinary Transvaal Boer. He lives in a way that would shock an English labourer at twenty-five shillings the week. . . . . His home is but too frequently squalid and filthy to an extra-ordinary degree. He himself has no education, and does not care that his children should receive any. . . . [The Boer makes occa-sional sorties on the neighbouring natives, just for the sport of it, and he detests foreigners, especially Englishmen. He has] a great idea of himself, and a corresponding contempt for all the rest of mankind. . . . [He hates laws and taxes.] He has no romance in him, nor any of the higher feelings and aspirations that are found in almost every other race . . . [and,] unlike the Zulu he despises, there is little of the gentleman in his composition.[10]

His anger spent, Haggard turns to the conditions in the Transvaal immediately preceding the annexation, and tells from first-hand experience about the political atmosphere in South Africa and of the events that led up to the annexation. He reports how Shepstone's party marched into Pretoria and took over the reins of government, he carries his history forward to the Transvaal under British rule, and then to the Boer Rebellion and the suffering of the colonial community in Newcastle during those tense months when he and his wife had lived at Hilldrop. The final chapter of this section he devotes climactically to the retrocession of the Transvaal, which he considers one of history's most humiliating political realities. He berates Gladstone and accuses him of having acted out of ignorance, dishonesty, and party motives. In abandoning the Transvaal and the loyal subjects within its borders, England, he feels, has committed 'an act of treachery' that 'marks a new departure in our history.'

There is no easy solution to the bungled situation in the Transvaal, Haggard realizes, and his indignant rebuke is not here accompanied by a constructive plan. He can only prophesy:

It will take but a small lapse of time for the Transvaal to find itself in the identical position from which we relieved it by the Annexation. . . . The only thing that is at present certain about the matter is that there will be bloodshed . . . [and] trouble, both from its white subjects, and the natives, who hate the Boers with a bitter and well-earned hatred.[11]

Though Haggard does not suggest positive steps in Britian's future policy with the Transvaal, he does put forward a very reasonable and constructive plan for Britain's future affairs in South Africa generally. All South African matters, he suggests, should be handled by a Board or Council 'composed of moderate members of both parties, with an admixture of men possessing practical knowledge of the country.'[12]

More than the Zulu War and the Boer Rebellion are fought out on the pages of *Cetywayo and His White Neighbours*, for the book also serves as the battlefield for two strains in Haggard's nature. Haggard is honest, feels a deep thirst for knowledge, and reveres any body of facts. *Cetywayo* draws heavily on official documents and eye-witness accounts and is uniformly accurate in tracing historical incident and presenting statistics. But Haggard's scholarship struggles, especially in the large section on the Transvaal, with his emotions. However much he may strive to be dispassionate toward his material, waves of feeling well up beneath the imposed academic exterior and break through the superficial restrictions. And how could he have expected to be detached? The tale would out – not in measured statements and scientific analyses, but in stirring prose designed to capture hearts as well as minds, and in a way that would enable Haggard, the traveller returned, to speak his piece, to rid himself of at least some of his anguish. Though Haggard disclaims 'party purpose,' he cannot write without bias. For *Cetywayo*, although it is unquestionably a unique historical document, is also a memoir and a tract. It is more a feverish attempt to put the record right than an effort to weigh that record objectively, and it is done with at least as fond a hope of influencing the future as it is with seeing clearly the past.

Although Haggard's philosophy battles with his scholarship and his heated language raised more eyebrows than hopes for his cause, all the same his history does not fade into fable. For *Cetywayo and His White Neighbours* is one of the very few authoritative reports of that period and as such is an irreplaceable primary source. Haggard's bias does not, in this case, invalidate *Cetywayo* for the historians – it may in fact increase its value for them (and certainly the polemic makes it a livelier volume) – because Haggard wrote boldly and bluntly from the point of view of an English colonial and made no effort whatever to conceal his opinions of the Boers, the British Home Government's record in South Africa, and the politicians on the contemporary scene. His opinions do not change the facts, and Haggard is faithful, in almost every instance, to the facts.

Other qualities that make the book important are its author's common sense, his political acumen, and his ability to predict the outcome of events. Disagreeing with popular opinion, he foretells accurately and devastatingly what would occur – and what later actually did occur – when Cetywayo was restored to the throne. He predicts also another war between Boer and Briton. And when he points a warning finger to a future where Britain's star will be in descent as a result of current political negligence and administrative complacency, he is again proved remarkably right.

Cetywayo was a 'first' of an unknown author and a book on a wearisome subject – reasons enough for the reviewers to ignore it. But many saw its merits, and it received favourable notices in most of the periodicals of the day. A strong religious organ, the *British Quarterly Review*, while anticipating that it would not receive the attention it deserved, called it 'a very able and judicious statement ... and [a] statesmanlike discussion of our leading difficulties in South Africa.'[13] The *Spectator* gave the book a lengthy and respectful review. It summarized Haggard's thesis faithfully, indicated that it disagreed with him on various points, and took him roundly to task for his intemperate treatment of the Boers. It said agreeable things about Haggard's writing ('charming description ... very striking picture'), and in devoting so much space to explain where it took exception with his views, it implicitly complimented him.[14] The *Saturday Review*'s politics differed with those of the *Spectator*, and it could say, in a long and agreeable notice, that *Cetywayo* 'thoroughly confirms ... [our] view ... on the subject.'[15] *Vanity Fair* gave it short but generous praise, noting especially that it contained 'a great deal of valuable and important information.'[16]

Perhaps as gratifying to Haggard as the good notices was a long letter from Carnarvon thanking him for his 'extremely interesting' book. 'A true statement of ... [the events is] very valuable,' wrote Carnarvon, 'and I am grateful to anyone who has the courage to say what really did occur.'[17]

In spite of its timeliness and the good notices it received, *Cetywayo* was a financial failure. South Africa was not a pleasant topic for hard-working, phlegmatic Londoners; they did not want to be chided about affairs in a strange distant land. Haggard's book was more authoritative than most of the other volumes on the subject, but that was no strong selling-point with an indifferent public. A year after its publication, Messrs. Trübner reported to Haggard that the book had sold 154 copies and that they were £32 15s. 5d. in the red, over and above the £50 Haggard had advanced them.

But this was not the end of *Cetywayo and His White Neighbours*, for in the mid-'eighties, when Haggard's adventure tales were the rage, Trübner saw to it that the unsold copies of *Cetywayo* were made available in bookshops. Haggard was by then so popular that the

public would read any title that bore his name, and some of the enthusiasts undeniably bought *Cetywayo* thinking they had found another
Haggard romance. In any case, the entire edition of 750 was sold and
Messrs. Trübner and Haggard recouped their investment. As time
failed to heal the wounds in South Africa and events moved towards
the Boer War, Trübner decided in 1888 to issue a second edition of
Cetywayo, for which Haggard wrote a new introduction, sixty pages
long, bringing the history up to date.

In the new introduction, the now-established story-teller points
with indignation and hurt pride to the auguries of the younger, unknown author of *Cetywayo*. In tighter, more forceful prose, Haggard
reviews the consequences of the Wolseley settlement and Cetywayo's
subsequent return. He tells how Cetywayo, after he had been restored
to his throne, was driven out of Zululand by his own people, and how
he ultimately died, probably a victim of poisoning. He traces the
events of the past five years through the chaos and civil war that
reigned in Zululand after Cetywayo's eviction and tells how the
Transvaal Boers infiltrated the torn country to their north to seize
control of the native house divided against itself. The Zulus were
powerless against the Boer aggression, but the British were not.
Whitehall then realized that if the Zulu was to be protected against
his Boer enemy and if the Boer was to be stopped in the scramble
for South African territory, Great Britain would have to act. All at
once, everyone saw clearly that Britain should have annexed Zululand
in the early 'eighties, just as Haggard had urged in his first book.
Now, hoping it was not too late, the British moved in to stop the
Boer, and on June 21, 1887, annexed Zululand. At last, Haggard
sighs, the British have taken up their true responsibility toward the
Zulus, although sadly late and after they had needlessly sacrificed
'many thousands of men, women, and children whose bones strew
the caves and whiten the veldt.'

Haggard's remarks on the Transvaal are of course bitter: England's
record of concession to the Boers goes on. The Boers are greedy
aggressors, and they will continue, by fair means or foul, to seek
more land. The big mistake was giving the Transvaal back to the Boer
in the first place, and the folly of that action has been seen more
acutely since the discovery of gold and other minerals there.

South Africa is still a boiling pot, Haggard reminds his readers,
and England must act wisely and quickly if she is to emerge from
the colonial scramble a winner. The 'mistakes and cowardice of the
past can still be remedied,' Haggard asserts in his conclusion, only if
the Home Government follows an enlightened course in the future.
Again he makes a constructive suggestion, calling for the Crown to

appoint a High Commissioner 'who would have charge of all Imperial
. . . interests,' who 'would study South African politics as a whole as
an engineer studies a map, and who would conciliate and reconcile all
interests for the common welfare and the welfare of the mother country.'

Haggard can never resist the temptation to prophesy, and his
crystal ball glows far more hopefully in 1888 than it did six years
earlier when he was studying law books in Norwood. 'The history
of the next twenty years, and perhaps of the next ten, will decide
whether this country is to remain paramount or whether South Africa
is to become a great Dutch, English-hating Republic.' If we conduct
our affairs properly, we might look forward to a 'South African
Confederation, strong in itself and loyal to England, that shall in time
become a great empire. For my part . . . I believe that such an empire
is destined to arise, and that it will not take the form of a Dutch
Republic.'[18]

The second edition of *Cetywayo* received respectful notices in the
Press, acknowledging almost without exception Haggard's sane
approach to South African affairs. The *Saturday Review* wrote, 'The
Introduction is very well worth reading by anyone whether he knows
the book or not, and the book by anyone who wishes to be acquainted
with one of the most ghastly stories of injustice and imbecility combined that recent times have seen.'[19] The *Westminster Review*, while
pointing out that Haggard succeeded best in the 'attractive medium
of fiction,' conceded that no 'writer of mark is better acquainted with
the affairs of South Africa outside of Cape Colony than Mr. Rider
Haggard, and no one has approached him in the power of exciting
interest in the fortunes of the people of that troubled region.'[20] The
Literary World apologized for devoting only two large, closely-packed
pages to a summary of *Cetywayo*. It called Haggard a 'charming writer,'
and asserted that 'to mention half the points of interest in the present
work would occupy too much of our space.'*

Cetywayo and His White Neighbours was not Haggard's only product
in print during 1882. Hardly a month passed that his name did not
turn up in the letters column of a magazine or newspaper, and between
September and November of that year, after *Cetywayo* had been
launched, six articles appeared in the *South African*. These letters and
articles all bore the same stamp. Haggard, now a zealot on South African
affairs, was determined to correct erroneous impressions and to bring

---

* *Literary World* (London), XXXVIII (July 27, 1888), pp. 76–78. As events developed in
South Africa during subsequent years, *Cetywayo* continued in demand, and new and cheaper
editions were issued. In 1899, when the Boer War broke out, the large section on the
Transvaal in *Cetywayo* (numbering over two hundred pages) was issued in paper covers
both in England and in the United States, and because of its topical appeal, sold by the
thousands.

before the reading public his idea of enlightened imperialism. While he gave all that was necessary to his law studies, he spent his remaining energies in writing on every phase of South Africa, from articles describing life in general to speculative essays on the prospects of South African confederation. By the end of the year, he had made a serious bid as an expert on South African affairs.

But something more spectacular occurred to the law student: before he and his family left Norwood, he had begun to write a novel, and before much time passed, it grew to be a driving force in his life. Nor is it surprising that he should turn to fiction at precisely this time. The pages of musty law books offered him meagre fare, and Haggard's pen worked overtime to compensate for the hours of dull self-discipline his studies exacted from him. However much his family and home life meant to him, his was essentially a solitary spirit; however much he realized that his legal studies offered him the most logical course, he was not entirely a practical man. Africa had become a symbol of freedom for him, freedom from the ordered English home life and freedom from the tyranny of his father. Africa and freedom became indivisible to him, and he could not live again entirely without that freedom. He had spent the whole of 1882 trying to return to Africa through scholarly channels; he had fed himself the contents of many government blue-books and had tried to make a scientific record of his memories and impressions. But this activity had not entirely satisfied him. Nor could it have, for though he made a respectable show at writing history, he was not really a scholar. One day Haggard stumbled casually and accidentally on the means that would give free rein to his pent-up feeling:

> Whilst we were at Norwood a little incident occurred which resulted in my becoming a writer of fiction. At the church which my wife and I attended we saw sitting near to us one Sunday a singularly beautiful and pure-faced young lady. Afterwards we agreed that this semi-divine creature – on whom to the best of my knowledge I have never set eyes again from that day to this – ought to become the heroine of a novel. So then and there we took paper and each of us began to write the said novel. I think that after she had completed two or three folio sheets my wife ceased from her fictional labours. But, growing interested, I continued mine.[21]

Soon Haggard was writing in great earnestness the story of the beautiful maid he had seen in church. This was not the labour he had grown accustomed to while working on *Cetywayo*. It seemed to have a force all its own that made the ink flow in a flood from his pen. Soon he had filled 554 foolscap pages with crowded writing, an amount he estimated would require a thousand printed pages.

While Haggard was still busy with this first effort to write fiction, he and his family moved to Ditchingham, Louisa's estate. The furnished house had been standing empty, and there was no reason why they should not take advantage of its spaciousness and comfort instead of paying rent in Norwood, especially when they were expecting another child. They went up to Norfolk in December, and on January 6 of the new year, Louisa gave birth to their first daughter. Choosing a name for the new arrival was a simple matter; she would be named after the first heroine of her father's romantic imagination – Angela.

The Haggards settled comfortably into the pleasant country life of Ditchingham. For Louisa it was a return to the home and surroundings of her girlhood; for Haggard a return to the Norfolk countryside he knew so well. The house afforded him the spaciousness for his studies and writing that he had lacked in Norwood, and he plunged seriously into the business of getting his novel into form for publication. This accomplished, he sent the bulky manuscript round to one publisher after another – but with no success. Determined to leave no stone unturned, he spoke to Mr. Trübner about it, who, in spite of the losses he had incurred on *Cetywayo*, took a friendly interest in the young author. He suggested that Haggard send the tale to John Cordy Jeaffreson, then a well-known novelist and biographer of Byron, Shelley, and Nelson.

Haggard followed his publisher's advice, and Jeaffreson, who by his own admission was a 'prejudiced East Anglian,'[22] replied with a detailed criticism of the manuscript. What is particularly interesting is that Jeaffreson was able to detect, this early in Haggard's career, both the strengths and weaknesses that were to characterize all of Haggard's later work. Jeaffreson's letter, written in 1883, can be read today not only as a criticism of Haggard's first novel, but as an evaluation of Haggard the writer:

> Your opening chapters have a superabundance of action, and several highly dramatic positions, but they lack dramatic interest, i.e. the interest that comes from an exhibition of the influence of character upon character. Novels being what they are just now, it is small praise to say that Angela's love-story is better than two-thirds of the stories that are published. . . . Still I urge you not to publish it in its present rude form. Indeed, the story has caused me to take so much interest in its writer that I could almost *entreat* you not to publish it.

I take it you are a young man. You are certainly a novice in
literature; and like most beginners in the really difficult art of
novel-writing you have plied your pen under the notion that
novels are dashed off. Inferior novels are so written, but you have
the making of a good novelist in you, if you are seriously bent
on being one. . . . I advise you to make your present essay,
what it might be made, a work of art and a really good
performance.

You have written it with your *left hand* without strenuous pains;
you must rewrite it with your *right hand*, throwing all your force
into it. If you rewrite it slowly . . . suppressing much, expanding
much, making every chapter a picture by itself, and polishing up
every sentence so that each page bears testimony to the power
of its producer – the story will be the beginning of . . . a literary
career. . . . You will succeed in literary enterprise if it be your
ambition to do so.

Your story disposes me to think you have that ambition.
It also causes me to hope that I may make the author's acquaintance.[23]

This is more than small praise or perfunctory courtesy from an
eminent literary man to an unknown, and Haggard's tragedy is that
he did not make Jeaffreson's advice the guiding rule of his life. He
did look upon Jeaffreson's recommendation seriously, for he immediately set himself to rewrite his novel, one of the very few works
he was ever to favour in this way. But even while he went through
one of the motions that Jeaffreson suggested, he blandly overlooked
the more serious and penetrating recommendations. Haggard took
little time to contemplate the ideas in Jeaffreson's letter; he did not
see that Jeaffreson was suggesting changes in his attitude toward his
craft as well as changes in the manuscript. What he saw was that
Jeaffreson had given him good advice which involved his making
certain mechanical revisions. These he would make immediately.
'Well, I took his advice,' Haggard asserts; he began to refashion his
novel on May 15, 1883, and he completed the task on September 5.
The quantity of the labour and the immensity of the task alone are
what his autobiography records:

In just under four months, in addition to my legal studies
and other occupations and the time taken in attending in London
to eat my dinners at Lincoln's Inn, I wrote nearly two hundred
thousand words. . . . I toiled at that book morning, noon, and night,
with the result that at length my eyesight gave out, and I was
obliged to finish the writing of it in a darkened room.[24]

He rewrote the manuscript at a gallop – but again with his left hand. He worked himself into a state of pain, but he simply would not take pains with his work. He did not rewrite it *slowly*, he did not polish every sentence, and by no means does each page bear testimony to the *power of its producer*, nor does the novel mark the beginning of a *literary* career. Jeaffreson had assumed that Haggard was interested in a career of letters, in devoting his life to literature and art. Jeaffreson was wrong.

Once the changes were made, Haggard wrote off to Jeaffreson for advice on how to get the novel published. Jeaffreson, without seeing the revised manuscript, sent Haggard a letter of introduction to Arthur Blackett of Hurst and Blackett. To Haggard's intense delight, Hurst and Blackett agreed to publish 500 copies, in three volumes, and to pay him £40 on the sale of the first four hundred copies and £30 on each succeeding hundred. Because *Angela* had been used as a title before, they asked Haggard to suggest another. He decided to call it *Dawn*.

'You lie; you always were a liar, and you always will be a liar,' is the opening sentence of the novel. It strikes the shrill tone that dominates the thousand or so pages of the book. Deception, as a matter of fact, is a mild vice compared to the parade of cardinal sins to follow. For *Dawn* is packed with a series of intrigues, treacheries, knaveries, and collusions, and with few exceptions its characters are villains. It is in fact a shapeless anthology of two-dimensional actors, vague symbolism, stringy plots, and blood-curdling horror stories. In its manifold pages, it seeks to engage every human emotion. As a novel it raises technical barriers which would be formidable for the modern reader to hurdle in a book half its length. The tale's greatest difficulty is that its author seems to know nothing about character motivation; as often as not, the people in *Dawn* seem to have no reason for behaving as they do, particularly when their deeds are overwhelmingly diabolical. Never does Haggard seek to understand his characters, nor does he seem aware of the influence they might have on one another. As a result they seldom come alive.

Haggard's attitude toward his work has much to do, of course, with his weak characters. His mind, even this early, is filled with formulae about life, and the people he creates are caricatures illustrating his maxims. He is more interested in making general observations than in studying human qualities. He has learned that life is hard and that man does not control his destiny. This is the philosophy Haggard writes into *Dawn*, and his characters are mere instruments to help him propound it.

Weak characterization is not the novel's only limitation. The numerous sub-plots that Haggard uses to engage the reader's attention are very often distracting, particularly those which do not relate directly to the main stream of events. And he has difficulty as well with minor figures, whose existence in the book he very often fails to justify. These irrelevant incidents and unaccounted-for characters, let alone the numerous philosophical digressions and direct author-to-reader chats, leave one with an impression of untidiness.

The young Haggard is a man who admires prophecy, omen, and symbol. He knows that these psychical devices have great power over the emotions, and he is determined to use them. His prophecies and omens are appropriate trappings for his melodramatic tale, but his symbols are confused. The only service they perform is to attest the autobiographical nature of *Dawn*. Haggard drew from his own psychological experience for the framework of his story. The setting is Norfolk, the old family hall is called Brantham Abbey (close enough in sound and description to Bradenham Hall), and the people who live and visit there are exaggerated images of England's country landowners. Angela (the heroine whom Haggard had seen first in the Norwood church), is a lovely, chaste maiden embodying heavenly qualities: she is Haggard's ideal woman. Arthur Heigham, the hero of the tale, is undoubtedly a projection of the author (one of Rider's favourite brothers was named Arthur, and Rider could easily clothe himself in his brother's name). A ferocious dog that Arthur gives to Angela is a fictional copy of Haggard's own favourite dog, Caesar. *Dawn*, the title, has no clear connection with the story, though it unquestionably symbolizes the beginning of a new life for the author as he makes his début as a writer of fiction.

And yet, although Haggard's pages contain innumerable faults, the book bears one quality that places it far above most first novels. The story is told exceptionally well, and each succeeding incident is another breathtaking dip on the roller-coaster tale. Through the narrative, Haggard invites us to experience a host of sensations, and once gripped in this world of suspense and tumult, we cannot turn back. *Dawn* does not engage our compassion for its characters, but the story does arouse our interest. Haggard's genius is narrative skill, and he shows it to its best advantage when he has action – even violent action – to write about. To this end, he amasses his interminable array of catastrophes, horrors, and grotesqueries. With these incidents he creates an atmosphere of suspense on almost every page, and although the reader does not become involved with the wooden people of the story, he does become intoxicated by the excitement. Plot and suspense are the inspired elements of the book and the qualities that would ultimately make a success of Haggard's writing.

Because *Dawn* was Haggard's first attempt at fiction, it was yet too early for the author to realize where his strengths and weaknesses lay. For that reason the book is an encyclopedia of Haggard's incidental observations, small philosophical comments, and a sounding board for his likes and hatreds, many of which are grafted upon the tale. But Haggard was hearing the sound of every note on a new instrument he had taken up for the first time – and it was not to take him long to decide which tunes he could play best.

The notices *Dawn* received were both good and bad. Writing in the *Academy*, George Saintsbury declares that

> there is altogether too much of it. It is too long. . . . It covers too great a stretch of time. There are too many heroines, and they are too beautiful. There are too many minor characters, and they have too much to do. The wicked people (of whom there are several) are too elaborately wicked. [Nevertheless, he asserts that the novel] . . . is well written, it has considerable interest of plot, and the characters are not borrowed.[25]

The *Athenaeum* had only back-handed praise. It suggested that Haggard wrote with 'a fatal facility,' and added: 'He accumulated a vast number of sensations, and has described in detail many repulsive incidents. He lacks neither imagination nor courage, and his achievement is such as need not call a blush to the cheek of the most melodramatic story-writer.'[26] The *Pall Mall Budget* judged it 'somewhat undisciplined,' but recommended it to its readers as 'above the average of first books.'[27] *Vanity Fair* thought 'this might have been an interesting book had it not been for its intolerable length and the unpleasantness of its characters.'[28]

Needless to say, *Dawn* was not a sell-out. There was a spate of first novels being issued, and fiction continued to flow from the indefatigable pens of Charlotte Yonge, Walter Besant, Margaret Oliphant, and Ouida. But Haggard had reasons for continuing his experiments with fiction. He was, after all, investing nothing more than his time, and he had plenty of that in quiet Ditchingham. He could, if he wished, see some progress in his writing, for where he had paid £50 to have *Cetywayo* published, *Dawn* had not cost him a penny. He was still plodding along with his law studies, and without doubt he continued to feel restless. Writing tales came easily and gave him the escape he sought. And certainly the prospect of authorship, even second-rate authorship, with all the publicity it brought, was not displeasing to him. Those reviews that were agreeable 'more than any other circumstances, encouraged me to try another novel.'*

Within a year after *Dawn* was published, Haggard's second piece of fiction, issued also by Hurst and Blackett, on essentially the same terms as *Dawn* in an edition of five hundred copies, was on sale in the bookshops. This one was called *The Witch's Head*, a title that, in its obvious sensationalism, embodies again Haggard's love of the grotesque.

The Witch's Head is another three-volume tale of country life, much like *Dawn*. But it differs from *Dawn* in two significant ways, one in a sense an outgrowth of the other. First, although *Dawn* had all the outer fittings of an autobiographical novel – Norfolk squire-archy, frustrated lovers, Madeira (where the Haggards had stopped on their way back from Africa), and so on – *The Witch's Head* is a much more personal book; in fact, it becomes for Haggard a device by which he can compensate psychologically for the blows he had to suffer in earlier years. Noteworthy is the change in character emphasis. In this story, we have a more fully developed hero, Ernest Kershaw – the story is about him, and, by and large, he lives the life Haggard had lived in his earlier years. Most pointed are the hero's failure to win his first love, Eva Ceswick, and his acceptance of a more practical relationship, though not one by any means lacking in affection, by marrying Dorothy Jones, the woman who manages the keys and accounts of Dum's Ness, an obvious replica (even to the contraction of the name) of Ditchingham House. Though Dorothy is second choice and though Ernest knows he can never love her in the way he once loved Eva, he looks forward to a quiet life of content-ment as a gentleman farmer.

The other difference between *Dawn* and *The Witch's Head* is that part of the story is laid in Africa. Here the grotesqueries vanish, and Haggard writes from the heart, with fresh strokes, about excitements he knows well. He no longer has to rely on the worn-out novelist's tricks – here he needs only remember and write. From the moment the reader sets foot on African soil until he leaves it, he is gripped by a new kind of story, one filled with three-dimensional pictures of a strange but real world; he becomes a tourist in a far-off land. He feels the hot sun and sees the strange people – and he is exhilarated by the new experience. The African interlude places *The Witch's Head* far above *Dawn* on the critical scale.

* Haggard, *Days*, I, p. 218. *Dawn* was reissued many times, for the first time in a single volume in 1887. As *Devil Caresfoot*, it was the first of Haggard's stories to be adapted for the stage (by C. Haddon Chambers and J. Stanley Little). It opened at the Vaudeville Theatre on July 12, 1887, and ran for more than a month. The critic for *Theatre* called it 'a play that will hold an audience for the length of a hot July afternoon not only interested, but that will bring tears to their eyes and a choking sensation in their throats . . . and more.' 'C. H.,' *Theatre* (London), X (August 1, 1887), pp. 100–101.

The reviewers, almost to a man, selected the African elements as those which made *The Witch's Head* much more than just another novel. George Saintsbury saw it as 'far above the average.' 'That Mr. Rider Haggard has very considerable powers as a novelist was evident from his rather extravagant book *Dawn*,' he wrote, 'and it is still more evident from *The Witch's Head*.'[29] The *Athenaeum* called it 'a lively story' with 'plenty of excitement and high colouring,' and although 'there is much that is ghastly in these three volumes, . . . they may be read without too many shudders, and the reader's attention is retained throughout.'[30] The weekly illustrated *Graphic* assured its readers that *The Witch's Head* 'is never for a moment dull,' and 'has plenty of individuality to give it a place outside the ordinary run of novels. . . . It is different, and that is saying a great deal.'[31] London's *Literary World* reported that 'some parts of the novel are really good. . . . The intervening chapters on South African life, including a rapid and vigorous sketch of the Zulu War, redeem the book from the commonplace.'[32] Boston's *Literary World* called it an 'extraordinary novel. Great amplitude of sensational incidents and considerable vigor and precision of style set it apart from current fiction into a certain standing of its own.'[33] The *Saturday Review* praised the African part, approved of Haggard's 'good taste,' and found that throughout the book the author 'exhibits a great deal of power and originality and knowledge of his subject.'[34] Greatest praise came from the *Pall Mall Budget*.

> Only one book is said to have got Dr. Johnson out of bed before he wanted to rise. Only one novel, for a very long time, has kept us out of bed when we were anxious to go thither. That novel is 'The Witch's Head.' . . . Mr. Rider Haggard has made us laugh and has made us cry. . . . Here is a novelist of Kingsley's school, not so much of a poet as Charles Kingsley, not so reckless a humourist as the author of 'Ravenshoe,' but still a successor in the art of truly patriotic and adventurous fiction.[35]

The weird excitements and eerie atmospheres which many critics deplored in Haggard's first two stories of English country life must have originated in the circumstances of Haggard's own life before he wrote the gruesome tales. Here was a young man who had felt his blood grow cold from the risks he had had to take on the African veld, who had on occasion come face to face with death, only to escape it by a hair's breadth. He had somehow outwitted the elements around him and made a success of life in the wilderness. Now he was back in England, shut away in a large house in the country, plodding through law books, beginning, as it were, from the beginning again. His reputation, the self-confidence he had acquired in his own ability to meet the challenges of South Africa, the security he felt when with his friends . . . all had vanished. He was not so sure of himself in his dealing with civilized men, with the kind of men who must have reminded him of his father. Getting on in civilized England was considerably harder than getting on in wild South Africa. He knew virtually no one in Ditchingham outside his immediate family circle, and because he had no income and his wife's estate was feeling the brunt of hard times, the young couple could not do much entertaining. Nor is the Norfolk country noted for its friendliness to strangers, and to Ditchingham and near-by Bungay, Haggard was a stranger who had married Louisa Margitson for her money. It would take time for him to be accepted. 'My recollection of this period,' Haggard later wrote, 'is that it was rather lonely, at any rate for me, since my friends were African, and Africa was far away.' Haggard clung to Africa, to his connections there, and when each morning, he went the rounds of his wife's estate accompanied by his bull-dog Caesar, he clung to a twisted Kaffir stick 'that reminded me of Africa.'[36] At placid Ditchingham, the only avenue to excitement was through his novels – and while he was writing novels about country houses and country people, the excitement would come only through the infusion of the exotic and the grotesque.

His restlessness had not abated with marriage and the passing of time. Fears and insecurities, planted in his personality as a child, filled him with resentment. He was still hurt, and to compensate for his weaknesses, he was determined somehow to succeed and make a name for himself. His energy soared, a fit companion for his determination, and he worked slavishly.

Early in 1885, after the publication of *The Witch's Head*, Haggard took stock of his career as a writer. He had written a history and two novels. The first had cost him £50, and he had received in payment for the two works of fiction exactly £50. This was obviously no vocation on which he could hope to support his growing family. He had finished his law studies and on January 26, 1885, he was called to the Bar; perhaps his road to fame ran through the courts of the land. There was only one course to take: 'I determined to abandon the writing of fiction and devote myself entirely to my profession.'[37]

The Haggards let Ditchingham House and packed themselves off to London, where Rider Haggard, at twenty-eight, was to try his hand at a new skill. They took a small house on Gunterstone Road in West Kensington, and he went to work in the chambers of Henry Bargrave Deane, a distant relative.

4

The Tale of African Adventure

RIDER HAGGARD was not destined to serve the law long. His whimsical strain made him unsuited for chambers and the routine of legal affairs. He grew restive and sought to occupy his leisure hours with non-legal matters.

The Haggard family recall how on a day early in 1885, Rider and one of his brothers were discussing *Treasure Island* on a London train. When Rider suggested that Stevenson's book was perhaps not so remarkable as many seemed to think, his brother offered to bet him that he could not do anything half so good himself. Rider took the wager, and that very evening sat down at the pedestal writing-desk in the dining-room of his Kensington house and began to write a tale of adventure for boys. Gone the resolution to put his writing ambitions behind him; the fervour of make-believe surged again, and each day, when he came home from the Temple, he turned to his desk and spent the evening on the manuscript. In six weeks he finished his first tale of African adventure, *King Solomon's Mines.**

* Haggard himself says that he happened to read a flattering review of *Treasure Island* and that he then 'procured and studied that work, and was impelled by its perusal to try to write a book for boys.' Haggard, *Days*, I, p. 220. Although *Treasure Island* was the model for *King Solomon's Mines*, Haggard drew on his African experiences to make the tale more than an imitation of Stevenson's. Martin Conway tells a story, revealing, furthermore, that Haggard drew upon childhood memories as well: 'One day when he and I were lunching together he produced a gold ring and told me that it was that ring that first opened the world of romance to him, and then he related the story which he incorporated in "King Solomon's Mines." The actual story was as follows. When Haggard was a boy there lived in the neighbourhood of his home a certain old retired sea-captain, who used to electrify him with all manners of wonderful tales of his own doings and experiences. The best of them, which he was never tired of hearing and hearing again, was the story of the Ring. The old skipper's ship had been laid up for some months in Callao. He relieved the tediousness of inaction by accepting the hospitality freely offered to him by residents in and about Lima. He was taken into the country one day to the sugar estate of a friend. Operations were going on there for the removal in whole or in part of a great mound. As they were watching the diggers a hole was breached into what proved to be a great cave or chamber within the mound, whose existence had not been suspected. What was their astonishment on peering in to behold a dozen or so of mummies seated as in life around a table, with the host or some superior person at their head. As the invaders watched in astonishment and some horror, the whole company fell to dust on the floor. Only one

In his efforts to have the tale published, Haggard got the manuscript into the hands of W. E. Henley, poet, critic, and editor of the Cassell's-owned *Magazine of Art*. Henley, in turn, brought the manuscript to the attention of Andrew Lang, at that time the English editor of *Harper's*. After reading it, Lang wrote Haggard:

> Seldom have I read a book with so much pleasure: I think it perfectly delightful. The question is, what is the best, whereby I mean the coiniest, way to publish it? As soon as possible I will find out what Harper's *Boys' Magazine* is able to do. . . . There is so much invention and imaginative power and knowledge of African character in your book that I almost prefer it to 'Treasure Island.'[1]

With Lang and Henley hailing it, the story was bound to find a publisher – and it did. Cassell's, delighted with the outcome of the risk they had taken in publishing *Treasure Island* at Henley's suggestion, was again inclined to follow the poet's advice.

Haggard received the good news in the post, and when he went round to Cassell's to settle the terms of the agreement, he was ushered into the office of the Chief Editor, John Williams. Williams offered Haggard a choice: £100 right off in full settlement for the copyright or a 10 per cent royalty on the published price of the book. One hundred pounds was a great deal of money for a chance story written in six weeks' spare time, and Haggard wondered whether this tale of his could ever earn that much money in royalties when his first three books had not brought him a penny of profit. 'After my previous experiences as an author £100 on the nail had great attractions,' he later recalled, and so he decided in favour of the lump sum. Williams went off to get the necessary legal form for Haggard to sign, leaving him alone with an unobtrusive clerk working at a desk in the corner.

> There was a clock ticking away on the mantelpiece. It seemed to be ticking happiness into my life. I thought this was the greatest hour of my life. I was going out of this place with a hundred quid. But the scratching of that quill pen at my back irritated me.

---

object survived. It was the golden ring which was on the finger of the chief. The ring was given to the skipper and he wore it to his dying day. When Haggard was grown up and his friend was long dead, he bethought him of this ring. After elaborate inquiries he discovered it in the possession of a lady, a descendant or relative of the skipper. Haggard bought it of her and used himself to carry it about. I have worn it on my own hand and examined it in every detail.' William Martin Conway, *Episodes in a Varied Life* (1932), pp. 255–256.

Kotzé tells, furthermore, that on one of their circuit tours, he and Haggard took a detour from Potchefstroom to visit the caves at Wonderfontein, containing a natural pulpit formed by stalactites. These caves were, in all probability, the basis for the Place of Death in *King Solomon's Mines*.

Presently it ceased. I heard the squeaky voice of the man at the desk say: 'Mr. Haggard, if I were you I should take the royalty.'

When Williams returned with the contract, Haggard told him that he had changed his mind and would prefer instead the royalty agreement. Though annoyed, Williams brought the alternative form, and Haggard signed it. Aided by the unidentified oracle, Haggard had made one of the wisest moves of his life.

With *King Solomon's Mines* coming off their presses at the end of September 1885, Messrs. Cassell printed a quantity of long broadsides, and one evening sent out a team of men to paste them up all over central London. The job was completed before dawn, and in the morning the posters hung everywhere, all shouting the same message. People in carriages, in horse-buses, on foot; people going to work, travelling to town for a shopping spree, out for lunch, and on their way home – all of them read the same message at every turn of the road and at every hour of the day: KING SOLOMON'S MINES – THE MOST AMAZING STORY EVER WRITTEN.[2]

But whether the public would consider this yarn 'amazing' was by no means clear in advance. Haggard's two erstwhile publishers and others to whom he had offered the manuscript had actually turned it down. Max Pemberton, the English editor, tells that on the evening before *King Solomon's Mines* appeared, a distinguished gentleman sitting next to him at a dinner-party said, 'There's a silly story of a diamond mine published today ... by a man named Rider Haggard. They offered me this book six months ago and I declined it. Some fool has bought it as you will see – and I'm sorry for him.'[3] The unidentified publisher did not know his public as well as he thought he did. He failed completely to appreciate how many readers were weary of the problem novel and how the demand for adventure and romance was again growing.

Tales of adventure were not, of course, new in the 'eighties. Scott claimed a wide audience throughout the Victorian Age, and almost every nineteenth-century novelist tried his hand at 'the novel as written by Scott.' Ainsworth, G. P. R. James, and Bulwer-Lytton made early successes with the Scott formula, and in the 'fifties and 'sixties, Reade and Charles Kingsley also told distinguished historical yarns. In other forms of adventure and suspense, Marryat, Ballantyne, and Collins made notable contributions at various times. In the 'seventies Blackmore, Baring-Gould, and Buchanan supplied some tales of adventure, and in the 'eighties, readers got more of what they were looking for when *Treasure Island*, *Kidnapped*, *King Solomon's Mines*, and *She* appeared within a period of four years (1883–87) and were followed by a new group of romances written by Quiller-Couch, Doyle, Hope, Hornung, Weyman, Munro, Hewlett, Mason, and others. Most of the popular romances of the 'eighties and 'nineties are, however, crude and formless. Their prose is often undistinguished if not actually substandard, their adventure incredibly wild. Only in the better ones can readers find some real literary qualities. But when these adventure tales first emerged, they all marked a change in pace from the three-volume society novel, a change many welcomed.

One would hardly expect the best of these open-air tales of romance to emerge from a sick room, but it did. The sick room was in the Braemar home of a young barrister, who in mid-1881 found himself confined by illness with his twelve-year-old stepson. For their amusement, the barrister drew a map of a strange island that looked like a 'fat dragon standing up.'[4] The map became the germ of one of the most exciting stories ever written, *Treasure Island*.

Stevenson and young Lloyd Osborne were old hands at make-believe, and hardly had the map dried when they started adding landmarks with nonsense names (Spyglass Hill, Skeleton Island, Foremast Hill, and the like). The map would be useless, of course, unless it revealed a great secret, unless, say, it was a pirate's map that led to hidden treasure. Stevenson drew three red crosses to mark the buried loot, and soon man and boy were dreaming up elaborate details to explain how the hidden riches had got there and inventing harrowing adventure for young Jim Hawkins to experience after he sailed off with Squire Trelawney and Long John Silver to the Barbary Coast in search of the pirate booty. The tale took shape, and Stevenson was fascinated by it. He had written numerous essays for literary periodicals and published the accounts of two tours he had taken abroad, but he had not yet published an extensive work of fiction. That fact did not deter him, however, and the morning after he had drawn the map for Lloyd, he wrote the first chapter of the adventure story. When he read it aloud, the boy reacted with overwhelming enthusiasm, and Stevenson resolved to write a fresh chapter every morning, a resolution he kept for some time. Every evening during the period when he was writing the story he would read aloud to the assembled family and visitors (among them Edmund Gosse and W. E. Henley) the chapter he had written that morning. The story now took on a much more important character than a mere pirate game with Lloyd, and Stevenson was delighted when a visitor suggested that the manuscript should go to the editor of a boys' paper. The first instalment of *The Sea-Cook*, by 'Captain George North,' appeared in *Young Folks* on October 1, 1881, even before Stevenson had finished writing the story, and two years later, Cassell's published it as a book.

But even though *Treasure Island* was a first-rate romance full of action, it took a year or two to catch on. Stevenson was not yet famous. Those who knew his name connected it with the literary *élite* and with a small volume or two, one with a Latin title. *Treasure Island* was, in fact, his first bid for the popular market. Stories of pirates were, moreover, old hat; Kingston and Ballantyne had done them very well, and now pirate tales were steady fare in the boys' papers. Although readers were yearning for a means of escape from their confined existence they did not respond quickly to a tale that seemed at first glance fantastic. They could not easily believe in a yarn that sent a ten-year-old English lad off on a schooner with a couple of artless English gentlemen and a crew of obvious thugs to the Spanish Main in search of Captain Kidd's pirate treasure. It strained the limits of probability, and not until readers got into the story and came to believe in Long John Silver, Pew, and the naïve Trelawney, not until they had been gripped by the power of the tale, could they suspend disbelief.

Another matter that puzzled readers was how to classify *Treasure Island*. Stevenson had called it a boys' book. It was primarily about a boy, told mostly by that boy in the first person, and printed initially in *Young Folks*, a boys' weekly. As a book for boys, it did not attract a large group of readers, at least at first. When the news got about that it contained a literary treasure that outshone its chests of pirate gold, however, and that like so many books written expressly for children, it suited the mature imagination as well, it began to attract a wider audience. All the same, two years passed before a second edition was called for.

On the other hand, when *King Solomon's Mines* appeared in 1885, bound as a matching volume to *Treasure Island*, it met with instantaneous success, both with the public and the Press, and suffered far less than one might expect from the inevitable comparisons. *Treasure Island* had actually helped prepare the reading public for more tales of adventure, had at least made adult readers less reluctant to pick up a book 'for boys.' Cassell's broadsides undoubtedly boosted sales for the Haggard story. And Haggard had already broken into the circulating libraries with two novels aimed at the popular taste. Nor was there anything 'literary' in *King Solomon's Mines* to put off the general reader. Allan Quatermain assures his audience at the outset that he tells his tale 'in a plain straight manner,' in his own 'blunt way of writing.'

Historical accident was also on Haggard's side. The telegraph and war correspondents were bringing to the English at home vivid descriptions of their far-flung colonies, and these readers grew eager to participate in the adventure of Empire. From November 1884

to February 1885, just a few months before *King Solomon's Mines*
appeared, England's attention was caught by the Berlin Conference
on African Affairs, where fourteen major powers laid down the ground
rules for dividing Africa's spoils. England's geographical borders
already extended to Africa; it was time for its literature to follow suit.

Only one African novel of note had appeared in London
before *King Solomon's Mines*, Olive Schreiner's *The Story of an African
Farm* (1883), a remarkable tale of Boer life in the back country.*
But London did not take to Miss Schreiner's work at first, perhaps
because, in its descriptions of spiritual struggles, its focus on family
relationships, and its strong feminist theme, it resembled too closely
the usual domestic novel. *King Solomon's Mines* was different. It appealed
to all readers, critics, schoolboys, housewives, and working men
alike, who found in it a story that was swift, terse, packed with thrills.
It was a tale of adventure and heroic deeds, and its hero was a well-
adjusted Englishman, competent, strong, sensible, in whom they
could believe. There was no heroine, nor should there have been.
Penetrating Africa was strictly a man's job. The adventure was the
thing, and there was plenty of it. *King Solomon's Mines* was just what
readers wanted.

The story begins aboard the *Dunkeld* as it sails down the east
coast of Africa. Quatermain, a distinguished elephant hunter, is a
passenger returning to his home in Natal from a hunting trip in the
wilds of Bamangwato. Also aboard the ship are Sir Henry Curtis,
a tall, blond-headed English gentleman, and Captain John Good,
a caricature of the punctilious retired naval officer. Curtis and Good
have come from England to search for Curtis's younger brother,
George, who, having quarrelled with Sir Henry, had gone to seek
his fortune in South Africa. Quatermain, as it happens, has heard of
the missing brother. Young George was last heard from when he set
out in search of the legendary King Solomon's mines, reputed to
exist somewhere deep in the interior. To these tidings Quatermain

* Haggard became acquainted with Olive Schreiner in 1885. In a letter to J. Stanley
Little, he wrote: 'Yesterday I made a bold effort. I am very anxious to make the acquaintance of the woman who wrote the S.A. Farm so I . . . sent her a copy of "Dawn" addressing
of course "Ralph Iron" [Olive Schreiner's *nom de plume*].' On May 17, 1885, Miss Schreiner
wrote to Havelock Ellis: 'This afternoon Philip Marston [1850–87; the poet] and Rider
Haggard called. I had such a dreadful time. In the middle of the visit my landlady burst
open the door in a rage – I'll tell you all about it when we meet. After they were gone
the two women turned on me and stormed. They asked me if I had so many men always
coming after me.' She records another visit from 'Haggard, Marston, etc.,' on October 27,
1885. Still another visit is mentioned in D. L. Hobman's study of Olive Schreiner: 'Rider
Haggard and George Moore called on her. The former suggested that she should write
something more cheerful, advice which she considered to come ill from one who had "a
murder or a suicide on every other page." As for the latter, she found him selfish and
frankly told him so.' *Catalogue 337*, Myers & Co. (Booksellers) Ltd., Autumn 1953, p. 30;
S. C. Cronwright-Schreiner, ed., *The Letters of Olive Schreiner*, 1876–1920 (1924), pp. 73–74,
84; and D. L. Hobman, *Olive Schreiner, Her Friends and Time* (1955), p. 42.

regretfully adds the chilling fact that no one has ever survived such a hunt. As a matter of fact, Quatermain himself has in his possession a crude map* which theoretically charts the route to the entombed treasure. The map, hardly more than a rag, was traced in blood on a piece of shirt by a Portuguese adventurer, one José Silvestra, who, having seen the mines in 1590, died on the return journey. The map had been brought to Silvestra's family by his servant and then, through the years, passed from generation to generation until another José Silvestra, a nineteenth-century descendant of the original, tried unsuccessfully to find the mines. Before José II died, however, he had crept back to Quatermain's camp and given the Englishman the map. Although he is convinced that the quest is hopeless, Quatermain joins the search for young George Neville. Among the five servants the men hire to accompany them is one Umbopa, a huge native who is willing to serve the white men without compensation, a fact that makes Quatermain suspicious of him.

The saga now begins, and the first adventure is an exciting hunt. Captain Good has a close call with a bull elephant, but the hunters succeed ultimately in doing in nine pachyderms. They bury the tusks in the sand, hoping to reclaim them on their return. Then they journey across a vast desert, barely surviving the heat and thirst, only to come face to face with a range of steep mountains which they must cross. Their privations and narrow escapes test their mettle. Trial follows hard upon adventure, adventure upon trial. At one point, the crippling cold near the mountain peaks takes the life of one of their servants in the night; at another, they find in a cave the body of the sixteenth-century Silvestra, preserved intact by the sub-zero temperature. Then follows the descent from the mountains on the other side, which leads the party into the hands of hostile natives who by tribal custom kill all intruders. But the captors are diverted by Captain Good's appearance. They marvel at Good's false teeth (whenever he is excited, he tugs at the upper set, then lets it fly back into place

* Haggard was very particular about the map, insisting that it be drawn on linen in real blood. He later tells an amusing story involving it: 'One day I took the manuscript of "King Solomon's Mines" to be bound by Mr. H. Glaisher the bookseller. In the carriage of the Underground Railway I perceived an old lady engaged in a close, indeed an almost ferocious study of the map printed at the beginning of the printed volume which rested on her knees. This was too much for me. Drawing the original map from my pocket, I placed it on *my* knee – we were seated opposite to each other – and began to study it with like attention. The old lady looked up and saw. She stared first at her map and then at mine, and stared, and stared. Twice she opened her mouth to speak, but I suppose was too shy, nor did I, apparently absorbed in contemplation of my map, written in blood upon a dirty piece of torn linen, . . . give her the slightest encouragement. The end of it was that she seemed to come to the conclusion that that railway carriage in which we were alone together was no place for her. Suddenly, as we were about to leave a station, she sprang up and leapt from the train.' Newman Flower, *Radio Times*, June 29, 1956, p. 6; and H. Haggard, *Days*, I, p. 234.

with a snap), his monocle, bare white legs, and half-shaven face (something of a dandy, he was in the midst of his elaborate toilet when the party was surrounded). Quatermain tells the natives that he and his friends possess strange magical powers and have come from the largest star in the heavens; and as proof, he shoots an antelope with his 'magic tube.' These unusual circumstances overwhelm the natives, and they readily agree to take Quatermain and his friends to their king. After a three-day journey, the Englishmen are led before Twala, a one-eyed giant, king of the Kukuanas, a Zulu tribe. At a dramatic moment in the interview, the quiet servant Umbopa steps forth and announces that he is in reality the true heir to the Kukuana throne, son of the king whom Twala had murdered years before, when Umbopa was a child. As evidence for his claim, Umbopa reveals a snake tattoo around his waist, the unquestionable sign of Kukuana royalty.

While Umbopa plots Twala's end, the visitors witness a spectacular witch hunt, the barbaric 'smelling out' ceremony, in which the tribe sorcerers, led by one of Haggard's finest creations, a mysterious, shrivelled female called Gagool, dance madly before Twala's twenty thousand warriors. In the midst of their ceremony, the witches stop before anyone they deem evil, and instantly he is stabbed to death. Quatermain and his party watch the ritual with amazement. Suddenly, the witches stop before Umbopa. For a moment the story hangs in the balance; Umbopa seems doomed. But Quatermain threatens to kill Twala, Gagool and all with his magic tube, a threat that persuades Twala to spare Umbopa. A number of the lesser chiefs defect to Umbopa's side when he secretly shows them the royal tattoo, and when, upon their demand for 'a sign,' Captain Good promises the chiefs that to prove Umbopa's claim, the white men will extinguish the sun in the middle of the next day (Good had had the sense to bring along his almanac, and he knew that an eclipse was due). The eclipse occurs: the white men and the petty chiefs take advantage of the darkness to flee Twala's camp. The renegade chiefs assemble their warriors on a mountain-top some two miles from Twala's seat and prepare for combat.

On the following day Twala attacks with thirty thousand men, and an epic battle ensues. Haggard calls it 'The Last Stand of the Greys,' and it reminded Andrew Lang of Scott's Flodden. Twala's forces are vanquished, and it remains for the golden-haired Sir Henry to fight in single combat with the black one-eyed giant. It is, of course, a first-rate fight, and Sir Henry finally decapitates the brute. Umbopa ascends the Kukuana throne, and in appreciation of the white men's help, he orders the ugly Gagool to lead the Englishmen to King

Solomon's mines in the mountains. Again the journey is long, but finally high in the hills, they come to the three ancient Colossi, deities carved out of stone, which Quatermain suggests might be the gods that Solomon 'went astray after.' The group enters the side of a mountain through a passage and arrives at an awesome stone cathedral, a sanctuary built by nature. No ordinary cloister is the Hall of Death, for here, round a huge table presided over by a giant skeleton gripping a spear, sit all the dead kings of Kukuanaland of the past four centuries, petrified by siliceous liquid dripping down upon them. Twala already sits in their midst – his head before him on his knees.

As Quatermain and his companions stand transfixed by this primeval Madame Tussaud's, Gagool pulls a secret lever, and a huge rock rises out of its setting to reveal a hidden cave containing chests filled with shimmering jewels. Gasping, the men move toward the treasure. But the unobserved Gagool touches the lever that returns the rock to its place, trapping the explorers in the treasure chamber. The witch pays sorely for her treachery, however, for she herself does not escape from the chamber in time, and the descending rock pins her to the ground, crushing her to death. Locked in the treasure den deep in a cavernous mountain, a few yards from the petrified kings, the men gradually resign themselves to death. But Quatermain comes once more to the rescue: he finds a ring in a stone slab that opens a door to a hidden tunnel, through which the party makes its way out of the cave. Umbopa arranges for a safe return across the mountains, and on the journey, they come upon a small makeshift hut by a stream, where George, Sir Henry's younger brother, is living. Hurt by a falling boulder, he could not move long distances without help. Finally, they all reach Quatermain's house in Natal, and at the end of the tale, the hunter-hero sets sail for England to see his son and 'to look after the printing of this history.'

Though they leave the wealth of King Solomon's mines essentially intact, the explorers come away with enough of it to make them rich men for life. For Quatermain, having kept his wits about him even when locked in the *sanctum sanctorum*, had put a handful of gems in his pocket.

Thrills and excitements are plentiful. But there is something else as well, for Haggard had produced more than another tall story of adventure. He wove throughout a web of realism so strong and intricate that had he wished to do so, he could have passed *King Solomon's Mines* off as a true story by one Allan Quatermain. After all, if the reader went to his atlas, he could put his finger on the very spot where Quatermain was exploring – at that time an unpenetrated wilderness. Who was to say the facts were not true, especially when

daily accounts in the Press told stories no less fantastic?* The Book of
Books even substantiated Haggard's tale, for there one could read
that King Solomon built the great Temple from ivory and gold brought
from Africa. All the details, the landscape, the accurate descriptions
of the equipment the adventurers take with them, the hunts, and
perhaps most of all the natives, their customs, their manner, their
speech – it is all believable, too vivid to have sprung from the imagination. So winning was Haggard's brand of realism that he was deluged
with letters from readers eager for assurance that the work was 'a record
of fact.' Even a prominent dealer in jewels approached him on the
subject. 'I believe,' Haggard later wrote, 'he actually sent an expedition
to look for King Solomon's Mines, or at any rate talked of doing so.'5
For many Englishmen, Africa became the Africa of *King Solomon's Mines*.

The book became a children's favourite immediately. Many
readers would agree with the observer who, writing recently in the
Illustrated London News, called it 'one of the greatest adventure stories
ever written' and remembered 'the strange seas – or, rather, strange
countries – which Rider Haggard opened up for a small boy straining
his eyes in the twilight of a first summer holiday, hours after official
bedtime, fascinated and held as he was, perhaps, never to be gripped
again.'6 But though Haggard had written *King Solomon's Mines* as
a boys' book and had even dedicated it to the 'Big and Little Boys
Who Read It,' its appeal went far beyond the slate-and-rule set. The
story had universal interest, for grown-ups as well as youngsters,
for women as well as men. Soon *King Solomon's Mines* was being read
in the public schools, even aloud in class-rooms.

The Press reaction was entirely favourable. Even before its notice
of the book appeared, the *Spectator* devoted a lengthy 'middle' essay
to *King Solomon's Mines* as the kind of story man needs to satisfy his
thirst for the wonderful. The writer of the essay finds great merits
in the tale and thinks it 'one of the most exciting' ever published in
a modern language, 'decidedly superior to the best of Jules Verne's,
and surpassing even Herman Melville's "Kaloolah," ' which 'we should
previously have placed at the head of this department of literary art.'7
The *Athenaeum* put *King Solomon's Mines* at the top of its 'Christmas
Books' and called it 'one of the best books . . . we remember to have
read. . . . There is some fighting hardly to be beaten outside Homer

---

* A two-column report in *The Times* told of a native raid upon a mission station in
Africa just as England was reading *Allan Quatermain*, which begins with a similar account.
Commenting on the coincidence, the *Spectator* wrote: 'After . . . [this] proof of Mr.
Haggard's genuineness . . . who will be surprised if some day . . . we hear that one of
those wonderful swords, with the back of the blade cut out in fretwork and inlaid with
gold, which Mr. Mackenzie [the missionary] showed to the astonished Allan Quatermain
is for sale in New Bond Street?' 'Reality and Romance,' *Spectator*, LXI (April 28, 1888),
pp. 569–571.

and the great Dumas. . . . In short, [it] is one of the earliest books
of the season, and we shall be surprised if it does not also prove to
be the best.'[8] The *Academy* called it 'a boys' book of the first class,
which holds the attention from the first page to the last.'[9] *Vanity
Fair* refused to see it as a boys' book at all and recommended 'this
clever and highly exciting story' unconditionally to its readers.[10]
The *Independent*, though it misspelled the hero's name, called the tale
'an exciting melodramatic romance' and 'a very clever piece of work,'[11]
and the weekly illustrated paper, the *Queen*, called it 'a romantic but
ingeniously contrived tale.'[12] The *Spectator*, in a review of the book
that appeared three weeks after the essay that judged it superior to
works by Verne and Melville, called it 'as effective a piece of writing
as we have seen for a long time' and asserted that its author is 'a
story-teller of no common power.'[13] *Public Opinion* and the *Saturday
Review* carried flattering notices, the latter an unsigned essay by
Andrew Lang. *Public Opinion* called the writing 'clever,' and assured
the reader that 'nothing of the kind has ever been better conceived.
It stands foremost as a work of art – we mean the art of drawing "long
bow." '[14] Lang's admiration went even farther. 'We have only praise
for the very remarkable and uncommon powers of invention and
gift of "vision" which Mr. Haggard displays. . . . To tell the truth,
we would give many novels, say eight hundred (that is about the
yearly harvest), for such a book as *King Solomon's Mines*.'[15] Thus
went the notices, and there were many as good.

Sales figures, too, reflected the general enthusiasm, as did the
comments of individual readers. In England alone *King Solomon's
Mines* sold 31,000 copies during the first twelve months[16] and was
clearly Cassell's best title for the year.[17] In the United States, at least
thirteen different editions appeared before the year was out.[18] Three
months after *King Solomon's Mines* appeared, the American *Book
Buyer* pronounced that 'Messrs. Cassell & Co. have . . . this year taken
the ring in the tourney for young folks' literary favor . . . [with]
"King Solomon's Mines." '. . . For simplicity, strength, and cunningly
devised chains of incident culminating in thrilling cries, we cannot
recall a bit of modern fiction to equal it.'[19] Henley said that he had
read it 'at a gasp';[20] R. L. Stevenson found in it 'flashes of a fine weird
imagination and a fine poetic use and command of the savage way of
talking: things which both thrilled me';[21] later Walter de la Mare
remembered the young ladies, 'like arum lilies, who dance the dance
of death before one-eyed Twala';[22] and Gerard Manley Hopkins
recommended it for boys in a letter to Robert Bridges: 'I have not
read *Treasure Island*. . . . However give 'em Rider Haggard's *King
Solomon's Mines*. They certainly will enjoy it; anyone would; and the

author is not a highflier.'[23] Four years after it was published, the *Scots Observer* waxed nostalgic over it: 'Who does not recollect,' it asked, 'the burst of genuine welcome with which *King Solomon's Mines* was greeted by all classes of readers?'[24] And Max Pemberton also remembered that 'we all loved *King Solomon's Mines*. . . . The author made children of us.'[25] Gladstone was one of its adult enthusiasts, and later Winston Churchill,* Maurice Baring, James Agate, and Evelyn Wrench recalled it as one of the books of their schooldays. Not only did the book establish itself firmly in boys' schools, public and otherwise, but in the girls' schools as well, as Haggard knew from his post that included a letter from a group of girls congratulating him 'with great earnestness' in having produced in *King Solomon's Mines* 'a thrilling book without a heroine.'[26]

For too long the reader's attention had been trained on London slums, prison houses, artists' attics, Manchester mills, and village vicarages, and *King Solomon's Mines* was one of the books that offered a 'way out.' It let the reader turn his back on the troublesome, the small, the sordid; and it took him on a journey to the Empire's frontier to perform mighty deeds he could believe in. If nothing more, *King Solomon's Mines* helped bring the story of adventure up to date.

For Haggard the story-teller, *King Solomon's Mines* stands as a milestone. There he eliminates many of the false elements that crowd his earlier work. Wild, warm, vivid landscapes supplant cold, gaunt Tudor country houses; realistic, hairbreadth escapes replace Gothic nightmares; a brave and confident hero unseats fainting damsels and male manikins; the memoir replaces the third-person narrative; and a crisp, taut, thrilling tale of deeds takes the place of a formless melodrama. At this point in Haggard's career, some observers saw in him the promise of an artist. But for Haggard himself, *King Solomon's Mines* stood rather as a landmark of financial success than literary

* A few letters that passed between Haggard and Churchill are extant. The first (undated) came from Churchill when he was still a boy. 'Thank you so much for sending me "Allan Quatermain," it was so good of you. I like "A.Q." better than "King Solomon's Mines"; it is more amusing. I hope you will write a great many more books.' Another pertinent letter (dated February 11, 1888) came from the boy's aunt, Lady Constance Leslie: 'The little boy Winston came here yesterday morning . . . [and beseeched] me to take him to see you before he returns to school at the end of the month. I don't wish to bore so busy a man as yourself, but will you, when you have time, please tell me, shall I bring him on Wednesday next, when Mrs. Haggard said she would be at home? . . . He really is a very interesting being, though temporarily *uppish* from the restraining parental hand being in Russia.' René Kraus, in his study of Sir Winston, tells us that the youngster 'was by no means awestruck in [Haggard's] . . . presence. "What do you mean by this passage in your new book?" asked the boy, quite without shyness. "I don't understand it." Mr. Haggard examined the passage, and did not understand it either. Of course a masculine friendship at once developed out of the incident.' Many years later, when, in 1924, the Labour Party's fall seemed imminent, Haggard wrote to Churchill, suggesting that he form a new government, and Churchill replied that Haggard's suggestion 'belongs to the most airy spheres of speculation.' Haggard, *Days*, I, p. 275; Maggs Brothers Collection; René Kraus, *Winston Churchill* (1940), p. 32.

accomplishment, and too soon he would come to see in it the formula for many of his later works.

Haggard's new-found success had a predictable effect upon him. Now that his labours were assured a just return, he worked steadily and within a year completed three more stories. He did not entirely forsake the law either. He continued in chambers and 'hung about' the Courts. But now he permitted his writing to intrude upon his daytime hours as he pressed ahead with his tales in the dingy room at 1 Elm Court, 'no easy task,' he later remembered, 'since young barristers . . . would enter and scoff at my literary labours.'[27]

He wrote *Allan Quatermain*, a sequel to *King Solomon's Mines*, and *Jess*, his first African 'novel,' before the end of 1885, and these were both taken up for serial publication, the former in *Longman's Magazine*, the latter in the *Cornhill*. But the first tale to emerge in book form after *King Solomon's Mines* was *She*.

Haggard wrote *She* during February and March 1886, in a little over six weeks. It virtually flowed from his pen of its own accord. 'The fact is,' he tells us, 'that it was written at white heat, almost without rest. . . . I remember that when I sat down to the task my ideas as to its development were of the vaguest. The only clear notion that I had in my head was that of an immortal woman inspired by an immortal love. All the rest shaped itself round this figure. And it came – it came faster than my poor aching hand could set it down.' When he had finished the story, he took it to A. P. Watt, whom he had engaged on the advice of Walter Besant* as his literary agent, and slamming the manuscript on to a table, he sagely proclaimed, 'There is what I shall be remembered by.'[28]

And he was right. For *She*, in spite of its weaknesses, has enjoyed a persistent popularity since it first appeared, more than seventy years ago. It was a best-seller from the first. On March 15, 1887, three and a half months after its publication, Charles Longman wrote Haggard

* Besant must have been one of Haggard's earliest literary acquaintances. Haggard sometimes consulted him about literary matters, and the two men met often at public functions and entertained each other at home and club. In 1887 Besant offered Haggard an opportunity to meet Brander Matthews, 'a critic journalist of the better kind who would very much like to know you.' In the following year, when Besant was recovering from an operation, Haggard regularly sent him flowers. In October 1891 Haggard must have asked Besant to suggest him for membership in the Athenaeum Club, for Besant replied that he certainly would put his name down (Haggard, though, was not elected until April 1895). When in May 1895 Haggard was guest of the evening at an Authors Club dinner, Besant, in introducing him, asserted that he was 'twice as successful as any other novelist of the day . . . [because of] the audacity and strength of his imagination . . . and, secondly, the quality of "grip," which his works . . . [possess] in an eminent degree.' And when Haggard testified in the Central Agricultural Chambers on May 30, 1899, about the rural exodus, he spoke of Besant, who he said knew the East End, telling him about the agricultural labourers who had migrated and were trying to find work on the docks. A series of twenty-nine letters (from October 1885 to May 1892) in the Huntington Collection; *Literary World*, LI (May 31, 1895), p. 515.

that ' "She" keeps on selling capitally. We have printed 25,000 already, and have ordered another 5,000, and I do not think we shall have many left when the printers deliver them. . . . Last week we sold over 1,000 copies!'[29] The enthusiasm of this experienced publisher conveys more clearly the dimension of *She*'s popularity than the sales data, for we have today grown calloused to astronomical publishing figures. *She* has never been out of print since it first appeared. In England today there are available at least four editions, and Macdonald & Co., publishers of a hard-cover reissue with new illustrations, admit that *She* is one of their best-selling titles. Hollywood filmed the tale as recently as 1935, and in the United States it is today in print in no fewer than five different issues. It is also available in Catalan, Czechslovak, Danish, Esperanto, Finnish, French, Gaelic, German, Hindi, Italian, Maltese, Norwegian, Polish, Portuguese, Rumanian, Spanish, Swedish, Tamil, and Urdu (and in some cases in multiple translations).

She is another tale told by a voyager returned. Ludwig Horace Holly, a 'scholarized' Allan Quatermain, a student at Cambridge University, sits studying mathematics in his rooms when, at midnight, Vincey, a friend, arrives with a heavy strong-box. Vincey confides that he is dying, and appeals successfully to his fellow-student to act as guardian of his son after his death. The next morning Vincey dies, and then the years roll quickly by until Holly's charge has turned twenty-five. But Leo Vincey has grown up to become no ordinary young man. He is one of Haggard's idealized heroes, a veritable Apollo, strong, handsome, and well versed in foreign languages. At the appointed time, he opens the box his father had bequeathed him and finds a broken potsherd, inscribed with ancient writings. The inscriptions tell a weird story: Leo is the sole descendant of one of the world's oldest families, tracing its roots back to ancient Egypt, to Kallikrates, a priest of Isis who had broken faith and fled his country with a young princess, Amenartas. The inscriptions also tell of the queen of a savage people, a white goddess, and of a strange Pillar of Fire which she had shown Kallikrates and Amenartas. The Queen had killed Kallikrates, but Amenartas escaped to bear Kallikrates's son, an ancestor of Vincey. The writing ends in Amenartas's plea that the son she was leaving behind or another courageous descendant avenge her against the Queen of the Pillar of Fire. Accompanying the clay fragment was a letter from Leo's father telling his son that he had journeyed to Africa but had not been able to travel to the interior because of a shortage of supplies and that his illness later precluded another journey.

Hardly three months pass before Leo, his 'uncle' Holly, and a servant, Job, are on their way to Africa. On their arrival they start inland in a whaleboat, making their way up a seething, crocodile-infested river that grows progressively narrower and shallower. Soon reeds obstruct their progress, and the men are forced to tow the boat. Suddenly, they are surrounded by natives and taken prisoner. They are about to be slain, when Bilali, an old man from among their captors, steps forth and orders their lives spared, reminding the Arabic-speaking tribesmen of the great Queen's dictum: all white men captured in her country are to be brought directly to her.

But the white men have far to travel before their interview with the great one, and during their journey, they are introduced to some gruesome native customs, in particular a cannibalistic drinking orgy, where the Africans prepare to kill the white man's native guide for their supper by placing a ceremonial red-hot pot on his head. A tussle ensues in which the guide is accidentally killed by a bullet from Holly's gun and Leo is wounded. Bilali restores order, and the three white men are carried on stretchers through the swamps, across plains, and led blindfolded through tunnels to the hidden city of Kôr, carved out of solid rock, where reigns the mysterious *She-Who-Must-Be-Obeyed*.

Holly alone is brought to her sumptuous apartments. Her questions are strangely anachronistic. She inquires after the ancient Egyptians and Greeks as though they were contemporaries. When Holly expresses astonishment, the veiled figure explains that she has been living in her hidden city for two thousand years without news of the outside world. Time means nothing to her; nor can death touch her. She reigns over the Amahagger Tribe only while she awaits the return of the man she once loved, for it was decreed that he would be reborn and come back to her. She tells Holly that her name is Ayesha, and casting her veil aside, she reveals to the Englishman her breath-taking beauty.

The next day, Ayesha visits Leo, who is dying of fever from his wound. When she enters his room and sees him, she draws back in astonishment. Leo has the features of the dead Kallikrates: he is the man she has awaited for two thousand years. Ayesha restores Leo's health, and then invites all three white men to a native ball, at which the illumination is supplied by burning embalmed corpses. Here a native girl, a reincarnation of Amenartas, who had fallen in love with Leo and, according to Amahagger custom, had proposed and been accepted, is killed by a fierce magical blast from the powerful Ayesha. The Queen then takes Leo and Holly to her apartments, where, drawing back the shroud covering a corpse, she reveals the body of Kallikrates, which she now destroys with acid; with Leo 'returned' she need no longer guard his ancestor's remains. Leo comes under Ayesha's spell, and that evening he, Holly and the Queen set out on

a journey to the Pillar of Life; for Leo is now to bathe in the sacred
fire and become immortal too.

They cross a vast plain and scale a cliff. After walking along a ledge,
they find themselves in a natural cave. Before them is a 'mighty chasm
in the black rock, jagged and torn and splintered through ... by
some awful convulsion of Nature, as though it had been cleft by stroke
upon stroke of ... lightning.' Leaning against the strong wind, which
wrenches Ayesha's dark cloak from her, they make their way along
a precipitous spur of rock. Standing on the brink, 'poised in the gloom
between earth and heaven,' they hear the winds roar through the
cavern and feel the driving mists. They must move to the very tip
of the spur and cross the ravine to the other side. They find that
Ayesha's ingenuity has brought them to the spot just as a great sword
of light from the setting sun pierces the gloom, lasting only a few
seconds, but long enough to help them set a narrow plank across
the pit and make their way over it to the other side.

Finally they reach the cave of the Pillar of Life. Leo, though,
hesitates to enter in the flame as it shoots up from the bowels of the
earth. To assuage his fears, Ayesha enters the fire where she bathed
two thousand years earlier. The flames shoot up along her limbs and
encircle her. Then, after a moment, they subside, and she steps out.
But she is not the same. And as Leo, Holly, and Job look on, she
changes more and more. Her features begin to shrivel, her arms
grow scrawny and wilt, and before the stunned audience, she shrinks
into a small bundle of skin and bones. Still she decays, until her frame
crumbles into dust and she is gone. Why? How? No one knows.
Perhaps the flame's magic has changed, or vanished. Or is it that the
fire's magic can be used only once in a lifetime? Ayesha's destruction
is so horrifying that Job dies of the shock, and Leo and Holly leave
his body in the cave beside the remains of She. Three weeks after
they penetrated the African interior in their whale boat, the two
white men emerge and make their way back to England.

She took London by storm. Writing two months after its publication, Henley informed American readers of the *Critic* that 'Mr. Rider
Haggard is still the hero of the hour' and that *She* had been 'received
with rapture.'[30] It enjoys a 'wildfire of injudicious enthusiasm,' wrote
the London critic of the Boston *Literary World* at about the same
time Henley was writing. It is 'impossible in any house to attempt
any conversation which is not interrupted by the abominable introduction of *She.* . . . Artist, author, pedant, politician, man of science, man
of the world, there is only *one* book that all of them just now are likely
to ask if you have read.'[31]

The reviews were longer and more analytical than those that

greeted *King Solomon's Mines*, and the praise was certainly as loud, though this time not unconditional. Haggard's imagination and inventive talent drew loud applause, his careless pen and shoddy execution evoked everything from gentle advice to stern rebuke. Time and again, critics were indignant over mechanical imperfections, violations of taste, weak character development. Even Andrew Lang, who had fallen in love with Ayesha, had to confess that '*She* is a book which it is hard to give any but a personal and subjective estimate.' He went on to say, however, that for him the book was a rare experience that took him ' "beyond the bounds of explored Romanticism." The more impossible it gets, the better (to my taste) Mr. Haggard does it.'[32] The *Athenaeum* judged Haggard 'a story-teller with a rare turn for romance,' and although it considered the conception of *She* 'original . . . weird, fantastic, and certainly fascinating,' it complained that the treatment was 'lamentably unequal' and that 'the language and dramatic force rarely rise to the level of a really great occasion.' 'On the whole,' it wrote, ' "She" is an original, attractive, bewildering, impressive, and withal disappointing work.'[33] The *Saturday Review* 'heartily' thanked Haggard for *She* and told its readers that in this romance they will have 'no cause to complain. It is a wonderful country "She" lives in, and inhabited by a wonderful people.'[34] The *Spectator*'s reviewer admitted 'a dislike for Mr. Rider Haggard's favourite literary method,' but conceded all the same that *She* is 'very stirring and exciting,' and 'shows remarkable imaginative power.' The story, he adds, is 'vivid and brilliantly told.'[35] The reserved *Blackwood's Edinburgh Magazine* devoted three full pages of measured prose to its notice. It is even 'stronger' than *King Solomon's Mines*, the reviewer asserts, and although Haggard is not the 'exquisite workman' Stevenson is, 'he has a great deal of power in his way, and rougher qualities which are more likely, perhaps, to "take the town." ' Haggard also has 'a distinct sphere which is his own. He "talks of Africa and golden joys" with a knowledge and certainty that few possess, and is able to . . . make the dismal swamp as recognizable as Princes Street.'[36]

Vanity Fair's review appeared in mock verse:

> This is the song of Ayesha.
> Weird, clever, exciting, full of strange
>   thoughts and true philosophy.
> Written by a dead Princess on a Cracked Pot.
> Price, six shillings for the lot. . . .[37]

The *Pall Mall Budget* deplored the 'bathos' and 'frequent torpors' but praised the 'energy and intensity of imagination.' 'It is as though a subject roughed out by Michael Angelo had been executed with an eye to New Bond Street popularity by Gustave Doré.' The reviewer likens Haggard's conception to Dante's, his writing to that of the *Daily Telegraph*.[38] The *Queen* praised the story's 'vividness and picturesque power';[39] and *Public Opinion* found it almost as fascinating as *Treasure Island*: 'greater praise than that we can scarcely give it. Few books bolder in conception, more vigorous in treatment, or fresher in fancy, have appeared for a long time,' the reviewer wrote and added that *She* is 'more fascinating' than Flaubert's *Salammbô* 'and is worth sitting up half the night to finish.'[40] The *Literary World* thought *She* more imaginative than *King Solomon's Mines*,[41] and *Murray's Magazine* called it 'a marvellously realistic tale of fantastic adventures.'[42] In the United States, where within a few months after its London publication, over a dozen pirated editions appeared, *She* was noticed in the *Critic* by Henley within six weeks of its London appearance. 'Haggard has the gift of invention to such a point as to be practically a man of genius,' the poet wrote. 'But he is not an artist. . . . I couldn't help regretting that Mr. Rider Haggard is not Mr. Stevenson, and has not taken seriously to heart the difficulties of his profession.' Nevertheless, Henley added, *She* had to be read 'in a gasp.' 'For my part I couldn't put it down until I had finished it.'[43]

She is such an unusual tale, so far outside the conventional limits of story-telling, that many people have speculated through the years about its origin. Where did Haggard get the idea of his enchanting Queen, and what enabled him to write such an enthralling bit of realism steeped so thoroughly in romantic supernaturalism? Some of the sources are quite obvious. Haggard had, after all, been to Africa and had experienced some unusual adventures. It is also true that through all his later years he was nostalgic about his African days and looked back upon them as a time of great personal freedom and vigorous accomplishment. It was there that he had grown to manhood, and in all probability it was there that he was first treated with dignity as a mature person. Accordingly the Dark Continent was one of his great passions, and certainly when it came to dreaming, he would dream about Africa.

None the less, his strange blending of narrative elements; the anthropological, cultural, and ethnic ingredients; and the psychological symbols present a challenging puzzle to the specialist as well as the casual reader. The story, furthermore, has a bewildering power, the sort one is accustomed to meet only in superior works of art such as 'Christabel' and some of Poe's masterpieces, a power that grips the reader so fiercely that he brushes aside Haggard's errors in taste, his occasional grammatical lapses, his imperfect character portrayal and lack of emotional unity. The power of his imagination is far stronger than the obstacles his writing puts in our way.

We do not get much help in tracing the origin of *She* from Haggard's own observations. His statements are at first hesitant, later weighty, and in all contradictory. He tells us initially that he wrote the story around a vague notion about an immortal woman, but how he came by the notion, let alone the other material he poured into the tale, we never really learn. Later on, after the book sky-rocketed to success, he tries to explain in a long, verbose, *ex post facto* statement the allegorical meaning of the tale, and finally he writes three sequels, each an attempt to work out the meaning of Ayesha for himself and his reader. All this is inconclusive for a real understanding of the tale, for, having written it as quickly as he did, Haggard was writing 'deep,' as though hypnotized. His later comments are all unsuccessful efforts to comprehend his own work. We must look, not in Haggard's statements about *She* for an explanation of the story, but in Haggard himself and in the forces working upon him.

Although Haggard was very much concerned with contemporary issues, he was never really content with his own times. From a personal and spiritual standpoint he was not modern. He yearned for the past and spent much of his time investigating ancient cultures. He was an amateur antiquary; ancient weapons, coins, odd bits of old writing, and anything with a patina, moss, or even a coat of rust caught his interest. Scott had opened history to colourful display and romantic interpretation; and growing up when he did, Haggard had come under Scott's sway. The concern with cataloguing and collecting the remnants of the past that became the vogue of Victorian scholars also rubbed off on Haggard. He had a great respect for facts and a deep feeling for ancient times, and his library contained books on Greek,* Egyptian, Nordic, Celtic, and African antiquity (some published even before *She*), many of them well annotated in Haggard's own hand. In 1907 the *Bookman* asked a group of authors which book each had enjoyed most during the past year. By and large, they chose either a work of fiction, a book on current events, a memoir or biography. Haggard significantly chose Breasted's *Ancient Egyptian Records*.[44]

Haggard's involvement with history was motivated by something stronger, however, than his spiritual incompatibility with the present.

---

* Haggard had read Homer. In the preface to *Mr. Meeson's Will* (1894), he points out how difficult it is for an author to create anything entirely new. 'For instance,' he writes, 'an author invents an immortal woman living in a cave, and prematurely rejoices, thinking that at last he has found a new thing. A little reflection shows his error. Homer found such a woman in the Odyssean myth, and sung of Calypso.' P. xii. See also *African Review*, VIII (September 19, 1896), p. 639.

He firmly believed that the past held the answer to the riddle of the present and the future; if one could understand the past, one could understand life. In primitive cultures lay the answers to universal problems, and in the wisdom of ancient times were eternal truths to enlighten us today. His search for ultimate meaning lay behind his attachment to the past, and his deep interest in primitive life and early cultures later led him to write the books some critics have called the romances of anthropology.

In *She* he displays some of his knowledge of primitive culture and society. His Queen is a beautiful, white woman of Arabic lineage ruling over a primitive tribe of Africans. She lives in seclusion, dedicated to love, tended by deaf mutes. She is worshipped and greatly feared by her people. She is immortal, or gives every indication of being so, having been rendered thus by the miracle of the Pillar of Fire. The city she lives in is one of stone caves, carved out of a mountain deep in the interior of impenetrable Central Africa, and the walls of the city are covered with ancient writings.

The worship of goddesses among primitives is of course commonplace. During their agricultural cycle and often before and after, all primitive groups celebrate the virtues and powers of a female deity. She is a symbol of fertility and is associated with fields and crops (as the corn goddess, the cloud goddess, the rain goddess, or something similar). She is worshipped often through rituals performed with the sowing of the seeds and the reaping of the harvest. With the advent of civilization, people's concept of the deity becomes more complex, and the primitive mother-earth goddess takes the place of her simpler predecessor, very often in a family of gods (as among the ancient Greeks and Romans, for example). In some cases, she herself gives birth to the male God (as among the Zulus). Ancient Egyptians worshipped many goddesses and particularly the great mother goddess Isis. The Greeks had goddesses a-plenty, and even as late as 204 B.C. the Romans worshipped the Phrygian Mother of the Gods because they believed, as a result of a Sibylline prophecy, that the great goddess would drive Hannibal out of Italy. Ayesha is not the conventional Great Mother by any means, but that the primitive Amahagger would worship an immortal woman is quite in keeping with tribal custom.

Why Haggard chose to make Ayesha a descendant of Arab stock can probably be answered in geographical terms. He was familiar with ancient Arabic civilization, and he knew that Arabs had migrated south from North Africa and Persia. Also in his reading about ancient Arabic religion, he found ample evidence for the worship of goddesses among Arabs. Herodotus, whom Haggard drew upon frequently, tells us that the ancient Arabs worshipped a Queen of the Heavens called Alilat or Alitta, who later became the great goddess Allat, a sun deity ultimately identified with Athene. Still later Allat is worshipped by the Arabs as one of the three daughters of Allah. Nor is it only the ancient Arabs who worshipped Allat. Allat is connected with the cult of Ashtar, the great ancient Semitic tribal mother (who inspired love and produced life) of virtually all Middle Eastern cultures. The Canaanites, Hebrews, and Phoenicians worshipped her as Ashtart; as Atargatis, she was goddess of Syria; the Greeks identified her with Aphrodite; as Ishtar she was the Babylonian and Assyrian deity; in Mesopotamia she was Attar; in Moab, Ashtar; in South Arabia, Athtar; and in Abyssinia, Astar. As Anat she sometimes appears as the wife of Baal, although in the Old Testament she is Asherah.*

Haggard not only gives his white Queen a name like that of the famous Middle Eastern mother goddess; he indicates quite clearly that he is familiar with her and her universal worship. Even before *She*, in *King Solomon's Mines*, he refers to her, and takes the opportunity to display his hard-bought erudition, which he attributes to Sir Henry Curtis.† There are also references to Ashtoreth in *She*.

When Haggard was in South Africa, he learned many native myths, some of which very likely found their way into *She*. The Baganda tribe of the Bantus believes in a family of gods at the head of which is Mukasa, a being of uncertain sex, often referred to as female. The Ashanti worship an earth goddess called Asase Ye, and among the southern tribes of the Nuba Mountains, God is referred to by the feminine pronoun. The Zulu people also worship a woman, one Nomkhubulwana, the daughter of the Creator or first Cause, Unkulunkulu (the old, old one). The Princess of Heaven is a corn goddess who lives alone in the forest. She occasionally appears to man to make known her wishes, but when she does so, man must not look upon her face, lest he die. Her word is absolute law, and the Zulus execute her laws faithfully, for, as they say, 'The Inkosazana has spoken!' Haggard was clearly familiar with the tales about this goddess. One of the most revealing statements about his sources for African tales is his Preface to *Nada the Lily*. Though first published five years after *She*, it applies to Haggard's early tales as it does to later ones.

---

* There are numerous references to Asherah (in various spellings) in the Old Testament, of course. See Judges 2:13, 10:6; I Sam. 7:3–4, 12:10, 31:10, and for direct connection with King Solomon I Kings 11:5, 33; and II Kings 23:13.

† Quatermain and his party, approaching the mountain where King Solomon's treasure is hid, pass three sculptured colossi. Quatermain and Curtis speculate about them. ' "Hum," said Sir Henry, who is a scholar, having taken a high degree in classics at the university, "Ashtoreth of the Hebrews was the Astarte of the Phoenicians, who were the great traders of Solomon's time. Astarte, who afterwards became the Aphrodite of the Greeks. . . ." ' And Haggard as editor of Quatermain's chronicle adds a footnote referring the reader to Milton's allusion to Ashtoreth and Astarte in *Paradise Lost*. H. Rider Haggard, *King Solomon's Mines* (Collins Classics, 1955), p. 208.

[In Africa, I] . . . was thrown in with men who, for thirty
or forty years, had been intimately acquainted with the Zulu
people, with their history, their heroes, and their customs. From
these . . . [I] heard many tales and traditions, some of which,
perhaps, are rarely told nowadays, and in time to come may cease
to be told altogether. . . . [In a note on Zulu mysticism, magic,
and superstition, he continues to say that he] well remembers
hearing a legend that told how the Guardian spirit of the Ama-Zulu
was seen riding down the storm. This is what Mr. [F. B.] Finney
[in *Zululand and the Zulu*, privately printed] says of her . . . : 'The
Natives have a spirit which they call *Nomkubulwana*, or the *Inkosazana-ye-Zulu* (the Princess of Heaven). She is said to be robed in
white, and to take the form of a young maiden, in fact an angel.
She is said to appear to some chosen person, to whom she imparts
some revelation; but, whatever that revelation may be, it is kept
a profound secret from outsiders. I remember that, just before
the Zulu war, Nomkubulwana appeared, revealing something
or other which had a great effect throughout the land, and I know
that the Zulus were quite impressed that some calamity was about
to befall them. One of the ominous signs was that fire is said to
have descended from heaven.'[45]

Among the Zulus, there is still another female deity, Uthlanga, the
wife of Unkulunkulu, by whom he is supposed to have begotten man.
Haggard later, in the series of romances where he tells the epic story
of the Zulu people, includes tales of Inkosazana or Inkosazana-ye-Zulu.

The worship of human females as priestesses or empresses is still
another matter, and pertinent, for Ayesha is, after all, not immortal.
But even here, Haggard could hardly avoid the congeries of myths
about the worship of woman. The ancient Germans believed that
women were holy and meant to be worshipped; they consequently
regarded as oracular the prophecies women said they heard when
they listened to rushing rivers or roaring seas. Some of these people
even worshipped women as true living goddesses, as in the case of
the goddess Valeda (of the Bructeri tribe) who lived in a tower on the
Lippe River. Women played no small part in the worship of the ancient
Egyptians, a fact that was not lost on Verdi when he wrote *Aida*.
Some Egyptian women were worshipped as prophetesses; others
had a place in the religious ritual as priestesses of music. In ancient
times Hatshepsut and Tiy were especially powerful queens of Egypt,
the latter believed by some authorities to have been a fair-haired,
light-skinned, blue-eyed Asiatic, and of course Cleopatra followed
much later. Priestesses attained high status in the religious cults in

Assyria and Syria, and they were worshipped also in Babylonia, Greece, and Rome. They also served in some Ganda temples (Central Africa). The Ethiopians, furthermore, believe to this day that Menelik I, the founder of their country, was the son of the Queen of Sheba, and they also believe that Queen Judith usurped the throne and reigned over Abyssinia for forty years. We have records and tales of more recent African queens and women chiefs. There are the heroic stories of the brutal Queen Nzinga of the Congo, whose carved footprint Livingstone saw when he arrived at a Portuguese fort in the Congo, and there are tales of chieftainesses on the slopes of Kilimanjaro, notably Queens Mamba and Juya. Nor could Haggard have overlooked the women who held a high place in the ritual of many African tribes; he certainly knew that among the Swazis (a people he had already written of in *King Solomon's Mines*), custom demanded, and does to this day, that a Queen Mother, or 'cow elephant,' be appointed, even if she be only of distant blood relationship to the chief. Haggard knew Zulu custom well, and he later wrote about Chaka's mother, Unandi, Mother of the Heavens, and other important tribal women.

But he did not even have to travel so far afield culturally for instances of both deified and immortal women, for there are many stories in Celtic myths which may have planted the seed of Ayesha in his imagination. In St. Patrick's hymn, the holy man prays against 'spells of women, smiths, and druids.' The women were feys who enjoyed eternal youth and unfading beauty. They were love-hungry and came from the Land of the Young to ensnare handsome men with their spells and carry them off as lovers. They appear in the story of Connla, a prince of Ireland in the second century. On one of his travels a beautiful damsel dressed in strange attire approached him. 'Come with me,' she cried '. . . a yellow crown awaits thee; thy figure shall not wither, nor its youth nor its beauty till the dreadful judgement.' Though he resisted for a time, the spell she cast was too strong, and he was finally lured away, never to be heard from again. Marie de France's *Sir Landeval* is an analogue of this tale, and it, in turn, was retold in England by Thomas of Chester (*fl.* 1430) in his *Sir Launfal*. There are many similar stories in Irish lore, notably the account of Tautha De Danann, where the youth and beauty of the women are also unfading, and the voyages of Bran and Maelduin, where mortals visit Elysium, an island inhabited by an amorous queen who heartily welcomes the visitor and hates to let him leave. Welsh lore also offers many parallels to these tales.

In the Arthurian legend, Guinevere means 'white phantom or fee' [from *gwen* (white) and *hwyvar* (a cognate of the Irish *siabur*, *siabhra* (phantom, fairy)]. In the *Vita Merlini* (attributed to Geoffrey), Morgan and her eight sisters rule in perpetual peace and harmony

mid eternal spring and flowers in a veritable Garden of Eden called
Insula Pomorum, an island that resembles the Irish Elysium. In this
Avalon, the people are all youthful, and there is no death. A beautiful
regia virgo rules, and it is she who heals Arthur. She is called Morgan
(though, of course, she appears more commonly elsewhere as his sister).
Giraldus Cambrensis calls her *dea phantastica*. How far Haggard read
beyond Malory in Arthurian literature we do not know, but even
in the twenty-first book of Malory – and in Tennyson's *Idylls* – the
queens on the barge come to take Arthur to the immortal isle, and there
is the mystical Lady of the Lake, keeper of Excalibur. We find women
with supernatural powers also in Chaucer, Lydgate, other medieval
writers, and later in Spenser.

There is another possible source for the idea that had grown to
the beautiful white Queen and her city of stone in Haggard's mind.
The notion may have been planted there when he himself was not far
from where he placed his African heroine. About 400 miles north-east
of Pretoria, near Fort Victoria in Southern Rhodesia, exist the
remarkable ruins of Zimbabwe, an inscrutable stone metropolis that
has puzzled archaeologists since its discovery in the late nineteenth
century. It is a city of walls, houses, palaces, passageways, and elliptical
temples – all built of rock. Even now, after the experts have studied
Zimbabwe, they disagree about its origin and meaning. Some still
claim it is the remains of a prehistoric civilization (*fl. c.* 4000 B.C.),
a white race that once ruled Africa. Others refuse to date it any farther
back than the fourteenth or fifteenth century and believe the Bantus
built it. Because of extensive mine workings in the area, Zimbabwe
(it is a Bantu name from *zimba* [house] and *mabgi* [stone]) is sometimes
thought to have been the distributing centre for the gold traffic
carried on in the Middle Ages between the Monomotapa and the
Mohammedans on the coast. But some who prefer the more anti-
quarian explanation insist that this is in fact the Biblical land of Ophir
where Solomon got the gold and ivory for his Temple in Jerusalem,
that it was where the Queen of Sheba reigned.

During the 'seventies and 'eighties, when Haggard was in Africa,
and later, when he was writing his first African romances, little was
known about Zimbabwe other than that it existed. The ruins had been
discovered by Adam Renders in 1868, and in 1871 Karl Mauch made
a risky penetration of the interior in the hope of uncovering more
facts about the strange ruins, but even he was not able to explore them
as he would have liked, for the natives in the area considered Zimbabwe
sacred and inviolable. Not until 1891, when the chartered Company
of British South Africa sent the explorer-archaeologist J. T. Bent
into the interior was Zimbabwe adequately examined. Earlier, when

Haggard was in Africa, stories about Zimbabwe could have been no more than legends, tales about a strange prehistoric city in the north, perhaps built by ancient white men, that would certainly appeal to the young Englishman's imagination. The similarity between Zimbabwe and Ayesha's city of stone is not literal, but it shows, if nothing else, how thoroughly Haggard assimilated the details of his African experience, creating a veritable storehouse of authentic information which he could draw upon when in later years he was writing his tales.

But Zimbabwe is not all, for in the north-east corner of the Transvaal to this day live the Lovedu, a tribe of negroid primitives, relatively unaffected by Western civilization. It is a small, weak tribe, but its fame has spread throughout the world because of its ruler, who had, from 1800 until recently, been a fair-skinned woman with great magical powers, living in seclusion among her people. Her very name provoked fear in the hearts of her African enemies and awe even in white Europeans who lived and explored in Africa. She was Mujaji (variously spelled), revered by the Zulus as the greatest magician in the world, queen of clouds, rain, locusts, and drought. Few ever saw her, and those who did could not tell about her, for, like Ayesha, she was served by a select inner circle, mainly mute women. Neighbouring tribes as well as her own people knew her to be immortal and all-powerful. She could summon clouds from the far side of the Drakensberg that towered over her domain, a feat she was said to perform with consummate skill. She could even arrange matters so that rain would fall on one tribesman's land and not on another's. Besides her power over the clouds, her fair complexion and her immortality added to her fame.*

The Lovedu is situated some 250 miles north-east of Pretoria, and in 1876, when Haggard travelled with the special commission to the kraal of Chief Pagate and, later, on his circuit court journeys with Kotzé, he came within a hundred miles of the tribe. Although later he specifically denied it, he may have heard about the marvellous Mujaji and her people, for there are clear similarities between the Lovedu and Ayesha's tribe, the Amahagger.[46]

Although the white queen of the Lovedu was rather special, there seem to have been a concentration of female chiefs among tribes of the north Transvaal, Southern Rhodesia, and Bechuanaland, just on the northern periphery of the area Haggard traversed in his stay in South Africa.

But apart from any possible carry-over from Mujaji, Ayesha is, in all, a unique figure, and the strange force she exerts upon most readers is in itself a tribute to Haggard's creativity. She is a rare

* There seem to be reasonable explanations for both her colour and her immortality. All white visitors were, by royal decree, ushered into the Queen's dwelling. White male offspring were killed at birth and female offspring were retained to serve the Queen. One of the Queen's entourage secretly replaced her when she died.

combination of unusual elements, basic life symbols. She is the
archetypal Great Mother. She is immortal, ever-beautiful, all-powerful,
wise – and inscrutable (she is veiled). Around her waist she wears
a serpent, as much a symbol of immortality and wisdom as of sexual
passion. One approaches her, after enduring many hardships, by
passing blindfolded through dark passages.

Clearly Ayesha is the intermediary between the divine and the
human; she is a female Prometheus. She not only knows where the
source of life is – she is the source of life. With her, and by means
of the bridge which she herself casts across the void, man may approach
the threshold of eternity, the divine fire, whence all life comes.

It is significant that Haggard chooses fire, not liquid, as his source
of rejuvenation.* True, having witnessed displays of natural pyro-
technics in Africa, he might easily imagine the fire bath. Furthermore,
on a continent of vast mountain ranges, the natives could well have
described some volcanic activities as 'magic fire baths,' just as the
Hebrews of the Exodus, travelling through mountainous terrain,
interpreted as a divine sign the 'pillar of fire,' which, according to
some theorists, may have been an active volcano. But regardless of
where Haggard got the idea to use it, fire symbolizes a great deal to mankind, and Haggard's use of it is meaningful. Fire, the eternal generator and
sustainer of life, is intimately connected with woman; it suggests motherhood, food, warmth, and the domestic hearth. It is, moreover, the sun,
light, and the symbol of the intellect. It is also tied to the emotions
and to love, spiritual as well as physical. It represents faith (the Hebraic
God in the burning bush and the eternal light at the ark), and it is worshipped by preliterate peoples as well as by the civilized. Fire is also
the universal mystery, for as great a force as it is, it is all the same
intangible. It is also related to death, for it is equally a consumer of life.†

---

* The rejuvenation theme occurs frequently in English literature. Haggard may have
taken it from any number of books he read, for it was a favourite with the Gothic School
(it occurs in Maturin, Godwin, and Shelley), with Hawthorne, and with Bulwer-Lytton,
one of Haggard's favourite novelists.

† Myth offers many instances of the connection between birth and fire, rebirth and
fire, and beauty and fire. Semitic mythology, for example, tells us of the cult of Melqart,
the solar deity (later the Greek god Melicertes), who, the Tyrians believed, sojourned
during the winter months in the lower world. In early spring they celebrated his rejuvenation by lighting a great fire, which consumes the god's age and replaces it with youth.
In prehistoric Ainu, *Fuji* means fire and is the name of the goddess of fire, one of the Ainu's
nature deities. Prometheus is of course connected with fire; the Greek god not only makes
prophetic utterances through a sacrificial fire, but also employs fire to create life out of
clay. Alexander the Great was conceived when a bolt of fire struck Olympias. In the
Atalanta myth, Meleager's life is tied to a brand; as the fire consumes the brand, so
Meleager's life wanes. Fire and ashes play an important part in the rebirth of the Phoenix,
and the ashes on Christ's head connect fire with death and resurrection in Christian belief.
In Philippine mythology, fire or bright glare is associated with a beautiful woman (a man
approaches his house, one story tells, and he thinks it is on fire; but when he enters the
house, he finds instead a beautiful maid in his bed). The connection between fire and beauty
is found in the myth of other cultures.

All these symbols come together for the reader in the Place of Life at the end of the story. But the reader never crosses the threshold to the divine, for the universe will remain, like Ayesha, veiled and mysterious. Instead one is forced to witness the flames consume rather than rejuvenate Ayesha. 'One is privileged,' writes Henry Miller, 'to assist at the spectacle of Nature reclaiming from her victim the secret which had been stolen from her.'[47] With Ayesha's destruction vanishes the secret of the universe, and the reader is once again bound by mortality.

Haggard, as we know, was always fascinated by the supernatural. From the time he was a young man, he dabbled with mystical matters, and even later, after rejecting spiritualism, he kept a careful eye on psychical research. Very early, furthermore, he leaned toward reincarnation as explaining the mystery of life and death. Haggard was one of the large number of thinking men in the latter nineteenth century who, seeing religious dogma shaken by the higher criticism and the advances of science, placed their faith in an undogmatic Christian animism. With Tennyson they believed in spiritual evolution, in a 'God . . . to which the whole creation moves.' It was a belief they could reconcile with the scientific theories of the times. It is not surprising, then, that Haggard uses metempsychosis in *She*, and it is also quite conventional for him to link, as did his literary forebears, true love with the eternal spirit. Both the spirit and the love it manifests would never cease to be. The idea of spiritual evolution through successive incarnations is of course old in Eastern myth, and it occurs occasionally in the fiction of the nineteenth century. Poe, whom Haggard undoubtedly read, used metempsychosis repeatedly. But although nineteenth-century animism and Poe's mysticism each undoubtedly influenced Haggard, he was, by the time he wrote *She*, already steeped in Egyptian lore and fascinated by Egyptian beliefs. His particular brand of metempsychosis comes primarily from ancient Egypt.*

We get further insight into *She* if we examine Ayesha in her literary setting. She emerges significantly at a time when the hero of Victorian fiction has been relegated to slumdom or is shown struggling with a weak will or an incapacitating conscience. The hero is in fact eclipsed, and what has eclipsed him is the heroine. Mario Praz, in his *Romantic Agony*, has offered an explanation of the eminence of the woman in

---

* There is a striking increase in the use of reincarnation and other types of spiritual transmigration in the fiction that followed *She*. Quiller-Couch (*The Mystery of Joseph Laquedem*), Edwin Arnold (*Phra the Phoenician*), F. Marion Crawford (*The Witch of Prague*), George Du Maurier's works, H. G. Wells (*A Dream of Armageddon*), Rudyard Kipling ('The Brushwood Boy,' 'The Last of the Stories') and many more used the motif. *See* Dorothy Scarborough, *The Supernatural in Modern English Fiction* (1917).

late Victorian fiction. According to Signor Praz, in the Byronic hero
we saw a combination of traits both admirable and despicable; he
was a fallen angel, a Satan. Some time after the decline of Byronic
heroes, their female counterparts appear – the *femmes fatales*, who are
of course beautiful, but also destructive and implacable. The more
the hero of Victorian fiction grows weak, impotent, and effeminate,
the more dominant the 'superwoman' becomes. There occurs a reversal
of roles, which aids the movement toward decadence. Exoticism
accompanies the reversal and is part of the strange woman's appeal.
Exoticism is furthermore allied to mysticism. By the latter part of
the century, the fatal woman turns up frequently in the literature of
the period: she is Rossetti's Sister Helen, Pater's Mona Lisa, Swinburne's Atalanta. She is the heartless beauty, the eternally pitiless
woman. Ayesha, huge, cold, and beautiful, passes in this parade of
fictional Victorian superwomen. She is a closer blood relative to
Wilde's Salomé (published seven years later) than to the fainting
heroines in Haggard's modern novels or to the characters in the books
for boys with whom she is often shelved.

The question of allegory in *She* has often arisen, and many moral
lessons have been ascribed to Haggard the preacher.* 'Whether . . .
[Haggard] is a philosopher with a turn for allegory the readers of
"She" must decide for themselves,' suggested the *Athenaeum* in its
notice of the book. But the facts are that Haggard was neither writing
a conscious parable nor preaching a moral sermon; as far as he was
concerned, he was simply telling a tale. On the other hand, there is
in *She* something more than the story he consciously wrote, and the
critics' efforts to grasp something beyond the narrative are perfectly
justified. *She* is undoubtedly a psychological allegory, and perhaps
more so than most works of fiction because of the way Haggard
let the tale write itself. Haggard, writing here just before the birth
of analytical psychology, innocently extends to the new scientists
an invitation to his unconscious. What is surprising is that not more
of them have delved into his books and translated the psychological
symbols to be found there. But some have.

Carl Jung selected *She* as a classic example of the *anima*, his concept
of the feminine force in man. Man's *anima*, according to Dr. Jung,
is the aggregation of all the feminine characteristics in him; the *anima*
enables him to understand the meaning of woman: it is his unconscious

---

* One book at least has been written to explain *She* in terms of Christian allegory.
The author, with dogged sincerity, explains that the ruined city of Kôr is the modern
world; Ayesha is the Church, the sole guardian of Truth and possessor of the Secret of
Eternal Life; Leo Vincey is Conscience; and Ludwig Holly is Science. The origin of *She*,
like that of the Church, is shrouded in mystery, and Ayesha's passion for Vincey is, alas,
the weakness of the Church. Leo Michael, *She, an Allegory of the Church* (1889).

idea of what woman ought to be. The *anima* is the image a man projects upon a woman when he falls in love with her, and thereby it becomes synonymous with the 'life-urge.' He falls in love with an ideal and remains in love as long as the real woman does not destroy the aura of the *anima* the man has created around her. Ayesha, as Haggard's *anima*, possesses the traditional ideal qualities of womanhood: unchanging beauty, perennial youth, and supernatural power. Complying even further with Dr. Jung's formula, she appears in historic dress and possesses sagacity (she is 'Wisdom's Daughter,' even though Ouida thought her banalities made her sound like a young woman of Kensington[48]). Jungian theory would make Ayesha the projection of Haggard's unconscious idea of the ideal love, an image that, varying only in minor details, all men possess, having inherited it as part of their 'collective unconscious,' or race memory.[49]

Nandor Fodor, a Freudian who believes man's life to be a working-out of the anxieties of pre-natal existence and the birth trauma, sees in *She* 'a beautiful allegory of the penalty attendant on our yearning to return into the womb.' Haggard's desire to return to that 'living fire' whence the newborn emerge 'in the splendour of physical perfection' is no more exceptional, according to Dr. Fodor, than the projection of Haggard's *anima* is to Dr. Jung; it is merely the search for pre-natal happiness common to all men. Since in the unconscious the ideas of birth and death merge into a single image, man's yearning for happiness becomes a yearning for death. But because the conscious mind rejects death, man's attempt to recapture complete bliss must be allegorical, not actual. Obviously no one can experience the living fire twice. Ayesha steps for a second time into the bath of flames from which she had once emerged a creature of flawless beauty and great power – and she pays the inevitable penalty.[50]

Convenient as it may have been for Drs. Jung and Fodor to use *She* to illustrate their theories, they are not of course addressing themselves to the relation of the story to its author. Modern psychology can, however, lend us some valuable insights. Ayesha is obviously tied to Haggard's childhood. In Africa she lives in an impenetrable cavernous dwelling, just as the forbidding rag doll had lived in the deep, dark nursery cupboard, and Ayesha possesses all the strange powers that the child might attribute to the mysterious doll. For Haggard the adult, she is the symbol of an invisible force. Ayesha is also tied to Haggard's adventures with spiritualism in the London séances. Ever since his encounters with Lady Poulett and her circle, Haggard brooded over the meaning of the strange forces he had then sensed, and he always strove to find a clue to the meaning of those experiences.

And just as the heroine is tied to Haggard's life, so the whole story expresses the essential qualities of Haggard's character. The hero's journey through wilderness and swamps, along precipices, over gorges, through ravines, to find the source of love and everlasting life in a huge cave city, is an obvious expression of the author's unconscious fears and desires. We know already that Haggard was an insecure person. The treatment he had received at his father's hands, his education, compared with his brothers', his failure in love, his numerous disappointments – all these left psychological scars. It is not at all remarkable that Haggard strove to gain security, nor is it surprising that *She* represents his search for psychological peace, his quest for success, the meaning of life, and immortality.

But in the end, Haggard knows, unconsciously if not consciously, that the answers to his questions about life, death, and immortality are not to be had in this world, just as he knows somewhere within him that even success is transitory, that there is no enduring security: Ayesha, the symbol of youth, love, knowledge, wisdom, and strength, turns to dust.

She not only appealed to the general public; it also attracted the attention of a good many eminent figures. Walter Besant considered it 'the greatest effort of pure imagination in the English language';* Edmund Gosse thought it 'simply unsurpassable' and said that he had never been 'thrilled and terrified by any literature' as he had by the latter chapters of *She*.[51] James Barrie 'read, enjoyed, and immediately produced a short skit on Rider Haggard's *She*';[52] Wilkie Collins praised it highly;[53] and Marie Corelli later wrote to Haggard to say that she was 'dazzled to my very heart's core by the splendour of "She"!'[54] Andrew Lang thought it 'one of the most astonishing romances I ever read.'[55] More recently C. S. Lewis called it a story that is 'in touch with the permanent nature of our imagination';[56] and Henry Miller wrote that Ayesha occupies a position in his mind 'comparable to the Sun in the galaxy of immortal lovers' against whom 'Helen of Troy is but a pale moon.'[57] Yet George Moore thought that *She* was 'paste' and not 'crystal,' 'Manufacture' not 'Art';[58] Henley both praised Haggard's imagination and damned his artlessness: Ayesha, he thought, was 'the heroic Barmaid – the Waitress in Apotheosis';[59] Henry Sidgwick, the philosopher, writing to Mary (Gladstone) Drew, said that he 'read *She*, but under protest and with firm resolve not to read any more [novels which the public "enthuse" about]';[60] and George Meredith could not even bear to read it.

---

* 'I read [it] in a single night,' he later said at a dinner of the Authors' Club; 'it was impossible while the book was in my hand to take my eyes from a single page.' 'Chronicle and Comment' *Bookman* (New York), II, (November 1895) p. 179.

The reason that many first-rank artists and critics disagree so sharply is intrinsic in *She*, for although it is a more remarkable story than *King Solomon's Mines*, it is at the same time a worse book. The flaws of *She* are no more numerous than those in *King Solomon's Mines*; they are merely more obvious, and what makes them so is a weakness in Haggard's point of departure. In both books Haggard poses as the editor of a manuscript written in the first person by an adventurer, a device that suits well his style of writing and lends the necessary credibility to the work. In *King Solomon's Mines* the person writing the story is the hero-adventurer Allan Quatermain, whose literary interests hardly go beyond the *Ingoldsby Legends* and the Old Testament. By his own confession he is a man of the gun, not the pen, and he finds difficulty in giving his tale the sophistication and polish he feels it demands. In this context the reader is fully prepared to overlook an amount of stylistic coarseness, a degree of bluntness in the manner of telling the story, and even occasional naïveté. Not so with *She*. True, as in *King Solomon's Mines*, Haggard is still the editor of a memoir. But the author of the memoir, although implicitly another Allan Quatermain, is in fact not a rough hunter who was reared on the African veld, but a Fellow at ———— College, Cambridge, a man who has spent his life studying languages and mathematics. Here Haggard makes a fatal error, for he is simply not up to producing the mind, emotion, or manner that a reader expects in a university man. From the first sentence of the journal, what we get is writing that would better fit Quatermain's rough pen: 'There are some events of which each circumstance and surrounding detail seems to be graven on the memory in such a fashion that we cannot forget it, and so it is with the scene that I am about to describe.'[61] Early in the narrative, soon after our heroes have entered Ayesha's country, Holly reports the following: 'At dawn we were aroused by a loud trumpeting sound, produced, as we afterwards discovered, by a young Amahagger blowing through a hole bored in its side into a hollowed elephant tusk, which was kept for the purpose.'[62] And much later, when the party has accompanied Ayesha to the Pillar of Fire, they find on the way the remains of an old philosopher. Holly picks up a yellow tooth from the dust at his feet and shows it to Ayesha. ' "Yes," she said, "it is his without a doubt. Behold what remains of Noot and the wisdom of Noot – one little tooth!" '[63] Convulsive sentences, flatulent prose, puerile descriptions, unfortunate metaphors, solecisms and slang – they are all to be found. Time and again the reader is forced to break through the prose barrier to the story.

But say what one will about Haggard's distracting prose, *She* is one of the most original of the romances that appeared toward the end of the century. To this day, it strikes the reader as an astonishing feat of invention, even after dozens of imitations have come from the pens of later writers and the white goddess has become a cliché among adventure stories. The story itself is at least as good as *King Solomon's Mines*, and often Haggard handles detail better here than in his earlier tale. The scholarly apparatus that accompanies the sherd of Amenartas, is, for example, a *tour de force*, easily outdoing the map device of *King Solomon's Mines*. So overpowering is its claim to authenticity that it assures the author a credulous reader from the start. Haggard handles the elements of romance well too. The mystery of distant lands and strange people, nature in the raw, the heroic behaviour of his characters, the clash of cultures are all managed convincingly. And the added mysticism gives *She* a dimension the reader did not find in *King Solomon's Mines*.

By 1887, Haggard's two African adventure stories placed him in the vanguard of the revivified romance. In February, a critic writing in the *Blackwood's Edinburgh Magazine* called Haggard 'the avatar of the old story-teller, with a flavour of the nineteenth century and scientific explanation,' and went on to say that his two romances are 'a strong pull upon the wholesome curiosity of the race.'[64] In May, the *Dial* devoted its leading article to an essay on 'Mr. Haggard's Romances.' Over and above his faults, the critic asserts, Haggard is 'a great story-writer. He has freshened and quickened literature by showing in a distinctive and original way that the stories are not all told.'[65] Later that same year, Saintsbury, in an essay on 'The Present State of the Novel,' acknowledged that

> Mr. Stevenson and Mr. Haggard have not only made themselves great names, but . . . have done a great deal to further that return to the pure romance, as distinguished from the analytic novel. . . . Both the writers have deliberately reverted to the simpler instead of the more complicated kind of novel, and have pitched away minute manners-painting and refined character-analysis. I hold that they have done rightly and wisely.[66]

Andrew Lang, a strong partisan in the battle between 'the crocodile of Realism and the catawampus of Romance,' hailed the revived genre in a set of verses (1887) which he dedicated to Stevenson and Haggard:

> King Romance was wounded deep,
>   All his knights were dead and gone,
>   All his court was fallen on sleep,
>   In a vale of Avalon!

· · · · · ·

> Then you came from south and north
> From Tugela, from the Tweed;
> Blazoned his achievements forth,
> King Romance is come indeed! ...[67]

Henley, too, looked upon the resurgence of romance with clear approval and saw Haggard as one of the central figures in bringing it back to life:

> Just as it was thoroughly accepted that there were no more stories to be told, that romance was utterly dried up, and that analysis of character ... was the only thing in fiction attractive to the public, down there came upon us a whole horde of Zulu divinities and sempiternal queens of beauty in the Caves of Kôr. ... Did the public, carefully educated to be calm and introspective, reject these funeral bake-meats with disdain? By no means. They fell upon them with incredible relish; and the waters were singing once more in the late-deserted channel of romance.[68]

Mrs. Oliphant, with more enthusiasm than critical acumen, captured none the less the attitude of many readers toward romance and Rider Haggard:

> [It is perhaps not so surprising that] the general reader should have gone back with a spring of evident relief to records of wild adventure, fighting, and bloodshed. This is a sort of natural recoil from fare too ethereal for human nature's daily food. ... And now the fine workmanship, say of Mr. Henry James, who carries that art to perfection ... naturally gives the fascinated yet unsatisfied reader an appetite for the downright effects of Mr. Rider Haggard. While the American Hamlet of the day wavers and hesitates, the Zulu's straightforward rules of action are delightful to the less sophisticated intelligence. ... This is quite enough to account for the sudden surging of the ancient legend of adventure and movement, amidst a society which has had its fill of philosophy of democracy, of criticism, and all the analytical processes.[69]

And in 1892, looking back upon the 'eighties, Saintsbury observed that 'we have revived the romance, if not on the greatest scale, on a scale which ... a whole generation had not seen. We have wound ourselves up to something like the pitch of Romantics of sixty or seventy years ago.'[70]

Haggard's role in this revival was clearly a central one, and *King Solomon's Mines* and *She* stood as milestones on the march of fiction in the 'eighties. '[They] are by far his most remarkable works,' wrote Hugh Walpole later, and show 'his gifts at their finest, surest, and strongest. . . . [They] read as though they had rocks for their foundations.'[71] Walpole's words echo the thoughts of the thousands of readers who, toward the end of the century, found themselves strangely gripped by the imaginative power of Haggard's two tales of African adventure. The appeal of *King Solomon's Mines* and *She* turned their author's name into a household word. By 1890, three years after *She* appeared, Haggard, at thirty-four, had already fashioned for himself a literary reputation and was well on his way to earning a fortune.[72]

5

Triumph and Tragedy

HE early years of success were happy ones. The excellent notices, the deluge of letters from readers, and most important the overwhelming financial returns were more than Haggard had hoped for. Wherever one turned there were articles by Haggard, articles about Haggard, and interviews with Haggard. The literary columns printed titbits about him, and the Press diligently accounted for his comings and goings. In the United States, the *Literary World* reported that 'ten thousand . . . readers demand imperatively to know the colour of Mr. Haggard's eyes.'[1] Walter Besant wrote in a letter that when the Library of the People's Palace opened, 'all day long the people demanded "Rider Haggard!" and there is not a single copy of any of your works on the shelves.'[2] In May 1887 a 'Spy' caricature of Haggard appeared in *Vanity Fair* over a terse caption: 'She.' The sketch shows Haggard in profile, standing with military erectness, hands behind back, feet spread at a forty-five degree angle. The hair is brown, a moustache extends to the mouth line, pince-nez sit gingerly on a heavy nose, the face is livid pink, and the mouth is open, as if indeed as a young barrister he were arguing a brief before the Bench. But perhaps the crowning note of recognition came as an official invitation to attend the Jubilee ceremonies in Westminster Abbey.*

Haggard took his success seriously. He accepted innumerable honorary posts in various specialised organizations, lent his support to any number of causes, joined clubs and associations with whose aims he sympathised, and was always ready to wield a gavel and make an after-dinner speech of welcome, thanks, approval, or disapproval. He proposed an endless number of public toasts and seconded as many motions. As a man acutely concerned with England and everything that touched upon her welfare, he had strong opinions about national events and contemporary movements, and he regularly

* It was forwarded from his London address to Norfolk too late for Haggard to attend.

expressed them in the letters columns of the daily Press on subjects ranging from hydrophobia to American copyright law.

Assured of a respectable income, he no longer permitted the law to master his life. He left the Temple, and in late January 1888, as soon as *She* was off the presses, he sailed for a three-month tour of Egypt, the land of his dreams. Leaving England now was very different from all previous departures. He was going south to relax, and he left behind him an enthralled public to whom he would return at leisure. For the first time in his life, he could look to the future with assurance. As he sailed south, not only was *She* selling well, but *Allan Quatermain* was running serially in *Longman's Magazine* and *Jess* in the *Cornhill*. Not many authors could boast three simultaneous successes. What is more, he had still another romance in mind. He would write a tale about Cleopatra, and his holiday in Egypt would supply the information and the inspiration for the work.

This holiday set the pattern for many similar journeys he took through the years to come, both alone and with his family. They were never pure holidays, for Haggard always journeyed with a purpose. He travelled as comfortably as possible and visited exciting places, but the destination was always determined by some particular interest he had in a country or a civilization and the practical end to which he would put the information he gathered there. He loved ancient ruins and strange lands, and he had a remarkable knack of soaking up exotic atmosphere. While abroad he was happy, even when his mind worked feverishly, taking notes, learning, thinking, hatching plots. His holidays were inspection tours of the world, and as such they were hardly restful – if anything, they were more active than the days at home. But they were active in a different way and at least added variety to his life. Haggard in his search for success and security lost the meaning of rest; the most he could ever hope for now was interesting and varied activity.

On his way to Egypt he stopped at the Louvre to examine ancient Egyptian holdings, and then went on by way of Rome and Brindisi to Cairo. On board the ship that took him from Italy to Egypt, he was pleased to find 'nearly everyone' reading either *King Solomon's Mines* or *She*. Egypt was no disappointment; all he had read about the ancient civilization suddenly came alive for him. The resident archaeologists welcomed such a devotee and showed him around the museums, tombs, and temples. In his letters home to Louisa he shared his excitement at seeing the gold signet of Meneptha, son of Rameses II, a 'ring that Moses must have looked upon.' And again, 'I looked . . . with feelings of awe and veneration at the dead faces of Seti and Rameses.' 'It is impossible . . . to begin to tell you the impression that all this has made upon me,' he wrote.[3] He crawled on hands and knees into newly opened tombs, and as bats flitted about his head, he saw by torchlight mummied figures that had been sealed up, out of sight, for thousands of years. Up the Nile he travelled from Cairo to Thebes (the 'most wondrous tombs in all the world'[4]), Luxor, and Aswan, inspecting at every point on the map. What he saw stimulated his imagination, and soon he wrote home: 'I am very anxious to get to my work again, my head is full of Cleopatra, for which I have got a very strong plot. I think and hope it will make the British Public sit up!' On the way back, he stopped at Cyprus, whose High Commissioner was now Sir Henry Bulwer, his old chief of African days. Nor did he overlook the opportunity of visiting Famagusta, the medieval city built by the Venetians, which later became the locale for his one travel book, *A Winter Pilgrimage*.

Rider had gone alone to Egypt; Louisa stayed behind in London with the three children. Making the voyage when he did, when the glow of success was still bright and fresh, he was bound to reflect upon his life and fortune, all the more objectively from afar. These musings he shared with his wife by letter. This is Rider at thirty, writing to Louisa six years after their marriage:

> I cannot tell you, dear old girl, how homesick I am – or how I want to see you and the kids again. I will never come on a trip of this kind again without you. I miss you very much and get quite low and lonely. . . . If it is feasible I shall go down to Ditchingham to write it [*Cleopatra*]. Kick that old Hampton out. I think we can afford to go there this summer. I forget when his lease ends, but when it does, dear, go down and see the place is put to rights. . . . We seem to be a good deal better off now, in fact, there must be a great deal of money due, though, of course, there are debts to pay. Still, I think we shall be justified. I cannot tell you, my dear, what a pleasure it will be to me if I find myself in a position to give you back the home again which in a way you lost by marrying me. I think that the best thing to me about such measure of success as I have won is that it has relieved my conscience of a great weight. I do not think I had any business to marry you when I did – it was pulling you down in the world. However, I think that I have now attained, in name if not in fortune, such a position you would not have been likely to exceed if I had not met you, and for that I am very thankful. I dare say that you think me a queer chap for writing like this, more especially as you have always been so gentle and considerate about things, but the matter taken in addition to my other weaknesses and failings,

has always pressed upon me, though it is only now, after all these years, when I have fought and to some extent won the day, that I can speak of it.[5]

Haggard returned to London in April and presented his wife with two molar teeth from a mummy he had himself excavated. She in turn had very good news for him, for his books had continued to sell in unbelievable numbers. Rider and Louisa now began to revise their way of life. In London they gave up their cramped house in Gunterstone Road and moved about a mile east, into larger quarters at 24 Redcliffe Square, near Earls Court, where they even permitted themselves to entertain a little. An interviewer wrote that their new home

> although quite in the city is surrounded by several acres of garden. Mr. Haggard's study is in the rear, overlooking the grounds. A large, solidly constructed table occupies the centre of the room, and at the table the author of 'She' does his writing. In a locked cabinet in the drawing-room is the famous 'potsherd' of 'She.' While talking . . . Mr. Haggard has a way of jumping up suddenly and walking about restlessly for a moment or two, though never interrupting the conversation by doing so.[6]

In 1887 Haggard was elected to the Savile Club, a gathering-place for writers, and here he met the literary lights of the day, laid the foundations of life-long friendships with some of them, and all in all spent some of the most stimulating and enjoyable hours of his life. On Saturdays, he regularly joined a small group of friends for luncheon, always at the same table reserved specially for them. There were Eustace Balfour,[7] Besant, Gosse, Lang, William Loftie,[8] R. A. M. Stevenson,[9] and others. It was also at the Savile that Henley insisted that Haggard spin for him an authentic tale of the Zulus every time they met.

Haggard retrieved Ditchingham House from its lessee almost immediately on his return from Egypt, and in May 1888 the family moved to Norfolk for the summer, returning triumphant to the gracious surroundings they had earlier been forced to surrender. During that summer, Haggard wrote *Cleopatra*. In the country, he concentrated well and wrote for long uninterrupted periods; he loved the land and rural Norfolk, and he felt at home in Ditchingham, not lonely or isolated as he had in 1883, when he had retreated there to study for the Bar. Having tasted the harassment of popularity, he welcomed the escape to the easier country life. Also, he had his town house, and he knew he could return there whenever he wished. Since he had made a name for himself, furthermore, he asserted his independence in the Ditchingham community. He could hold his head high among any men, and even the unfriendly East Anglians could not help taking notice of him. Soon he gave them ample reason for respecting him, for he began to settle into the rural aristocratic pattern of life that had characterized his forebears. He enjoyed this picture of himself as a squire-adventurer, and he was determined to engrave it on the pages of British history.

But the days between 1885 and 1890 were by no means filled with unmixed joys. Haggard, determined to be shrewd in all business matters, and sometimes succeeding, nevertheless had an impetuous temperament and an impractical streak in his nature which often clouded his judgement and led him astray. These weaknesses combined, in 1887 and 1888, with a large share of bad luck to subject him to an arduous series of financial reverses, professional attacks, and personal depressions.

In financial matters he grew rash. He quickly forgot the advice given him by the thin-voiced clerk in Cassell's office, and he sold *Jess*, *Cleopatra*, and *Colonel Quaritch, V.C.* for lump sums, not without considerable regret later, especially when he lost some of his earnings on poor investments. These financial miscalculations were as nothing, however, compared to a misjudgement he had made earlier that came back to haunt him at this time. In 1885, after *The Witch's Head* had been published and fairly well received, Haggard looked about for a publisher to bring it out in a cheap edition. He found one who brought out both *Dawn* and *The Witch's Head* in two-shilling copies. Haggard received one-third of the profits, but he also agreed to let the publisher bring out, on the same terms, any other novel he might write within the following five years. The shadow of that agreement cast itself over *King Solomon's Mines*, *She*, and the other tales Haggard had written, and his folly troubled him. Only after much consultation was A. P. Watt, agent and guardian angel of the innocent literati, able to appease the publishers with different terms. Haggard would write two new tales for them, and they would relinquish the right to his other works.[10]

In December 1889, Haggard's mother died, an event that unsettled him considerably. As a boy at Bradenhan, he had found in her alone the sympathy and love he needed, and he had given in return almost all the affection a child ordinarily divides between two parents. Now she was gone. Over twenty years later, when working on his autobiography, he could still not bear to write of her death. Later still, when he paid his last visit to Bradenham, he stood with his youngest daughter in the empty room that had once been his mother's, and he tried to tell her what his mother had meant to him. He spoke 'of the feeling that with her went something of himself; that there had never been a day when he did not remember her and pray for her. He who spoke so seldom of the things which lay nearest his heart, tried,' Miss Haggard writes, 'but he could not go on, and turning, walked out of the room and out of the house.'[11]

Another kind of distress came from still other quarters during these early years of fame, in the form of attacks in the Press, which, once they began, rained heavily upon him. They were, in part, inevitable. Rider Haggard was one of the few names added to the rolls of fiction in the 'eighties, and his quick success caused deep resentment in some literary circles, for more than any writer at the time, he gave the English middle class books that satisfied their palate, books they could understand and enjoy.

Flushed with success, always ready to express an opinion, Haggard himself gave the signal for the attacks to begin. Before leaving for Egypt, he had written a lengthy, indiscreet article called 'About Fiction' for the *Contemporary Review*[12] which appeared just after he set sail. Haggard was generally outspoken, and his directness, while it added virility to his fiction, made his critical remarks appear rude and dogmatic and turned the essay into an intemperate, pretentious assault upon fiction *en masse*, in England, France, and America. The world could do without three-fourths the novels written, Haggard insisted, and he accused the poorer novels of lowering public taste and obscuring the true end of fiction. Americans were destroying their own literature by reading so many English works. French naturalism was an 'accursed thing'; 'whatever there is that is carnal and filthy, is here brought into prominence, and thrust before the reader's eyes.' English fiction was all being written for sixteen-year-old maidens, and everything unsuited for these rosy-cheeked damsels was deemed improper for the novel. Romance alone satisfied; it was the *ne plus ultra* of all art, and 'really good romance writing is perhaps the most difficult art practised by the sons of man. It might even be maintained that none but a great man or woman can produce a *really* great work of fiction.' He called for a 'higher ideal' in English fiction and asserted finally that romance was the form of literature that would outlive naturalism, Mr. Howells, and the 'society novel.'

This volley from a newcomer on the literary scene not only demanded a rebuttal; it exposed Haggard to a counter-attack. For his own work was by no means invulnerable to criticism. Haggard, by denouncing his fellow-craftsmen, had assumed a privilege his success did not grant him. His contemporaries bristled and sent him packing to Coventry.

'About Fiction' appeared in February 1887, and in the months to follow the critics pounced concertedly upon him. March was a hard month for his reputation. Denunciations of his work and charges of plagiarism appeared on both sides of the Atlantic. W. T. Stead, editor of the *Pall Mall Gazette*, a master of sensational journalism, led boldly on March 11 with an attack entitled 'Who Is "She" and Where Did "She" Come From?' and he continued the attack into April, opening wide the letters column of the *Gazette* to the controversy.* Stead's fever spread, and the *Literary World*, the *Spectator*, the *Whitehall Review*, and the *New York Post* in turn accused Haggard of plagiarism in *King Solomon's Mines*, *She* and *Jess* from sources as varied as the Japanese legend of Urashima and Thomas Moore's *Epicurean*.[13] At the end of the month, George Moore, writing in *Court and Society*, accused Haggard of creating 'the literature of gross excitements and vulgar display,' and stated that 'my difficulty lies not in exoneration of him from having read . . . [Moore's *Epicurean*] but in conceiving him to have read anything, saving, perhaps, the *London Journal*.'[14] Elsewhere he wrote that 'to contrast Mr. Rider Haggard and Mr. Robert Louis Stevenson is like comparing a worm to a star.'[15] April brought no decrease of activity in the *Pall Mall Gazette*, and the controversy spread to the letters column of *The Times*. In May, *Time* printed an eleven-page, tale-by-tale analysis of Haggard's work by Augustus M. Moore—a plethora of Moore's was involved in the polemic—which accused Haggard of having 'crammed' for *She*, sinned against good taste, committed banalities, and also demonstrated that he could not 'construct and parse simple sentences.'† Disapproving notices of Haggard's stories were, furthermore, more numerous and less polite (e.g. James Barrie's review of *Allan Quatermain* in the *British Weekly* on August 5, 1887). And the attacks continued into the following year, when two more lengthy essays appeared, 'The Culture of the Horrible: Mr. Haggard's Stories,' in the January issue of the *Church Quarterly Review*,[16] and 'The Fall of Fiction,' in the *Fortnightly Review*.[17]

In his absence, Haggard's family and friends came to his defence. Charles Longman, J. Stanley Little, Andrew Lang, Rider's brother Alfred, and Louisa all upheld Rider's honour in the letters column of the *Pall Mall Gazette*, and when Rider learned of the tempest, he added his own rebuttal from Cyprus. Lang went even farther and wrote a long article on literary plagiarism for the June issue of the

---

* On February 23, 1887, appeared Andrew Lang and W. H. Pollock's parody of *She*, called *He*, in which Stead figures as one of the dramatis personae, under the name of 'Old Pell-melli.' Stead's ensuing attacks upon Haggard were certainly provoked by *He*.

† Moore himself exhibits singular erudition (and imagination) in citing a remarkable array of sources for *She*, all the way from Bishop Hall's *Mundus Alter et Idem* to the stories of Théophile Gautier. See 'Rider Haggard and "The New School of Romance," ' *Time*, XVI (May 1887), pp. 513–524.

Contemporary Review, a sensible and lucid defence of Haggard's originality. Lord Curzon also came to Haggard's support. Curzon did not know Haggard, but according to the story-teller, Curzon was attracted by the accusations, read all the evidence, and then wrote a letter to the editor—Stead?—who had made the accusations, which, in Haggard's words, 'absolutely, finally and utterly destroyed, squashed and obliterated the whole false case that had been set up against me.' The editor involved refused to publish Curzon's letter, and so Curzon sent the letter on to Haggard.[18]

Both Haggard and his reputation were damaged irreparably by the attacks. They hurt him because they cast a shadow upon the quality of his life he valued most, his honour; and they made Haggard the writer the fashionable target of parody, farce, and rebuke. Anyone examining the charges of plagiarism can recognize their absurdity at a glance. Haggard was accused of stealing from books he had never read and from authors he had never heard of. If any similarity actually did exist between his work and the books he had read, the similarity would today be called literary influence. If he had drawn upon his reading, he had done no more than any other author. But it would take the humility and honesty of Rudyard Kipling to suggest, with impunity, that borrowing from other writers was not necessarily immoral:

> When 'Omer smote 'is bloomin' lyre,
> He'd 'eard men sing by land an' sea;
> An' what he thought 'e might require,
> 'E went an' took—the same as me!

Confronted with the accusations, Haggard could only protest and say he was not guilty of the charges. But his assertions of innocence did not excite the literary gossips of the day—only the accusations against him did.

Haggard had made two mistakes: he had written an intemperate essay, and he had included in *Jess* a set of verses someone had sent him in the post, which he believed written by an amateur poet. The verses, as it turned out, had been copied by his correspondent from some already in print. Haggard deleted the verses from subsequent issues of *Jess*, but not before he paid heavily for his carelessness. He had alienated the people he should have befriended, and he was punished for his sin. What is more, he remained in bad odour in literary circles all his life. A good story-teller, Haggard was neither critic nor sage. He realized this in later years when he termed his writing the article on fiction 'very little short of madness.'[19]

Nor could Haggard take criticism lightly: 'The unceasing public and private attacks upon him embittered his whole existence at this period, until, at length, his health began to give out,'[20] his daughter writes, and he himself said, 'About this time I must have become rather sickened of the novel-writing trade and despondent as regards my own powers.'[21] He took up again the idea of re-entering the Colonial Service—Lang had earlier arranged a luncheon with Balfour, thinking he might be able to help, and Haggard had already written an application—but his efforts failed. The Colonial Office under Salisbury's premiership was not interested in dispensing patronage to colonial servants of Gladstone's days. Haggard brooded at Ditchingham and grew more depressed as the attacks continued. But one consolation was the reports from his publishers, which were encouraging, in spite of the attacks. Longman wrote that *She* kept selling 'capitally.' And in July 1887, within a month after *Allan Quatermain* was published, Longman again sent good news to Ditchingham: 'You have broken the record. . . . We have subscribed over 10,000 copies of "Quatermain" in London, which they say is more than has ever been subscribed of a 6/- novel before.'[22] *King Solomon's Mines* also continued to sell. Haggard may have lost the favour of his critics and his literary confrères, but he was not deserted by his reading public. Nor by his friends, for Lang and others were ever faithful during these difficult months. 'Merry' Andrew wrote frequently to buck him up.

> If you jack up Literature, I shall jack up Reading. *Of course* I know the stuff is the thing, but the ideal thing would be the perfection of style, and we don't often get that; except from Henry Fielding. Yes, I believe in 'Jess'; but you can't expect me to be in love with *all* your women, the heart devoted to Ayesha has no room for more. Probably I think more highly of your books than you do, and I was infinitely more anxious for your success than for my own, which is not an excitement to me. But Lord love you, it would be log-rollery to say that in a review.[23]

In May Lang wrote again:

> I've seen August [*sic*] Moore's [attack in *Time*]! Splendid, not a rag left of *you*, and *I* am 'corrupt.' . . . The whole shindy is now explained: it was your *Contemporary* article and the blood of the Moore's, thereby aroused. Of course you won't notice him in any way. You steal from Bishop Hall, Campanella, via Lord Bacon, and I don't remember who (or is it whom?) besides.[24]

To top off the entire affair, Lang wrote a bit of doggerel parodying the attackers:

The Critics, hating men who're Dabs
At drawing in the dibs,
Declare that Haggard cribs his crabs,
And so they crab his cribs.[25]

Although the critical attacks continued in the Press and his later books received nothing like the unconditional acclaim the reviewers had given *King Solomon's Mines*, Haggard's popularity did not diminish; instead it soared. What the Press said pained him deeply—he wanted to be accepted and was hurt anew by each bit of criticism he read—but the assaults had no effect upon his popularity. For Haggard's work stood in the van of a new body of writing that appealed to a public whose reading habits were independent of official critical verdicts. A vast new working-class audience had come into being, moulded by the reforms of the mid-century, by universal education, by the cheaper processes of publishing, by the advent of free libraries, and by a rising standard of living that brought greater comfort (especially electric lighting) into the working-man's home and gave him more leisure. For these people, Haggard, in the 1880s and 1890s, was what the radio, the films, and television have become today: an inexpensive evening's diversion. In time, Haggard himself turned his back on literary matters—he refused even to read the notices—and he worked breathlessly. Tales poured from his pen: not only *Cleopatra*, but *Maiwa's Revenge* and *Mr. Meeson's Will* were finished and *Beatrice* and *The World's Desire* begun within a year of his return from Egypt. Once completed, the stories were sent off for serial publication in one of the weeklies or monthlies. Then before they had a chance to cool, Longman's (or in exceptional cases another house), published them, Mudie's stocked them in vast numbers in London and sent them off in equal quantity in library boxes to the provinces—and the royalties mounted.* Haggard may have thought his occupation stale and flat—but it was never now unprofitable, and as long as the money poured in, he persistently wrote.

The idea of writing a saga kept recurring to him, and finally, encouraged by Andrew Lang, he decided he would write one. He always had a strong affinity for Icelandic lore. He had read the sagas himself and then to his children. But he could not write a saga without

---

* Harcourt Matthews of Mudie's Select Library said that Haggard's tales were always good for a 400 or 500 first order. Raymond Blathwayt, *Looking Down the Years* (1935), p. 198. George Gissing, writing to his sister Ellen (July 8, 1887), just after the publication of *Thyrza* and Haggard's *Allan Quatermain*, compares bitterly the demand for the two books: 'Mudie, I hear, took sixty copies of *Thyrza* to begin with, and has sent for another twenty-five since. Over against this put the fact that he has just taken 2,000 of Rider Haggard's new book.' Algernon and Ellen Gissing, eds., *Letters of George Gissing* (1937), p. 196.

visiting the land of the midnight sun and the scenes of the primeval slaughters. Thus on June 14, 1888, he set off with his friend, A. G. Ross, on a journey to Iceland. But before he left he went to see William Morris, told him his plan, and came away with letters of introduction and the name of a particularly able guide.

Roughing it in Iceland must have reminded Haggard of his younger days in Africa, and though the north country was black and drear, he was mesmerized by it as he had been by the beauty of the veld. Book in hand, he visited the landmarks of the ancient tales. 'This is an interesting but God-forgotten country,' he wrote home, and he recorded his thoughts in considerable detail in his diary:

> I am writing this on the site of Gunnar's hall, which I can distinctly trace. . . . To the north is a large glacier-mountain. . . . The lark now sings over where Gunnar fought and fell betrayed by Hallgerda. . . . Dug last night and found various relics of the burning. The floor of the hall seems to have been sprinkled with black sand (see the saga). . . . What man who has read the Sagas can look upon the site of Thingvellii without experiencing the most lively emotion? . . . There is the Holmgang Island in the middle of Oxara's stream, on which champions without number have lost their lives in duel, there the pool where faithless women met their doom. . . . It requires but a small exercise of imagination to repeople the entire scene; almost can one see Gunnar. . . . Where are they all—Gunnar, Hallgerd, Grettir[?] . . . And a raven flies croaking from the drift, a wild duck passes swiftly to her nest upon the lake. That is the answer, the only answer given to those who seek what has been in what is.[26]

He and Ross had some good fishing, salmon by the eerie light at midnight and trout so large they broke the tackle. Haggard soaked up atmosphere, and he waited for the moment when the story he would write would appear to him in a flash. For five weeks, he surveyed the naked landscape surrounding the ruins of Njal's Hall; saw the geysers whirl with foam and steam, the eddies bubble and boil; watched and wondered at the shimmery colours of the midnight lights; filled his mind with the images of the barren, craggy land; filled his imagination with the tales of the ancient Norse which he re-read as he went from landmark to landmark. He travelled on, scanning, collecting, noting —confident that the inevitable would occur. It did. Standing by the remains of what he believed was Gunnar's tomb, the tale of Eric Brighteyes took shape, and he was ready to return to England.

In the months following the voyage to Iceland, Haggard devoted himself to his saga. He took four months to write *Eric Brighteyes*, and though it is one of his least read books, it is one of his best. The additional care he lavished on the tale helped to distinguish it from some of his earlier six-to-ten-week productions. He was in fact done with writing romances in six weeks. Undoubtedly the attacks in the Press tempered his speed, and his success lessened the need for haste.

Eric Brighteyes, despite its unfortunate title, is a thoroughly successful Anglicized saga that deserves a place alongside Scott's *The Pirate* and Kingsley's *Hereward the Wake*. It is an Icelandic love story of broad dimensions filled with heroic vikings and a long succession of bold actions thwarted by witchery and vengeance. The saga is so convincing that Haggard here seems to write instinctively, as though his notion that in some previous incarnation he himself had been a viking were true. Again he displays his own peculiar creative force, but this time he is on new ground and brings forth a fresh and powerful story. Nor was the time he spent polishing the work wasted. There is less to offend the reader here, and the language rises to artistic heights more often than in his other tales. Students of Icelandic literature say, furthermore, that Haggard's dialogue reminds them of the original sagas, and one commentator goes so far as to place *Eric Brighteyes* ahead of all English novels written in the saga style.[27] Certainly, in its day, it lacked no admirers. The Prince of Wales and his family preferred it over all other Haggard tales,[28] and Andrew Lang also thought it belonged to Haggard's best.[29] Of all Haggard's neglected stories, *Eric Brighteyes* deserves most to be read.

Haggard's steady income continued to provide him and his family with the traditional comforts of the British upper classes and enabled him to indulge other interests. He continued investing some of his earnings according to the advice of friends in the City, mostly in mines and wildcat schemes, he continued reading and answering the letters he received from his public, and when in London, he enjoyed the fruits of his popularity. On September 6, 1888, a dramatized version of *She* opened at the Gaiety, and Haggard obliged with a speech from his box.* His circles of friends increased, and he grew close to a few men in politics.

It was through his connections in the City that in 1889 he met J. Gladwyn Jebb, managing Director of the Santa Fé (Chiapas) Copper

---

* Sophie Eyre played Ayesha. The *Illustrated London News* (XCIII [September 15, 1888], p. 306) praised the production. The critic for the *Athenaeum* wrote: 'So many intentional burlesques have been played at the ... [Gaiety] that one unconscious burlesque which surpassed them all in extravagance and drollery could scarcely provoke ... [anything but a favourable verdict].' Reprinted in *Critic*, X (September 29, 1888), p. 157. *She* was also produced in New York (November 29, 1887) and in San Francisco (1898). In 1898 a ballet of *She* was produced at the Royal Opera House in Budapest, without Haggard's permission: the Hungarians thought the author was dead. Six films have been made of *She*, the most recent in 1935.

Mines in south-east Mexico. Jebb was another rugged adventurer, one of that breed of muscular romantics devoted to the strenuous life and to exploring the uncharted, uncivilized areas of the world. He was continually risking limb and fortune on the world's frontiers, seeking excitement and hoping to find hidden treasure or natural wealth that would make him a million. He owned a home in Mexico, then a country of unexplored mysteries and untapped resources. Jebb and Haggard hit it off well, and soon Haggard was investing in Mexican mine schemes Jebb recommended.

But more than investments drew them together, for in 1890 a tale Jebb told Haggard induced him to join Jebb in Mexico on what was an absolutely fanciful treasure hunt. The tale had roots that reached back into the sixteenth century, to the last days of the Aztec empire in Mexico. Cortez, the defiant Spanish conquistador, after having captured the Aztec kingdom and subdued Montezuma, suddenly found the Aztec Indians in open revolt against Spanish rule, and in 1520 was forced to flee with his soldiers from the Aztec capital, Tenochtitlan, on the famous *noche triste* (August 13). Before retreating, however, he saw Montezuma slaughtered, and the soldiers filled casks with the ruler's jewels and gold to take away with them. But they had to fight their way out of the city, and their treasure horde proved a disadvantage. Outnumbered by the attacking Aztecs, they fled, leaving the casks behind, sorry they did not heed Cortez's famous words: 'He travels safest in the dark who travels lightest.' The Aztecs, led by Chauhtemoc, Montezuma's nephew, gathered up the treasure, which contained a famous and precious gold head of their late emperor, and buried it in a cache sixty feet deep somewhere on the shore of Lake Tezouco. For centuries speculators and adventurers sought to discover the buried treasure, some of them even torturing local Indians who reputedly passed the secret of the treasure's hiding-place by word of mouth from generation to generation. The treasure, however, never turned up. And now Jebb added an engrossing note: a friend of his, a Cuban geologist named Anselmo, had learned from an Indian who lived on the lakeside the secret of the hidden treasure. Anselmo did not have the funds to buy the land in which the treasure lay buried, but he had acquired instead a permit from the owner to prospect on it for sulphur. Anselmo, Jebb said, had uncovered the old shaft which certainly must lead to the treasure, for on the inner rock door he found carved Chauhtemoc's owl emblem. He had excavated farther and found a passageway and a flight of stairs ending at a wall. But Anselmo could not blast away the wall for fear of revealing his secret. Instead, he filled in the shaft and left. Anselmo, knowing that Jebb was a friend of the owner of the land, approached him and poured out his tale. Jebb had written his friend for

permission to dig on his land for 'antiquities,' and Haggard was with
Jebb when the letter arrived granting the permission. Haggard did not
need much more encouragement, and in a moment, he and Jebb were
sworn brethren in a wild scheme to unearth the treasure. He could later
rationalize his commitment easily enough. He was interested in the
ancient Aztec civilization and would enjoy digging in the ruins. The
trip to the New World would be his first and could be something of a
holiday for Louisa – this time she would accompany him – and certainly
he could write a romance about Montezuma after he had exposed
himself to the local colour and drunk in the atmosphere.

The family spent Christmas (1890) together at Ditchingham. Jock
was now nine, a handsome lad with 'a nature of singular sweetness,'[30]
and the girls were growing up too. Angela would very soon be seven,
and Dorothy soon thereafter six. After a happy, festive yuletide, the
children were left in the care of close friends, and Rider and Louisa
sailed on the *Etruria* for New York. They arrived on January 10 and
were immediately besieged by reporters. They gracefully submitted to
the rigorous hospitality to which New York, even then, subjected all
visiting dignitaries. The *New York Times* gave an interesting account of
Haggard's arrival:

> In the parlor of the Victoria Hotel last night, from 7 to 7:30,
> a tall, lank, middle-aged man was fidgeting about in an alleged easy
> chair, tying his legs into bowknots and doing everything with his
> hands that the hands of a naturally awkward man ever did do when
> he was in a state of nervousness.
>
> He ... had just reached the hotel. ... During the half-hour
> [interview] ... he was undergoing examination by eight or ten
> newspaper men, and he apparently enjoyed the inquisition as much
> as he would have enjoyed ... furnishing data for an obituary notice
> that was to appear in the Sunday morning papers.
>
> 'How did you enjoy your interview with the customs officer?'
> 'How do you like New York?' 'Where are you going when you
> leave here and what for?' 'How old are you?' 'What is your opinion
> about the elevated railroad?' 'How do American reporters compare
> with the reporters in England?' These and scores of other questions
> were fired at the victim of newspaper enterprise. He said that ... he
> guessed that he should like New York ... and he affirmed positively
> that there were no reporters in England.
>
> '... Do you consider that you have exhausted Africa [in your
> stories]?'
>
> 'I guess not,' said Mr. Haggard, giving three quick turns to the
> collar button at the back of his neck.

'How do you do your work?' asked another man.

'Oh, any way that I can. Sometimes one way, sometimes another.'

'Dictate it?'

'No, I write it.'

'Work nights?'

'Oh, yes, sometimes, but I don't do much night work.'

'... Do you make your plots before you write your stories, or do you write the stories first?'

'Undoubtedly,' said the novelist, throwing a pitying glance at the enquirer, 'I make the plots before I finish the stories.'

Mr. Haggard did not urge his torturers to remain after they showed their readiness to leave. . . . [He] is a tall man, probably six feet high, somewhat loosely put together, with a slight stoop of the shoulders. He has dark hair, but the delicate mustache which adorns his lip is quite light in color. A long pointed nose gives his face a thinnish appearance, but a careful look at him shows that he has a full forehead and that his eyes are well apart. He has an agreeable manner and a pleasant smile. When he shakes hands he gives a quick, nervous grip and he simultaneously gives a pull sufficiently strong to take a man who has not good understanding quite off his feet.[31]

From New York the Haggards went by train to New Orleans, where they enjoyed another social whirl, and then on to the Jebbs's house in Mexico City. Here the men prepared to explore the wilderness, and in the months that followed, while the ladies busied themselves in Mexico City, they hunted, inspected, and dug into the rough country. Everything from the Aztec ruins to the native farming methods interested Haggard. They travelled by horseback over precipitous mountain ledges to inspect a silver mine deep among the Chiapas, beyond Vera Cruz. The risks were many – yellow fever and malaria were prevalent, and there were real dangers in travelling on these mountain paths, for they might easily die a mountaineer's death or be attacked or killed suddenly by local bandits – but adventure lured them on. The beauty of the country, the attraction of the ruins, and the romance of the expedition were ample for Haggard. Damn the tarantulas, the mosquitoes, the ticks, the bandits, and the precipices. Haggard made mental notes (he found he could not easily make a record in his diary) of it all, of the beautiful fauna and flora, admiring particularly the palms and orchids. He collected many samples of plants. 'Only, because of the snakes . . . it was necessary to be very careful in gathering these floral treasures,'[32] he wrote. He succeeded also in shipping a sackload of roots back to Ditchingham, and many of these Mexican plants thrived for decades in his Norfolk greenhouses.

But although Jebb and Haggard prepared to leave Mexico City to excavate Montezuma's treasure on February 9 (1891), they abandoned the project entirely on the day before. On Sunday morning, February 8, in the Jebb home in Mexico City, Mrs. Jebb read the Haggards the contents of a cable that bore a simple message: little Jock, their eldest child, had 'passed away peacefully.'* The news was a staggering blow and turned Rider Haggard's world into confusion. In a moment, his life had been shaken to the core; while he was away searching for gold in Mexico, his handsome boy, his only son and heir, had vanished. Life could never be the same again.

'I can see the room now,' he recalled in later years. 'Jebb weeping by the unmade bed, the used basins – all, all. And in the midst of it myself – with a broken heart!' Louisa, always withdrawn in the face of tragedy, paced the roof speechless, and Rider threw himself into wild activity with Jebb on their journeys. There was no point in returning home to face the empty sorrow, not yet in any case – they might as well stay out their time in Mexico. But there was no taste left for the Montezuma treasure hunt, and a planned journey to the pre-Aztec Palenque ruins was also abandoned. Finally in April, after weeks of inner trial, the Haggards returned to Ditchingham, by way of New York and Liverpool, to 'two little girls dressed in black and – a grave.' Although racked by misery and physical pain, Rider plunged into his writing. Bent over his work, he wrote in the later summer of 1891 the historical romance his trip to the Aztec ruins had suggested, *Montezuma's Daughter*, the tale of the buried treasure he never found.[33]

In later years he told how he had had a presentiment about impending disaster before he left England:

> When I went to Mexico I knew, almost without doubt, that in this world he and I would never see each other more. . . . The parting was bitter indeed . . . I went through the agony of a separation which I knew to be the last. With a cheerful face I kissed him – I remember how he flung his arms about my neck – in a cheerful voice I blessed him and bade him farewell, promising to write. Then he went through the door and it was finished. I think I wept.[34]

At the time Rider assumed that if anyone would come to grief, it would be himself.

Another irony was that Haggard only four years before had dedicated *Allan Quatermain* to 'my son . . . in the hope that . . . he . . . may . . . reach the highest rank . . . we can obtain – the state and dignity of English gentlemen'; and had made Quatermain begin his tale with the

---

* Jock had been left in the care of the Edmund Gosses at Delamere Terrace. The boy died 'suddenly of a perforating ulcer after an attack of measles.' Haggard, *Days*, II, p. 46.

prophetic words: 'I have just buried my boy, my poor handsome boy of whom I was so proud, and my heart is broken. It is very hard having only one son to lose him thus.'[35]

Haggard's conscience would not let him rest; he had been blind not to read the signs and presentiments more clearly. He was alternately torn with unbearable feelings of loss and guilt. On the one hand he could not bear the waste of such promise as young Jock had shown, he could not take easily the fact that his one son, his only true line of descent, had been wiped out, and he brooded over the loss. Nor could he bear the guilt that grew within him or refrain from implicating his wife in that guilt. His daughter later suggests that

> there was undoubtedly the psychological obsession that his child's life had paid the price of the father's sin; that it was required in expiation of transgression, and being so required increased his guilt. The belief (to judge from chance remarks and pencilled passages in his well-worn Bible) he carried with him, an unhealed wound, until the day of his death.[36]

So profound was this tragedy that Haggard lived for years in utter dejection. He sold his town house and shut himself and his family up in Ditchingham, where he sank into a deep melancholy from which he never completely emerged. He was incessantly ill with influenza, digestive disorders, and headaches, and he suffered 'acute mental depression.' He took little interest in the old delights, in hunting, in adventure, in creating romance; and he found writing distasteful. He took no solace from family or friends and even resented their efforts to cheer him up. On Jock's grave he carved the message 'I shall go to him,' and he undoubtedly spent many hours standing by the grave gazing at those words, 'full of comfort and meaning to me.'[37] He put out of sight everything that reminded him of his son and imposed a hard rule upon the family: never to speak Jock's name in Ditchingham House. Jock's memory retreated to the shadowy corners of the Haggards's lives and hovered over all they did, a cloud of sadness over a home that had once echoed with laughter. Rider's nephew has written about the effect of Jock's death:

> There was . . . a super taboo – the subject of his only son. Although it was assumed that Jock's memory was for ever in Rider's thoughts, years passed without his name being mentioned. It was unnatural so to bottle the thing up, especially in a talkative family like ours. . . . It should have been dragged out into the light as a measure of relief.
>
> . . . Rider had the dynastic sense. To leave a son, and lands for

him to inherit, to perpetuate his name; these were strong prepossessions with him. They were disappointed. Jock was dead and so he must not be mentioned. To come on a book or a toy that once had belonged to my young cousin . . . was to strike a hush over the room such as might almost have been observed towards a relative who had been hanged for murder. There was a guilty silence. Jock haunted the house the more obtrusively because everyone there pretended they could not see him, and the poor schoolboy wraith seemed to be begging piteously for some notice, so that at last he might be laid to rest.[38]

The Haggards spent most of their time in Ditchingham now and lived 'in a very quiet and retired fashion.' Rider gradually turned to the land and occupied himself with farming and gardening 'for which occupations I have always had an instinctive taste.' He did not often go up to London to see his friends whose company he had so enjoyed in earlier years. No letters to *The Times* appeared over his name for more than two years, and there exists no record of a single public appearance through a longer period. In April 1892, a little more than a year after Jock's death, Rider's father died, an event that must have awakened many turbulent emotions within him, for although his father had been an arbitrary, tyrannical parent, Rider had found much to admire in him. But though he 'grew heartily tired of the writing of stories,' somehow throughout these years of seclusion and strain, Rider ploddingly worked away at his romances.[39] They were, after all, his livelihood.

After a reasonable time had passed and Rider showed no signs of overcoming his sorrow, even Louisa grew resentful. She too had felt the terrible loss and knew a mother's grief. But being a sensible woman, she saw no point in making her life, or permitting her husband's, to become a monument to the death of their nine-year-old son. One simply had to face life and make the best of it. She tried determinedly to console Rider, but he would not respond. His wife, his family, his home, his career – none of these any longer ruled his life: he was now the tragic mourner, and so he would remain. Louisa 'had done her best to comfort him, but when he persistently turned away from all the things they had enjoyed together, she . . . went her own way with her many friends.'[40] In 1891, as Rider approached his thirty-fifth birthday, he gave the impression of a man old before his time.

For about two years, this dull, isolated life endured. But it was impossible even for Haggard to remain a recluse for the rest of his life. He was by nature an active, intense person: beneath his conscious sense of loss still raced a swift mind, and his body welled with energy. He could don the mourner's cloak, but he could not suppress for ever his innate curiosity about man and the world. Jock's death actually quickened his search for the meaning of life, and Rider was still faced with growing responsibilities, for Ditchingham took a great deal of money to sustain properly, and his family still had to be cared for. These proddings worked on him in such a way that although his aching loss never left him, over a period of years he slowly emerged from his depressed state of isolation and loneliness. As 1892 came to a close, Rider showed distinct signs of recovery. Ditchingham and the greenhouses did not offer enough outlet for his restlessness, and by his own admission he 'longed for a change, for this humdrum existence in a country parish, staring at crops and cultivating flowers, was, I felt, more suitable to some aged man whose life's work was done than to myself.' The fact that Louisa was again with child, while it discouraged her, helped to restore in him some of the hope and interest in the future that he had lost. On December 9, 1892, almost two years after Jock's death, Louisa bore Rider another child – a girl. Rider had unquestionably wanted a boy – the family 'wrote letters of condolence instead of congratulations' – but he suppressed his disappointment and took a warm, fatherly interest in the infant. His health improved instantly, and he began to think constructively about his life. Again he gave serious thought to changing his occupation ('the unrealities of fiction greatly wearied me'), and though he continued, relentlessly forcing himself to create romance after romance, he at least took steps that lightened somewhat the physical strain of the work. He hired a secretary, Ida Hector,* instructed

* Haggard had two secretaries in his life. The first, Agnes Barber, the sister of Marjorie Barber ('Michael Fairless,' who wrote *The Road-Mender*), was a school acquaintance of Louisa's. She was 'a woman with...[a] fine...literary sense and...all-round ability,' wrote Haggard later. Her critical talents came to his attention early, when his sister Mary forwarded a letter in which Agnes analysed *Dawn* and disagreed with Jeaffreson's advice that he change the ending. After she came to work for him, Agnes helped concoct the Sherd for *She*, reproduced as the frontispiece of the first edition. So cleverly antiquated were the inscriptions on the piece of clay pot that it almost passed for an authentic ancient fragment, even among experts. Admiral Vernon H. Haggard, Rider's nephew, remembered that when, as a young boy of about ten, he spent the summer at Ditchingham, he was permitted on rainy days to sit in his uncle's study while Rider worked on his stories with Miss Barber. The author either dictated or read aloud what he had already written. ' "And then he said to her," ' Rider would read from his foolscap and on occasion turn to Miss Barber to ask, 'What did he say to her anyway?' and the secretary might make a suggestion. In January 1888 Agnes married Rider's brother Jack. But before this event, some Haggards say, there had been a slight tiff between Agnes and Rider. She had read one of his tales in manuscript and told him in no uncertain terms what she thought about it and how he had better improve it. Rider is reputed to have lost his temper – and thrown a book at her. Ida Hector, Haggard's second secretary, was herself the daughter of an author (the Irish novelist Mrs. Annie [French] Hector [1825-1902] who wrote under the pseudonym of Mrs. Alexander), and she remained with Haggard until the end of his life. She too was efficient, a good horsewoman, took her place easily in the family circle, and became, in Haggard's words, 'a very faithful friend and companion.' Occasionally, it seems, she invested some of her earnings in the mining schemes in which Haggard himself sank some of his fortune. Haggard called her 'Wisdom's Second Daughter' ('Wisdom's Daughter' was, of course, Ayesha). Haggard left her £1,000 in his will, and she lived out her last days in a flat in Kensington.

her to buy and learn to operate a typewriter,* and he himself learned
to dictate aloud to the rhythmic punctuations of Miss Hector's clatter-
ing contraption.† The method proved a great success, and after *Montezuma's Daughter*, Haggard rarely wrote by hand. His interest in little
Lilias and his desire to assist Louisa as much as he could helped bring
him back to reality. Exactly one week after Lilias's birth, he penned a
letter to *The Times*. Though the subject of the letter, the relative merits
of burial and cremation, was dreary, the letter itself signalled his return
to the outer world and its controversies.[41]

While the Haggards continued to live in Ditchingham, their life
now took on a more normal aspect. Although Jock's name was still not
to be mentioned, and although the tragic stance, the sorrowful gesture,
the wrinkled brow would be Haggard's henceforth, he could now at
least function as a human being, as a husband and a father again, and
most important as a man of affairs. For it was mankind and its plight on
earth that was to interest him in later years, and this interest would lead
him to exhibit a compassion for suffering that owed its meaning if not
its inception to the pain that he himself felt for the first time in 1891.

With the birth of Lilias, with the coming of Ida Hector, and with
the arrival of Christmas, Ditchingham House takes on a less gloomy
air. Later it is to become a capital of activity and jollity, but in late 1892
it still presents a quiet domestic scene, one in which we have a glimpse
of Haggard taking the new-born babe from his wife's bedroom into
his study next door and pacifying the infant in his arms while he strides
back and forth, reciting another episode in his tale of adventure, to the
accompanying pizzicato of Miss Hector's typewriter.

The new year brought a new spirit with it, and the revived Haggard
became somewhat more visible in the Press, commenting on developments in South Africa, writing an occasional article, and permitting an
interview or two. By 1894, his activities returned to the feverish intensity that characterized his earlier years and that was quite normal for
him. Rider Haggard had lost himself when he lost his son in 1891; in
1893, he was able, at least, to retrieve something of that lost self, enough
certainly to live an active, meaningful life for another thirty-two years.

---

* The first commercial typwriters were placed on the market in 1874, but in the
early 'nineties, they were still quite novel. An instructor came with the machine to Ditchingham to teach Miss Hector how to use it.

† About dictating, Haggard wrote: 'Personally I have always found . . . [it] easy,
provided that the dictatee, if I may coin a word, is patient and does not go too fast. I
imagine, for instance, that it would be impossible to dictate a novel to a shorthand-writer.
Also, if the person who took down the words irritated one in any way, it would be still
more impossible.' Haggard, *Days*, II, pp. 81–82. In an interview he said, 'Sometimes I write
a first draft with my own hand, and then dictate to a typist; sometimes I dictate straight
off, sometimes I write and don't dictate at all. I am not a slave to any one method.' 'A.D.,'
'An Interview with Mr. H. Rider Haggard,' *Christian Commonwealth*, November 1, 1906,
pp. 75–76.

6

Lord of the Manor

IN 1889 the Haggards returned to Ditchingham House, this time
to make it their permanent home. Ditchingham itself is a small
parish in a quiet corner of south-east Norfolk, twelve miles from
both Norwich and Lowestoft. The closest village is Bungay, which,
though only a mile away, is actually in Suffolk. Bucolic and picturesque,
Ditchingham is distinctly a farming parish, its cottages scattered among
hillocks, its people labouring in the fields and living modest lives within
earshot of the toll from St. Mary's Church, an old Perpendicular structure with 240 sittings across the road from the Haggard home. These
people cling strongly to tradition, speak their own distinct dialect, and
look upon strangers with suspicion.

The 'House' – in the parish the Haggard home is called just that –
is a red-brick Georgian edifice, built in the last days of the eighteenth
century and bought by Louisa's grandfather about 1830. A three-story
structure, utterly square and plain, it was for a time irreverently
called 'Mustard Pot Hall.' When Louisa inherited it, it was in poor condition, because of her guardians' neglect, and now that the Haggards
were moving back there from London, Rider set about making his
home attractive and comfortable by renovating, ornamenting, and
beautifying it. He broke its squareness by building large bow windows
on three sides which reached up to the first floor; and he turned the
billiard room that Louisa's father had added in a 'new' wing into his
private study.

Haggard's love of carved objects, particularly oak, and his collector's impulse transformed the inside of the house. He had grown up
surrounded by oak panelling at Bradenham, and he was determined
that Ditchingham should have no less. He bought all the oak panels,
beams, and fittings he could put his hands on and turned them over to
Williams, the craftsman on his estate with an inherited 'oak thumb,'
who dutifully worked them into the house. Perhaps Williams's
greatest achievement was fitting into Ditchingham House the doors

from Queen Victoria's yacht that had been built on the bias to fit the ship's specifications.

Nor did it take Haggard long to amass a vast collection of exotic ornaments. From each holiday he returned with trunks full of trinkets, mementoes, and souvenirs of far-off places and ancient times. These he hung about him in his study and against the wainscot. Friends and relatives knew his leaning toward the unusual and very often sent down to Ditchingham weird items they had picked up on their holidays abroad. Haggard found it difficult to discard any curiosities, for they were the trappings and the inspirations of his tales. Surrounded by his strange clutter, he wrote the romantic stories of the people it reminded him of. An illegible inscription, a piece of parchment, a rusty engraving, a string of ancient beads found in a tomb encouraged him to spin his tales ('I hold [a relic] as I write'[1]). What is more, these physical objects, faithfully and realistically described, helped give his stories the ring of authority. They were, in a sense, the proof of his dream visit to the exotic world he wrote about and of the events he experienced there. Where many Victorians surrounded themselves with souvenirs that reminded them of the grand moments in their own lives or those of their ancestors – a white bearskin from Burma, a collection of Venetian glass, a handful of shells from the Bay of Naples, an album of daguerreotypes – Haggard assembled the objects that reminded him of the greatest moments in man's history on earth. He turned Ditchingham House into a private museum.

Oak cornices crowned displays of gongs, stuffed animals and birds, heavy earthen vases, and ugly crescent knives. Here and there were seats of twisted wood, curious footstools from Lamé, and throne-like chairs of inlaid ebony and ivory. Lamps hung precariously from African royal redwood trees, a wood restricted to the use of kings and princes of the Zulu nation. Their light fell on Arabian shields, Egyptian swords, African spears, primitive bows and throwing sticks. An ancient Greek head served as a doorstop and sent many a visitor crashing to the floor. On a ledge was a row of ostrich eggs, and not far away the hideous head of a Mexican god, the skull of an eland, a priest's wand from Achamine, and a cedar rod believed similar to the one Moses cast before the Pharaoh. Above a carved Scotch settle hung a whip made of hippopotamus skin, and two huge Burmese figures stood against a window holding a gong between them. Placed here and there were native war horns, Zulu kerries, a buffalo head, a shield of rhinoceros hide, a much-carved cabinet with forty secret drawers, boxes of rings (one from the mummy of Queen Taia of Egypt), ancient coins, spearheads, Mexican combs, a caged rat that cracked nuts for the amusement of visitors, Greek vases, beads from the necks of mummies,

Zulu battle-axes and assegais, a bronze jar from the tomb of an Etruscan monarch, a green jade Mexican idol, clocks of all shapes, sounds, and sizes, boxes of Mexican cigars to be smoked after dinner, large ox-hide shields, a solid bronze head of Sappho five or six times larger than life, an ebony dinner-table inlaid with ivory images of Roman emperors, Indian masks, to mention only a few – and all this mixed in with Louisa's houseful of late-Georgian furniture, portraits of Norfolk worthies, oil paintings of her Royalist ancestors and one of Louisa herself, a Charles Dickens desk (bought at the Gad's Hill sale), a white enamelled chimney-piece, cushioned corners, a portrait of Rider, a Reynolds in the dining-room, china knick-knacks, exquisite embroidery, and elegant fans.

Tales of Haggard the world traveller and collector are numerous. When he travelled, he took along huge trunks containing all sorts of supplies and clothing an ordinary voyager would leave behind. Ofttimes his luggage disappeared en route, no doubt on occasion lifted by souvenir hunters who mistook 'H.R.H.' for a sign of royalty. And everywhere he went, he accumulated his own souvenirs, particularly curiosities of bygone days.

> My father loved collecting things – for choice of the largest possible size, [recalls his daughter,] so his family were obligated when accompanying him about the world to keep up a constant chant, 'It won't go in – it won't go in!' We narrowly escaped Napoleon's (reputed) four-poster of gargantuan proportions and covered tastefully with bees, which we regretfully abandoned in a Naples curio shop, and always mourned. He always said that looking back on life, what he regretted were not his extravagances but his economies.[2]

As the years passed, Haggard added in the remaining interstices on the walls the illustrations Maurice Greiffenhagen[3] drew for some of his romances and a rich collection of Dutch tiles that hung attractively against the panelled oak. The overall effect the house gave was of being lived in and enjoyed – and so it was, nothing delicate, nothing barred from the children, nice big pieces of furniture, and plenty of oddities. Houses were made for people, Haggard believed, not people for houses; and his house was one he and his family could live in comfortably and informally. Certainly it was a clutter, but an interesting and homely clutter.

Haggard on his return to country life found his Ditchingham lands in 'scandalous condition,' and in a few years, he not only turned the House into an attractive home, but added outlying farms to his Norfolk acres and turned the whole into a model farming estate. To the grounds surrounding the House he gave particular attention. He planted creepers to break the monotony of the red brick, he sowed lawns and gardens, and built greenhouses to alleviate the austerity of the square structure. By 1902 he could boast a walled kitchen garden of three-quarters of an acre; a large flower garden (more than an acre) of thick lawns, a lily pond, shrubbery, three treasured greenhouses; and an orchard with more than three hundred fruit trees. Beds of grass, perennials, and shady beech trees framed the colourful flower beds, and at the foot of the garden, a tennis and croquet lawn afforded many afternoons of pleasure to the Haggards and their guests. The greenhouses were Haggard's particular delight, and in them he grew tomatoes, peaches, figs, grapes, mustard, cress, radishes, and other fruits and vegetables. But Haggard never was so relaxed as when he was working in the long house he had built for growing orchids. Here he pottered with the delicate, tropical plants and experimented in hybridizing. His orchid house was his private flower world, his African jungle transplanted to Norfolk, and here, in the hot, glassed-in, heavy air he found rest and diversion.

Staffed with seven servants for the house and five workers for the grounds, the estate, bearing seasonal splashes of daffodils, tulips, iris, Solomon's seal, saxifrage, roses, and many other flowers, was indeed a handsome model of its kind that all could enjoy. The children grew and their parents re-accustomed themselves to country life, their eyes engaged by the beauties of nature, their ears charmed by the melodious parliament of Norfolk fowl, and their bodies nourished by the wholesome produce from the land.[4]

Although the Haggards gradually became a part of the Ditchingham landscape, they were never entirely assimilated; just as Rider's orchids could not be mistaken for the ordinary Norfolk iris; so the Haggards, strident and trumpet-toned, could not be mistaken for the simple run of Norfolk folk. But Haggard's fame had overcome the indifference of the community; the villagers were now accustomed to watch unruffled the somewhat eccentric behaviour of the Haggard clan and expect an occasional outburst from the House. Their huge parties, shoots, and cross-country paperchases, that brought to Ditchingham guests from all over England, were soon, if not unnoticed, also accepted.

Rider grew a beard and looked very much the country gentleman,[5] and Louisa enjoyed living among the people and fields familiar to her. 'Shortcomings in the household routine were one of the few things over which . . . [Rider] could assert himself with no uncertain voice,' but Louisa looked after the house and the children quietly and efficiently. She was by no means a docile, demure, or delicate wife. She was eminently a creature of common sense, 'not in the least imaginative,' a woman with an 'orderly mind,'[6] and, one senses, very much a person with a will of her own. She lent solidity to Haggard's world, for her outward manner reflected her inner strength; she was firm and decisive. Although no beauty, she was, in her husband's estimate, 'the most courageous woman I ever met ... most upright and straightforward ... in fact, good, sensible, and true-hearted, as few women are, [and] she was also that rare thing – a staunch and loyal friend ... entirely ... trustworthy in every matter, either public or private.'[7] She liked people and made many friends. As hostess, she welcomed freely the hundreds of relatives, friends, literary and agricultural associates, newspaper men, and the like, who poured into Ditchingham; and she supervised the many family gatherings with a pleasant vigour all her own. She was a strong-minded feminist who much preferred the active out-of-doors to the study. Country sports were her favourites; she enjoyed a good croquet match – in later years she won a number of champion bouts – and played golf along with the men (she even gave some thought to devising a special golf club for women). A person of strong will and opinion, she thought nothing of riding right into the town of Bungay on a Safety bicycle instead of the more conventional tricycle.

Though a devoted wife (she acceded to her husband's wishes as a matter of rule) and mother, there was something in her nature that made her less than perfect in either capacity. For Haggard she fell short of being the ideal companion, for she was not really interested in books and probably read very few of the tales her husband wrote. Nor could Haggard come to her for literary advice or critical comment. She had no real understanding of what went on in his study, and, as a result, we must wonder whether she realized what went on in his mind. Nor was she the conventional 'motherly type.' Though thoroughly devoted to her children, she could never express emotion openly. Her daughter puts it succinctly: 'She was in no sense a maternal woman. She loved her children, and did her absolute duty by them, even when it entailed no small self-sacrifice, but the deeper sympathies and ties of motherhood passed her by.' There are other indications that difficulties arose from the coupling of the impetuous, imaginative, ambitious Rider and the steady, practical, unhesitant Louisa. 'In later years the faults which sprang from her virtues sometimes troubled the relationship of their married life,' we read, and 'an irritability ... grew on her with the years.' Rider's nephew, writing in 1950, makes the conventional family assumption that his aunt and uncle were not ideally matched:

Had he found the perfect mate, whose general characteristics may be gathered from the collective heroines of his romances, would his spirit have been so free to roam? His marriage went as far with him as it needed to go, and for the rest of the time he was with his own thoughts. He was thrown in upon himself, and his novels were his principal outlet.[8]

But even though Louisa could not share Rider's pursuit of the imagination, even though she may have fallen short of his image of the ideal wife, he still asserted that in marrying her he had done 'the wisest and best deed of my life.'[9]

With time Haggard settled into a daily routine and kept somewhat regular hours. The day began with family prayers in the hall which the entire household, family, servants, and guests, were expected to attend. Rider of course officiated, reading from the old family Bible in his resonant voice. Before breakfast, he might go out to look in at the orchids in the greenhouses, to check any experiments in progress, or in season he would go out to the garden, where he probably gave instructions about flower-cutting for the House. Then back for breakfast punctually at nine, and after breakfast to his post, dictating or writing replies; next to the affairs of the estate and whatever commission or other government tasks demanded his labours. At about eleven (although this varied) he dressed for his walk, often in knickerbockers and boots. Then, a pipe in his mouth, his hand clutching the old Zulu stick by its huge knob head, Haggard, either alone or accompanied by one of the children, a relative who was staying at the House, or by his waddling bull-dog Caesar (and later by Caesar's successors), made his daily rounds of the land. About the farm he went, exchanging hard-crusted Norfolk words with some of the tenants he met at work; inquiring of Longrigg, his bailiff ('with red cheeks like apples and an accent as hard and harsh as some of the bargains he drove'), about the bull he had just bought, or of Rough Jimmy ('with fingers gnarled ... black and rugged like the stumps he dug up') how repairs on the fence were going; or chatting with Rolf, the King of the Norfolk Poachers, or Williams, the skilled carpenter.[10]

Only after taking care of all practical matters did Haggard turn finally, in the later afternoon, to his yarn spinning. Usually he sat down to write at 4:30, wrote till dinner, and then resumed for an hour or two at night. When he was able to turn to his study before tea-time, he would not interrupt himself, but would have a large cup of weak tea brought up to him. He wrote between three and four thousand words a day, and each of his books occupied him for about six months. He needed little preparation for his work. He had read a book or two for background detail, he had the plot fairly well worked out in his mind, and he could take up easily at the point where he had left off the day before. He wrote at 'fever heat' as a rule, for 'when once I have started a new book I am in a state of unrest until it is finished.' 'I think the thing to do is, first, to get an idea, and then to let it take possession of you, surrender yourself absolutely to it, and keep as closely to it as you can until you have bodied it forth.' He worked just as well in London as at Ditchingham, but winter was best for writing ('In the summer time I like to enjoy the country'). 'You notice that I have two tables for writing,' he told an interviewer in 1894. 'I use both alternately, as I like to have a change of position. When I have written my novel on fools-cap,' he continued, 'I . . . dictate it . . . making any necessary correc-tions as I go along. This plan saves me much trouble with the proofs.' 'Do you write easily?' another interviewer asked, and Haggard replied, 'Yes, usually; sometimes more readily than at other times. For instance, when you are full of practical business it is not easy to shunt on to the imaginative track.' Although he did revise some of his work, he generally believed that romances should not be rewritten, for 'wine of this character loses its bouquet when it is poured from glass to glass.'[11]

The study was a large room set off somewhat from the main part of the house with its own stairway leading from the main entrance hall. Facing south, away from the road, it offered a quiet air and a magnifi-cent view of the rich Norfolk fields through which ran the River Waveney. It was bright and sunny, for Haggard had kept the skylight when he converted it from the billiard room. Here he dictated aloud to Miss Hector. As voices went, his was extraordinary, and yet a typical Haggard voice, and when he chose to use its full thunderous strength, as he sometimes did when he had a grievance against one of the family, a servant, or tenant, the walls of Ditchingham quaked. The Haggards 'could chat quite easily across a field,' a neighbour observed. When Rider was working in the study, he was, to the rest of the household, just the Voice, distant and forbidding, that penetrated the oak door and flowed down the private staircase. The study was of course sacrosanct, and under no circumstances, was Haggard to be disturbed during the hours he spent there. The children learned soon enough to keep a safe distance from the study window, and if they dared use the 'offices' directly under the study, they approached and left on tiptoe. The study was large and, like the rest of the house, comfortably cluttered. In the room was a huge oak desk from which Haggard commanded an excel-lent view of his lands. To one side of the desk was a large table on to which his papers and books overflowed and at which Miss Hector undoubtedly sat. On the desk was a vase of flowers in company with many knick-knacks and souvenirs from hither and yon. A statuette of the Madonna and Child was a favourite item. The floor was well carpet-ed, and there were a settee and half a dozen or more upholstered chairs.

J

The Dickens desk stood in an alcove, and on all sides were many small tables, chests, and curiosities. He had himself designed the gun cupboard against the wall for his fishing rods, guns, and ammunition. The study walls were covered with family portraits and photographs, above the chimney-shelf hung a pencil sketch of D. G. Rossetti, and the sherd Miss Barber had helped Rider make for *She* was on the mantel. Also on the mantel stood an old Egyptian bust, and on the wall hung an Egyptian coffin lid bearing in bold relief a sculptured head 'in a calm expression.' The bookcases contained the manuscripts and first editions of his works, all bound, a collection of about fifty United States pirated editions, as well as reference books he used in writing. But even more than other rooms, this one was Haggard's treasure house for curios. There were little chests of rings carved with hieroglyphics that he had collected, coins, Greek vases, ancient pots, and empty cartridge cases he had picked up on the battlefield of Isandhlwana. There were a score of pipes and huge tobacco jars.

Haggard and Miss Hector emerged from the study before dinner (about 7.30 or 8), which the family and whatever guests were present took together. Though the Voice was unapproachable and the study where it dwelt inviolable, Haggard the person, once he had descended the half-flight of stairs, was a very human creature indeed, human and unpredictable. All his life he tried to keep the Man and the Voice apart. His writing had little to do with his home life, and he liked to confine it completely to his study. In his home he did not want to be the successful author, but the relaxed human being.

Haggard ruled majestically over the dinner-table. He had had it built, of solid oak of course, to his own design, and down the two sides ran long linen slips on which the settings of shining glass and silver were laid, leaving the polished wood exposed in the centre. At the far end of the table stood a six-branched candlestick and vases of flowers, and round the table sat the Haggards, rarely fewer than ten or twelve of them. The food was usually on the sideboard, and family and guests got up to help themselves. Wine and beer normally accompanied the meal. Rider's taste leaned to simple foods well cooked, but he liked exotic drink and had cases of Cyprian wine in his cellar. At the table he could be an extremely engaging person and delightful host, but he could also be a tyrant. He was moody, delightfully entertaining at one meal, brusque and bombastic at others. But on the whole, the Haggards went at conversation with gusto. Louisa was the one who felt rather lost at table, letting her spouse carry off the laurels for the clan, remaining herself, as her nephew put it, 'Wife of the Life of the Party.' Actually she had neither the ability, the vocal power, nor the desire to compete.

As the earlier sad years passed, Ditchingham more and more housed guests, very often close relations of Rider's, with whom he felt a strong kinship. His many nephews and nieces came on frequent visits in the summer or during school holidays. Rider's quick mind usually put him well ahead of the others, and he sometimes revealed an impatience with their less agile faculties. Everyone was welcomed into the conversation at dinner if he had something to say and the courage to say it, but his 'wits had to be on the alert if he meant to enter the lists,' Sir Godfrey tells us. Almost any subject was fair game (aside from the 'unacceptable ones': Jock, Haggard's work, and religion). 'But a fatuous remark, particularly one of those exaggerations unsupported by fact to which unthinking youth is prone, drew thunderbolts from heaven.' For Rider did not suffer fools easily, dismissing them with, 'Small Beer, my dear, Small Beer.' 'There was no mercy. You were hacked and hewn to pieces before them all.' It was not literary talk, for Haggard found writing hard work, and at dinner he did not wish to be reminded of it. Talk of the harvest and agriculture, of hunts and grouse drives, news of expeditions and discoveries of mines and ancient cities, tales of far-off places, reports of family happenings, and gossip about local characters all had their place. But if a bull had been bought for the farm, or a sow had produced a litter, the talk dwelt on that event. 'Maybe it was all a little barbaric,' Sir Godfrey writes, 'with Rider's loud . . . voice and laugh, and when he was pleased with some remark (not necessarily his own) his explosive "What hey! What hey!" which shook the rafters.'[12]

When there were guests, they all went into the drawing-room after dinner. In season they munched 'great Ribston pippins picked from the tree only an hour ago.'[13] But when nothing special had been planned for the evening, Haggard and Miss Hector withdrew to continue working for an hour or two, and Louisa and visiting relatives often played bridge. At ten, the family frequently came up to the study, joining the head of the household for an appointed hour of leisure before the end of the day. But even after everyone had gone to bed, Haggard remained awake, to read, to think, to smoke his pipe quietly and alone. He rarely retired before one in the morning.

He was a tall man, about six foot in height, with broad shoulders, 'a Norseman in looks.' He was slender, 'well set up,' and had bright blue eyes, a delicate mouth, and a ruddy complexion. It was not a perfect face – there was too much nose and not enough chin – but it was an interesting one, in youth full and round, in middle-age, when the beard was still new, longer and pointed, regal even, anticipating somewhat the image of George V. Many descriptions survive of Rider Haggard; one, by his daughter, captures the spirit of the bicycle age and describes how her father looked in it. She examines a photograph as she writes:

My parent [is] on one side in a striking attitude, holding a
bicycle of terrific and archaic build. He is clad in very tight white-
flannel trousers which dwindle at the ankles to mere drainpipes,
and a straw boater, both much too small . . . [Beside him in the
picture,] on a stool, is an exotic-looking lily in a pot, with about a
hundred flowers bunched on a single stem . . . We think this photo
was a celebration of 'learning to ride'. Being entirely unmechanic-
ally minded, this fact was only achieved by the intensive labour of
the postmaster, who nearly cut short a promising career labouring
long and faithfully behind my parent, supporting him when he
wobbled and catching him when he fell off. As to the lily, it was,
I suppose, the horticultural triumph of the moment; a photo being
taken – 'Let's put it in!' An example of the warring traits of the
practical and picturesque, whose marriage in my father's mind
sometimes produced astonishing offspring.[14]

Harry How, who visited the House in 1892 for an interview that later
appeared in the *Strand Magazine*, found Haggard looking his age (thirty-
five), passionately fond of gardening, and not at all suggesting a literary
man. 'His kindness makes one happy, his modesty is impressive. . . . He
tells you nothing but what is worth remembering.'[15] At a dinner James
Barrie gave at the Garrick, young Cosmo Hamilton, shepherded by
Barrie, was thrilled to sit at a long table with many literary lights of the
day, including Rider Haggard 'with the cavalry face and the jangle of
imaginary spurs.'[16] A description of him that appeared in 1906 tries to
capture the inner man as well:

If you saw . . . [him out] of doors, where he loves to be, say on
his Norfolk estate – tall, large-framed, straight- and strong-shoul-
dered, dark and bearded, altogether a commanding figure – you
would regard him as a representative of the best type of English
country gentleman; and you would be right. But you probably
would not suspect him of being much addicted to writing, still less
of being one of the most famous novelists in the world. It is only
when you come to close quarters with him, within four walls, with
doors closed, and observe, as you cannot help doing, his physical
and mental restlessness, his eyes that seem to be wandering through
eternity and at the same time taking keen and minute note of immediate surroundings and proceedings, the quick transition of his
moods, his rapidity of thought and directness of utterance, sometimes having the appearance of bluntness and even brusqueness,
and especially when, at length, the deeps within him are stirred, and
he pours out a stream of words impelled by burning and long-settled

conviction; – it is only then that you begin to get an adequate idea of the scope and measure of the man. And as you feel the impact of his eager, tense, nervous personality, you can easily understand how needful to the equipoise between mind and body are plenty of physical exercise, copious draughts of fresh air, and a free and spacious environment.[17]

He was, undoubtedly, more gifted than most men, possessing a power to focus sharply and concentrate intently. He had a keen eye, and he could get at the core of anything quickly and incisively, whether a book, an idea, or a person. To the people around him he seemed instinctively to know things, almost as if he had second sight. He had a habit of 'getting fey' and foretelling the future, a nephew recalls.[18] Haggard himself believed that he was uncommonly attuned to spiritual forces. 'A turn of the wheel might have sent him into a trappist monastery,' wrote *The Times*.[19] Mysticism had taken hold of him early, and as he grew older he tried to reconcile his inner perceptions with modern science. He sought some certainty about the fate of his soul. He carefully unwrapped and examined Egyptian mummies, he read Oliver Lodge's books on psychic research, he studied Eastern religions, and he followed the proceedings of the Psychical Society. Sometimes he was carried away by his fancy. On occasion he made the heroes of his novels return to previous incarnations, and reincarnations occur frequently. Once he is even reputed to have said quite seriously to a young lady visitor, 'I can see you are the reincarnation of an Egyptian princess.' But most of the time, his approach to questions about life and immortality was quite rational.

He frequently exchanged letters with people who claimed to have had direct contact with spirits, and his most extensive correspondence on the subject was with William T. Horton, an illustrator who, in Haggard's words, was 'a mystic of the first water.'[20] Over a twenty-year period Haggard quizzed Horton through the post about his spiritual experiences. On December 14, 1910, Haggard writes:

It's all very interesting – oddly enough I was lying awake last night thinking of a mystical romance I have it in my mind to write in which two modern people get *back* to a former life in old Egypt. But it's a difficult business to do. I suppose your spiritual wanderings haven't brought you in contact with the Court of Meneptah (son of Ramases II) have they? If so I shall be thankful for some details as I want to write a story of the Exodus of the Israelites! Joking apart I should be glad to hear more of your experiences. Do I understand you to refer to separate *incarnations*? If so they seem to have come round more rapidly than would please me. Still I have always had a kind of instinct that there is something in the reincarnation business.

In a postscript, Haggard adds, 'I suppose there isn't any receipt for getting oneself back to old Egypt. How do you do it? *I* should like to go.' In another letter, Haggard reflects the struggle within him: 'If only one could get the real hang of this reincarnation business: if only one could be *sure*. It seems reasonable, a quarter of the inhabitants of the world believe in it to this day, it explains things, there is nothing against it (and one or two things for it) in the Bible, and yet if one could be sure!' Again and again Haggard wonders whether Horton's contacts with the other world are not products of his imagination, and yet he remains interested and curious and as late as 1916 sends Horton a list of questions he was to ask during a 'communication.'[21]

Haggard's mysticism alongside Horton's seems sceptical and bland, but it was nevertheless strong enough to take him into strange areas of thought and experience and ultimately to make him believe in reincarnation. For him reincarnation did not conflict with Christian dogma; in fact, he saw the Resurrection as further evidence of its truth. Haggard explored far and wide spiritually, but he saw his wanderings as healthy pursuits of answers to the universal riddle, and he reconciled them easily with his Christian faith.

Obviously two essential qualities composed his personality, and these were always in conflict. He was at once the dreamer and the pragmatist. He dreamed about the past, asserting that he 'understood the Scandinavians of 800 A.D., and the Egyptians from Menes to Ptolemy, far better than his neighbour of the next street in London, or the next property in Norfolk.'[22] In his autobiography he wrote, 'With the old Norse and the old Egyptians I am at home. I can enter into their thoughts and feelings; I can even understand their theologies. I have a respect for Thor and Odin, I venerate Isis, and always feel inclined to bow to the moon!'[23] He could look into the future with equal ease and predict the outcome of government policy with surprising accuracy. And he could project himself into imaginary worlds as well. But the dreamer also felt the pressures of his environment. He had grown up in an age which, bound by the doctrine of duty, taught him to emphasize the utilitarian and to reject his dreams as impractical. It was important to live a fruitful, Christian life as loyal husband, providing father, and hard-working citizen of the Empire. He might dream only after duty was done.

The conflict within him between the fanciful and the practical made his character complex and inconsistent. There is ample evidence that in his everyday life he was charitable toward his fellow-man, and yet he also had his prejudices. We know that for a long time he hated the Boers but that he was later able to develop some understanding of them. He also spoke out against Dissenters (see his *Joan Haste*, for example). He believed the conventional stereotypes of the Jews (see *Benita*), although he clearly admired ancient Hebrew civilization and learning and wrote a number of tales favourable to the Hebrews; furthermore, in a letter to *The Times*, Haggard asked that Palestine be made a home for Jews under British rule.[24] He could hardly be called a xenophobe, but he did believe in the superiority of the Anglo-Saxons as a race. During World War I, he expressed his hope that the Empire would 'cease to be so fond of admitting Germans and other foreigners within its gates and . . . stick to Anglo-Saxons.'[25] He had nothing good to say about the naturalistic novels, which he felt reflected 'petty social conditions,' and were boring and unedifying,[26] though he too devoted much energy to improving the social conditions the naturalists described. He was a strict and narrow moralist and could not condone any violations of his code. He could not enjoy smoking-room yarns, and when some readers accused him of advocating infidelity in *Beatrice*, he was so shocked that he tried to have the novel withdrawn; and to guard against future misunderstanding, he swore not to write another modern novel. In spite of his stern morality, he was all the same capable, as he himself tells us, of resorting to language he did not want recorded. There is, moreover, no doubt that ambition ruled his life and that he was, at times, a victim of pride and self-pity.

He was also capable of honest exaggeration. He liked to think, for instance, that he was known in the Ditchingham district as 'the Squire,' a circumstance that was less true than he led people to suppose. He tended to dramatize and romanticize the events in his own life, and sometimes he was so carried away by his own narrative skill that he confounded fact and fiction. A good example is Haggard's oft-repeated story, from his South Africa days, about the execution of a Kaffir petty chief. In his autobiography (and in a number of interviews for the Press) he recorded his version:

> In the grey morning light he was then led to the scaffold erected in the prison yard. . . . The executioner proved to be hopelessly drunk. . . . The High Sheriff, Juta, overcome by the spectacle, retired into a corner of the yard, where he was violently ill. The thing had to be done, and between a drunken executioner and an overcome High Sheriff it devolved upon me. So I stood over the executioner and forced him to perform his office.[27]

Justice Kotzé, taking great pains to point out that Haggard would never distort the truth intentionally, gives us, all the same, a very different account of the execution:

> Haggard came into my chambers, which were next to his own room, on the previous day, and told me he wished to be present at the execution early on the following morning. . . . I intimated to him that . . . there appeared to be no objection to his presence. . . . Everything was in readiness, and when the condemned man was brought from the cell and mounted the platform Sir Rider, before the final drop, was overcome and moved away towards the corner of the yard. The Sheriff . . . an old sailor . . . was not the kind of man to be overcome in the discharge of his duty. . . . The sentence was carried out by the executioner without any hitch. Later that same morning Sir Rider himself mentioned to me that he felt queer and upset and could not look to see the end. Mr. Juta, the Sheriff, also told me that Haggard's nerves had failed him.[28]

Kotzé's account of the hanging would perhaps be less meaningful had Haggard himself not paid tribute to the Judge's exceptional memory. Haggard tells that when Kotzé visited him at Ditchingham some twenty years after their association in Africa, Kotzé pointed to a coat and recognized it as the one Haggard had worn when they went on circuit together. At another place in his autobiography, furthermore, Haggard significantly admits that 'memory is a treacherous thing.'[29]

The fault is not necessarily serious. Had Haggard been a dry-as-dust collector of facts, he would not have written his romances. In his case, fancy not only spun his tales of adventure, but occasionally crossed the boundary into fact.

Certainly Haggard cut a colourful figure, for he often wore unusual costumes. 'His fancy ran to flowing capes and voluminous tweeds,' writes his daughter, and his clothes 'rather hung than sat on him.'[30] She tells of a visit by W. H. Davies, the poet-tramp, to her father. After they had talked for a while, it seems, Haggard offered Davies a suit of clothes. The tramp hesitated, for, it would appear, Haggard was himself dressed rather shabbily. He finally accepted the gift.

> However, when he undid the parcel he found a perfectly good suit 'of some extraordinary close hard-woven material which I have never seen elsewhere, and when the sun shone on it it glittered like silver.' He goes on to say he wore it for years and that it was regarded with surprise and suspicion by many. How well we knew those suits! If in his many wanderings my father discovered a local

industry he would return in triumph with lengths of handwoven material. In remarkable hue and design they may have differed, in one respect they were all alike – they were indestructible. . . . They were apt to be slightly odd in cut, but whatever you did to them they emerged brighter, fresher, and . . . more extraordinarily startling. After a period of parental enthusiasm they retired to the depths of some cupboard, and were in due course secretly bestowed upon the needy.[31]

In the atmosphere of Ditchingham, Haggard preferred to be informal, and very often, when photographers and newspaper interviewers were not expected, his hair was untidy and his trousers not creased. Frequently his costume consisted of odd and unmatched trousers, coats, boots, and hats. But he could enjoy this casualness only when he was alone with his family and close friends. In London, or even at Ditchingham when a stranger or formal acquaintance was staying, he dressed meticulously and formally. But always, formal or not, he wore at least one of his treasured trinkets, an ancient Pharaoh's gold ring knotted in his tie, a charm on his watch chain, and in later years the Egyptian ring that Andrew Lang left him as a keepsake.

Haggard's speech was like his mind, quick and decisive; it was always fluent and sometimes blunt. Not often did he stop to ponder a question, nor contemplate a problem; he had a ready answer, and sometimes gave it even too abruptly. He never had to search out an expression or phrase. 'He always popped out the right word,' a villager recalls. From childhood he had an unusual manner of speaking which added colour to everything he said. He pronounced his r's as w's, and he could not pronounce th at all, substituting either v or f for it. Thus, 'a very thorough rogue' might sound rather like 'a vewy forough wogue.'[32] Or, as a New York reporter once noted, he might say that the records last year surprised everybody 'wiv a hundred and fifteen fousand on ve rates.'[33] This same newspaperman found the overall effect of Haggard's speech 'quaintly pleasant.' For, in spite of the difficulty, his speaking and reading voice was resonant and dramatic. He read aloud a good deal, at morning prayers in the House and occasionally at bedtime to the children. As Churchwarden on Sundays he read the Lessons in the little church. His reading was a high point in the service, for he always read with personal interest and deep feeling. The Bible was, for him, a possible key to understanding the universe, and each time he read from it he tried to extract new meaning by giving different emphasis and searching out the words. One of his Sunday hearers described him as reading with 'sincere and moving eloquence, helped by his vigorous tones and an occasional glance at his audience over the top of his book which kept him in touch with us.' 'How he loved those rolling periods,'[34] wrote his nephew in later years.

Children loved this tall, withdrawn figure of a man. And he, while often aloof, shy, and fumbling with youngsters (his reputation and his memories of Jock set up natural barriers between them), was nevertheless drawn toward the young and tried to be friendly with them, often with success. He would tell them stories, and watch their faces light up. In his presence the children listened to his animated tales and to his Bible readings with glee, and when he was gone, they took 'guilty joy' in imitating his 'dwiving is as the dwiving of Jehu the son of Nimshi, for he dwiveff fuwiously!'*

Just as he was sometimes shy with children, so too he was ill at ease with women; in their presence he would rarely say the right thing, and as a result they generally disliked him. The exception to the rule was the intelligent woman who would not be badgered by the male and stood up for her rights and ability. This type he liked, and he would engage her in conversation on many subjects. All in all, though, he was not a tactful man, sensitive to other people's feelings but occasionally, perhaps when his own ego was not involved. His tactlessness conspired with his eccentric leanings, his fame, and the fact that he had married into Ditchingham, to make him a subject of parish gossip, and some neighbours talked of him as overbearing and conceited, an impression that very active people often give to less active onlookers. The consensus, however, was favourable; most people in and out of Ditchingham respected him as a man, valued his friendship, and admired his generosity.

For he was generous. The brothers who had got better educations were not so successful in their life's work, and Rider, who was expected to give help, gave it willingly. Nor did his generous spirit move within the family circle only. He actually supported destitute friends and neighbours over long periods of time. One neighbour, speaking of Haggard's generosity, said, 'Though . . . compared with us they were indeed wealthy and well-placed, it was not at his home that I learned how salty is the bread another person gives and how steep the steps of other people's stairs.'

Perhaps the most revealing indication of Haggard's success in human affairs comes not from family, friend, or neighbour, but from the men and women who worked for him and around him. And even here, one finds only an occasional deprecation. He may have been a 'crotchety squire,' but this reservation is soon drowned in praise. He

---

* As reported by an acquaintance and neighbour. Parishioners also remember that when Rider returned from his visit to the Holy Land he had new pronunciations for Biblical names.

was in his dealings with his servants and tenants eminently fair. He respected an honest man's work, no matter what that work was, but especially if it was work on the land. He dealt with other farmers with complete honour, as fellow-farmers, regardless of their station. He was, in the estimates of the labouring folk of Ditchingham, a good landlord, an honourable 'maister,' and an upright Christian. The old clockmaker in Bungay can still think back to the days when he cycled over to the House to wind the clocks every Thursday: 'A fine man, a fine man, one what grows on you, a fine man.'

All in all, however, Haggard's character is elusive; it defies definition. In his daughter's words, his was 'a nature both bafflingly complex and childishly simple.'[35] But the many forces that struggled within him certainly made him the interesting man he was.

7

Agricultural Reformer

IN 1894, having emerged from the spiritual isolation which followed Jock's death, Haggard grew restless again, and now that the estate was in good condition and required less of his attention, he searched for some new outlet for his energies. He was 'utterly weary of a retired life and of the writing of books,' and he 'sought eagerly for some avenue of escape.'[1] One such avenue that suddenly became available to him was politics. Haggard was well qualified for a political career. He was after all a barrister with legal experience in Transvaal and English courts; he was of the respected, traditionally Conservative squirearchy; he owned land and was familiar with landowners' and farmers' problems; he had travelled and knew a great deal about England at home and abroad; his fame as a story-teller reached not only beyond Norfolk but even beyond the shores of England; and he was a personable, sincere gentleman who spoke easily and effectively and made a striking appearance in public. Early in 1892 Haggard was asked by the Tories to contest King's Lynn, a 'safe seat,' but the offer came too early, while Rider was still brooding over the loss of his son and just after his father's death. He refused. But in 1894, when he was asked to stand for Parliament in East Norfolk, he accepted, although this was far from being a safe Tory district and he knew that it would be a difficult campaign. Haggard hitched his wagon to a political star – he would return to serve his country in Parliament.

As with everything he undertook, he gave this venture all he had. Month after month of 1895 he travelled in a drag up and down the Broadlands, Louisa and his partner of ostrich-farming days, Arthur Cochrane, by his side, making speech after speech on subject after subject. He was unanimously accepted as the Unionist and Agricultural Candidate, and huge campaign broadsides presented his programme to the people as early as March for a July election. So intense were the issues and so divided public opinion that Haggard's speeches were often accompanied by violent displays of approval or, more often, disapproval, both in his constituency and out. The London Press followed the contest closely, reporting each new outbreak with relish. Haggard's firm but ticklish stand on taxing imported grain was at the bottom of the bitter controversy. He was trying to protect the farmer, who could not compete with low-priced imported grain, and swinging far afield from Tory policy, he advocated a tax on some imports. The tax could, he claimed, serve as a source of revenue for a government-sponsored pension scheme. All this sounded too much like Protectionist and Socialist doctrine to win Haggard many friends among his fellow-Conservatives and stimulated a good deal of invective from the Tory Press. True, the *Pall Mall Gazette* welcomed Haggard's candidacy ('The sitting member . . . is an average Radical who knows as little as may be about farming'[2]), but the *Saturday Review* felt that Haggard 'should content himself with [the traditional advantages of the squirearchy] . . . and leave the weary task of politics to others.'[3]

At home in Norfolk, his programme appealed to the farmer, but it alienated another large segment of East Norfolk voters, the wherrymen, who made their livelihood ferrying imported wheat up the reedy inlets and rivers to the cities. These stalwarts, accustomed to a hard life on the Broads, did not think twice about flexing their muscles at political meetings, and they made life for Haggard and his companions difficult indeed during July. 'Disgraceful Radical Proceedings,' read a headline in the *Norfolk Chronicle*,[4] reporting Haggard's speech at Horsford 'which was interrupted continually by an organised gang of youths and eventually broke up in disorder.' On July 17, at Walsham, a 'meeting in favour of Haggard was again broken up when held in the Market Place.' On July 19, when the voters went to the polls, Haggard and his party travelled relentlessly from town to town and 'met with very rough treatment.' At Sodham a shower of mud and stones greeted them, and at Stalham such commotion raged that the day has gone down in local history as the Battle of Stalham Bridge. Haggard, riding into town, came up against a solid wall of club-carrying wherrymen bent on over-turning his drag. He took refuge in the Swan Hotel until members of his party and the local police formed a guard to escort him safely out of town. For months after the election, there were still repercussions of these violent proceedings, and two men, one a lord, were fined for common assault.[5]

Haggard did not mind the hard work of the campaign, the expense (over £2,000),[6] and even the indignities, because winning 'seemed to me about the most important thing in the world.' Had he won he would have embarked upon a new profession, where 'he felt he could exercise those talents for public life and service he knew that he possessed.'[7] But he lost, and not very gracefully either, by a small but unconsoling margin of 198 votes. Some of his public comments and letters to the Press showed his resentment. He tracked down misstatements, put the record right on every point, and insisted that he had been defeated by the calumny that he paid his farm labourers only nine shillings a week. The picture of Rider Haggard embittered is not a pleasant one, and there were those who shared the views of the *New York Times* correspondent who wrote from London that 'Rider Haggard's tempestuous boohooing about the way that the rustics chivied him and his swell turnout in Norfolk lanes might have been funny if it had not been angering to see a grown man so little able to take a beating with decent grace.'[8] But Haggard had been much abused in the campaign, and defeat did not come easily to him. Never again would he stand for public office. Dejected and bitterly disappointed, he turned back to Ditchingham, to his family, his farms, and his romances.

But not for long, for Haggard was eager to prove to himself and the world that he could do more than write fiction. The part of him that enjoyed the world of affairs and strove to be successful there drove him hard during the early 'nineties: 'The desire haunted me to do something in my day more practical than the mere invention of romance after romance.' Opportunity came soon enough. First he helped edit a weekly paper called the *African Review*, and then he entered a partnership with his co-editor, who was a financier in African trade, to buy and sell imports on the open market.

Haggard's family urged him not to undertake so risky a venture. They argued that the Haggards were traditionally inept at money matters, and that he had himself already displayed much imprudence on the business side of his literary dealings. Even Rider's eldest brother, William, wrote in an effort to dissuade him, urging him to consider his 'ignorance of business and distaste for business detail,' and warning him that 'if you give up writing novels others will spring up and take your place.'[9] But Haggard heeded his inner discontents more than his brother's appeal to reason – the old restlessness he knew when tied to the law books demanded something more exciting than the natural beauty and rural routine of Ditchingham and the palling occupation of grinding out romances.

Leaving his family behind, off he went to London again, where, for 'nine long and tumultuous months the unhappy Rider toiled in a gorgeous city office' while an 'anxious circle of family and friends watched his city career with awe and apprehension.'[10] But nine months was long enough for Haggard to learn that the City would not satisfy his love of adventure. His nerves were torn and his ease of mind shattered by the need to make decisions involving vast sums of money, and he soon learned that his imagination thrived better creating romantic tales in his Norfolk study than trying to amass a fortune in London. When Haggard's partner told him that he was going abroad for some time, leaving him to carry on alone, Haggard had the good sense to call a halt to the venture. He fled – back to the glasshouses of orchids and ferns, to the oak panels, to the shade of the beech trees, to the morning walks, to Miss Hector's typewriter in the afternoon, to the security of the placid Norfolk fields, back to Ditchingham.

Haggard frankly admitted that his London sojourn was a mistake. He realized that in the City he had got his fingers burnt, and he knew now that, after disappointing tries at politics and high finance, he would have to be content with County life and with the story-teller's trade. He settled down, 'as . . . far as any one of his nature could ever settle down' and turned again to Africa, 'for which he was always homesick,' studied those parts of the map which were still mysteries and, one after another, spun tales of adventure about the deep unexplored areas. He was elected Chairman of the local Bench of Magistrates, and as the years passed he came to accept more and more his role as writer-squire and to relinquish slowly the image of himself as world adventurer and explorer. He learned to compromise with life and became reconciled to his particular abilities, the accidents of fortune, and the craft he could ply with success. Ironically he found the place where he could do 'something . . . more practical' than 'the mere invention of romance upon romance'[11] right at his own back door, in agriculture.

Farmers have never been very quick to alter their ways, and rural reform in England in the nineteenth century was very slow indeed. Distance and provincial custom still cut the farmer off from the hub of activity, and it took time for progress to break through the city-country barrier. The 'what-was-good-for-my-father' philosophy and the proud agrarian tradition still dominated rural thought and feeling. Innovation was foreign and suspect, in part because there was no real need for revolutionary change between 1850 and 1871, when the English farmer enjoyed one of the most prosperous periods in English agricultural history. A rising population, the discovery of gold in California and Australia, the Crimean War, the U.S. Civil War, and the Franco-Prussian War, kept farm prices soaring. Come what might, the farmer fared well: 'a short crop meant high prices, low prices meant an abundant crop.'[12] England for the farmer was an earthly paradise. Foreign imports did not really threaten the English farmer; they merely augmented and corrected any shortages on the home market. As late as 1871, the Census found slightly over two million people employed on the land in England and five and one-half million in industry and commerce, a fair distribution for a balanced economy. Farm wages in England were higher than anywhere in Europe, and rents were also

high. Nor had landowners merely sat back and waited for the milk and
honey to flow in. These 'grandees,' born to the remnant tradition of
feudalism at a time when Arthur Young's cries of land-patriotism still
rang in people's ears, sought, in the 'forties and 'fifties, and later as well,
to advance the interest of their tenant farmers along with their own by
farming scientifically. So successful had they been that England, with
its rich and beautiful fields, its large farm production, its contented
farmer and rich landowner, became, in the third quarter of the century,
the model for all Europe.[13]

But the prosperity did not last, and by the 'seventies the agricultural
decline had already begun. A giant spectre had appeared on the horizon
to threaten the very life of the British farmer. Foreign competition had
never really challenged English produce on the open market, primarily
because transport was difficult, and large nations were too far away to
bring their crops within competitive price range. But the United States
had been building railways across its vast prairies with cheap immigrant
labour, and the railway companies transported farm crops at less than
cost in a campaign to encourage farm settlement in the West. New
ocean-going steamers with improved marine engines and farm machinery that enabled one man to do the work of four made it possible for
the United States to flood the European market with grain at ridiculously
low prices with which the English farmer could not hope to compete.

England was not alone in this agricultural setback. It affected all
Europe, and farmers everywhere sent up a cry for tariffs. France and
Germany responded to their farmers' demands instantaneously, for in
those countries the farmer was the backbone of the army, not only
because he fed the military but because he himself made the best soldier
in emergencies. Duties were slapped on imports and the continental
farmer was saved. But England, primarily a naval power, did not see her
farmers as potential soldiers and turned a deaf ear to their cries. 'British
agriculture, which till then had . . . led the world, was thrown over-
board in a storm like an unwanted cargo.'[14]

But competition, bad as it was, gave the English farmer only part
of his difficulty. Nature took a hand also when from 1875 to 1879 she
sent wet, poor-crop summers. Then came the monetary depression,
forcing the prices of meat and dairy products down. To add to the
farmer's problems, in 1877 England was visited by rinderpest, in 1879
English sheep suffered liver-rot, and in 1883 cattle fell victims of foot-
and-mouth disease. Between 1871 and 1881, nearly a million persons
emigrated to seek a better life elsewhere. During the last two decades
of the century, English agriculture, the major industry of the nation,
employing more people than any other, was reduced to a mere by-
product of English life.

Rider Haggard had grown up in the flush of agricultural prosperity. Rents were at a peak and profits excellent, and his father bought up numerous outlying farmlands. But as the 'seventies came to a close, the signs were clear. The squire was not getting the return he should have from land-invested capital, and there were many indications, particularly the industrial depression, that the future would be grim. These facts may have influenced William Haggard's decision to ship his son off to Africa. There was, after all, little for a young man to do in an overpopulated country with a tightening economy.

If the agricultural slump was not clearly defined in 1873 when Rider left for Africa, it was certainly apparent by his return in 1881. His struggle to keep Louisa's estate properly tenanted taught him at first hand some of the economic difficulties the landowner was facing. In 1886 his tenant left him, and he sat down at the Windham Club and wrote a letter to *The Times* proclaiming his dismay over the agricultural economy. The privilege of owning his farm, he wrote, cost him £50 a year. He would simply sell the farm and retire from agriculture. But we may infer that he found no buyers, only another tenant, and in 1889, when that one left him, he decided to farm his own land – and so he did into his old age, at a continuing loss. The 'nineties were the worst years of all for the English farmer, and although Haggard liked to think of himself as a country gentleman by profession and a novelist by accident, he knew that his farming depended for its life-blood upon the income from his writing. Haggard's romances afforded him the luxury of remaining a farmer through the hard years.

When, in the mid-'nineties, he returned to Ditchingham from the City, the farming communities of England were in their worst doldrums. Haggard knew this when he decided to devote his attentions again to his own farms. It was an easy decision, for Haggard, though an impatient wanderer, was also irrevocably tied to the soil. Always drawn to the beauty and mystery of nature, he was a sharp observer of everything that grew. With the land came a sense of dynasty: his father had owned and lived in Norfolk fields, his children should also – the land was the one unchanging factor in man's life. For him, it was a symbol both of the past about which he dreamt and of the future about which he speculated and prophesied. The land was his dominion, his piece of England, and working on it soothed him as nothing else could. He felt closer than ever to it after his unpleasant experience in the City, and in that sympathetic frame of mind, he devised a plan for a book he 'enjoyed' writing and consequently could write from the heart, a book which better than anything else offers a picture of Rider Haggard the Norfolk squire, the 'maister' of Ditchingham, and captures the flavour of a way of life that has fairly vanished.

At the outset of *A Farmer's Year, Being His Commonplace Book for 1898*, Haggard tells his reader that

> this book shall be a journal of a farmer's year rather than a work
> about farming, setting forth with other incidental things the
> thoughts and reflections that occur to him, and what he sees day by
> day in field or wood or meadow, telling of the crops and those who
> grow them, of the game and the shooting of it, of the ways of wild
> creatures and the springing of flowers, and touching, perhaps, on
> some of the thousand trivial matters which catch the eye and occupy
> the attention of one who lives a good deal in the company of
> Nature.[15]

This, then, when Haggard took up his pen 'with very real humility,'
was to be a chatty, homespun chapbook – and so in large part it is.

He takes us through the succession of months and the cycle of
seasons with ease, arousing our compassion at the scene in a marsh of
a beautiful mare standing over the dead body of her infant foal, and
filling even the city dweller with tense expectancy when the veterinar-
ian arrives to snip the lambs' tails. He invites us to enjoy with him the
excitement of a week-long shoot, to share the bag, and to listen to anecdotes about shooters; and he permits us to chuckle at him hiding behind
a bush to watch 'a most curious form of courtship in progress between
a cock and a hen turkey.' Haggard's style is relaxed and he creates a
congenial atmosphere throughout; often the prose is actually charming.
He paints a warm picture of a rent dinner (with landowner, agent, and
tenants enjoying the traditional rites and eating traditional foods; he
even includes the menu), he tells us in great but engrossing detail how
his outlying Bedingham farm is bush-drained, he takes us back into his
youth to tell a story of a horse he owned in South Africa, and he
explains how he cut hay and made bricks with his own hands on his
farm there. He talks about the grass that grows in Iceland, and he takes
us on a trip to the Hebrides. He stumbles upon curious epitaphs in
churchyards and searches out old church registers and discovers scraps
of information about the people who worked these same Norfolk fields
years ago, sharing it all with the reader: the story of the clerk who, able
to write, had to travel from church to church to make entries in the
register; and the long succession of little marks made by illiterate trembling brides on their wedding days. He tells us too how, as Bench
Magistrate, he judges a case on egg stealing, fining the defendant – the
case against him was perfectly clear – a shilling for each stolen egg. In
February he tells about winter ploughing, in April about sowing
carrots, and in June about sheep shearing. In August he goes to a

Ditchingham Primrose League country fête, with its shooting gallery, dull speeches, and evening dancing; in October we accompany him on a pheasant shoot, from which in six hours the party returns with over four hundred birds; and in December he takes us on a visit to a near-by workhouse.

Although it is not an almanac, Haggard wants the book to be useful to the farmer. Early in the volume he assures the reader that there will be 'a practical side to this book. I am a farmer, and engaged in a desperate endeavour to make my farming pay. Perhaps the chronicle of my struggles may . . . teach . . . [others] what to avoid.'[16] But it is more than a chronicle of his struggles to make his farm pay, for he includes a meticulous record of figures, charts and maps, so that the individual farmer can follow him about his work and see for himself where Haggard makes money and where he loses. Furthermore, as he performs and directs the various farming operations, he explains them minutely, telling why he chooses one particular method or time over another for the operation. As a result, *A Farmer's Year* was a very informative handbook. The advice Haggard gave was sound (some of it still is), the instructions and descriptions for performing various farming tasks clear and detailed. An ample supply of illustrative material accompanies the prose, and the writing is never overtly technical. A long table of contents, a comprehensive index, and a chronological arrangement allow the reader to find advice readily on any subject. How does Haggard shed barley in dry seasons, what price does he get for his beans, which method of lifting beets does he prefer, what does he have to say about pond water for drinking purposes, or what and how to feed toads? It is all there, and can be found in a jiffy.

But before Haggard is finished, *A Farmer's Year* becomes something more than a delightful excursion into the country and a practical handbook for farmers. In his effort to write a useful book for the 'reader of utilitarian mind,' he sought to record as accurate a picture of rural life as he could. His 'research' threw him into closer acquaintance than ever before with his neighbours, his tenants, and Ditchingham labourers. He learned at first hand about the state of English agriculture and about the people who tried to make a living on the land in the days of agricultural depression. What he learned was even more appalling than he had imagined, and he had not been unacquainted with the difficulties of the English farmer. He was stunned by what he saw at first hand, by what, he was forced to conclude, was the ruinous decay of a treasured part of English life; and immediately his shock and concern were reflected in his chronicle. As the year wears on, furthermore, and he examines his own financial figures, kept most systematically now because they would be the backbone of *A Farmer's Year*, he faces the reality that even he, with all his care, cannot farm his own lands at a profit. Particularly towards its close, the misery that Haggard has observed in the countryside, coupled with the despair over his own accounts, turns *A Farmer's Year* into a record of the English farmer's plight. Not that Haggard becomes a reformer – he merely sets down the facts which so astonish him and which he is sure will astonish his reader. As a result of his experiences on the land while he writes the book, the end product becomes something different from what Haggard originally intended. But it is more valuable than it might otherwise have been. For the reader gets more than the aura of country life, more than a quiet ramble through a wooded grove; he also gets an interesting picture of what agricultural life is like in England in 1898 – the practical side, the financing of the farm, the prices of the produce, the hopes and disappointments of the farmer. The record of Haggard's experience as farmer for a year is also a picture of English farming for a year, a morose picture of a way of life deteriorating before the onslaught of 'progress.' *A Farmer's Year*, intended to be a congenial conversation about farming, turned out to be a plea for the English farmer.

The book is not hurt because it serves a practical and a historical purpose; in fact it emerges as one of Haggard's most engrossing works. There is neither haste nor tension here; the prose meanders as gently as the River Waveney through the fields of Ditchingham, reflecting the blue sky, the trees in the meadow, and the birds flying overhead. It is charming in its shapelessness and simplicity. The mood often varies, the light changes, but the quiet pleasure remains throughout. And the writer himself is here a craftsman of distinction. He seldom offends with harshness, he never forces the language or the pace; he writes from the heart. Haggard is at home, writing for neither money nor fame. And because he is relaxed, composing at leisure about things he loves, he himself emerges in a better light. Humbled by his experiences in politics and finance, he is an attractive, genuine person; mellowed by Norfolk and the daily walks around his farms, he is an engaging raconteur. Haggard interested in the soil, in cattle, in his neighbours, is a man who demands respect. Haggard the landowner, the planter, the breeder, the magistrate, the agricultural experimenter, is far more interesting than Haggard the prospector, the world traveller, the treasure hunter, the politician, the financier, the adventurer – and indeed more exciting than the man locked in his study persistently dictating romances.

A Farmer's Year got a very good Press. The reviewers were invariably surprised by Haggard's departure from story-telling, but they were also impressed. Here was no sham farmer, no collection of rustic jottings. The *Athenaeum* called it 'a most delightful and useful book,' written 'with a breadth of judgement and with a power of accurate observation which are unusual, . . . a book of which we have formed a high opinion.'[17] The *Literary World*, while dubbing it a 'Protectionist "tract of the times" ' – in *A Farmer's Year* Haggard actually rejects Protection as a means of solving the farmer's problems – and noting that 'Mr. Haggard as a farmer is naturally a subject of curiosity,' concedes that the book is 'ably enough written' and that there is 'no . . . monotony'; it is, the reviewer writes, 'of permanent value as portraying the agricultural life of the times.'[18] In a review entitled 'Pegasus at the Plough,' the *Bookman* greeted *A Farmer's Year* with uncommon whimsy:

> Mr. Rider Haggard as a farmer ought to be a curious spectacle, as curious, say, as 'She' peeling potatoes at the back door. But he is not. He is, very simply and naturally in his place. We own we scarcely expected it. We even own that at first we felt disappointed. Our delicious anticipatory creeping of the flesh at the mention of his name was thrown away upon this chronicle of the fields. There is some climbing down to be done before you can appreciate Mr. Haggard among the wheat. But when you are on the ground beside him you will find yourself rewarded. He knows what he is talking about.[19]

Even in the United States, the *New York Times* noted that 'the merits of it are unquestionable,' and found that 'the simple notes taken by him of work in English fields, make most delightful and composing reading.' He tells about farm life 'in the happiest manner,' and 'you understand old England better as Mr. Haggard writes it.'[20] Not only farmers and reviewers found *A Farmer's Year* interesting; literary people enjoyed it as well. The Kiplings read it with delight, and Swinburne gave an inscribed copy as a gift to Theodore Watts-Dunton.[21]

By the time Haggard had finished writing *A Farmer's Year*, he had a cause on his hands. He could not bear to see the English farmer suffering from grave economic injustice and English rural life deteriorating. But not only his love of the land and his concern for justice spurred his ire. With men like Chamberlain, Milner, Rhodes, and Kipling, Haggard saw England as a land of destiny and the English as a people with a mission. The isle in the North Sea was really the heart of a vast domain that encompassed all climates and people of various colours and convictions, and it was ordained that the small nation of people, the Anglo-Saxon race, was to spread enlightenment, justice, and Christianity everywhere. This was England's calling, and each

Englishman must do his share. If the Empire were to become unified and strong, the heart of that Empire must be strong, pumping the life-blood powerfully and regularly to the colonies. And the island's strength, Haggard knew, depended first and foremost upon its natural resources, upon a strong agrarian population standing behind the civil, the industrial, and the military. Without a strong agricultural industry, no economy could ever hope to be independent, and independence was necessary if England was to lead the world. Unless something were done to strengthen the farmer, England would lose her economic independence, the heart would deteriorate, the colonies would fall away, the Empire would be lost, and the light would fail. In *A Farmer's Year* Haggard sums up his position: 'The practice of Agriculture . . . means . . . the engendering and achievement of patient, even minds in sound, enduring bodies, gifts of which, after the first generation, the great towns rob those who dwell and labour in them. And when those gifts are gone, or greatly lessened, what does history teach us of the fate of the people who have lost them?'[22] The importance of the farmer to the welfare of a nation is today an accepted political fact, but in 1899, Haggard's concern was unusual. But he got his ideas merely from examining the nation's economy; he was simply using common sense, and again the combination of his common sense and imagination enabled him to see the future clearly. Something had to be done to save England, and although Haggard was not yet sure what it was, he knew that some action would have to be taken, and soon.

A Farmer's Year was not a political tract; it did not offer a concrete point-by-point programme for change. It showed the degradation of the English farmer, and Haggard, sensitive to the needs of all human beings and prepared to lend a helping hand to those less fortunate than himself, urged various general measures. He felt the Government should give financial aid to agriculture, revise the various land taxes, alter the ratings, take stronger measures against adulteration of farm products, and do something to enable the farmer to get his produce to market at cheaper transport costs than in the past. But these at best were general suggestions; at this point Haggard knew the ills better than their causes or remedies.

Although he was much occupied with the letters concerning *A Farmer's Year*, which poured in 'almost without number,' Haggard found time, at the turn of the century, to buy a summer house at Kessingland, on the east coast of Suffolk, near Lowestoft, a many-windowed, two-storied house on a cliff, with nine acres of land, a private beach and a magnificent view of the churning North Sea. A refashioned coastguard station, U-shaped and lonely, filled with the sounds and the smells of the sea, the house was a strange place altogether, quaint and rambling 'where one loses oneself immediately with the greatest of ease.' Everywhere inside the house were creaking doors, 'wandering passages, queer cubby-holes, and unexpected rooms.' Haggard renamed it from Cliff Grange to Kessingland Grange, called each of the cabin bedrooms after a British admiral, planted a garden, dug a new well (operated by a windmill), and furnished the rooms with more of his collected display pieces. He proudly exhibited a bust of Nelson which bore the date 1812 and had been carved out of the timbers of the *Victory*. An old pewter platter of the Norwich Nelson Club, dated 1806, was another treasure. More illustrations from his romances, family photographs, and a collection of samplers adorned the walls. In 1914, when Haggard let the Grange to the Kiplings for a summer, Rudyard Kipling recorded his own description of it in a letter to a friend: '[It] is for all practical purposes the side of a ship. The garden runs about fifteen yards to a cliff – then the sea and all the drama of the skirts of war laid out before us.'[23]

As owner of the Grange, Haggard grew particularly interested in coast erosion, for his own beach and the shore on all sides of him were being eaten away by the sea. He experimented with various grasses, hoping they would be effective in stopping the erosion where concrete walls had failed. And he succeeded with marram grass. In five years, he managed to raise his own beach twelve feet in height. At Kessingland he was free of the responsibilities of Ditchingham and the routine of writing, and here he came to get away from the intruding world, to busy himself with the encroaching sea and his garden, less complex matters than faced him daily at home. He 'generally enjoyed himself with improvements and additions,' and was able to 'think thoughts to the accompaniment of the roaring waves.' But Kessingland was not always quiet and lonely. Like Ditchingham House, it became the site of 'large family gatherings in the holidays, which always seemed to start at tea-time, with brown bread and shrimps, and huge cos lettuces with hearts such as never could be produced at home.'[24]

In January 1900, Haggard took his family for a holiday to Florence, and it was there, his mind still teeming with the agricultural problem, that he devised a scheme for continuing his service to his country and mankind. Like Archimedes, 'I was taking my bath one morning [when] . . . an idea struck me. It was to the effect that I should like to emulate Arthur Young, who more than a century before had travelled through and written of the state of agriculture in the majority of English counties.' Here was a practical mission to perform, and the mission became ever clearer when he dwelt on the 'considerable similarity between [his own and Arthur Young's] aims and circumstances.'[25] An accident that occurred even while Haggard was in Florence pushed the notion along the road to fulfilment. Haggard had signed a contract to go to South Africa on the completion of the Boer War and write a series of articles on 'The New South Africa' for the *Daily Express*.* But since the war dragged on terribly and everyone was fed up with the Boers and South Africa, Arthur Pearson of the *Daily Express* asked Haggard to cancel the contract. Haggard saw fate operating and suggested that the contract be modified. He would, instead of writing about South Africa, do a long series of articles on rural England. 'Otherwise I would proceed to South Africa,' he told Pearson.[26] Pearson had little choice; he took the less undesirable course.

Haggard left his family in Florence and went on to Cyprus and Palestine with his nephew, Arthur Maddison Green,† intending to carry out a verbal agreement with Moberly Bell of *The Times* to do a series of articles on the Near East. Green, who travelled as Haggard's secretary and did in fact bring along a typewriter ('all he did with it was to drop it on my toes out of the rack of a railway train'[27]), made any real work quite impossible. He was, as Haggard put it, 'in the heyday of his very fascinating and festive youth,' and for the most part, master waited on helper, struggling to get the youngster up in the morning and 'generally attending to his wants.' He never wrote the articles for *The Times*, managing only to take some notes which he would later use for two historical romances (*The Brethren* and *Pearl Maiden*).

When in late spring he returned to England from his sojourn in the Near East, Haggard made immediate plans for what he later called 'the heaviest labour of all my laborious life,' an investigation of the English countryside and the state of English farming. For large parts of 1901 and 1902, Haggard, accompanied by the indomitable Arthur Cochrane, travelled up and down England, from county to county, village to village, by train, horse, and ship, gathering data. 'What a toil was that!' Haggard later recalled. Once they were gone from home gathering facts

---

* Negotiations between Arthur Pearson, its editor, and Haggard were carried on through A. P. Watt, and a series of unpublished letters from Haggard to Watt in the Huntington Library reveals Haggard's attitude toward the Boers and tells us something of his business approach. In the first letter, dated November 23, 1899, Haggard replies to Watt's initial feeler. Haggard protests about all he would have to sacrifice to undertake the venture and about how expensive the journey would be. He also insists that he would require a free hand, for he sees points in the Boers' case, 'without hoping (as some do) that they will drive us out of South Africa.' Another letter (December 5) acknowledges that Pearson is to pay all expenses for Haggard and his family to, from, and while at the Cape; and pay £20 per 1,000 words for what he writes, for a total of about 100,000 words. Haggard asks for a minimum guarantee of £2,000 for serial rights. In a third letter (December 8), Haggard agrees to dine with Pearson on Monday night. He here seeks to increase the limit of his projected prose from 100,000 to 120,000 words; and he estimates his expenses (while assuring Watt that he will undoubtedly have to add funds from his own pocket to meet them) thus: travel, £550; rent at Cape, £600; secretary, etc., £500. He adds that it would be nice if Pearson would be willing to pay his estate something if 'I come to grief on this undertaking.'

† The son of the Reverend Mr. Green who had examined Rider as a boy.

for eight months at a single stretch. All day they questioned the people close to the land, landowners, land agents, public officials, tenants and labourers. Haggard put the questions to the rural citizens, and Cochrane, off on the side, faithfully recorded almost every word of the questions and answers in a huge notebook. To corroborate the personal interviews, Haggard collected figures on population, prices, and costs, and assembled maps of the areas in which he worked. In the evening the two men retired to the inn, hotel, farmhouse, or manor where they happened to be staying and worked late into the night assembling the material, Haggard writing the articles that were already running in the *Daily Express* (and the *Yorkshire Post*) and Cochrane making the charts and drawing the maps that accompanied them.

Hundreds of interviews were recorded in twenty thick notebooks as they travelled on their survey of twenty-seven English counties and two Channel Islands. Over fifty articles in the newspaper series appeared between April and October, 1901. Haggard's letters home to 'Dearest Lou' tell of the 'continually lost luggage, the strange and astonishing establishments, the peculiar meals, the damp beds and chills and stomach aches, the appalling discomfort of historic old houses, the surprising comfort of modest farms, and the unvarying kindness with which he and Cochrane were welcomed by all and sundry.'[28] And when the interviewing was done and the facts gathered, Haggard returned to Ditchingham with his notebooks and maps and set himself to assembling the material into book form. Less than half of what he considered the complete survey had appeared in print, and he wanted to finish the task. To this end, he spent the early months of 1902 assembling and arranging the material and writing introductory and explanatory paragraphs and a concluding chapter for it. Finally, in November 1902, the heavy two-volume tome appeared as *Rural England, Being an Account of Agricultural and Social Researches Carried out in the Years 1901 & 1902.*

Some minor flaws exist in *Rural England*, and we must acknowledge them. There is nothing wrong with Haggard's journalistic style, but the way he reports material as he finds it leads him into some difficulty. The arrangement of the counties follows Haggard's itinerary rather than any geographical plan, and that makes for some rather abrupt and unreasonable jolts. At one point, for instance, he jumps from Kent to Devonshire, and later from Yorkshire to Suffolk. Treating counties individually creates unnecessary repetition, also, as Haggard records similar circumstances in different parts of the land. Nor does Haggard's thoroughness extend to the index as it ought to, where cross-references are noticeably lacking.

In spite of the faults, however, the reader cannot but stand in awe of the display of energy, the magnitude of the task, the endurance and devotion the two volumes attest. Haggard completed the survey in something more than a year, and the volumes appeared hardly two years after he started his study – formidable evidence of his capacity for hard and close work. For *Rural England* is an immense document, a permanent reference book for historians, economists, agricultural specialists. A detailed survey of agrarian conditions in England at the turn of the century, it is invaluable to the student of rural life. Its thoroughness sets it apart from most surveys before and since, and its value is increased by Haggard's stern objectivity.

Anyone who ventures to read in *Rural England* will be shocked by the condition of English farmers and farmlands at the beginning of the century. Haggard enters upon his study with an open, curious mind and draws conclusions only from evidence he discovers. As the details accumulate, the picture of English rural life and farming industry emerges as one of neglect and decay. Haggard's conclusion today seems to be a conservative statement of the needs of the time, well stated and judiciously defended. 'The impression left upon my mind by my extensive wanderings,' Haggard wrote at the end of the work, 'is that English agriculture seems to be fighting against the mills of God.'[29] So disturbing were the facts that they drove him to devise a detailed programme of reform for agricultural England.

Haggard finds two causes at the root of all the difficulty: the general practice of agriculture on the land and the rural exodus. The rural exodus is by far the worse of the two. Agriculture always supplied England with her best men, but now the men leave the fields for the towns. 'Free Trade has filled the towns and emptied our countryside; it has gorged the banks but left our rickyards bare.' Unless something is done, England will find itself industrialized but hungry, facing 'the progressive deterioration of the race.' One way to stop the flow of land labourers to the city is to make life on the land more profitable, more comfortable, and more alluring. The Census figures clearly show that in the second half of the nineteenth century, the number of agricultural workers had been cut in half – and this with a rising population.*

Haggard's assertion that he offered nothing 'new, startling, or revolutionary' is inaccurate. His blueprint for rural rejuvenation was thirty-five years ahead of its time; it was startling also, as a good deal of the reaction to *Rural England* proved; and it was revolutionary, for it adumbrated the role of Government in the lives of farmers.

* Haggard, *Rural England*, pp. 536–576. There were, to be sure, forces other than the lure of machine industry sapping the land of its strength. England's military commitments, in war and peace, were world-wide, and many of her rural youth went off to India, Africa, and elsewhere. Also new discontent appeared in rural areas as news sifted in from the towns of higher wages and of jolly town life. Primitive rural dwellings and a general shrinking from the hard life on the land also helped the rush. 'Human action quickened by wider knowledge,' *The Times* called it. 'The Deserted Village,' August 24, 1905, p. 57.

The socialist movement had been on its feet for some time, to be sure. The *Clarion* blared; Lawrence Gronlund's *Cooperative Commonwealth* (1884) and Edward Bellamy's *Looking Backward* (1887) had appeared; and Henry George and the Fabians were getting much notice. But while the socialists were enthusiastic utopians, they were seldom practical; they seemed to put more effort into shaking shameful fingers at city poverty and slums than devising schemes for changing matters, and very few bothered about the farmer at all. Haggard would be the last to see his programme as one based on socialism, but that is exactly what it was; for the initiator, executor, and father-protector of his plan for reform, in each instance, whether direct or indirect, is the Government. Haggard sees that the Government, and only the Government, can save English agriculture, sees it clearly long before most men, and he says so. He calls upon Parliament to enact legislation that would bring about two major reforms and a dozen or so minor ones. First, the Government must give active and generous support to a system of small holdings to enable the people who farm the land to own it; and second, the Government must establish an agricultural parcel post to help the farmer get his produce to market efficiently and inexpensively. These two essential measures – small holdings and rural post – will bring the farmer sustained prosperity.

Haggard's programme is based on his own strong feeling for the soil, which he knows most rural people share. The farmer, born on his farm and loving it, ought to be able to own it. If he were given the chance to be the lord and master of the soil he worked, or even if he were given a hope that his son or grandson would one day own it, he would labour with pride and devotion in dignity and security. He would himself be a better man for it, and he would help to build a better England. Small holdings were not new – there had been a Small-Holdings Act in 1892 – and Haggard asserts that 'wherever small-holdings exist in England there is comparative prosperity, great love of the soil . . . an increasing as compared with a diminishing population . . . and a considerable addition to the supply of local labour.'[30] But Haggard wants the Small-Holdings Act revivified, and he asks the Government to supply the wherewithal to make England more a nation of small holdings than it has been in the past. Capital for buying, stocking, and maintaining small farms must be available as loans from the Treasury at low interest rates. Not for a moment does he suggest any outright give-aways, however – he is still rooted in the Conservative camp – he envisions instead a system of 'indirect aid' only. Since direct aid 'pauperizes and is foreign to our character and traditions,' the farmer will need to have some capital from his own means or savings, and the rest he should be able to borrow from cooperative credit banks. Because

Haggard believes that the small landowner has suffered most in the agricultural depression, this small-holdings scheme is designed to get him back into operation. He in turn will improve conditions for his tenants, so that their lives on the land will be comfortable. The tenant will be free to use all his capital in stock, rather than tie it up in investment or use it to pay mortgage interest. A network of holdings will bring back prosperity and dignity to the countryside, will abate the rural exodus, and will begin the rebuilding of England's agricultural industry and society.

The second vital change, the agricultural parcel post, would be a new Government bureau, a branch of the Post Office, that would operate like ordinary parcel post. He considers this 'the greatest and most far-reaching of the remedies that I have to propose.'[31] This post would carry all farm produce, including milk in churns, in units up to one hundred pounds in weight, at the lowest possible rate 'without loss to the Country.' It is a particularly crucial measure, he claims, because the English railways were then giving preferential rates to foreign goods and thereby setting up competitive price obstacles against English produce. If the new post were put into effect, the English farmer could hope to compete with foreign prices. The overwhelming expense of transport is one of the farmer's worst enemies, and because of it, many farm products are left to rot, for it is not profitable to ship them to market. If the farmer had a chance to get established under a small-holdings scheme, an agricultural post would then help him get his produce to market, compete successfully with foreign imports, and get a fair return for his labours.

Haggard asks for other reforms, and although subsidiary to his two main proposals, they also are important. He wants the Government to revise completely the tax laws that cripple the English landowner and farmer; he urges them to abolish Copyhold and to cheapen land transfer; he wants the Government to increase and strengthen the powers of the Board of Agriculture; he suggests more light railways be built; he asks for a law requiring that foreign meats be branded as such, thus preventing their sale as home produce; he feels the Government must help solve the problem of preferential rates on railways; he wants it to promote cooperative societies for the manufacture of butter; and he demands a review of rural education (a country lad should become acquainted with the land and animals before he is twelve; he should spend the winters with book and slate, the summers working on the land).

Programme now in hand, Haggard addresses himself to the means for carrying it out. And he is firm about where the responsibility lies. The Government must bear the burden, for only it has the necessary money and power. It must take a strong initiative along the lines he has proposed. But the Government is traditionally indifferent to change, he realizes. 'English Governments . . . cannot be brought to recognize that the matter is one of real importance.' They 'shrug . . . [their] shoulders, say that any party or Cabinet that attempted remedies would lose popularity in the cities, and leave things to take their chances.'[32] As a result, the Government is doing far less for 'loyal English farmers than . . . [for the] disloyal Irish ones' significant to party politicians. It would be an uphill struggle for those who wanted to bring about change. Haggard knew from his South African experiences what governmental apathy meant, but he would not be content to surrender at the shoulder shrug of a Home Office official; he would go beyond Government offices and take his case to the English people.

A Farmer's Year showed Haggard as a man of strong feeling for the land and its workers, one well attuned to all natural phenomena and seeking justice for people on the land. *Rural England* shows him as something more. Here he is not only the census-taker, the indefatigable surveyor, the incisive interviewer, the historian, but also a fist-pounding social reformer. Haggard throws before the English public a blueprint for progressive reform of all rural areas of their land, and he tells them straight away that either they do something about the conditions he describes or prepare to surrender England's powerful place among nations. In *A Farmer's Year* Haggard found his cause; in *Rural England* he devises his programme for remedy and change.

Rural England appeared at the end of November 1902, about four months after the Fourth Colonial Conference, at which the colonies had passed resolutions opposing free trade and favouring imperial preference. The battle of Protection versus Free Trade interested the British public at that time more than any other question and split the Balfour cabinet wide open. Where the reviews could deal kindly with Rider Haggard the farmer and call *A Farmer's Year* pleasant and charming, they had to deal with the Haggard of *Rural England* as a political commentator. *Rural England* was noticed everywhere and provoked long and argumentative essays, crammed with polemics and statistics, devoted less to reviewing Haggard's book or explaining his position than to delineating the particular essayist's own political position. Most of these observers commended Haggard for his hard work, thanked him for his service to English history, but styled him an alarmist who drew much too black a picture of English rural life. With confident optimism, they invariably pointed to a statistic here or a fact there that seemed to indicate that prosperity was on its way back, that agriculture was best left to take care of itself. The *Edinburgh Review* devoted many of its pages to a detailed summary of Haggard's work, however, and

even went on to agree with some of Haggard's analysis. But after all
was said and done, it could not concur with Haggard's conclusions;
the 'picture . . . is painted in colours altogether too dark,' it insists.
The critic writing the article is sanguine about foreign trade and competition, his own private agricultural Utopia is an England composed
of cooperatives, and he completely rejects the idea of small holdings,
small tradings, and the agricultural parcel post as answers to the problems. There are no heroic remedies, he insists, and above all, England
must not rely upon the Government for aid. If farming methods were
improved, both the quality of farm products and the farmer's chances
of competing successfully on an open market would improve. 'There is
nothing disheartening in the outlook for agriculture in this country
. . . [in spite of] the croakings and forebodings of some friends.' All we
need is the determination to do the job. Self-reliance will save England's
agriculture.[33] The *Contemporary Review*, one of the few not to take issue
with Haggard's analysis, conceded that it

> is not a cheerful picture that Mr. Rider Haggard presents, [but
> asserted that he] . . . is no irresponsible alarmist, [for] . . . he gives
> chapter and verse for every statement he makes. . . . [It is] interest-
> ing and . . . packed with information . . . [not a] 'dry book.' On the
> contrary it cannot fail to be of fascinating interest to everybody
> whose heart is in the country. It is an 'open-air book' in the truest
> sense of the term, written with a professional charm and a whole-
> hearted love of the soil, of growing things, of country sights and
> sounds, that despite its ballast of facts and figures, carries it into the
> domain of literature . . . . It will live for many generations to come.[34]

The *Spectator* attacked Haggard mercilessly. The only concession it
made was that as 'a record of present modes of farming, local custom,
crops, prices, breeds of cattle, transport, and rent of lands his work will
remain valuable.' But it insists that Haggard's conclusions are based on
shaky evidence treated injudiciously. 'The writer does not distinguish
his conclusions from his preconceptions. . . . His judgement seems con-
stitutionally pessimistic. . . . But though we must make our protest
against . . . [the] book, we admit to the full not only its literary charm,
but the great interest of much of the information contained in these
volumes.'[35] The *Quarterly Review* had high praise for the work: 'We
cannot recall an instance, except that of Mr. Haggard, in which a
distinguished writer has beaten his inkstand into a ploughshare. . . .
[These] portly volumes take their place by the side of the works of . . .
Young, Cobbett, and Caird.' Still, even the *Quarterly Review* felt obliged
to add that 'its message is too negative and too half-hearted to excite

enthusiasm,' and as 'it is, his gospel of dependence on the government is a confession of failure.'[36] There were many more reviews, much in the same vein.

Haggard was not alone in his outcry, for other men who lived close to the land and witnessed the ruin of country communities could not help being moved to shout out against it. R. W. Hanbury, President of the Board of Agriculture, faced the realities squarely, read the signs properly, and spoke out for change, and the *Morning Post* championed the farmer's cause. Joseph Chamberlain saw the need for agricultural reforms, and when Haggard sent him a copy of *Rural England*, he wrote: 'I judge from what you say that we are very much at one [on agricultural matters]. I am, and always have been, in favour of Small Holdings.'[37] Another important voice was Thomas Hardy's. Hardy said with fiction what Haggard said with facts; five of his novels[38] written during the agricultural depression are tragic and accurate accounts of the ruin of English country life and the collapse of the English peasantry. Hardy treats the economic crisis in terms of personal, Haggard in terms of national tragedy. But the theme is the same; the men see eye to eye.*

Their views of agriculture and rural life formed a real tie between them. When Haggard came to Dorset in the course of his travels for *Rural England*, he called upon Hardy, who gladly gave him his impressions of conditions in the shire. In *Rural England* Haggard quotes verbatim[39] a long letter from Hardy, in which he described in detail some of the changes he has witnessed, and with Hardy's permission, Haggard also quotes from Hardy's little-known article 'The Dorsetshire Labourer.'[40]

But the voices were too few and Parliament was intransigent. Given Government apathy and the unpopularity of his reform programme with the Press, Haggard might have turned his attention away from farming toward other things. After all, he could have reasoned, he had

---

* Hardy had met Haggard at the Savile Club in the 'eighties, and the two remained friendly through the years that followed. In a letter dated December 21, 1904, Hardy writes Haggard 'to thank you heartily for the Christmas present of pheasants you have been been [*sic*] so kind as to send, my wife joining me.' He regrets not being able to send something in return, 'but a freehold estate of under 2 acres does not yield any game larger than sparrow or starling.' In 1910 Haggard and Hardy sat together on a balcony of the Athenaeum Club in London as the hearse bearing the body of Edward VII passed, and in 1911 Hardy wrote again to say that he thought Haggard's *Mahatma and the Hare*

a strangely attractive book . . . . I am, as you may know, entirely on the side of the hare . . . . I feel certain that you are too, in spite of your reserve; and that delights me. There is not the least doubt that blood sport will have to go. To teach boys to like it, in the 20th Century, is monstrous.

I hope very many people will read the book, and be as much moved by it as I was and am.

Both letters are in the Lockwood Collection. See also Haggard, *Days*, II, p. 214.

presented the facts, and it was now England's job to help herself. But he loved England too much to sit by and watch her grow weak. If there was something he could do to bring people to their senses and keep his country strong, he would. In the years that followed *Rural England*, Haggard tried desperately to revive public interest in the land and to win Government assistance for rural needs. His letters to *The Times* and other journals multiplied. Whenever he was interviewed, either for a literary portrait, for an article on the writer at home, or for some notable personalities series, he invariably turned the interview into an agricultural discussion and made it part of his campaign to get the alarming facts before the public. Persistently and forcefully he depicted the rural crisis for a citified England and showed over and over again how England without her agriculture was England without her strength. 'You will understand what labour all this means,' he wrote to Stanley Weyman, 'and I have to write novels in the cracks (for two years past there have been no cracks).'[41] He took every opportunity to speak in public for the destitute farmer and the depleted farmlands, and his frequent testimony before the Norfolk Chamber of Agriculture and before the Central and Associated Chambers of Agriculture received good coverage in the London Press. Wherever Haggard went, he took his banners with him, so much so that a commentator in the *Literary World* suggested that 'Mr. Haggard's position as a social reformer has become almost apostolic.'[42] So intense was his concern that, by his own confession, he became 'an agricultural bore.' In 1905 he told a Letchworth audience that on entering a room, 'I have heard people say, "Here comes Rider Haggard, for goodness' sake do not mention the word agriculture." ' He coined phrases and rallying calls, he stormed the bulwarks of conservatism, he shouted, pleaded, and pounded. The Press was full of Rider Haggard the farmer; Rider Haggard the romancer seemed to withdraw into the background. The storm brought some eminent people rallying to his side, but turned a good many against him.

And to what avail? To what purpose the speeches, the letters to newspapers, the articles, the books he wrote and the complimentary copies he sent, the pamphlets, the long, carefully phrased letters to influential people of the day, the exhausting political discussions at dinner-tables and in clubrooms – did all this do any good? Haggard, impatient as always, in 1905 said, No.

> Personally I have done my best to . . . enforce . . . my ideas of agricultural reform on those in high places, and to impress them on the minds of the people of this country, [he told the Letchworth gathering.] . . . I have written a book on the subject, so big and so

fat that whenever I open it . . . it makes me shiver at the recollection of the labour which the writing of it entailed. . . . Well, what has been the end of it all? Failure. I have failed. I cannot say that the ideas I have advocated are one bit advanced. . . . Our Government will not listen to anything that has for its object the good of agriculture.[43]

Also, writing a preface to a new edition of *Rural England* in January 1906, he gloomily said that now 'after four years are gone by I must with humiliation report that nothing of consequence has happened.'[44]

But Haggard, even as early as 1906, was more successful than he knew. The letter columns and editorial pages echoed his name as more and more they discussed agricultural questions. Even as Haggard was writing his gloomy second preface to *Rural England*, the *Review of Reviews*, in an article entitled 'Where Is Mr. Rider Haggard?' not only called for 'immediate action' in agriculture reforms, but insisted that 'Mr. Rider Haggard ought to be despatched at once to report upon all that has been done [in land reform] . . . in Denmark, Holland, Belgium, and Bavaria. . . . There is no more capable agricultural commissioner than Mr. Rider Haggard, and . . . it is to be hoped that Lord Carrington will have despatched him on the Continent before Parliament assembles.'[45] Haggard had not got his reforms, but neither had he failed completely. One thing was certain: he had helped to create an atmosphere of controversy in which people talked and argued over the nation's responsibility toward the farmer. By 1906 few doubted that the farmer was in trouble.

Actually neither Haggard nor his message had been unduly pessimistic. Agricultural conditions in England in the early years of the twentieth century continued to decline. The estimated worth of agricultural lands reached a new low in 1908, and the numbers of arable acres decreased by three million between 1885 and the outbreak of World War I, when the Government was jarred out of its lethargy and lent a helping hand. In spite of rising prices in industry, a fact that helped distort the picture of England's overall economy, the rural exodus continued, imports rose steadily, and farm produce prices remained low. The *Agricultural Returns* for these years tell a sadder tale than Haggard's *Rural England*, and the mismanagement of England's agricultural problems in the early years of the twentieth century is universally deplored by historians. Not until 1910 did English agriculture, now largely a meat-growing, not a crop, industry, rise to a level of subsistence, and not until the war years did the English farmer see a profit. Haggard lived to see what he feared most: an England where farming was no longer significant.

Facing this reality, the Press no longer suggested that time alone would take care of the farmer, that all he needed was an ounce of self-reliance. The tenor of opinion had changed noticeably in a short time, and Haggard had played his role in bringing about that change. Agricultural issues by themselves may not have defeated the Unionist Party in 1906, but the Party's failure to pass major legislation to benefit the farmer could have contributed to its defeat. With the Liberals' victory, Haggard and the English farmer looked for increased concern in official circles on rural matters, and they got it. In 1907, the Liberals took up the question of small holdings, and when a major controversy ensued over the issue of compulsory surrender of land, Haggard found himself at its centre and, astonishingly enough, pleading for moderation. Haggard, a cross-bencher, retained his earlier position and continued to campaign for indirect Government assistance. Small holdings had to grow up naturally, not by confiscation and allocation of land. He 'always aimed,' he said at this time, 'not at revolution, but reform.'[46] The *Spectator*, having lashed out at Haggard for his programme five years earlier, found his policy now the one sound statement among all the 'windy denunciations of wicked landlords and indiscriminate accusations of Radical rapacity.'[47]

In 1909, Parliament passed what Haggard saw as the essential reform of his programme. It was the Development Bill, which authorized the Treasury to make grants and loans for forestry, agriculture, rural industries, and transport. Agriculture's capital could be replenished by this plan, and small holdings could grow up across the land quite naturally. It had taken many years to make this act a reality, but it was done, and Haggard could take a good deal of credit for it. With a sense of pleasure and fulfilment, he rose on the evening of November 25 before the Bungay Farmers' Club and proclaimed that 'British agriculture has turned the corner, and ... [is] once more on an upward trend.'[48]

8

Friends

HAGGARD's boundless energy, his diverse interests, his eagerness to make a contribution to his Country, and his quest for fame brought him to the notice of a wide public. His striking appearance, eloquent speech, and agreeable manner helped keep him in the spotlight for many years. For more than a generation, his name was on everyone's lips, and he himself was a force that men in every walk of life had to reckon with. The chronicle of his associations with fellow-farmers, agriculturists, politicians, miners, explorers, antiquaries, archaeologists, financiers, and publishers could in itself fill a volume and might provide some interesting insights. But in his relations with literary figures we find the facts that illumine Haggard the writer.

Five men were largely responsible for the surge of interest in romance in the 'eighties and 'nineties, Stevenson, Haggard, Kipling, Henley, and Lang. In 1883 *Treasure Island* gave new vigour to the genre; in 1885 and 1887 *King Solomon's Mines* and *She* helped romance claim a vast new reading public. Although Kipling did not appear upon the London scene until 1889, it was he who brought originality and artistic authority to the new school of romance. Henley performed two offices: he was the movement's troubadour, singing romantic ballads ('I was a King in Babylon / And you were a Christian slave'); and he was the helmsman who steered his contemporaries' earliest romances into print (after *Treasure Island* and *King Solomon's Mines* found a publisher with his help, he himself published *Barrack-Room Ballads*). And Andrew Lang was the crusader on behalf of romance: he boomed it in his columns. It was inevitable that these five writers, drawn to a common centre from different poles, should become acquainted and that their paths should cross frequently. Two of them, Lang and Kipling, became Haggard's intimate friends. The friendship with Lang developed early and lasted until Lang's death in 1912; Haggard and Kipling, although acquainted as early as 1889, did not become close friends until after the turn of the century, and not until the war years did a strong bond grow between the two.

Haggard's friendship with Lang dates back to *King Solomon's Mines* days. They probably became acquainted in 1885. But before they met, Lang, as English editor of *Harper's*, received a story from Haggard in the post. Lang replied by letter that all such material was considered by the New York office. He doubted, all the same, that the American editor would be interested because he had a large backlog of stories by English authors. The only out-of-the-way item in the letter is the postscript: 'I am glad to take this opportunity of thanking you for the great pleasure "The Witch's Head" has given me, I have not read anything so good for a long time.'[1] In his next letter to Haggard, probably written after Haggard and Lang met, Lang expresses great enthusiasm for *King Solomon's Mines*, which he had read in manuscript. The book was published in September 1885, and another letter from Lang to Haggard acknowledges his complimentary copy. 'Many thanks for "K.S.M." How grand the map is.'[2] A week later Lang's favourable notice of the book appeared in the *Saturday Review*. With the success of *King Solomon's Mines*, the two men were jubilantly united in the cause of romance.

It was a meaningful relationship for both, and at the height of their literary careers, Lang had no closer friend, and Haggard, who could make friends more easily, valued no other more. The two men were very different, but their differences, though obvious, were superficial and complementary. Lang admired Haggard's self-confidence almost as much as his flashes of imagination, and Haggard respected Lang's learning and judgement. But what they had most in common was something else. They both believed in the reality of the imagination, and all their lives, together and apart, they sought to explore the unexplorable, to travel in the world of fancy and capture its essence. This deep sympathetic understanding annihilated the other surface differences between them and drew them together. As the months and years passed after *King Solomon's Mines* was published, Haggard and Lang spent much time in each other's company and soon came to draw freely on one another's peculiar resources. In time each became the other's literary mentor.

From a purely practical point of view, the relationship did Haggard a great deal of good, for, when he came upon the scene in 1885, Lang was already an influential critic and established writer; Lang added considerable prestige to Haggard's reputation. The relationship, on the other hand, did not benefit Lang's standing in literary circles. Lang's defence of Haggard when he was under attack linked their names irrevocably, and together they often became targets of ridicule and condescension.

To many, Haggard stood for the 'low-brow' school of writing, and anything associated with him was pooh-poohed, particularly among the fastidious amateurs. Lang none the less stood strongly on the side of the romancers in the literary squabbles that raged between them and the forces of realism and naturalism in the novel. He was, for instance, displeased by the 'ingredients of the blackest misery' in Hardy's *Tess of the D'Urbervilles*, and although his review of the book was generally polite and called Hardy's style 'pellucid', he suggested that 'if [Hardy] . . . be too good for us, or good in the wrong way, if in short, we are not *en rapport* with him, why there are plenty of other novelists.' Earlier in the same review, Lang admitted that 'Umslopogass . . . is one of my dearest friends in fiction: "I will never desert [him]." '3 The double-barrelled confession and the juxtaposition of Hardy and Haggard, coming as they did when Hardy was the man of the hour, caused a furore, and for the remainder of his days, Lang saw recurring jibes in the Press about his criticism of Hardy and knew that men privately joked about his preferences for 'other novelists,' meaning Haggard, over Hardy.

While Haggard was writing *She*, he began to call upon Lang for help with manuscript details. Lang's letters to Haggard record for us the translation of *She* from foolscap to printed volume. Although none of Haggard's letters to Lang survives, we know that he must have asked Lang's assistance in charting the history of Leo Vincey's ancestry, for Lang wrote explaining how the ancient Greeks named their children. 'My Greek prose has 20 years of rust on it,' he continued, 'but I'll get you a piece by an Ireland scholar.' For tracing the line from Roman times, Lang suggests that 'Vindex, Vindici, Vincey would knit.'4 In July 1886 Haggard sent *She* to Lang in proofs, and although Lang was immensely impressed with it, he sent back numerous criticisms:

> I have pretty nearly finished 'She.' I really must congratulate you; I think it is one of the most astonishing romances I ever read. The more impossible it is, the better you do it, till it seems like a story from the literature of another planet. I can't give a better account of the extraordinary impression it makes upon me; as to the Public I never can speak.

But he also points out weaknesses caused by Haggard's hasty execution:

> You really must look after the style, more when it comes out as a book. I would also, if it is not impertinent, reduce the comic element a good deal – it is sometimes so sudden a drop as to be quite painful. For my own part (and I am pretty sure many readers will agree)

there is too much raw heart . . . and other tortures. I'm saying
pretty much what I would say in a review, only beforehand. I'd
like to see it polished up a bit and made more worthy of the imagination in it.

Still working on the proofs, Lang wrote again to caution Haggard
against facetiousness:

> I'm *sure* the note about a monograph on Ayesha's Greek pro-
> nunciation for the use of public schools, will show the Public you
> are laughing – a thing I never can help doing, and the B.P. hates it.
> [He also questioned the propriety of 'hot potting':] As to the
> pot, I never heard of it, historically, and even now I'm not sure
> whether it is one of the Cannibal myths . . . I thought the potting
> might be modified slightly in the *selling* interest of the book, as
> many people funk giving children or boys anything of that sort. . . .
> Not that I want to disestablish the pot, but to *glisser* him a little. . . .
> When I say *style*, I mean that it is risky to bring in colloquialisms
> with abruptness, after flights into the ideal.

On the following day, Lang wrote again:

> I have just finished 'She.' . . . I certainly still think it the most
> extraordinary romance I ever read, and that's why I want you to be
> very careful with the proofs, before it goes out in a volume. I will
> read them over again, and annotate. I'm perfectly certain most of
> the chaff about Gladstone must go [it did], it entirely disturbs the
> mood of the reader – any reader can be a judge of that much. I
> nearly cried over Ayesha's end. . . . There is a difficulty about Leo.
> He is not made a very interesting person. Probably he was only a
> fine animal . . . some of the chaff in awful situations lets one down
> too suddenly. I'd take other fellows' advice about it, in some of the
> marked places. . . . By George, I'd have gone into the fire and
> chucked in She too, perhaps it would have picked her up again.[5]

Because Lang helped so much with *She*, Haggard wished to dedicate
it to him. Lang did not protest, simply reminding Haggard of his
responsibility as a critic: 'I consider it a great distinction. The only
thing is that, if you do, I shan't be able to review it, except with my
name signed thereto and my honest confession.'[6] The book was
published in January 1887, and Lang wrote a review of it in the
Academy,* where, although he praised the tale in general terms, he also
expressed some reservations.

She was an immediate success. Lang had fallen irrevocably in love

* *See* p. 101 above.

with Ayesha, and he was delighted to see her fame spread. He wrote a
sonnet called 'She.'* Then he went even beyond the sonnet: in collaboration with W. H. Pollock (at that time the editor of the *Saturday
Review*), and 'aided by the kind, but wholly impracticable advice of
H. R. H.,' he composed a gentle parody of *She* called *He*, 'By the author
of *It*, *King Solomon's Wives*, *Bess*, *Much Darker Days*, *Mr. Morton's
Subtler*, and Other Romances.'†

During the days when the Press was in full cry against Haggard,
Lang sent almost daily communiqués to Ditchingham, where Haggard
had gone on his return from Egypt in 1887. Haggard carefully planned
his counter-statements, and Lang advised him judiciously on what to
do, whom to write to, and, even more important, whom not to
write to. Also, Haggard was busily at work on his first historical
romance, and he needed help from Lang. He asked where he might
find background material, and Lang sent him Theocritus (good for a
picture of Alexandria two hundred years before Cleopatra, he told
him), Apuleius (good for 120 years later), and a list of authorities on
Cleopatra.[7] Lang also wrote lyrics to be included in the tale, read
proofs and advised Haggard at great length:

> You will loathe me for the advice, but if I were you I'd put
> 'Cleopatra' away for as long as possible, and then read it as a member
> of the public. [In part] . . . it is too long, too full of antiquarian
> detail, and too slow in movement to carry the general public with
> it. . . . I would condense a good deal. . . . I see pretty clearly where
> and how the condensing could be done. You don't want a reader's
> interest to fall asleep, and now it would in places. I am writing with
> perfect frankness because, of course, I want it to be A1 in its
> *genre* – a dreadfully difficult *genre* it is. . . . The main thing is, at any
> expense, to hurry on more – to give the impression of solemnity
> but at more speed, and with much fewer strokes.
>
> [Some] inverted constructions might be re-verted [Lang says in

---

* Ayesha prompted more sonnets: Lang parodied his original 'She' with 'Twosh,' at
least two versions of which are extant. The better version, dedicated to Hyder Ragged,
is included in Roger Lancelyn Green, *Andrew Lang, A Critical Biography* (1946), p. 123.
The Comtesse de Bremont wrote a sonnet also called 'She,' and dedicated it to Sophie
Eyre, who played Ayesha in the original London production. See her *Sonnets and Love
Poems* (1892). Another poem, 'To the Author of "She," ' by 'Theophilus,' appeared in
the *Month* (September 1888).

† The parodies of Haggard's works would in themselves make an entertaining study.
Punch was the major contributor to this collection, but there were many other entrants.
Some of the titles, at least, must be noted: *King Solomon's Wives; or The Phantom Mines*,
by 'Hyder Ragged'; 'A Proposition and a Rider'; 'Adam Slaughterman,' by Walker
Weird, author of 'Hee-Hee,' 'Solomon's Ewers,' etc.; 'She-That-Ought-Not-To-Be-
Played, A Story of Gloomy Gaiety'; 'The Book of Kookarie,' by Reader Faghard, author
of 'Queen Bathsheba's Ewers,' 'Yawn,' 'Guess,' 'My Ma's at Penge,' 'Smallum Halfboy,'
'Gen. Porridge, D.T.,' 'Me a Kiss,' 'The Hemisphere's Wish,' etc., etc.; 'Allan Quatermain's Farm,' a parody of *A Farmer's Year*. See Scott, *Bibliography*, pp. 230–233.

another undated letter, and] . . . I still hanker after [some shortening in speeches.] . . . Do reflect that a lady with a love affair 1,000 years old is very like another interesting lady who lived in Kôr.

I gave all my morning to 'Cleopatra' [Lang writes in still another letter]. . . . I have marked a good many minutiae of style, or expression. In a few places, a judicious shortening of moral reflections [would help]. . . . I think even more than before you should lighten the ship by greatly shortening. . . . I venture to suggest some alterations where modern words come in out of tune.

Screw it a little tighter, and I think it is undeniably an artistic piece of work. . . . I'd like, if you don't mind, to read over the early part with you as I feel a good deal turns on adding energy to that, and on condensing. . . . I don't see whom they can say you stole your plot from. They'll say the parts from Plutarch are from Shakespeare, probably they never read Plutarch!

After finishing *Cleopatra* (August 2, 1887), Haggard came up to London for the autumn, and some time before the end of the year he and Lang hatched a plan to write a romance together. Although we do not know who suggested the partnership, the idea to collaborate was a perfectly natural one for them, close as they were in literary interests and tastes. Lang's letters are full of disclaimers about his own creative ability; but Haggard brushes aside all his misgivings. We may infer that Lang suggested a sequel to *She*, for Ayesha had completely captivated him. But Haggard rejected that idea, because he had already decided to write a sequel by himself, although twenty years would have to pass, he felt, before he would be ready for it. Haggard seems to have made a counter-suggestion that took the subject more into Lang's camp: he thought they might write a romance about Odysseus. But Lang did not at first seem to welcome the idea, suffering, as he often did, from doubts about his own talent. 'Bother Odysseus,' he wrote Haggard. 'You may tackle him. I daresay you can, but pancakes are imaginative, compared to me.' But Haggard prevailed, and some time between January and March 1888 the two men set out seriously to write the tale. They were both in London, meeting at the Savile frequently and exchanging bits of manuscript and plot suggestions through the post.[8] The partnership was not an easy one, all the same, and while Haggard's work on *The World's Desire* did not diminish his own independent output, he was involved in this single undertaking for over two years.

The vicissitudes encountered by the manuscript almost equalled Odysseus's own, and as many words must have gone on to letter paper as on to foolscap. At one point, Lang even lost the manuscript, and the partnership was abandoned until he rediscovered it in a folio volume where 'it was put to keep it clean.'[9] The record of the collaboration, as one sorts it out of Lang's undated letters and Haggard's account in his autobiography, is fascinating. Haggard's personality is dominant throughout, but then it would be, for he was the more flamboyant of the two. But beyond this, it is Haggard's characteristic drive that keeps the manuscript going and gets it finished, though once Lang becomes interested and involved in the work, even his recurring diffidence is dispelled.

When *The World's Desire* appeared in December 1890, it made quite a stir, for this sort of collaboration inevitably set afire the curiosity of the literary set of the day. Readers tried to sort Haggard from Lang, and the book became a popular item. None the less it got a poor Press. Henley's *National Observer* called it 'a tortuous and ungodly jumble of anarchy and culture.'[10] James Barrie wrote in the *British Weekly* that 'the crowning misfortune of *The World's Desire* is that it is sometimes dull, a failing that we should not find in any book written by Mr. Haggard or Mr. Lang alone.'[11] The *Spectator* called the collaboration an 'audacious scheme,' and guessed it to be Haggard's conception. 'We think so well of Mr. Lang,' it wrote, 'that what would please us best would be to be told that his name on the title-page is his principal contribution. . . . The whole thing is a failure in which each of its authors has so wasted as almost to extinguish his natural genius.'[12] The *Athenaeum*'s reaction was hardly better: 'Why should Mr. Lang lend himself and his genius to such unreal stuff?' it asked, and suggested that Haggard's touch was fatal.[13] Only an occasional voice, such as the *Literary World*'s, praised it.[14]

Stevenson wrote to Lang about the book, and Lang reported to Haggard: 'Stevenson says he is "thrilled and chilled" by Meriamun [the evil Egyptian queen who, in the tale, destroys Odysseus]. He thinks much of it "too steep," bars Od(ysseus) killing so many enemies – exactly what Longinus says of Homer – and fears Meriamun is likely to play down Helen. He is kind enough to say "the style is all right," and adds a poem on Odysseus.'* Lang did not think very highly of his effort and later versified his own opinion about the book:

> It did not set the Thames on fire,
> It is not quite 'The World's Desire'!
> Much rather do the public scoff,
> And yell to Nature, 'Take them off!'
> While critics constantly conspire
> To slate the hapless *World's Desire*.[15]

* See p. 212 below for the poem.

To Haggard, Lang wrote with characteristic self-depreciation: 'I brought you worse luck than you would have done alone.' In 1907 Haggard wrote to Lang: 'I think you were a bit discouraged about *The World's Desire* because a lot of ignorant fools slated it, but in my opinion you were wrong. That work I believe will last. It is extraordinarily liked by many who can understand. I told you about the American Egyptologist I met, for instance, who reads it every night!'[16]

Although *The World's Desire* has been in print almost continuously from the day it was published, it is hard to agree with Haggard's prediction or with the poet William Canton, who wrote in 1895 that it is 'one of the most strikingly picturesque and imaginative of recent romances.'[17] For *The World's Desire* is too many things in one. Lang's and Haggard's efforts detract from each other. The reader cannot pass easily from Lang's Ithaca to Haggard's Egypt, or from the *Odyssey* to the Bible – the distance is never satisfactorily bridged. The tale gives the impression that the walls of time have been torn down. What is more, although it is on the surface Odysseus's search for the immortal Helen, Odysseus is basically just another one of Haggard's true-bred Victorian adventurers. He lacks wisdom, depth of character, and breadth of spirit. Furthermore, although Odysseus is a Hellenized Allan Quatermain, Helen is not Helen at all, but Ayesha, simply transplanted from Kôr northward to Egypt and renamed. While Ayesha is herself no small accomplishment, she does not blend well with the Graeco-Egyptian landscape. From time to time, Lang and Haggard's combined talents soar, and the reader is rewarded. But these moments do not come often enough, and the result is rather a hodgepodge, a ragbag of myth, legend, history, anthropology; Greece, Egypt, and Kôr. It is *She* tacked on to the *Odyssey*; Haggard piled on Homer.

The years that followed their work together on *The World's Desire* often put many miles between Haggard and Lang; yet the friendship endured. They exchanged letters often and visited with one another whenever they could. They met frequently at the Savile and at other clubs, went away from London on fishing trips together, often with C. J. Longman, and entertained each other at their homes. When they travelled abroad or got involved in work that demanded their entire attention, as was often the case with Haggard in his agricultural and government undertakings, there were long gaps when they did not come together; but the reunions were always warm. To the end of Lang's life, their strong feeling for one another did not abate.

After *The World's Desire* was published, Lang continued to be Haggard's literary adviser, not only in matters of Haggard's relations with the public and the Press, but in planning, executing, and selling his romances. Though Haggard did not always follow Lang's promptings, so important to him was Lang's judgement that for a long time, it would seem, proofs automatically went to Lang from Haggard's publishers and agent. Some of Haggard's romances Lang read two and three times, either in manuscript or proof or both. 'Delighted to look over any proofs' is a phrase that recurs in the letters, and in one written in 1890 Lang assures the abused and maligned Haggard that no one can accuse him of plagiarizing *Eric* from Kingsley's *Hereward*. 'Delighted to read *Beatrice* . . . in proof,' and 'I shall be *delighted* to read proofs of Eric. . . . May I use a free hand . . . I mean, if a line or two seemed superfluous to the critical understanding, might they go out?'[18] 'Please let me see the proofs, as two pairs of eyes are better than one.'[19] 'I'd like to read it [*Eric*] again, in pages.' [20] 'They [the publishers] have sent me a lot of *Allan's Wife* I corrected before.'[21] 'Have you the proofs of *Beatrice* yet? I might as well read them over, if two pairs of peepers are better than one.'[22] 'Proofs to hand. . . . My remarks on proof will refer to publication in book . . . where you can edit as much as you like.' 'What is this Roll of Proofs? Am I to read and critically mark, and how long have I for that purpose, if so?'[23]

Lang gave Haggard the benefit of his own reading and scholarly pursuits: 'The Fates have led me to read Scott's preface to Ivanhoe (1830). I suppose it is in most editions. Do read it. It is the reflections of a successful novelist who was a man of business. What he says about varying the *venue*, and about *names* of novels . . . is good and interesting.'[24] 'Jebb's version of Œdipus Colonnus and Tyrannus are the only good prose cribs, and expensive. For Sophocles in verse, Lewis Campbell and for Æschylus Milman are about as good as any. Bohn's cribs are awful, but better than verse, may be.' 'Scott's notes to Marmion, where they brick up Marmion's young woman, are likely to be useful.'[25] 'Certainly Homer has the "whizz of arrows . . . and the sound of spears" – Iliad XVI, 361.'[26] 'For Heaven's sake, *corpus vile*, not *vilum* as your printer hath it. I have many unkind suggestions to make, for book form. Do read [name illegible] – it needs a light hand like hers.'[27]

Lang was ever on the lookout for plots he could suggest to Haggard. At one point, he suggests St. Germain as a 'grand subject . . . a male She of the last century,'[28] and at another he urges a novel about West Africa based on the *Proceedings* of the Society of Psychic Research about a white man in native service who had learned the natives' magic.[29] It was Lang who put Haggard on a train of thought that led him to write some of his best fiction, the four tales of the Zulus. Lang wanted a story about the natives, one with no white men, and writing in the *Scots Observer* at the same time that he was urging Haggard to try such a tale, he speculates about 'how delicious a novel *all* Zulu, without a white face in it, would be!'[30] Four months later, Haggard began to write *Nada the Lily*, just such a story. In one letter Lang told Haggard, 'I think you could make a romance of Meleager.'[31] And at another time, he suggests the legend of the golden bough: 'the priest who slew the slayer and shall himself be slain . . . any Roman period would do. . . . If you fancy it, read the opening chapter of Frazer's *Golden Bough*.'[32]

Lang gave other help as well: 'Shall I bring your . . . ms. down, and go through it with you? If I am not to be critical, I'd rather wait and read it in print. You go a rare howler in Chapter 1, with your dates.'[33] When he was reading proof on *Allan Quatermain*, he wrote: 'When you get them in such a tight place, for goodness' sake (& Good's), let them live up to it.'

Frequently Lang sought to curb Haggard's excesses: Lang found 'too much gore' in *Montezuma's Daughter* and thought that 'the murder of the children may stodge the reader.'[34] After reading *Allan Quatermain*, he suggested that 'perhaps it would be well to mop up a little blood, is it not going to be rather sanguinary?'[35] Another time: 'I return *Eric*: I have still an impression that . . . murders are a little too common.'[36] And again: '[Your manuscript] . . . appears to be overcome by reflections on Boers, Land, the Prince of Wales, wicked millionaires, and the decay of British bowling.'[37]

Lang also helped in matters of style, custom, and taste: In *Eric*, 'I would look carefully after phrases like "the pitiless waters", they are quite useless, and don't *really* add anything to the sense . . . [and] much will be got by a serious consideration of the epithets, adjectives I mean, it's wonderful how much is gained often by cutting them out.'[38] 'The thing I like least in [Beatrice], is where Godfrey is rather schoolboyishly talky with her, it may be in nature, but it is not good manners. Perhaps, married men in love are unmannerly. Perhaps reviewers in manuscripts are unmannerly too. I daresay one is.'[39] 'I am marking little turns of expressions that I think might be bettered: *clichés* of phrase like "rising to the occasion", etc.'[40] 'I hope *Beatrice* will come off. But I prefer your males. Don't let her flirt. Frank fornication were better.'[41] 'Here are some piddling attempts at bettering a few sentences or phrases, à prendre ou à laisser. I've read it very carefully, and the changes suggested satisfy my ear a little better than the text as it stands . . . the opening sentence should be broken up as too long.'[42] When Lang was writing some poetry for one of Haggard's tales, he responds to a suggestion from Haggard with this: 'I'll try – I'm not so sure about making the moral so awfully obvious though. The *sonnet* could not be added to, sonnets are only of 14 lines.'[43]

But perhaps the most valuable service Lang performed was to keep

Haggard's self-confidence up with little, genuine flatteries and the praise that Haggard particularly needed when he found himself under attack. Of *Cleopatra* Lang wrote: 'I know *I* couldn't write it, and I doubt if anyone could.'[44] When Haggard showed some misgivings about *Eric Brighteyes*, Lang wrote: 'Bosh! It is a rattling good story. . . . It is chock full of things nobody else could have done: indeed nobody else could have done any of it. . . . For heaven's sake, don't be disgusted with it, or me because I look at it through a microscope.'[45] On another occasion: 'You are in the same boat as Scott and Byron.'[46]

But the friendship did not benefit Haggard only. Lang stood in constant awe of his friend's prolific imagination, and sought to profit from it. Haggard in turn was delighted when he could be of service to Lang. Consequently Lang discussed the plots of his own imaginative ventures with Haggard and frequently sent Haggard plot outlines, manuscripts, and proofs for his opinion. For Lang knew that his strength lay in his critical powers, and although he needed no help in his scholarly work, he often asked Haggard to lend some fire for his imaginative works. Time and again, Lang's letters indicate that he sent Haggard proofs of his own – 'I send you five chapters of my romance' – asking that they be sent on to the publisher if Haggard found them adequate. 'Can I get any more flesh on the dry bones?'[47] 'I've worked in your dodge in my fairy tale; it's no more an extravaganza than anything you like. . . . Could you read it when typewritten?'[48] 'Don't worry your eyes with my stuff. . . . Indeed I don't know why I should bother you with it.'[49] 'I've written an article on Realism and Romance for the *Contemporary*. I'd like you to see the proofs, for various reasons when I get them. I *hope* it won't hurt Howells' feelings!'[50] In *Prince Prigio* (1889), Lang says in the Preface that ' "The Return of Benson" (Chapter XII) is the fruit of the research of the late Mr. Allan Quatermain,'[51] undoubtedly his way of acknowledging Haggard's assistance. Furthermore, there are in the fairy tale similarities to elements in Haggard's writing, and it is entirely probable that Haggard rewrote some of Lang's dialogue. There is also ample evidence that in 1895–96 Lang and Haggard were in close correspondence over Lang's romance about Joan of Arc, published as *A Monk of Fife*.

The two men never collaborated again after *The World's Desire*. They had talked a great deal of another partnership, particularly of doing another tale about Kôr. As early as 1890 Lang wrote: 'As to a Kôr romance wait to see if they'll stand the W.D. . . . I'll make a Kôr plot for fun.'[51] Later he wrote: 'I'll enter into a partnership on Kôr, whenever you like, if only one can get a good plot. . . . It's a good theme.'[53] In another letter, he writes: 'If we ever do *Kôr*, I must try to be more copious.'[54] But nothing ever came of it; each grew much too involved with his own work, and neither could take the time to give it serious thought. Even in Lang's later days, when Longman and Haggard grew worried about his low spirits, and Haggard tried to involve him in another collaboration, in hope of revivifying his old interests, Lang answered: 'Faire des objections c'est collaborer, but I don't think I could do more. Had I any ideas of Kôr long ago? "She," I think, is not easily raised.'[55] Haggard was too busy to keep after Lang, and the idea slept. Not until after Lang was gone did Haggard take up the idea of writing the tale they might have written together, *Wisdom's Daughter*, the last romance of She-Who-Must-Be-Obeyed, and dedicated it to Lang's memory.

On July 22, 1912, when he was working on his autobiography at Ditchingham, Haggard read in his morning paper that Lang had died suddenly in Scotland. So moved was he by the news that he sat down and wrote a chapter in his autobiography as a memorial to his dear friend. 'It is odd that only last Thursday, when I was in London, some vague anxiety concerning him prompted me to make an effort to see Lang. Having an hour to spare before my train left, I took a taxi-cab and drove to his house in Marloes Road, to find which his direction of many years ago used to be, "Walk down Cromwell Road till you drop, then turn to the right!" ' It was their last visit together. Not all men warmed to Lang, but to Haggard he was 'among men my best friend perhaps, and the one with whom I was most entirely in tune. . . . I reckon it as one of the privileges of my life to be able to call him [a friend].'[56]

The two men had been friends a long time: it was twenty-seven years since *King Solomon's Mines* had appeared. The attacks upon Haggard and Lang, the coupling of their names in parodies, the false accusations that Lang had written dozens of reviews for each of Haggard's books – none of these marred the friendship between them. An occasional letter from Lang, written at times of crisis either in his or Haggard's personal life, shows the deep affection Lang felt for his friend. On the death of his younger brother, 'my little brother,' as Lang called him, he turned to Haggard: 'I tell you because you are a good fellow if ever there was one and so was he . . . but please do not reply to this.'[57] On another occasion, Lang wrote Haggard that 'you have been more to me of what the dead friends of my youth were, than any other man, and I take the chance to say it, though not given to speaking of such matters.'

Although Haggard's and Lang's names were often linked humorously, not one of these expressions is remembered so well as a bit of doggerel by J. K. Stephen joining Haggard's name to Kipling's. Deploring the state of contemporary writing, Stephen wonders:

Will there never come a season
Which shall rid us from the curse
Of a prose which knows no reason
And an unmelodious verse:
When the world shall cease to wonder
At the genius of an Ass
And a boy's eccentric blunder
Shall not bring success to pass:

When mankind shall be delivered
From the clash of magazines,
And the inkstand shall be shivered
Into countless smithereens:
When there stands a muzzled stripling,
Mute, beside a muzzled bore:
When the Rudyards cease from kipling
And the Haggards ride no more?[58]

By February 1891, when this gentle abuse appeared in the *Cambridge Review*, Haggard and Kipling already had a good deal more in common, and they could both be amused by Stephen's wit.

Kipling, who was ten years younger than Haggard, provides the single exception to the latter's practice of associating with men older than himself. The two met in 1889, while Haggard and Lang were putting the finishing touches to *The World's Desire*. Though Kipling had achieved some literary fame in the East with his tales of Indian life, he arrived in London in October 1889 virtually unknown both to English literary circles and to the reading public. It did not take seasoned critics like Henley and Lang very long, however, to see in this moustached, bespectacled youth the makings of a literary giant, and they quickly took the twenty-three-year-old in tow. Lang shepherded him into the circle of Savile wits, and it was here, unquestionably, that Kipling and Haggard met.

Kipling read Haggard's *Cleopatra* even before he met its author, for he quotes from it in 'Her Little Responsibility,' which was published before he arrived in London.[59] Later, furthermore, in a parody of Bret Harte's 'Truthful James' which Kipling wrote to amuse his ever-widening circle of friends at the Savile, he alludes to Haggard's historical tale. But this was all in good fun, for Haggard entertained Kipling at a party in Redcliffe Square probably in early 1890, and in the following year Haggard supported Kipling's nomination for membership in the Savile. Even earlier, however, in a letter Kipling wrote, he alludes to three literary friends. 'London is a vile place,' he complains, 'and Anstey and Haggard and Lang and Co. are pressing on me the wisdom of identifying myself with some set.'[60]

But Kipling did not have to bother with planning a career; his fame was assured from the start. Within six months of his arrival in London he was the literary man of the day. Editors scrambled for his stories and verses, critics praised them and sought to meet the young genius from the East, and the reading public was star-struck over the new cadences and colloquial language in his verse.

Such observers saw Kipling's sudden rise as a threat to Haggard's fame; they predicted that Kipling would eclipse his contemporary. As early as November 18, 1889, John Addington Symonds wrote on the subject: 'Did I tell you of my making the acquaintance of Rudyard Kipling . . . a very extraordinary young man. . . . The Savile was all on the *qui vive* about him, when I lunched there once with Gosse. Rider Haggard appeared really aggrieved at a man with a double-barrelled name, odder than his own, coming up. Literally.'[61] Also, Henry James wrote from London to R. L. Stevenson in Samoa: 'We'll tell you all about Rudyard Kipling – your nascent rival. He has killed one immortal – Rider Haggard.'[62] But while Kipling and Haggard often appealed to the same audience, the texture, imaginative quality, and subject matter of their work were so different that one did not hurt the reputation or sales of the other. Neither the literary chitchat nor their own fame created any personal rivalry between the two, and both men later had only pleasant memories of their early acquaintance. Kipling recalled that 'I took to him at once, he being the stamp adored by children and trusted by men at sight; and he could tell tales, mainly about himself, that broke up the table.'[63]

Just as Andrew Lang destroyed all incoming letters, so did the Kiplings. Because the rule of burning in-letters was seldom broken, the friendship between Haggard and Kipling, like the one with Lang, is chronicled mainly in the letters written to Haggard,[64] and these give, at best, only a partial picture. The earliest extant letter must have been written in late spring 1891. In it Kipling thanks Haggard for a copy of *Eric Brighteyes*, which Haggard had left at the Savile for him. 'It's all as strong as wire rope,' says Kipling and, alluding to a minor objection he makes earlier in the letter, adds, '& 'twere impertinent of me to criticize.'

Haggard and Kipling, it seems, kept in touch through the years that Kipling and his American bride lived in Vermont (1892–96), though only one of the letters that passed between them survives. But after the Kiplings returned to England, and particularly after 1902, when they bought Bateman's, the home in Sussex where they would live out the remainder of their lives, the correspondence resumed and the friendship took on new depth. In July 1897 Kipling wrote to Haggard about an early draft of a poem and in the same letter asked Haggard's advice about housekeeping in South Africa, where he and his wife were planning a winter holiday. And in 1899 Kipling wrote enthusiastically about *A Farmer's Year*. But the two men not only wrote to each other; they must have met often in the mid- and late-'nineties. For Haggard these were years of politicking and business dealing in the City; he was much in London. Kipling, living in Rotting-dean, was within easy reach of London, and he too got up to town often. Meetings at the Savile, the Society of Authors, and at the homes of mutual friends were frequent. On May 20, 1898, Haggard was Chairman at a dinner of the Anglo-African Writers' Club at the Grand Hotel, and Kipling was guest of the evening. Haggard introduced Kipling to an overflow audience that included Sir Henry Bulwer, Sir Walter Peace, Agent-General of Natal, Sir B. W. Greenacre, Mayor of Durban, and other notables, and he read a telegram from Cecil Rhodes expressing his regret at not being present. Kipling had just returned from his second visit to South Africa and was to share his impressions with those present. Haggard toasted Kipling and called him 'a watch-man of our Empire.' Along with the report of the occasion in the following week's issue of the *African Review* appeared an anonymous poem in honour of Kipling in which Haggard was also mentioned:

A Humble Tribute

'I am but a 'umble waiter, Mr. Kiplin', that is all,
But I'm 'uman tho' I'm 'umble, an' I've got a 'eart an' brain;
An' I does a bit o' readin' of a evenin', off an' on,
An' on Sundays, for a instance, when I'm kept indoors by rain.

'I'm acquainted with your stories, an' by Gom, sir, they're A1!
I 'ave laughed, an' I 'ave cried, *an'* felt as creepy as can be.
There's Mulvaney, why, Lor' bless yer! 'e's a reg'lar pal o' mine,
So are Ortheris an' Learoyd, they are real live pals to me.

'I am not much 'and at poetry, but I 'ear as you're a poet;
(Once I 'eard a chap recitin' somethin' called "The Bolivar,"
But I can't say I remember what the verses was about,)
Still they say that you're a poet, sir, an' I'll take my oath you are.

'I 'ave always said, "Now Kiplin', 'e's a genius out an' out,
There's no bloomin' doubt about it, an' I'd say so to 'is face!
But o' course they're ain't no chanst o' that, cos why? well 'e's a gent,
While I'm a 'umble waiter, which I 'opes I knows my place."

'At the *Grand* on Monday evenin' I was fairly took aback,
An' I got no end excited when they said as you'd be there;
But you might 'ave knocked me backwards when they all flocked in to
       dine,
An' I found you at my table an' a-sittin' next the Chair.

'Oh! I waited on yer proper from the soup right to the end,
There was nothin' as yer wanted but you got in 'arf a mo.,
You'd the nicest cup o' saddle, you'd the pick o' the *menoo*,
An' I kep' yer glass a-brimmin'—tho' you takes yer liquor slow.

'Then I listened to yer speakin' (I was 'id behind the screen)
An' I said, "Well, this 'ere Kiplin', 'e's a *man*, an' no mistake";
An' I said, "Oh —— this waitin', chuck it, let's go out an' fight,
I should like to punch some fellow's 'ead for good old England's sake!"

'Now the Chairman, Mr. 'Aggard, 'e's a hauthor I admires,
I 'ave read 'is stories many times, I fairly dotes on "She,"
All the same—an' Mr. 'Aggard, 'e'll agree with this, I know—
For a general good all-rounder you're a greater man than 'e.

'Mr. Kiplin', Mr. Kiplin', ah! you little knew that night
'Ow I wanted just to speak to you an' tell you what I thinks,
I'd 'ave given my night's earnins' to 'ave 'ad a word with you,
I'd 'ave given up my week's, sir, to 'ave treated you to drinks.

'I am but a 'umble waiter, Mr. Kiplin', that is all,
But I'm 'uman tho' I'm 'umble, an' I've got a 'eart an' brain;
An' you've got one constant reader who can swear that you're a brick,
An' I'll say so to your face, sir, if I waits on you again!'[65]

When the Kiplings settled in the country, away from London, they needed practical advice about their land, and they sought it from Haggard.

> Rider Haggard would visit us from time to time [Kipling wrote later of this period], and give us of his ample land wisdom. I remember I planted some new apple trees in an old orchard, then rented by an Irishman, who at once put in an agile and hungry goat. Haggard met the combination suddenly one morning. He had gifts of speech and said very clearly that one 'might as well put Satan in an orchard as a goat.' I forget what he said about the tenants, but I know I acted on it.[66]

The letters that passed between them were full of practical questions and answers – not about literature, but about crops and vineyards, and show how Kipling appreciated Haggard's know-how.

I – alas! – hold land now which I trust you will see next summer [he writes on December 22, 1902]. An old house and a 25 acre farm of good hop land and fruit and a mill (water) that dates from 1196. The farm is let down and neglected: the tenant is a glib-tongued impostor and the buildings are disgraceful. I shall probably lose much in getting the farm into shape because if I grub out the hops no one will take it and if I don't I might as well keep a small Monte Carlo for hops are a demoralizing gamble. Now you see why your book [*Rural England*] touches me nearly. I shall have to put up at least two decent cottages in the place . . . and I *do* want to make it possible to rear clean & healthy men on my fraction of England. That is why I want to see you when we come back from the Cape.

Kipling obviously valued Haggard's advice about how best to manage his estate.

Yours is advice of gold [he writes a few days later]. Apples, as you say, are likely to be the game. I have 335 trees bearing already mostly good sorts but grievously in need of oil and lime-wash & salt and soap & shaping which they will get this spring.

But it's difficult about the tenant. You see there's that blessed mill which is a convenience for grinding pig food and any man who takes that wants a few acres of land. However I will lay my woes before you in the spring. Meanwhile I have to spend £239! (two thirty nine pounds!) on making neglected cottages habitable! Dog kennels aren't in it with their present state of filth.[67]

In 1904 Kipling took Haggard's advice about buying a vineyard. Kipling's failures and successes with animals, trees, and tenants are catalogued in his letters through the following years, and Kipling evinces respect for Haggard's advice on practical matters in 1916, no less than he had in 1902.

You know your letters are family possessions with us. . . . It's good to get in touch with you again. You'll be badly wanted down here in the spring to hear what we've tried to do in the farming line. . . . We all send our love, especially Elsie, and when spring comes (D.V.) we'll meet and collogue and let the years go by. I'd like to hear the gist of what Roosevelt said to you if you would dictate it.[68]

Haggard's farming books delighted both Rudyard and Carrie Kipling, and they both read them avidly.

I wish you knew how much the wife and I have enjoyed your 'Farmer's Year,' [Kipling wrote on November 12, 1899]. . . . In our tiny way we also have made experiments with land: and your figures made us groan sympathetically. Over & above the actual facts I don't think there has ever been a better book of the sane, common (which is uncommon) quiet humorous real country life in England. I've been going back & re-reading it slowly & leisurely: for the mere taste of it – same as Gilbert White.

Three days later Kipling added, 'I think the Year book [*A Farmer's Year*] will last – as a study of certain facts and conditions at a certain date in our history – like Tusser.'[69] When *Rural England* appeared, Kipling bracketed Haggard with England's two greatest agricultural economists.

Dear Cobbett-Young-Haggard. For the last week or more the wife and I have been reading *Rural England*, with deep joy (I don't mean on account of the state of things revealed) and admiration. I bought it lawfully in market overt and it stands with your Farmer's Year between Young's Agriculture of Sussex and Selbourne. I take off my hat to you deeply and profoundly because it's a magnum opus and altogether fascinating and warning and chock full of instruction. . . . Of course like all the people who have written to you from other countries, I am exceedingly disappointed and wroth and all the rest of it that you did not devote at least 200 pp. to my own county. Sussex, Sir, has been badly treated by you. You have neglected the fattening grounds of the Ouse and the meetings of the curious old riverleet or whatever they call it, which apportions the rental of these pastures once a year I think. Likewise you haven't made enough of our down shepherds nor of our fruit: nor of our most primitive peasantry. . . . I am going to have my Rural England bound in pigskin for real use. Have you thought of selling each county separately for a shilling with an appendix consisting of letters and information which have reached you later from men explaining industries & situations which you may have overlooked. I think it might be rather a success . . . it's an immense book in every way.[70]

When *A Gardener's Year* was published, Kipling again expressed his enthusiasm for Haggard's work. 'Everything in the book delights my sympathetic soul except your orchids,'[71] he wrote. But Haggard even got the Kiplings to share his love of orchids by giving them some of his plants.

The two men found common interests in more than farming. Their love of England made both of them bristle at the incompetence displayed by the denizens of Whitehall. Kipling and Haggard held like beliefs on many contemporary issues, and they took most seriously both England's mission to civilize the backward parts of the world and her struggle for supremacy among nations. Kipling, less by nature a campaigner than Haggard, did not stump the countryside making speeches and rarely expressed his indignation publicly in prose. His poetry was the medium for his sharp and stinging commentary on political events, and Kipling's collected verse is today a gallery where the monuments of England's political blunders are exhibited and bitterly denounced. Kipling's letters to Haggard reflect his indignation over the government's bungling through the years and his great concern for the national good. They show also that although Kipling himself would not sit on commissions, he read Haggard's reports eagerly and followed his friend's activities with keen interest.

I was glad to get your letter of the 4th and to learn that you approved of operations as conducted on my flank of the attack [Kipling wrote from Cape Town on January 28, 1902]. . . . Your side of the attack – the question of food supply – is as you say *the* vital one. You have the figures & facts & the influence: and for goodness sake keep on hammering at it. What makes me sick is what makes you sick – the way, to wit, in which the responsible politician admits the cold truth of one's contention & then explicitly says that he doesn't dare 'go in advance of public opinion' & so on.

Well here's luck! We need it.

Later that same year, a month after *Rural England* was published, Kipling was willing to help the cause of English agriculture with his poetic talents.

Your suggestion about the Rural Muse appeals to me mightily. I am slowly discovering England which is the most wonderful foreign land I have ever been in. As you say it has no grub and no trained men except a few days' supply of each and it spends its time telling ornate velvet-plush lies. But the man-question is serious. I entirely agree with you about the town-bred person. He has to spend half his time keeping fit outside his employment which ought to be making him fit while he works. If there is any way in which my Agriculture Muse may be of service later, why then as Virgil says 'Come on, oh (young) husbandman' and command me.

Six years later, after Haggard's report on afforestation had been published, they still shared the old indignation over the Government's blindness.

I am as you know *not* a lover of the present Govt [wrote Kipling]. . . . But what an England we could make if we could only get 1/2 of your programme put through. Forgive me if I seem a pessimist. They are all such a set of flagrant and persistent liars that I can't believe in their rectitude over anything. I shall be enormously pleased tho' if they develop any sparks of decency or gratitude towards you.

And later that same year, Kipling warned Haggard again against the ingratitude of politicians. 'You've got a long and a hard, but a very good row to hoe. Only remember that sooner or later you will be let down and given away and generally repudiated by the Beasts with whom you do now associate. They are only united on one thing and that is lying.'[72]

Already seeing eye to eye on many things, Kipling and Haggard found another cause in common in 1920, when a group of eminent Englishmen founded the Liberty League to combat the advance of Bolshevism. A long letter explaining the League's intentions appeared in *The Times*, above the signatures of its chairman, Haggard, and other founders, including Kipling, and on the following day, *The Times*[73] reported the League's inaugural meeting. This public joining of Haggard and Kipling led to another set of mildly satirical verses:

> 'Every Bolsh is a blackguard,'
>   Said Kipling to Haggard.
> 'And given to tippling,'
>   Said Haggard to Kipling.
>
> 'And a blooming outsider,'
>   Said Rudyard to Rider.
> 'Their domain is blood-yard,'
>   Said Rider to Rudyard.
>
> 'That's just what I say,'
>   Said the author of *They*.
> 'I agree; I agree,'
>   Said the author of *She*.[74]

Politics and agriculture aside, Kipling thought highly of Haggard's imagination, an opinion he expressed often.* Commenting on Haggard's *The Way of the Spirit* (1906), which was dedicated to him, Kipling testified to the power that Haggard's tales held over him. 'I did as I have done with a many of your books – simply surrendered myself to

---

* For Kipling's general opinion of Haggard's story-telling ability, see p. 15 above.

the joy of reading & read on. That's better than any criticism.'[75]
Returning the manuscript of *The Wanderer's Necklace*, Kipling praised
it too. 'The Necklace I like *immensely* – it all goes with a rush
& a whirl & holds like all the others of yours.'[76] Later, commenting on a play Haggard had written, Kipling shows himself
fascinated by the working of Haggard's imagination even in drama
form. ' "Oro" promises well. Gad what an undefeated and joyous
imagination you have! I want fuller details, please, of what Oro did
when he reentered upon life on the earth. . . . Can you send me a
typed scenario.'* Haggard's power to captivate Kipling was evident
time and time again, even during the war years. 'Thank you!' Kipling
wrote on January 9, 1916. 'I'd have to be pretty far gone before a
book of yours didn't take me altogether out of myself.' And returning
the manuscript of *When the World Shook*, the response is similar. 'A
thousand thanks for the privilege. As I told you yesterday it's as fresh
and as convincing as the work of a boy of 25 and it held me like a
drug. That's your d—d gift!'[77] Haggard's books were favourites not of
Kipling alone, but of his entire family, and Kipling reports that the
arrival of a new tale caused some pleasant competition at Bateman's.
'Dear old man – Just back from Edinburgh to find (and I've told
Elsie she isn't to touch or look at it till I've done) "Finished." Any
book of yours takes one out of oneself more potently than any drug.
I know and as soon as I'm finished with a d—d pile of accumulated
mail, I go to my study, and up & enjoy myself. Thank *you*, Sir.' Another
scramble took place over Haggard's *Moon of Israel*; after it appeared
Kipling wrote from Brown's Hotel in London.

* This letter, dated January 7, 1916, refers to Haggard's tale *When the World Shook*,
which he may, at the time, have been trying to adapt for the stage or screen. But I have
found no evidence that a drama or film version was ever produced. Haggard made other
unsuccessful efforts to turn his tales into stage productions, as two letters from W. B.
Yeats (Lockwood Collection) prove. The first is dated September 8:
   Dear Mr. Haggard: I have kept your plays too long for it to be right for me to
keep them longer. Neither would be possible at the Abbey, as I feared when I saw
you in London. I find that I have so much to say about them (or rather about the first
[word illegible] one) that I must wait to say it in person if you wish to hear it. I have
kept putting off writing thinking a few times to write at length but my sight has been
worse than usual, and there has been so much to do (Mr. Shaw has just left) that I
have given up the thought. Before I get to London you will probably have sent your
first play to some manager from whom my long delay has kept it. Yrs sy W. B. Yeats.
The second is undated:
   Dear Mr. Haggard: I send your two plays in the same post with this letter.
Have you thought of offering 'The Star of Egypt' [*Morning Star* (1910)] to Tree [?]
It is full of wild phantasy. It may interest you to know that a certain [name illegi-
ble], a Polish man of science was investigating what looks like a modern case of the
Double – the Ka I think you call it. A medium who is one of his patients is haunted
by a Doppelgänger [?] image of herself 3 feet high. . . .
In a letter dated March 21, 1910, Haggard wrote his Egyptologist friend, E. W. Budge:
'I am amusing myself dramatising "Morning Star." . . . Do you know of any instance of
a Ka demonstrating itself and assuming physical form during the life-time of its companion body, or are its manifestations purely post-mortem.' Huntington Collection.

E[lsie] bagged it first tho' I got it for myself. What *is* your secret, old man? It goes, and it grips and it moves with all the first freshness of youth and – I got into a row with the wife because I had to finish it in bed with the electrics turned on. It's ripping good and I'm d—d jealous . . . you've developed [that] which Scripture makes plain but which no one else dwells on – the essential turbulence & unaccommodativeness of the Israelites in their captivity. . . . Next time you come along bring your diary with you. I want to see how it [World War I] struck you day by day.[78]

The scuffle for Haggard's books continued, with, it seems, Carrie participating. When *The Virgin of the Sun* arrived, Kipling wrote, 'E. – trust her! – has swiped and stands guard over it! I shan't get it till she & Carrie have done. (My God! I wish I had your flaming vitality.)'[79]

It was not just Haggard's historical knowledge or story-telling ability that Kipling admired. Writing about a tale in the *Smith and the Pharaohs* volume, Kipling said, 'Best of all . . . I like Little Flower for its power and justice and humanity (it's a young gem) but, as ever, it is the amazing freshness of your work that always hits me between my envious eyes.'[80] Kipling was not completely uncritical of his friend's work, and often he made suggestions for improving the manuscripts he read. His opinion of Haggard the man was obviously high, and when he felt that Haggard the writer was not fulfilling himself, he would say so. Of *Wisdom's Daughter*, the last of the Ayesha tales, Kipling wrote at some length:

> The more I went through it the more I was convinced that it represented the whole sum and substance of your convictions along certain lines . . . the whole book is miles and miles above the head of the reader at large. . . . Damn it man – you have got the whole tragedy of the mystery of life under your hand, why not frame it in a wider setting? (This comes well from a chap who could not write a novel to save himself.)
>
> . . . You are a whale on parables and allegories and one thing reflecting another. Don't cuss me. You wanted to know what I thought and so I send it to you.[81]

The many similar experiences the two men had in common, the resemblances in the external circumstances of their lives, and a strong inner affinity strengthened the ties between them. Neither had had a university education, and both had spent the impressionable years of their youth in one of the distant colonies of the Empire, where they had gained experience and knowledge of imperial affairs. Each in turn had suffered the pangs of unrequited love, but both had made suitable matches for themselves. Both men had small families with whom they lived on country estates, close to the land. Each had lost his first-born child, and with the loss of Kipling's son in the war, the men shared another grief, the loss of an only son. Though Haggard was by no means the artist Kipling was, this fact did not divide them and seems even to have eluded them. What is more, both insisted that they were essentially 'un-literary,' and it was easy for them to see the superficial similarities, if not the qualitative differences, of their literary output. Each had written of new places and new things, each had grown popular with a newly shaped reading public, and to each fame had come overnight. They also shared a deep feeling for the land, the land as a symbol of England, not England the island but England the Empire, the England of Allan Quatermain and Umslopagaas, of Tommy Atkins and Kim.

But Kipling and Haggard had something else in common. Haggard shared with this friend something he could not share even with Lang, the gift of imagination. Haggard, and even more Kipling, could not discuss his literary promptings with many friends, and certainly neither Haggard nor Kipling explored with anyone else outside his immediate family the shadowy recesses of what Haggard called his 'second sight' and Kipling his 'daemon.' Generally, Kipling shied away entirely from discussing matters of a deeply spiritual or psychic nature, for his sister, 'Trix,' had suffered greatly because of her attraction to psychic phenomena. The shadowy problems never really left Kipling and crept into his tales time and again, but Haggard was the only human being with whom he talked about them at length. Haggard, on the other hand, fanned the psychic spark within himself, indulged it and let it influence his life in many ways; but it seemed that he, too, saved most of his thoughts on the subject for Kipling. There is no question that the long afternoons they spent together in Kipling's study were full of talk about reincarnation, spiritualism, and fourth-dimensional psychic promptings they both felt, and that these afternoons invariably gave rise to much of the strange atmosphere of mystery that infuses many of their stories.

Haggard never wrote a *World's Desire* with Kipling. But although the two did not collaborate in the formal sense, they quite naturally consulted each other about their own work, often helped each other in plotting tales, and even wrote in each other's company. Speaking of Haggard in his short autobiography, Kipling said, 'We found by accident that each could work at ease in the other's company. So he would visit me, and I him, with work in hand; and between us we could

even hatch out tales together – a most exacting test of sympathy.'[82]
Writing some two decades earlier, before the friendship had grown to
maturity, Haggard said much the same thing.

> Among my pleasantest recollections during the last few years
> [Haggard is writing in 1912] are those of my visits to the Kiplings,
> and one that they paid me here, during which we discussed every-
> thing in heaven above and earth beneath . . . we do not fidget each
> other. Thus only last year Kipling informed me that he could work
> as well when I was sitting in the room as though he were alone,
> whereas generally the presence of another person while he was
> writing would drive him almost mad.[83]

An entry in Haggard's diary of the same period reports specifically on
one such occasion. 'On Sunday and Monday I sat in his study while he
worked and after a while he got up and remarked to me that my
presence did not bother him a bit; he supposed because we were two of
a trade. He told me I was the only literary person with whom he could
associate at all.'[84] In later years, after Kipling suffered the loss of his
son, he kept even more to himself, and his circle of friends grew much
smaller. His study at Bateman's, lined with books and filled with hard
wooden furniture, a long work-table, a settee, and two or three globes,
became more and more inviolate to family and friend alike. But Haggard
still needed no invitation to visit, and he would spend an occasional
long week-end with the Kiplings, sometimes on his way from St.
Leonards to Ditchingham, or else when he made a point of going
down from London expressly for a visit. These days he spent largely
with Kipling himself in the study, discussing the philosophical problems of life, Empire, religion, immortality, reincarnation, and other
matters. Here they wrote out plots together, and sitting at the long
table, passed papers back and forth, for the one or the other to read and
perhaps add to. Here they read their tales aloud to each other, here they
speculated on the outcome of the war, and here they shared the grief it
brought.

Haggard's war diary, some of the letters that passed between the
two men, and a few quarto sheets of stationery with scribbled plot outlines and other jottings which Haggard judiciously saved from extinction
enable us to recapture the atmosphere of Kipling's study when both men
worked there together and something of the thoughts and feelings they
shared. After one of his visits to Bateman's Haggard wrote in his diary:

> Most of the day I have spent with the Kiplings at Bateman's.
> Rudyard is not well. . . . Seated together in his study in the

old house at Bateman's, we had a most interesting four hours together while he fiddled about with fishing tackle with which he tries to catch trout in the brook. There are two men left living in the world with whom I am in supreme sympathy. Theodore Roosevelt and Rudyard Kipling. The rest . . . have gone. What did we talk of? So many things that it is difficult to summarize them. Chiefly they had to do with the soul and the fate of man. Rudyard apparently cannot make up his mind about these things. On one point, however, he is perfectly clear. I happened to remark that I thought this world was one of the hells. He replied he did not *think*, he was *certain* of it. . . . As for the future he is inclined to let the matter drift. . . . His humility is very striking. We were talking of our failings. I said that what grew on me from day to day was a sense of my own utter insufficiency, of complete humiliation both in the case of those things that I had done and left undone. . . . I commented on the fact that he had wide fame and was known as 'the great Mr. Kipling,' which should be a consolation to him. He thrust the idea aside with a gesture of distrust. 'What is it worth – what is it all worth?' he answered. Moreover he went on to show that anything which any of us did *well* was no credit to us: that it came from somewhere else: 'We are only telephone wires'. As an example he instanced (I think) 'Recessional' in his own case and 'She' in mine. 'You didn't write *She* you know,' he said. 'Something wrote it – through you!' or some such words.

. . . He opined in his amusing way, that if the present taxation, etc., goes on much further, he and I should be seen on opposite sides of the Strand selling 'Recessional' and 'She' for our daily bread. How interesting it would be to have a shorthand report of such a three hours' conversation as ours, . . . of which I can only recall a point here and there. . . . I believe honestly that outside of his own family, there is no one living to whom Rudyard opens his heart except to myself. Practically he lacks intimate friends, it is not in his nature to make them; he said he could count those he cared for 'on my fingers', although all mankind interested him.

. . . He parted from me with much affection and said how delighted he was to have had the opportunity of a good mental and spiritual clean out. So was I.[85]

Later that year, just after the armistice was declared, Haggard recorded his impressions of another visit

I have been spending the day at Bateman's. . . . As usual, we discussed all things in Heaven and earth. . . . I took this diary over, as R. had asked me to do, & read him passages of it, till I was tired. These interested him greatly.

After the reading I happened to say to him that I wished I were a poet, as so many things occurred to me of which I should like to make poems. R. answered in these words, as nearly as I can remember them: 'Don't you see, Rider, that much of what you write, in your reflections, etc., is poetry, & very fine poetry? Only the rhyme is lacking; the fall of the sentences and the essentials of poetry are all there, also the poetic imagination. You do not chance to have the gift of rhyme as I have it, & I'm glad of it, as I should not like your competition.' (This he said jokingly.) ... He and the others were full of the 'Moon of Israel,' which they seem to know much better than I do myself; no single point in the tale has escaped R's piercing attention.... 'All the same,' I answered, 'seeing how poorly many of the critics seem to rate me, you would not dare to say over your name that you thought me a great writer?' '*Wouldn't I just*, if it came my way to do so!' he exclaimed. Well, it is pleasant to have one competent admirer left now that Andrew Lang is dead.

... A long talk with Kipling is now one of the greatest pleasures I have left in life, but I don't think he talks like that with anyone else; indeed he said as much to me.[86]

In the course of their association, Kipling suggested the idea for at least one of Haggard's tales (*When the World Shook*), he took a considerable hand in plotting five others (*The Ghost Kings, Red Eve, Allan and the Ice-Gods, The Mahatma and the Hare, The Way of the Spirit*), and he read (or was read[87]) at least six stories in manuscript (*Child of Storm, The Wanderer's Necklace, When the World Shook, Wisdom's Daughter, The Way of the Spirit*, and *Moon of Israel*). For this much we have evidence. 'On my return to England [from his second trip to Egypt in 1904],' Haggard tells us, 'I wrote "The Way of the Spirit" ... [a book] that interested him [Kipling] very much. Indeed he and I hunted out the title together in the Bible, as that of "Renunciation," by which it was first called, did not please him.'[88] But of all the help Haggard received from Kipling, the most interesting is in the plotting of three of Haggard's tales, *The Ghost Kings* (1908), *Red Eve* (1911), and *Allan and the Ice-Gods* (1927). Because these tales are so widely separated in time, it is quite possible that Haggard got help from Kipling on other tales that he wrote between 1908 and 1927. The evidence of these three, however, is quite clear. Haggard himself mentions Kipling's assistance on *The Ghost Kings* in his autobiography. He reports that late in 1905, he entered a nursing home for an operation. 'When I escaped from that nursing home,' he later wrote, 'very feeble and with much shattered nerves, I went to stay with my friend Lyne Stivens[89] to recuperate, and thence for a day or two to Kipling's. Here I remember we compounded the plot of "The Ghost Kings" together, writing down our ideas in alternate sentences upon the same sheet of foolscap.'[90] The foolscap Haggard mentions is preserved.[91] Actually there are four pages (three quarto sheets) on which the story is plotted in precise detail. At the top of the first page, in Kipling's handwriting, are two titles. 'The Shapes' is crossed out and over it is written 'The Ghost Kings.' Then seventeen lines in Kipling's hand outline the beginning of the tale; Haggard's hand then takes up the plot and carries it on for some fifty-four lines, leaving off in the middle of a sentence, where Kipling's hand again takes up and finishes the plot in some additional twenty-eight lines, ending with the word *curtain* and a flourish of the pen. On the reverse side of the second sheet, some plot emendations appear in Haggard's hand.

Just how much Kipling helped with *Red Eve* is not entirely clear; we are certain, however, that he created or helped create the character of Murgh, as a sheet of Bateman's stationery indicates. For evidence there is the derivation of Murgh's name, looking like a genealogical chart. The two men, we may infer, started with the idea of 'Death' and worked their way through 'Morgue' to 'Murgh.' It is all in Kipling's writing, and is arranged thus:

Death's name

	Takht		Adm		
Taung			Adam		
Maung	Rukhm		M ada		
Paung	Mar		Fa		
	Tarkoth		Koth	Kaf Salm	
	Koth	Koth	Kaf		
	Murth		Morg		
Morgue		Murg			
	Murg		Murg		*Murgh* (name chosen)

In addition to the name chart, there is a pencil sketch of the head of Murgh made by Kipling and very like the word description of Murgh in the book. In Haggard's hand are the following notes:

Title — El Murgh
     The Herald
     The Ambassador

Wears gleaming black furs ——
His hands hid in perfumed gloves [illegible word in parentheses after *gloves*]
Big quiet large boned man
Had interview with Pope

And over on one side, in Haggard's hand, is written: 'Bateman's/ Kipling's idea of *Murgh, 5.10.08.*'[92]

Kipling seems to have given Haggard the most elaborate assistance on *Allan and the Ice-Gods*, which they worked over on Haggard's visit to Bateman's in February 1922. The evidence rests in a group of seven pages (four quarto sheets) containing detailed plotting, alternating between Haggard's and Kipling's handwriting; three pencil sketches; a list in Kipling's hand of the characters of the tale, with accompanying phrases that either explain the meaning of their names or give a thumbnail description (e.g. 'WHAKA – a kind of ill-omen – one who howls; PITOKITE – a churl[;] one of the unlucky'); and a series, also in Kipling's hand, of suggested manuscript changes. On the reverse side of one page, Haggard wrote: 'Synopsis of story drawn up by Rudyard K & myself at Batemans [Feb. 1922] H. Rider Haggard.' Of particular interest is the fact that the larger part of the writing is in Kipling's hand. When Haggard returned from the visit to Bateman's, he acknowledged his debt to his friend in an entry in his diary: 'I never knew a man so full of "light" as Kipling, nor anyone quite so quick at seizing and developing an idea. He has a marvellously fertile mind. We spent a most amusing two hours over the plot and I have brought home the results in several sheets of MS. written by him and myself.'[93]

Because we know that the two men were sympathetic, that Kipling enjoyed reading his work aloud to close friends and family, and that he helped Haggard with his tales, it is hard to believe that Kipling did not consult his friend about his own work and that Haggard did not return the courtesy of letting Kipling benefit from his own prolific imagination. Carrie Kipling's careful selection of the papers that would be kept for posterity may have put an end to the possibility of determining the extent to which Kipling accepted help from Haggard. But some threads of evidence do survive, and these lead to interesting speculations.

In late June and early July 1897, Kipling (in Rottingdean) worked over a poem around the refrain 'Lest we forget.' There were many interruptions, and the verse did not shape easily. Not until July 16 did he arrive at a satisfactory version.[94] The poem was his 'Recessional,' and when it was published in *The Times* on July 17, it immediately became the hymn of the nation. A week earlier, before he had arrived at the completed version, Kipling wrote to Haggard to explain what he wanted to get across in the poem.

> Dear Haggard Your note did me much good – and thank you for it.
>
> I've just come off a fortnight with the Channel Squadron off the North Coast of Ireland – rather a jolly time. Now, any nation save

ourselves, with such a fleet as we have at present, would go out
swiftly to trample the guts out of the rest of the world; and the fact
that we do not seems to show that even if we aren't very civilized,
we're about the one power with a glimmering of civilization in us.
As you say, we've always had it somewhere in our composition. But
my objection to that hymn is that it may be quoted as an excuse for
lying down abjectly at all times and . . . seasons and taking what any
other country may think fit to give us. What I wanted to say was:—
'Don't gas but be ready to give people snuff' . . . and I only covered
the first part of the notion. [95]

The letter clearly implies that Kipling had sent 'Recessional' in an even
earlier letter, undoubtedly to get Haggard's opinion of it, and that
Haggard had already commented on it once.

In two different places, Kipling acknowledges that reading Haggard's
Nada the Lily helped give him the idea for the *Jungle Books*, his most
popular tales to this day.

It chanced that I had written a tale about Indian Forestry work
which included a boy who had been brought up by wolves [Kipling
writes in his autobiography]. In the stillness, and suspense, of the
winter of '92 some memory of the Masonic Lions of my childhood's
magazine, and a phrase in Haggard's *Nada the Lily*, combined with
the echo of this tale. After blocking out the main idea in my head,
the pen took charge, and I watched it begin to write stories about
Mowgli and animals, which later grew into the *Jungle Books*. [96]

Closer to the time when he composed the *Jungle Books*, Kipling acknowledged his debt in a letter to Haggard. 'It was a chance sentence of yours
in *Nada the Lily*,' he writes from Vermont in 1895, 'that started me off
on a track that ended in my writing a lot of wolf stories. You remember
in your tale where the wolves leaped up at the feet of a dead man sitting
on a rock? Somewhere on that page I got the notion. It's curious how
things come back again, isn't it? I meant to tell you when we met: but
I don't remember that I ever did.' [97]

Both Haggard's and Kipling's tales of wolf men are remarkable
expressions of their individual imaginations, but there is a striking
similarity between characters the two men create (Mowgli and Galazi,
for example) and a close relationship between some of the incidents.

Haggard's notebooks and war diaries reveal that Kipling sometimes
discussed his plots with him and read his tales aloud to him before
publication. In one such entry Haggard wrote: 'We talked a great deal
on many subjects, making plots for books etc. He read me some of his

plays and we discussed others, especially one that would deal with the fall of the British Empire.'[98]

And there are many more suggestions of Haggard in Kipling's tales. Anna M. Weygandt, in her study of *Kipling's Reading*, realizes that Kipling's 'genuine enthusiasm' for Haggard's tales was bound to have an effect upon his own imagination. 'If Haggard could supply an impulse . . . [for the Mowgli stories],' Miss Weygandt says, 'he must indeed have meant much to Kipling.' She recognizes the influence of *Allan Quatermain* (though she misspells the hero's name), *She* and *King Solomon's Mines* in other works by Kipling,[99] but there are also similarities in the stories of reincarnation the two men wrote, in their Boer tales, and in a remarkable tale each wrote about communicating with spirits in their cosmic resting-places by means of telegraphy.

Haggard's affection for Kipling and the kinship between the two men is perhaps best reflected in Haggard's dedication to his friend in *The Way of the Spirit* (1906). It is worth noting that it is dated August 14, 1905, quite early in the annals of the friendship:

> My dear Kipling, – Both of us believe that there are higher aims in life than the weaving of stories well or ill, and according to our separate occasions strive to fulfil this faith.
>
> Still, when we talked together of the plan of this tale, and when you read the written book, your judgement thereof was such as all of us hope for from an honest and instructed friend – generally in vain.
>
> So, as you found interest in it, I offer it to you, in token of much I cannot write. But you will understand.

Kipling and Lang supplied Haggard with the understanding he seldom got within his family circle and with the firm props his ego required. Haggard, in turn, offered them a friendship and companionship they enjoyed and appreciated. Haggard's relations with Lang and Kipling were vastly different, of course, because Lang and Kipling were vastly different men. But in each of his two close literary friends Haggard found the qualities of person, mind and imagination that he much admired. That Haggard could enjoy the friendship of both speaks for his own breadth of character and interest; that he could make his way so firmly into their lives and evoke the devotion and affection from two men so staunch in principle, so firm in taste, and so discriminating in friendship attests perhaps more than anything else to his remarkable appeal as a human being.

One contemporary man of letters Haggard never met was Stevenson 'To my sorrow I never met . . . [him] face to face,' Haggard wrote, 'always we just missed each other.' But Stevenson read Haggard's tales with enthusiasm, and soon letters passed between them. Some of these, again the ones which Haggard received, have survived. The first, undated, came from Skerryvore, Bournemouth, soon after *King Solomon's Mines* appeared.

Dear Sir, – Some kind hand has sent me your tale of Solomon's Mines; I know not who did this good thing to me; and so I send my gratitude to headquarters and the fountainhead. You should be more careful; you do quite well enough to take more trouble, and some parts of your book are infinitely beneath you. But I find there flashes of a fine weird imagination and a fine poetic use and command of the savage way of talking: things which both thrilled me. The reflections of your hero before the battle are singularly fine; the King's song of victory a very noble imitation. But how, in the name of literature, could you mistake some lines from Scott's 'Marmion' – ay, and some of the best – for the slack-sided, clerical-cob effusions of the Rev. Ingoldsby? Barham is very good, but Walter Scott is vastly better. I am, dear sir,

Your obliged reader,
Robert Louis Stevenson[100]

Haggard wrote back (he had not sent Stevenson the book, he tells us in his autobiography) pointing out that Allan Quatermain's 'habit' of attributing various quotations to the only two works of literature he knew, the Old Testament and the *Ingoldsby Legends*, was a 'literary joke.' Stevenson, in his turn, replied, with the kind of advice Haggard often received and too often ignored:

Dear Mr. Haggard, – Well, yes, I have sinned against you; that was the part of a bad reader. But it inclines me the more to explain my dark saying. As thus:

You rise in the course of your book to pages of eloquence and poetry; and it is quite true that you must rise from something lower; and that the beginning must infallibly (?) be pitched low and kept quiet. But you began (pardon me the word) slipshod. If you are to rise, you must prepare the mind in the quiet parts, with at least an accomplished neatness. To this you could easily attain. In other words, what you have still to learn is to take trouble with those parts which do not excite you.

Excuse the tone of a damned schoolmaster, and believe me,

Yours truly,
Robert Louis Stevenson

But Haggard could not be remade, or even altered, not by Stevenson, Lang, Henley, or anyone else.

The next letter from Stevenson is almost meaningless to us, its frame of reference lost, and even Haggard did not know in later years what it referred to. It also is from Bournemouth and undated; it strikes a decidedly more friendly tone than the earlier letters. These are the intelligible passages:

> I come rarely to town, and am usually damned sick when I do. But if I can, I'll try to see you. (I know a cousin of yours here by the way.)
>
> What are you about? I am again at a boys' story; but I've been a year at it already and may be longer. [In a postscript, he adds] ... Further reflection on 'K.S.M.' makes me think you are one who gets up steam slowly. In that case, when you have your book finished, go back and rewrite the beginning up to the mark.
>
> My case is reverse: I always begin well, and often finish languidly or hurriedly.

Another letter from Stevenson to Haggard must be dated about 1892; it comes from Vailima Plantation, Samoan Islands, and it too bears a friendly tone:

> Dear Haggard, – In cleaning up the hideous mess which accumulates about the man of letters I came on the enclosed sheet. Its filthiness will indicate its age. But there is internal evidence which to me dates it still further back; and that is the reference to your brother Bazett. I now know him well and regard him with the most sincere and lively affection and respect. Indeed we are companions in arms and have helped each other back and forth in some very difficult and some very annoying affairs. This has given a wonderful jog to my sense of intimacy with yourself until I begin to have a difficulty in remembering that I have never seen you. Two remarks and I leave my filthy enclosure to speak for itself. First, the equations on the fly-leaf were not in the least intended for you – they're pieces of a lesson in the Samoan language – and you must kindly regard them as non-existent. Second, 'Nada the Lily' is AI.

Unfortunately, Haggard could not in later years remember what 'the filthy enclosure' was. Bazett, Haggard's elder brother, had taken a government post in Samoa, and as Lord Commissioner became a friend of the Stevensons.* In 1893 the Stevensons and some of their friends, by way of a jest, concocted a community romance in which Bazett is the hero, which when they finished they had printed. It is a satire on Samoan life entitled *An Object of Pity; or, The Man Haggard,* 'A Romance. By Many Competent Hands. Imprinted in Amsterdam.' A second volume, written entirely by Bazett Haggard, is *Objects of Pity; or, Self and Company.* 'By a Gentleman of Quality.' Stevenson sent both of these to Haggard with a letter.

> Dear Rider Haggard, – I send you herewith a couple of small (and, so to speak, indecent) volumes in which your brother and I have been indulging in the juvenile sport of shying bricks at each other. *Honi soit qui mal y pense,* say I. And I hope you will say the same. We were a large party, with nothing to do – Lady Jersey, my wife, Captain Leigh, your brother and I, and Mrs. Strong,[101] my daughter in law – and that which we wrote was not according to wisdom. I have heard some of yours called in question for steepness; here is your revenge.

A letter from Bazett accompanied Stevenson's and the volumes.

> Dear Rider, – Enclosed letter from R. L. Steven. speaks for itself. He says we all had nothing to do. He is wrong there. *They* wrote the 'Object of Pity' on the days I was at work at Comn. I did not write my letter till 3 [word illegible] after, when Stevenson insisted on having it printed and took it to Sydney and had it printed. I was riled at being called 'an object of Pity' *rather,* so set to and gave them a Roland for their Oliver. . . . These books are R.L.S.'s gift to you – write him a line. . . .
>
> Your loving brother,
> Bazett M. Haggard.
>
> Stevenson and I are great friends; he is such a good chap, but *as* I say of him in my book.

* Fanny Stevenson wrote of Bazett as 'a determinedly patriotic Englishman . . . [who] wants an English protectorate [in Samoa].' But more important, he was a most cheerful person with a devil-may-care attitude, and as 'the gaily indiscreet British Land Commissioner' fitted well into the Bohemian circle which grew up around the Stevensons. Fanny Stevenson recalled an occasion when Bazett 'had had more drink than was good for him, and besides was quite intoxicated with excitement and romantic feeling.' He was a frequent visitor at the Stevensons', and at one point inherited a Moslem cook of theirs. '[Bazett] Haggard was rather a bull in a china shop in relations with his government,' writes an eminent Stevenson scholar. Another member of the Stevenson circle in Samoa remembered him as 'a great character . . . [whose] universe . . . revolved round his native county, Norfolk, whence sprang all that was finest in the British race, particularly the Haggard brothers . . . [who] had, he said, all loud voices, and on some occasion won a contested election by the simple process of shouting. . . . Apart from this quaint strain of simple satisfaction with himself,' the observer added, '. . . he was the kindest of men.' Fanny and Robert Louis Stevenson, *Our Samoan Adventure,* ed. Charles Neider (1955), pp. 117, 199–200; Furnas, pp. 37–38, 380, 399; and Dowager Countess of Jersey [Margaret Elizabeth Child-Villiers], *Fifty-One Years of Victorian Life* (1922), pp. 293–294.

Rider studied the volumes 'with zeal' but was 'unable to make head or tail of them.'

That Stevenson and Bazett should appear together in print is ironic. In a postscript to the first letter on page 210 above, Stevenson asks, 'How about a deed of partnership?' The suggestion was probably made in jest, and a collaboration between Stevenson and Rider Haggard would hardly have been congenial, considering their extremely different temperaments and literary attitudes. Certainly Haggard would have welcomed the opportunity to meet Stevenson, and for that matter, the chance to collaborate with him. His explanation of Stevenson's 'partnership' suggestion is interesting:

This 'deed of partnership' on the face of it would seem to suggest some scheme of collaboration. Yet I do not think that this could have been the case – for the following reason. I remember that my late brother Bazett, who was afterwards an intimate friend of Stevenson's in Samoa, told me that someone, I know not who, had written to him [Stevenson] suggesting that he and I should collaborate in a story, and that he had returned an angry and offensive answer to the suggestion, as I daresay it was quite natural that he should do. This answer, it seems, had however weighed upon his mind. At any rate Bazett informed me that Stevenson on several occasions spoke to him with deep regret as to his petulant reply. This is all I know, or at any rate all that I can recollect, of the matter.

The only other extant items touching the relationship between Stevenson and Haggard pertain to *Nada the Lily* and *The World's Desire*. On May 25, [1893?] Lang wrote to Haggard, 'I have just had a letter from Samoa, only I've mislaid it, in which Stevenson expresses devotion to your brother, and to Chaka, as in the scene where he bewails his mama. He adds a lot of matter not very intelligible about my own work, but asked me to send this message on Chaka and your kinsman.' Stevenson's reaction to *The World's Desire* also came in a letter from Lang, accompanied by a poem which Stevenson had penned for the occasion. The poem, dialect and all, is a typical Stevenson prank.

1.

Awdawcious Odyshes,
Your conduc' is vicious,
Your tale is suspicious
     An' queer.

Ye ancient sea-roamer,
Ye dour auld beach-comber
Frae Haggard to Homer
    Ye veer.

2.

Sic veerin' and steerin'!
What port are ye neerin'
As frae Egypt to Erin
    Ye gang?
Ye ancient auld blackguard,
Just see whaur ye're staggered
From Homer to Haggard
    And Lang!

3.

In stunt and in strife
To gang seeking a wife —
At your time o' life
    It was wrang.
An' see! Fresh afflictions
Into Haggard's descriptions
An' the plagues o' the Egyptians
    Ye sprang!

4.

The folk ye're now in wi'
Are ill to begin wi'
Or to risk a hale skin wi'
    In breeks —
They're blacker and hetter —
(Just ask your begetter)
And far frae bein' better
    Than Greeks.

5.

There's your *Meriamun*:
She'll mebbe can gammon
That auld-furrand salmon
    Yoursel';
An' *Moses* and *Aaron*
Will gie ye your fairin'
Wi' fire an' het airn
    In Hell.

I refuse to continue longer [Stevenson adds in the letter]. I had an excellent half-verse there, but couldn't get the necessary pendant, and anyway there's no end to such truck.[102]

All in all, it is a great pity that Stevenson and Haggard never did meet, for one feels that Stevenson, who grew to adore Lang, collaborated at length with Henley, and had great affection for Edmund Gosse, would have taken to Haggard and that each would have helped fan the other's imagination.

The Edmund Gosses were the Haggards's close friends from early London days when the Haggards lived in Redcliffe Square. Actually Haggard and Gosse must have been acquainted as early as 1886, for on December 29 of that year Haggard sent Gosse a copy of *She* with a friendly note. When the Haggards went to Mexico, they left Jock in the Gosses's care, and it was they who had to report the news of his death. Very little correspondence survives between Haggard and Gosse, probably because the men met frequently in London. But we do know that the Haggards visited the Gosses often and that the Gosses came occasionally to Ditchingham. Edmund Gosse was a photography enthusiast in the early days of the portable camera. He took pictures almost everywhere he went and assembled photographs of almost everyone he knew. Some of these survive of the Haggards and their friends in striking poses on the Ditchingham lawn.[103]

There is however another record of the friendship. The Gosses, from the earliest days of their marriage, gave Sunday afternoon tea parties at their home at 29 Delamere Terrace, across from the Paddington Canal. For forty-five years, these Sunday gatherings were a London institution, particularly among literary people. Edmund Gosse, a very orderly person, kept a record of each of the parties in a thick, narrow book known now as the 'Book of Gosse.'[104] Here are recorded the dates of each occasion and lists of all the guests present. The groups vary from small, intimate dinners to assemblies of eighty-five, and they span the years 1875 to 1920. Some of the entries are underscored, Gosse's way of indicating those who stayed on for supper. Rider and Louisa Haggard appear frequently. Haggard appears alone as early as March 25, 1888, and he reappears either alone or with Louisa (sometimes Miss Hector is with them) on dozens of occasions through the years, until March 30, 1906, the last entry of Haggard's name.

Although the Book gives only the guests' names, it is interesting to note who was present with Haggard at Delamere Terrace. One early entry reports an interesting collection of literary lights: Thomas Hardy, Henry James, Andrew Lang, Walter Pater, Robert Bridges, and Rider Haggard;[105] and later entries show that Haggard shared the Gosses's hospitality with the following: Mr. and Mrs. Humphry Ward, Austin Dobson, Max Beerbohm, Walter Raleigh, J. K. Stephen, Aubrey Beardsley, Carrie Balestier (before she became Mrs. Rudyard Kipling), Lawrence Alma-Tadema, the Dutch-English painter, Sir Walter

Armstrong, the art critic and biographer of Millais, A. C. Benson, and Sir Henry Redvers Buller, the general who commanded English forces in the Boer War. Haggard had dinner at the Gosses' with S. R. Crockett and Frances Hodgson Burnett, author of *Little Lord Fauntleroy*, among others. The Book also contains entries for the club luncheons Edmund Gosse gave for friends. Haggard appears at three of these, the first two at the National Club and the third at the House of Lords.[106] Also present at one or more of these were Sidney Low and Aubrey Beardsley.

W. E. Henley does not seem to have been present at any of the Gosses's Sunday gatherings, but he and Haggard were, all the same, well acquainted. True, they could not have been close friends, and yet there was more than a business relationship between them. Henley was clearly responsible for getting Cassell's to publish *King Solomon's Mines* in 1885. But in 1887, when *She* appeared, he was disillusioned by Haggard's careless craftsmanship, and he said so in the 'London Letter,' a column he wrote for the American journal, the *Critic*. He minced no words about Haggard's latest romance: 'So many "foolish faces of praise" have not, that I remember, been crowded about a book. With Ayesha, the heroic Barmaid – the Waitress in Apotheosis – numbers of intelligent men are in love, as the author himself appears to be; and what is bad in the record of her adventures is, as it seems, as much admired as what is good.'[107] Haggard probably did not see the column, and if he did, it is not likely that he knew who its author was. At any rate, a friendliness continued between the two men. On June 8, 1888, Haggard wrote Henley to tell him that he very much enjoyed his recently published *Book of Verse*,[108] and on the following day, Henley replied: 'I *do* care for your approbation very much; for I do not think I should have it if my verses hadn't a kind of basis in life. Lang hates 'em, I believe; and I shall tell him of your note with pride and glee.'[109]

In 1889 Henley became editor of the *Scots* (later the *National*) *Observer*. Lang contributed to the *Observer*, Henley continued to praise Lang's work as he had always done, and soon the *Scots Observer* suggested that Lang be appointed to the Chair of English Literature in Glasgow University.[110] But in that same year, a break occurred between Henley and Lang. Henley 'was impatient with ... Andrew Lang,' John Connell tells us, and about this time Henley wrote to Charles Whibley: 'I am completely sick of Andrew Lang and care not if I never hear from him again. I do *not* believe he wishes me well.'[111] The last of Lang's signed contributions to the *Observer* appeared on May 4, 1889, and his subsequent letters to Haggard also reflect the harsh feelings that had grown up between him and Henley.

But the break between Henley and Lang did not, it seems, affect Haggard's relationship with Henley. Though the *Scots Observer* slated

Colonel Quaritch, V.C. in December 1888,[112] four months later it devoted its 'Modern Men' feature to a profile of Rider Haggard, where it hails him as an innovator and gives him the palm for bringing romance back to life. The article is worth noting at some length, for though unsigned, it is (as are the notices of Haggard's books in the *Scots* and *National Observer*) written in Henley's distinctive style.

> Why should the critics be so much scandalized and astonished at Mr. Haggard's success? . . . It is no new thing for the novel of analysis and the romance of action to flourish side by side. . . .[Yet] no author in our time has had an odder fate. Accepted with open arms by the great mass of readers – accepted, as numerous signs would seem to indicate, by the responsible leaders of his profession – Mr. Haggard has been forced, to a degree scarcely paralleled of late, to run the gauntlet of petty newspaper criticism. If one should believe certain sections of the London evening press, for instance, one would say that there was no novelist of our age who had been so completely broken, crushed, pulverized, and blown away for ever by the Rhadamanthuses of Grub Street as the author of *She*, who, nevertheless, in a mysterious fashion, like some heroine of his own, after undergoing all forms of extinction seems to reappear smiling and as fresh as ever, to be reduced to powder once more on the following evening. [The article continues with elaborate praise for Haggard, accusing his critics of being both jealous of and impatient with his talents. It points out that Haggard's popularity has come to him suddenly, that three years ago he was an unknown, and today he is 'if the gossip of clubs and book-shops is to be believed, the most popular writer of fiction of the day.'] . . . [Haggard] has the 'prevailing eye' [the writer continues] of the true creator of fiction; he thoroughly believes in the wonders that he tells. If his style would but deposit more rapidly the crude tartar that floats in it, and if we could but be sure that he would confine himself to narratives of grandiose empires of the past and the up-heavals of colossal civilizations . . . we could look forward with absolute confidence, as we do with considerable hope, to his becoming one of 'the glories of our blood and state.'[113]

A month later Henley read *Cleopatra* and wrote Haggard about it.

> I got a week at Windermere and took 'Cleopatra' with me. I was alone, and found her very good company.
>
> You were terribly handicapped by the inevitable comparison [with Shakespeare]; but you come off better (to be frank) than I'd

expected you would. The invention throughout is admirable – is good enough indeed to carry off the archaeology and the archaical style, though they are both large orders.

And in Charmion you have given us, I think, your best creation. . . . And you know that I mean a good deal when I say that.

I am glad to have read the book, and glad to have it by me to read again. It has plenty of faults, but it has an abundance of promise and some excellent – some really excellent – achievement. There is never a sign of exhaustion, but on the contrary no end of proof that you have scarce got into your stride.[114]

Haggard must have replied immediately, for within a week he had another letter from Henley, this the friendliest of all:

It is pleasant to know that I have paid a very little of my debt. I think the *Romance and Fame*[115] in the current S.O. [*Scots Observer*] will not displease you. The writer is a strange old, brilliant creature whom I have found here* and whose opinion is worth having. Meanwhile, you may put down the attacks partly to envy (for you can't deny that you've had a dam [*sic*] good innings) and partly to the inevitable reaction – for I don't know that your admirers have praised you in quite the right way. And you need bother yourself no more about them. Why should you? You are bound to win, and you need not care three straws for anything they say. You need only do your best, and leave the rest to time.[116]

The notice appeared within a day or two; it was indeed favourable. 'The book is the highest of its author's achievements – the most artfully constructed, the most evenly sustained, the most passionate, impressive and poetic . . . a daring and, with all its defects, a successful essay in the loftiest sphere of romance.'[117]

A year and a half later, when the notice of Haggard and Lang's *The World's Desire* appeared in Henley's *National Observer*, it struck a very different note indeed. 'Mr. Lang we know and Mr. Haggard we know: but of whom (or what?) is this "tortuous and ungodly" jumble of anarchy and culture?' it asks. 'This critic,' it continues, 'was moved to curse his literary gods and die at the thought of the most complete artistic suicide it has ever been his lot to chronicle.'[118] Both Lang and Haggard were much hurt by the notice, which seemed to them to go beyond the bounds of literary criticism, but in time, they overcame their disappointment. Lang wrote to Haggard: 'I was an ass to vex

---

* The review is almost certainly Henley's own writing, and so this is either his private joke or one he does not mind sharing with Haggard.

myself about Henley: he seems to me to be possessed with a desire to insult everyone he knew in town: I can't imagine why, but he was more offensive when he was patronizing. Also the laws of the game prevent me from having a shot at him, if ever there was an opportunity, and I think I could do it sweetly!'[119]

Still relations between Henley and Haggard continued quite congenial, even though Haggard may not always have caught Henley's critical insinuations:

> I remember once driving to the British Museum with him . . . in a four-wheeled cab [wrote Haggard in his autobiography] to see some Japanese prints that were on show. On the way I told him that personally I admired statuary, and especially Greek statuary, much more than I did pictorial art. He was greatly astonished.
>
> 'I think it wonderful,' he said, 'that you being what you are, and your work what it is, you should prefer form to colour.'

Haggard also tells us that Henley 'was extremely fond of war and fighting . . . and at the club [the Savile, of which Henley became a member in 1890] would insist upon my telling him stories by the yard about Zulus and their blood-thirsty battles and customs.'

In 1890 and 1891 the *National Observer* found good things to say about both *Eric Brighteyes* and *Nada the Lily*. As late as 1912, Haggard thought back pleasantly to his associations with Henley. 'I was well acquainted with this able and interesting man,'[120] he wrote with some pride.

9

The Story-teller

AGGARD'S activities in agriculture, politics, finance, and
travel did not reduce the steady flow of his fiction through the
years. The quantity and variety of his output are another index
of the man's vigorous energy and imagination. He wrote a total of fifty-
eight volumes of fiction. From the time *She* was published in 1887 until
his death, thirty-eight years later, only two calendar years went by without a new work of fiction appearing in book form.* More usually each
year saw either one or two new works of fiction (in each of twenty-five
years a single work appeared; in each of ten, two works), and in each
of two years, 1887 and 1888, there were actually three. Four volumes
of tales were issued posthumously, the last as late as 1930.†

Of the fifty-eight volumes, forty-seven are conventional Rider
Haggard adventure romances, and twelve are novels of contemporary
life. One is a propagandist novel.[1] Of the romances, almost a dozen can
be called historical novels, and four comprise a loosely knit story of the
rise and fall of the Zulu dynasty in South Africa. Allan Quatermain
appears in eighteen adventures (four of them short stories), Ayesha in
four romances, in one of which they appear together. Haggard's romances are not restricted to Africa and England; he also wrote about other
lands, Iceland, Mexico, Peru, Denmark, Spain, the Holy Land among
them. Yet, even though the landscape changes, the quality differs, the
subject matter varies, and theme and texture alter as Haggard ages, there
is in almost all his work a fixed combination of basic ingredients.

The world that Haggard creates is new in the geographical sense,
but it is actually the old, conventional world of the medieval romance

---

* 1897 and 1902. *Rural England* appeared in 1902.

† There is ample evidence that Haggard wrote far ahead of publication, and after
his initial success spaced the appearance of his tales to insure that only one would come
out in a given calendar year. He sometimes had as many as four unpublished manuscripts
in Longman's or Watt's vaults. Although some of his tales appeared first in the United
States, these computations are based on the first English appearance of the tales in book
form.

adapted to modern tastes and contemporary attitudes. There is the knight at the centre not in shining armour but in a flannel suit from New Bond Street, carrying not a spear and shield but a Winchester rifle. The mission, as of old, is always there and ever noble: sometimes to rescue a damsel in distress, sometimes to help a friend, sometimes to right a wrong, sometimes merely to seek adventure and try one's strength, and very often to search for riches, a respectable Victorian pursuit. The mission does not take the hero pricking on a plain, but takes him instead across a veld, a desert, a range of mountains, or into the jungle. The obstacles he meets along the way are often the usual ones, mountains, gorges, rivers, and waterfalls. And very often he has to endure hunger, thirst, cold and heat. Because of these trials, the hero gets ample opportunity to demonstrate his superhuman strength of body and character and to perform feats. If there be no dragons (though crocodiles come very close), there remain lions, tigers, elephants, snakes, spiders, and even more exotic creatures like sorcerers and witches. The unknown cities, the temptations of the devil, the massive battles, the incredible achievements – they are all there. And in the end the hero emerges victorious, unhurt but broadened by his experience, humble in the presence of his fellow-man and obedient and grateful to God.

Haggard takes us back to the bold, uncomplicated world of the nursery, where being a strong, brave knight was quite enough, where a man won his laurels by brawn and rectitude, where virtue always triumphed and evil always lost. He tells his readers that the ancient chivalry has not completely disappeared, that off in Africa, Mexico, or on the other frontiers of civilization, it still lives. Not all is daily drudgery there, not all is narrow living yoked by political intrigue and high finance – freedom and excitement still dwell upon the heights or on the horizon, at least in the imagination. Haggard helped to Victorianize the medieval romance and allowed the bored reader to see himself strapping his canteen round his waist, flinging his rifle across his shoulder, and going in search of – if not his layde grace – then at least adventure and fortune.

On the whole Haggard's characters are not elaborate; we do not know the inner workings of their minds. When Haggard tells his story in the third person, he places a strict limit on his omniscience. In the first-person tales, the character who acts as narrator occasionally lapses into 'speculation,' pondering the nature of the universe, the meaning of life and its various problems. But these musings are never psychological revelations; they are monotonous reflections, conventional for their time, hackneyed today, told by a dull old codger in a stuffy West End club or by an African hunter as he lies awake on the open veld looking up at the stars. The reader never really gets beneath the character's surface, into his mind; we learn nothing about him that Haggard, or his characters, could not politely tell us over a glass of port.

And yet Haggard lavished considerable care on at least one character in each book, a person whose motives are more ably constructed and more carefully revealed than most. He is Haggard's hero, Allan Quatermain or any of his confrères in other tales. His role as hero is, however, subtly devised, for there is often a more apparent protagonist, a youthful Adonis of romantic proportions, the *beau idéal* with great physical strength, courage, and pluck. But he is only two-dimensional, a papier-mâché hero. And though he gets his woman, his treasure, his wish (or in some cases he does not), the tale is only superficially about him.

The real protagonist is the narrator, an aging, experienced, wise gentleman who is more complex than his youthful companion. Between him and Rider Haggard there is always a very strong family resemblance. He is not the universal man. He is far better with a machete in the African bush than with a tea-cup in the English drawing-room; he has learned more from nature than from books; but if he is somewhat coarse, it is only because in pitting his wits against raw nature he has grown rough and rugged. No matter what his negative qualities, he is essentially an excellent person of unimpeachable honour and genuine feeling. And, despite modest disclaimers, he has a glittering eye and can tell a cracking good story. His superhuman strength is well concealed, but his power rescues him and his companions from certain death even when the Adonis's strength has failed. He is clear-minded in all situations, prudent, practical, strong-willed, decisive, humble, ingenious, resourceful, sporting, and a devoted friend, a kind master, and of course an expert rifleman. Though well on in years, Quatermain (who appears in the role more than any other Haggard hero) cuts quite a figure. He is tall, trim, with a head of scrubby hair and a neat Van Dyke. He takes an occasional drink and he smokes a pipe. But he possesses minor physical defects. He speaks with a 'curious little accent' and in later life he is slightly lame. He reads the Bible and the *Ingoldsby Legends*; but as a man of action he has no use for fiction.* The emotions he displays are conventional. He knows fear and is capable of trembling when facing it – but it never unmans him; it only sharpens his faculties. Personal tragedy he keeps sealed within his heart: he rarely speaks of the death of his first wife or of his son. He gets on with most men very well, regardless of their colour or nationality, and although he was reared on the Dark Continent (he has learned Dutch and three or four

---

* In *She and Allan* (1921), Captain Good brings Quatermain a book and urges him to read it, but Quatermain declines on the ground that it is a novel. He does, however, read it, because, as the book lies beside him, his curiosity is engaged by the Egyptian hieroglyphics on the cover. The book happens to be *She*.

Kaffir dialects perfectly), he is an Englishman staunch and steady, and England is his home. He is in fact the Englishman of Empire, the crusader who takes England's divine mission to heart and carries the white man's burden of spreading Christian love and Anglo-Saxon justice to the far corners of the world.

But Quatermain is more than the masked Haggard, the silent hero of the tales, and the model Englishman abroad – he is the Modern Man, and as such he lends verisimilitude to the Haggard adventure. Quatermain believes in scientific realism: all unusual phenomena must be proved before he will believe them. This is not a world of cock-and-bull ghost stories, of fairies and wraiths – this is a man's world, and science is man's tool for proving or disproving. From the outset Quatermain is a hard-headed cynic who has no use for humbug, will not tolerate magical hocus-pocus, and absolutely abhors superstition. He is a detached observer, a phlegmatic judge of the universe and its natural operation. He is the last man in the world to believe in subterranean cities, eternal goddesses, hidden civilizations, in any form of miracle, and he says so freely and frankly. He is, in a word, a sceptic, and since he usually is the teller of the tales, he tells them from a sceptical point of view.

In the 'eighties, 'nineties and later – even today – a reader, disillusioned by the unfulfilled promises of progress, watching the new technology turn the world around him into an ugly, shapeless chaos, could easily appreciate Quatermain's scepticism. And in associating with the hero and his disbelief, he is won over to Haggard's brand of romanticism, which leads him across the great divide that separates reality from fancy, smoothly and easily, on a bridge of scepticism. Prudent Quatermain and shrewd reader are invariably induced to go upon their adventure by hard-headed honourable considerations: in *King Solomon's Mines*, Quatermain goes not only because he wishes to search for a lost Englishman but because he has signed a contract whose provisions guarantee a fortune for his only son, should he not return; in *She* Holly accompanies his fair-haired ward, Leo Vincey; in *The Ivory Child* (1916) the hero goes to rescue a beautiful titled English lady from savages; and so on. The reader, constantly sharing Quatermain's doubts and misgivings, goes along with him, not with the Adonis. And then suddenly (but never too soon), the sceptic comes face to face with the impossible, the imponderable, and his reaction is just what we would expect: he does not believe what he sees. But there it is before him, and he looks for some explanation. He subjects the phenomenon to all the tests of reason: Ayesha is after all there before his eyes, and her story is air-tight; King Solomon's treasure is not something he imagines: he runs his fingers through the cold, glittering gems. Perhaps, dear reader, the sceptic is forced to suggest, there is more in heaven and earth than is dreamt of in our scientific realism. Perhaps. And how can the reader, trusting implicitly in Quatermain's detachment, refuse to believe in what Quatermain experiences? He believes – in subterranean cities, in eternal goddesses, in hidden treasure, in lost civilizations, in African magic, in Peruvian sorcery, in Tibetan alchemy, in castles in Spain. He believes so strongly that he closes the book wondering whether Haggard's imaginative flight has not perhaps a basis in fact, whether this is not more than a romantic tale.

Haggard adds to the impact of his adventures by putting them in the form of memoirs; by writing errors into the text so that he, as editor, may correct them in footnotes; by introducing a mass of meticulous detail in describing far-away places, the people who inhabit them, the costumes they wear, even the utensils they eat with. The formula is a psychological powerhouse, and in Haggard's hands it seldom fails, no matter how steep his tale or how flat his minor characters, to draw the reader into a strange and distant world. Allan Quatermain is more than a revived Saint George and a man of modern times. He is Rider Haggard, a man who found the unrealities of romance distasteful, who insisted that a stalwart Englishman had to be a pragmatic Englishman, who knew that doubting Quatermains not only hunted on the African veld – that they walked in great numbers on the pavements of London and the country lanes of Norfolk.

The variations in Haggard's heroines are so many that it is hard to lay down any rules. Roughly, however, one detects three kinds. In the novels they are often beautiful, talented, desirable maidens who frequently meet tragic ends because of calculating, bankrupt parents or guardians who insist on marrying them off to wealthy, villainous suitors. They are often trapped by the strange and cruel workings of circumstance or fate, and if they swerve from the straight and narrow, they inevitably pay the price of sudden and often violent death. In Haggard's day, his women were sometimes praised for depth of soul and complexity of character, and some critics even thought them far superior to his men. Although Haggard does in fact probe their minds more than those of his heroes, they are, with some few exceptions, conventional Victorian maidens, indistinguishable one from the other. Haggard's heroines suffer the ravages of time, and they do very little today for the tales in which they exist.

Besides the romantic heroine, there is often another woman in the Haggard novel. She usually moves in the shadows of the tale in the first twelve to twenty chapters and emerges as a force to be reckoned with only towards the end, when the hero has lost his heroine and realizes, on the rebound, that perfection may not be all in life, and perhaps a young miss who truly loves him, is a good manager, and is plain but devoted, might not be such a bad companion after all. The hero marries her, and the couple live in perpetual contentment, if not bliss, ever after. Haggard's frequent use of two heroines only points up the deep disappointment he suffered at the age of twenty-two. Because of his failure in love, Haggard repeatedly condemned beautiful heroines to death in his novels, reasserting the wisdom of his decision to live his life with a woman who, though she fell short of his ideal, was a dutiful wife and agreeable companion. In the romances, however, where he strays far from his own experiences, a single heroine often triumphs over adversity (or the female villain) and wins her man, as a rule the Leo-type hero.

A third feminine type, a supernatural projection, is however the most important of all Haggard heroines. She is the superhuman woman with superfeminine qualities: eternal beauty, eternal life, eternal wisdom, eternal charm. She lives in a physical and spiritual no-man's land, and she is the goal of a quest, also both physical and spiritual. She has supernatural powers of attraction, and the hero, forced to suspend all reason, is drawn to her, ready to surrender irrevocably to her charms and forgo all worldly things. She is the essence of romance, the antithesis of practicality. The hero finds her only after encountering and overcoming many obstacles. Her presence overwhelms his doubts, dissipates his scepticism. He succumbs and yearns to be united with her – but just at the moment when they are to experience eternal union, she vanishes. For she is actually unattainable, and the hero, jarred back to a mundane consciousness, is left nursing a dream.

The search for Ayesha is an important symbol for Haggard. It is a Faustian as well as a Freudian quest for a universal guiding principle of life and spiritual behaviour. Haggard, essentially a humanist, is not content with the answer of 'God'; he seeks to know His nature, he seeks to prove Him. His gropings into Egyptian and Nordic archaeology, his scrapings in prehistoric temples and tombs, his toying with spiritualism and psychical phenomena, his strong belief in reincarnation – all are part of his quest for the answers. He felt within him deep spiritual soundings which he could not understand, and he firmly believed that, as one of the few men on earth gifted with 'a second sight,' it was his duty to explore the spiritual neverlands and deduce what he could. Haggard was a man in doubt, and his fictional sorties were often attempts to vanquish that doubt. Although he eventually settled upon a working faith, which included a Christian God and devil, an Egyptian belief in reincarnation, and a concept of love reminiscent of Socrates's definition in the *Symposium*, Haggard always sought ultimate proof. If in his African adventures he gave the Victorian reading public a 'way out' of their narrow distress, in Ayesha he gave them something more, a symbol of the mystery of their existence. For the story of the goddess-spirit, the quest for the feminine universe, is mankind's quest for truth and understanding.

In Allan Quatermain and Ayesha, Haggard has given us engaging character studies; the scepticism of the one and the mystery of the other, when Haggard manages them deftly and effectively, bring us close to essential verities. These two, and perhaps some of the Zulus, repay close examination. For the rest, Haggard created little more than pasteboard images to suit his major purpose, to tell a story.

The quality of Haggard's settings varies. Haggard knows his England, Africa, Egypt, Iceland, and Mexico, and he also knows that accurate backdrops are crucial to his tales. He is, as a rule, a stickler for precise detail, and when he has the information for the setting well in hand, he paints it realistically and well. Haggard would often go to great lengths to achieve credibility. He would travel far and endure much to get a first-hand picture of the geography and people he was to write about. He supplemented this material with knowledge he got from books, for he frequently steeped himself in historical, archaeological, and sociological treatises on the subject to hand. When he knows his landscape, his imagination sparkles, and he creates some magnificent scenes. But Haggard is in the main a hasty writer, and in later years, a bored and tired writer, and he sometimes glosses over the setting and omits the details as the price of getting on with the tale. Far too often he permits his narrator modestly to disclaim the power of words to do justice to the scene, and much too frequently the reader's appetite is whetted by a reference to a striking landscape or to a strange natural configuration without being satisfied with a description. But, conventional sunsets aside, when Haggard lets his imagination feast on the scene before him, he often rises to a distinguished level of expression. Let the reader turn to Chapter 16 of *King Solomon's Mines* and judge for himself; Haggard's description of the Place of Death, a sacred, terrible tomb-cathedral, endowed by nature for the glory of Kukuana kings, can stand beside some of our best descriptive writing. The innumerable scenes of wild war dances, tribal trials, and single combats; the great sweep of impis screeching down upon an outnumbered foe and the epic battles that follow; the hushed moments in cavernous temples where one's very thoughts seem to reverberate – these Haggard manages convincingly, conjuring up with them an atmosphere simultaneously magical and real. And when Haggard creates these exotic moments, he hits his stride and writes with unusual power. His talent for words and their happy order emerges most often at the crest of a dramatic incident, as though an inherent sense of drama sharpens his

ear and makes his faculties sensitive to texture and cadence. At these
moments, somehow Haggard the artist transcends Haggard the man,
and the result is gratifying.

But Haggard's writing is more often not of a high quality. His
sentence structure is frequently cumbersome and unnecessarily involved, and he repeatedly shows an insensitivity to subtle meanings,
usage, and rhythm. He is often prolix, and he does not command the
variety of words and images he needs to make his prose engaging. He
lacks wit almost completely, and his writing, good or bad, is never
schooled. Too often he employs personifications: Life and Death, Love
and Hate, Sea and Sky, Fate and Destiny, Truth and Beauty, and War
and Peace. And interjections: Ho! Ha! Hee! Crash! Bang! Rip! Phut!
Wow! The rhetorical question goes hand in hand with his direct address
to the reader, of course, and although these two devices stand well in
the tradition of Victorian fiction, they do not help his prose.

Nor are his faults only stylistic, for some of the ingredients of his
tales are out of place, particularly his chats with the reader. Too often,
he stops his narrative to rant against political intrigue, the dullness of
American novels, the unprincipled Press, and the like, or he takes time
to discuss thoughts on life, death, immortality, reincarnation, or some
other large problem. But Haggard is not a moralist in the grand sense.
He has nothing new to say, and by giving pedestrian answers to great
philosophical problems, he invariably seems pompous. Not that trying
to understand the universe makes him so; it is rather his habit of sounding as if he first invented or discovered the universe and the manner
in which he examines it, as if it were an odd Egyptian coin he had
picked out of the dirt, that is unsettling. Too often he tells us that life is
sad and then stops to admire his sagacity. Haggard takes himself much
too seriously, and though Lang and Kipling warned him against musing
and moralizing, he did not always listen.

Haggard's 'gore' presents another problem. He could draw massacre well, but he drew it too often. As early as 1888, when, by their very
numbers, the attacks upon Haggard seemed the fashion of the day, the
Fortnightly Review found in Haggard's pages a 'reek of blood that rises
like an exhalation from the gratuitously detestable details,' deplored
'depths of degradation a sensational novelist can coolly descend' to, and
objected to being 'regaled with slaughtered humanity served up in
every variety of appetising ways – speared, brained, caught in lion
traps, torn in twain by elephants, and so forth.'[2] In 1892, the *Pall Mall
Budget* called Haggard 'in imagination a very Attila or Tamburlaine,
rejoicing in cruelty, revelling in carnage. . . . He must wipe out an
"impi" or two every morning before breakfast, devise new methods of
massacre as he chips his eggs, wade through gore at luncheon. . . . Can

he sleep o' nights, one wonders, with his brain in this homicidal ferment?' And assessing Haggard's latest romance, the writer continues: 'Take it all in all, "Nada the Lily" is probably the most sanguinary work of its size in existence. It is drenched, sodden, dripping with blood.'[3]

Haggard was aware of the criticism, but it did not deter him. In the Dedication to *Child of Storm*, he says that he seeks to write of the Zulus 'as a reigning nation . . . and to try to show them as they were, in all their superstitious madness and bloodstained grandeur.' In 1912, before *Child of Storm* was published he wrote to Kipling that he will see it 'described as a boys' "story as usual too bloody for most tastes." . . . Piff!,' he continued, 'What is blood in Zululand?'[4] For Haggard reporting the facts was quite enough. When it came to death and massacre there was never a question of taste. He knew that in the parts of the world he wrote about life was cheap, and he knew too that blood and death had a strange fascination for his readers and drew their attention to his work. Haggard liked critical approbation, but he wanted an audience more.

These weaknesses in Haggard's writing stand between him and immortality. And when we ask why they existed and why Haggard did so little to change, we find ample reasons. Had the boy been given an adequate schooling, had he been conditioned by a literary environment, had he been taught the refinements and graces of the English language, had he been steeped in the classics and grown conscious of his own shortcomings, had he not to struggle so for financial independence, and above all had he been more secure psychologically, he might have woven his tales into a finer fabric.

With so many faults, it is indeed remarkable that Haggard's stories are so compelling. Yet they are – and unquestionably because of Haggard's unusual imagination. The reader cannot resist the force of the story: right from the start, when the narrator sits before the hearth with a scrap of parchment or an ancient relic in his hand, we become partners in the adventure to come. The incidents that follow keep us fast in Haggard's spell. We feel sharply the rush of air through the gorge we must cross on a narrow ledge, and we breathe heavily the cloudy vapours that rise from the crocodile-infested waters we must ford. The movement is swift, the invention fertile, and all rushes towards an exciting and fresh conclusion. And when we close the cover of the book, we do not feel that this has been a shapeless series of incidents ending with arbitrary success or failure. For there has been a strong dramatic unity. Haggard creates cohesive entities, with beginnings, middles, and ends. His canvases are blemished, but the bold strokes, the bright colours, and the movement make us linger over them.

At least the better ones. For Haggard's work is uneven and many of his stories are undistinguished. A few, however, deserve particular mention. Of his early works, those he took pains with have literary merit. The best of these is his Icelandic saga, *Eric Brighteyes*, and his first Egyptian tale, *Cleopatra*, is still worth reading. Though Haggard did not really grow in artistic stature with the passing years, his later work does become more fluent and taut, as narrative kinks and some of the stylistic faults disappear. Of the later tales, *Lysbeth* (1901), *Ayesha* (1905), *Queen Sheba's Ring** (1910), *Red Eve* (1911), *The Holy Flower* (1915), *The Ivory Child* (1916), *When the World Shook* (1919), and *The Virgin of the Sun* (1922) at least, are outstanding. And in a series of African tales, he also achieves a high level of story-telling.

These are his Zulu stories, his saga of the black nation, *Nada the Lily* (1892) (Lang called it an 'epic of a dying people' and Besant thought it 'splendid, the best thing . . . since "She" '), and *Marie* (1912), *Child of Storm†* (1913), and *Finished* (1917), which he wrote as a trilogy. 'Rider Haggard did a great service for South Africa by accurately portraying the Zulu character,' writes one authority, 'and no one has ever succeeded in doing this better. . . . [His tales] are a perfect mirror of the Zulu as he was before he was touched by civilization.'[5] Free of conventional moral limitations and British restraint, remembering the simple, dignified savages he knew as a young man in South Africa, he reconstructs the rise and fall of the Zulu dynasty. He writes of giants and their deeds in the deep African wilderness. He works on a broad scale, spanning almost a hundred years, centring his tales on the royal house of Chaka, the black Alexander. He tells of the Zulu people's

---

* The editor Eveleigh Nash tells us how Haggard came to choose this title. The story was to appear as a serial in *Nash's Magazine*, and Mr. Nash suggested that the original title, *Maqueda*, be changed to *Queen Sheba's Ring*. Haggard went to Nash's office to see him about the matter. 'I felt a thrill at the thought of meeting the author of "King Solomons' Mines" and "She," for as a boy I had read these great romances,' writes Nash. 'He entered the room and remained standing in spite of an invitation to take a seat. "Why do you prefer 'Queen Sheba's Ring' to "Maqueda"?' he asked. "Because," I replied, "there's romance in the title, and women love a story about a ring." "Good," he answered, "call it 'Queen Sheba's Ring,' " and took his departure. It was the shortest interview I ever had with an author.' *I Like the Life I Lived* (1941), pp. 108–109.

† In 1913, when Haggard was in Brisbane, he met Oscar Asche, the actor, and persuaded him to dramatize *Child of Storm*. The play opened in the Globe Theatre as *Mameena* in October 1914, after rather elaborate preparations. Captain James Stuart, the former Assistant-Secretary of Native Affairs in South Africa had been 'roped in with a bag of gold' to supervise costumes and weapons and to teach the cast the manners and customs of the Zulus. Three Zulu kraals were engaged for three months to make authentic costumes and props. Forty oxen were killed to supply the necessary hides. A representative of the production was sent to the Berlin Museum to borrow additional material, and two Zulu chiefs were brought to London for dances and songs. Special lighting and stage effects were devised, particularly for the wedding dance, performed by eighty dancers. 'The book does not lend itself well to dramatic treatment,' wrote the reviewer for the *Athenaeum*; 'in fact,' he continued, 'the play would have been as effective if acted in a dumb show.' Nevertheless it played 133 times, although it lost £8,000. Oscar Asche, *Oscar Asche; His Life* (n.d.), pp. 142, 156–160; *Athenaeum*, CXLIV (October 10, 1914), p. 364.

unification under the military leadership of the great warrior-king and how the nation fell into oblivion under the sons' divisive jealousies and the white man's advance. Much of the material is factual, much based on oral legend which Haggard himself heard in South and Central Africa, and much is Haggard working most creatively. Chaka emerges a classic figure, a medley of militaristic greatness and primitive brutality, a man whose personal force enabled him to unite the Zulu tribes into a single nation, organize their finest youth into mighty battalions and lead them with a military perfection and crusading determination rarely excelled in history. Chaka and his armies took a million lives, and Haggard makes us feel the meaning of that statistic, gives us the emotion to accompany the fact.

In these tales Haggard does for the Zulus what Cooper does in his Leatherstocking tales for the American Indian. But there is a difference. Cooper tells of a people now so thoroughly subjugated that they can no longer hope to emerge as a cultural entity or national unit, whereas Haggard writes of a people with a future. In Africa the overpowering majority of black people are restless and eager to assert the authority of their numbers; they still aspire to national unity and cultural recognition. When they assert their independence and rule once more in their native lands, Haggard's Zulu saga may come into its own. For he captures in it a clear, engaging picture of Zulu life and comes to terms with the turbulent Zulu spirit. As the African nations continue to take their place in the modern world of states, during the late twentieth century and in the twenty-first, their writers will, if they follow the pattern of those in other new or reborn nations, try to portray the glories of their people's past. Among their sources will most likely be found Haggard's works.

But there is more in these four volumes than the raw material for a later writer to use. Haggard himself, when writing of Zulu life, achieves some distinction. There is little on the Haggard shelf more convincing than these tales. The people, the language, the landscape – they all ring true. Zulus could not be otherwise than Haggard pictures them; Africa must have been exactly as he paints it. Out of these pages come his ostrich-plumed warriors. They stamp their salute to Chaka on the ground and then, assegais raised on high, sweep over the crest of a mountain and with a shriek rush down upon their enemy. Haggard had known the black man, and his knowledge combined with his imagination to give rise to an eloquence he seldom reached in his other work.

But the tales that display Haggard at his most original are, after all, *King Solomon's Mines* and *She*. Their unchanging freshness has commanded a reading audience for seventy years now and will continue to do so. In them Haggard has come closest to capturing universal elements and satisfying an essential need in mankind. The imaginative quality of these two stories makes them classics of a kind, and many readers feel, as Stuart Cloete does, that it is 'amazing to read *She* again at the age of sixty and recapture the charm and excitement I felt at fourteen,' or as the reviewer who recently wrote in the *Times Literary Supplement* that 'on the strength of *King Solomon's Mines* alone . . . [Haggard] deserves a place higher than is generally reserved for him.'[6]

Haggard's impact upon his time was probably greater than has been estimated. Almost every tale of wild adventure in strange lands that appeared after *King Solomon's Mines* – and they appeared by the hundreds – showed the Haggard stamp. For generations, whole magazines were devoted to this kind of story, and to this day, many tales of hunts, explorations, and encounters with savages, and some stories of reincarnation and other supernatural phenomena, owe a debt to Haggard. His influence upon his contemporaries is most easily discernible, for it seems that in the late 'eighties and early 'nineties, almost every English novelist tried to write at least one adventure story à la Haggard. In the mid-'nineties, romance was the thing. Readers flocked to it to escape realism and naturalism, and a flood of romance fiction emanating from the New School of Romance satisfied them. As early as 1887, Quiller-Couch, faced with debts totalling £308, told A. E. W. Mason and J. C. Brinton, 'I shall pay it somehow! It seems to me the best thing I can do is to write an adventure story – a cross between Robert Louis Stevenson and Rider Haggard, shall we say: those are the sort of novels people read nowadays.'[7] And *Dead Man's Rock* was the result.

But 'Q' was not alone. In the late 'eighties and 'nineties many writers, young and old, tried their hand at romance. Some of the tales that resulted from these efforts are better written than Haggard's, but it is hard to select even one that shows the imaginative quality of Haggard at work.[8] Nor did romance die in the new century, when a vast reading public, Haggard trained, went on to read works by younger writers. Some are obvious imitators,[9] but others are products of fresh genius writing merely in the context of Haggard's brand of romance.[10] And still today, one sees advertisements for adventure tales by writers who try to recapture the strength of the older giants. 'Stevenson plus Rider Haggard plus John Buchan equals Robert W. Krepps,' reads one such advertisement, quoting a review that sums up in a sentence the author's formula: ' "[It is] a fast-paced, chattering, lusty and enchanting story of white men after Solomon's treasure in the land of the Zulu." '[11]

Many prominent people, furthermore, have acknowledged their familiarity with Haggard's work – King Edward VII preferred Haggard to Hardy and Meredith – and some writers openly recognize a debt to it. D. H. Lawrence devoured Haggard tales when he was a young man in Manchester, training to be a teacher, and he did not hesitate to use an occasional phrase from Haggard in later years.[12] C. S. Lewis read Rider Haggard, and still does; and he admits to an influence exerted by Haggard upon his tales.[13] Gilbert Murray read Haggard and wrote a single romance very much in the Haggard vein, *Gobi and Shamo*. Henry Miller considers Haggard's tales a strong force in his life, and he has given us an essay of rhapsodic appreciation of *She* and another of Haggard himself.[14] Stuart Cloete tells us that he 'was brought up on Rider Haggard and G. A. Henty' and that their books 'were the literary milk of my boyhood from which I have never been weaned.'[15] Graham Greene, looking back to his boyhood days, remembers 'the missed heartbeat, the appalled glee I felt when I found on a literary shelf a novel by Rider Haggard . . . which I had not read before.' What is more, he credits *King Solomon's Mines* with influencing his career: 'If it had not been for that romantic tale . . . would I at nineteen have studied the appointments list of the Colonial Office,' and 'wasn't it the incurable fascination of Gagool . . . that led me to work all through 1942 in a little stuffy office in Freetown, Sierra Leone?'[15] And there were undoubtedly many other young Englishmen before Greene in whom Haggard awakened a thirst for adventure that helped settle the Empire.

During the last fifteen years of the nineteenth century, Rider Haggard's immense attraction held fast, and in the new century that appeal continued strong. The statistics of Haggard's popularity in both centuries show that it was not by any means restricted to any particular section of the reading public and that it paid no heed whatever to national and language barriers. It was universal. What is especially interesting about the response to Haggard is its force after the turn of the century. After Africa and the other undiscovered areas had been explored and exploited, and although the reading habits and tastes of the world changed radically as man's technological horizons widened, Haggard still commanded an audience.

Records of sales and returns for the years before 1900 are both difficult to come by and deceptive, and before the International Copyright Act of 1891, they are also chaotic. Many English novels in those days were pirated in the United States before the ink of the first edition was dry, and not a penny went to the author. Popular writers suffered especially from these abuses, and Haggard was no exception. In 1907 he complained that in the United States *King Solomon's Mines* 'is frequently given away by grocers as flavouring to a pound of tea';[17] and on another occasion Boston's *Literary World* reported that nearly 200,000 copies of the story were sold in the United States, with Haggard getting a mere £13 for them.[18] Sales data are further distorted because the reading world was still rather limited, universal education not having been in force long enough to make England a nation of readers. Moreover, today's sales figures make those of the nineteenth century seem insignificant by comparison, and of course a guinea was worth a great deal more in Haggard's day than it is today. But even in view of these circumstances, those facts of Haggard's popularity that are available are illuminating.*

In September 1885 *King Solomon's Mines* was published in an edition of 2,000 copies. In England alone 31,000 were sold during the first year, and by Christmas 1886 Haggard had received over £750. Because of the demand, within two years a total of 53,000 had been printed; in eight years 100,000 copies had been issued; and by 1905, 300,000 had been sold in England. From a recent history of the House of Cassell, we learn that, all in all, 'more than 650,000 copies, in one form or another, were printed in . . . [Haggard's] lifetime: there is no record of his ultimate receipts, but it is clear that they must have amounted to a small fortune.'[19] The story has never gone out of print; it is in fact Haggard's most frequently reissued title. It has been read by children and adults of all generations since it appeared and has even been used as a textbook in many schools. One issue, printed in 1938 in Afrikaans, comes equipped with lessons and questions at the back. Today there are no fewer than twelve English-language issues of *King Solomon's Mines* in print. The B.B.C. has dramatized the tale from time to time, celebrating Rider Haggard's centenary in 1956 by serializing it on the Light Programme. The adventure story has been filmed at least four times, most recently in 1950 in Hollywood Technicolor.

More than any other Haggard story, *King Solomon's Mines* has become a boys' book classic. It shows no sign of aging or of losing its audience. A reviewer, noticing the Puffin Book edition in the *Times Literary Supplement* recently, was not being over-optimistic when he predicted that the story 'will find thousands, perhaps tens of thousands, of new readers.'[20]

She enjoyed an even greater success than *King Solomon's Mines*. In a few months it sold 30,000 copies,[21] and we can understand why if J. P. Collins's experience was characteristic of his generation. 'I can remember,' he wrote in 1926, 'one provincial lad with an exiguous allowance of pence per week rashly mortgaging the income of months in order to burst into a bookshop and buy "She." . . . There are no such thrills

* Perhaps the best way to gauge Haggard's popularity is to compare the sales figures of his books that are available with those of classic best-sellers. *Waverley*, published in an edition of 1,000 in 1814, sold a total of 57,000 by 1836. The original issue of *David Copperfield* (1849-50) was 25,000, but later a penny edition sold 83,000 in three weeks. *Tom Brown's School Days*, published in 1857, sold 28,000 in six years, and *Alice in Wonderland*, published in 1865, sold 180,000 in forty-three years. *Robert Elsmere*, published in 1888, between *King Solomon's Mines* and *She*, sold 70,5000 in three years. Richard D. Altick, *The English Common Reader* (1957), pp. 381-390.

now,' he continues, 'and sometimes we feel as if we would give the whole of Paternoster Row for but one hour of the breathlessness with which we saw Ayesha arise in her vesture of cool white flame.'[22] W. T. Stead, who had earlier accused Haggard of plagiarizing *She*, did not hesitate, in 1903, to take advantage of its popularity. When his publishing venture of the Penny Poets ceased, Stead brought out a series of condensed novels (*Punch* called them 'Penny Steadfuls'), and the first of the series was *She*. It sold half a million copies very quickly.[23] At least eight reprint issues are available today in England and the United States, and when, in 1949, Dell Books brought out the 'retold' (meaning *abridged*) paperback, it sold its complete issue of 250,000 copies. Besides being dramatized, *She* has been filmed at least six times. Alice Payne Hackett, in her *Sixty Years of Best Sellers*, includes *She* in her list of ninety-five books published before 1895 which have certainly sold more than a million copies.[24]

Some figures are available on other early books. *Jess*, one of Haggard's earliest anti-Boer novels, remained popular for decades. It was translated into French the year it was published (1887), and when Haggard was writing his autobiography in 1911, he received in the post a copy of the twenty-seventh edition of the story. It has been translated into numerous other languages, and as late as 1923 into Urdu. Its publisher's records show that between 1911 and 1916, over 64,000 English copies were sold.[25] *Allan Quatermain* sold 10,000 subscription copies before publication. A few weeks after it was published, J. M. Barrie complained that '2,000 copies of "Allan Quatermain" are in circulation in Mudie's and not a single copy of Hardy's "A Pair of Blue Eyes" ' and that Mudie's customers 'read "Kidnapped" when the 2,000 copies of "Allan Quatermain" are all out.'[26] In 1934, the story, 'simplified' by Michael West, was issued as A New Method Reader, and in 1956, the full story was read on the 'Book at Bedtime' series of the B.B.C. It remains one of the more popular titles to this day, and there are at least six issues now in print. *Maiwa's Revenge*, published in an issue of 30,000 in August 1888, sold 20,000 copies on the day of publication,[27] and in a letter of uncertain year, Lang reports to Haggard that *The World's Desire* had sold 227,000 copies.[28]

Royalty figures are especially hard to come by, but we have some. During its first three years, *King Solomon's Mines* earned for its author £1,346,[29] and it is certain that John Murray paid Haggard £900 for the copyright to *Jess*.[30] By 1890, Haggard had made £10,000 on *She* alone.[31] His daughter tells us that over a three-year period (either in the late 'eighties or early 'nineties), her father made a total of £20,000 on his books;[32] and we know also that in November 1902, Haggard sold the British rights to *Ayesha*, his first sequel of *She* for £1,000 plus 25 per cent of selling price.[33] In 1925, an American commentator noted, furthermore, that Haggard had made $10,000 on *King Solomon's Mines* and $50,000 on *She*.[34]

Haggard's popularity was of course reflected in various compilations, lists of recommended books, and in popularity contests. In 1891 *A Guide Book to Books*, recommending 'books of value,' listed *King Solomon's Mines*, *She*, and *Jess*,[35] and in 1912 *Books that Count, a Dictionary of Standard Books* included *A Winter's Pilgrimage* and *Regeneration*.[36] In 1925 the *Bookman* reported that a 'great competition' had just been held (by an English newspaper, probably), and that prizes of eight automobiles had been awarded 'to decide the grave question of the most popular authors in England. . . . The prize-winners were those entrants who placed the authors in the order established by their numerical appearances in the lists of all the competitors.' The final order of the authors is interesting, and especially because the contest occurred in the year of Haggard's death, when his popularity was at its lowest. Rudyard Kipling heads the list, and Rider Haggard is sixth of the twelve finalists. Between Kipling and Haggard fall Thomas Hardy, Hall Caine, Arthur Conan Doyle, and H. G. Wells in that order; below Haggard come Arnold Bennett, Ethel M. Dell, Joseph Conrad, W. J. Locke, G. K. Chesterton, and Ian Hay.[37] Haggard would have been pleased to know that nine of his books got into William S. Sonnenschein's *The Best Books* in 1935, and happy for the selection, for they are his books on agriculture and history. Ernest A. Baker's *Guide to the Best Fiction in English* listed thirty-three of Haggard's novels in 1913 and forty works in 1932. As recently as 1950 Kathleen M. Lines recommended *Allan Quatermain* and *Eric Brighteyes* for youngsters in *Four to Fourteen, a Library of Books for Children*, and in 1953 *King Solomon's Mines* and *She* were among the 3,000 choice selections in *The World's Best Books* by Asa Don Dickinson.

There is ample evidence that Haggard's tales had a wide appeal in public schools and universities as well as grammar schools in England and abroad. '*She* is a great success at Eton and Oxford,' Lang wrote to Haggard after its publication.[38] Maurice Baring gives us an interesting look into the reading life of a couple of young scholars at Eton:

> Dunglass and I used to read a good many books. Rider Haggard and Edna Lyall were our favourite authors; Stevenson got a second or third place. . . . [I] enjoyed my breakfasts with Mr. Impey [his master] most; he used to tell me about books, and we used to discuss Rider Haggard and Stevenson. I greatly preferred Rider Haggard, and I had just read *King Solomon's Mines*, and had one night sat up late reading *She*.

Baring kept a list of books he read in the year 1889, 'marked according to merit.' On it were *King Solomon's Mines*: 'excellent'; *She*: 'thrilling'; *Jess*: 'worth reading'; *Allan Quatermain*: 'exciting'; *Mr. Meeson's Will* and *Maiwa's Revenge*: 'trash.'[39] 'I have used, as a schoolmaster, *Nada the Lily* in many English classes at prep. schools and always with over-whelming success,' writes Peter Gamble in 1945. 'Let me commend it to the notice of sympathetic teachers as a welcome relief from antho-logies and collections of polite, but worthless, animal stories.'[40] An authority on South African literature writes that the most popular of Haggard's works in South Africa are *King Solomon's Mines*, *Allan Quatermain*, and *Nada the Lily*. 'The first has been prescribed for schools and the last broadcast by the South African Broadcasting Corporation,' he continues. 'Few educated South Africans have not read these three works, and most have also read *She*.'[41] The ladies read Haggard books. Winifred Graham recalled that Rider Haggard's books 'fascinated me in my youth. . . . I thrilled when I read of adventures in darkest Africa and longed to lie in a tent at night listening to the roar of lions.'[42]

From the first Haggard had a great success in the United States, even though in the early years it brought him virtually no financial return (by 1891 he was paid a mere £13 by publishers for the privilege of putting his books on the American market in dozens of issues and thousands of copies). In 1887, when *Allan Quatermain* appeared, an American critic boldly wrote in *Epoch* that 'we drop our Howells and James as readily as Sandwich Islanders doff their civilized garments, and plunge gleefully into the sea of melodramatic romance with Mr. Haggard as our guide.'[43] And Walter Snow reported that when Haggard first visited New York (1891), 'his works were read and dis-cussed by everyone, and his latest novel was one of the current topics for conversation in clubland.'[44]

In 1893 Messrs. J. Delwin Tait and Sons, Publishers, conducted a survey of all major United States libraries to determine which were the 150 all-time favourite novels, and *She* ranked 117th.* In the list of authors' popularity (determined by the number of times their names appeared on the library lists), Dickens again led, Scott was third, Cooper fifth, George Eliot sixth, Hawthorne seventh, Howells twenty-sixth, Haggard forty-third, Hardy forty-sixth, Stevenson forty-ninth, and Zola and James were conspicuously absent.[45]

In 1895 six Haggard titles appeared in the *List of Books for Girls and Women and Their Clubs*,[46] and in the same year the *Ladies' Home Journal's* publication, *Five Thousand Books, an Easy Guide to the Best Books* (selected by 'a corps of experienced editors'), recommends fifteen

---

* *David Copperfield* led the list, and it was followed by *Ivanhoe*, *The Scarlet Letter*, and *Uncle Tom's Cabin*. *Waverley* and *Pride and Prejudice* fell beneath *She*.

Haggard stories. In 1928, the *United States Catalogue* listed seventy-seven different issues of Haggard's works in print, and in 1930 *A Guide to Books for Character* recommended *Eric Brighteyes* for teaching personal honour, sincerity, courage, integrity, devotion to friends, and magnanimity to enemies.[47] *Five Adventure Novels*, a Haggard miscellany issued in New York in 1951, was immediately listed in the *Standard Catalogue for High School Libraries* among a selected 3,610 books.

She made quite a splash in the United States. It was published by Harper & Brothers mimediately after it appeared in London, and the cheap 'libraries' immediately pirated issues. In 1887 alone there were at least ten editions, most of them priced at twenty or twenty-five cents. There were dozens of immediate imitations and parodies, all eager to cash in on Haggard's popularity. On April 30, 1887, the New York *Journalist* observed that 'a host of imitators has sprung up, like toadstools, in a single night. *He, It, Me, Her* are on the news stands in gaudy covers.'[48] Another report in the New York *Herald* tells of its vogue among the ladies. One observer on holiday in the Catskill Mountains that summer 'paused one afternoon on a knoll where he could look down on the lawn of the hotel. A hundred women were lounging in various chairs. It was an Adamless Eden where every Eve had a book. And of the hundred women eighty-five were reading "She." ' [49] *She* was dramatized by William Gillette and produced 'with great success' at Niblo's Garden in New York. In spite of a bad Press, it ran for four weeks. *She* remained a popular title through the years. In 1896, a commentator in *Chips* queried:

> Where is there a man who has not been staggered
> By the great *She*-demon of Rider Haggard?[50]

There is ample evidence that Haggard is still read today. In England alone there are more than thirty different issues of his titles in print, and although sales figures are hard to come by, library circulation figures and information supplied by education officials indicate clearly that his works continue to be popular. A tabulation supplied by three of London's twenty-eight metropolitan libraries shows that they have a total of 151 copies of Haggard's fiction in stock and that each copy averages two issues a month. Of these 151 copies, only twenty-one were not being used by readers on October 9, 1958. The issues per year of all 151 copies is estimated at 2,476.

Comments of some schoolmasters and schoolmistresses indicate that Haggard remains a favourite of boys and girls. The Head of the English Department of the Secondary Modern School at Daventry, Northamptonshire, for instance, writes that

Allan Quatermain and *King Solomon's Mines* have become mile-stones in a child's literary progress. . . . For many years, I have taken [them] as class text books . . . [and] both have been thoroughly enjoyed. . . . Scarcely a year passes without it [*Allan Quatermain*] being studied by one or other class in the upper age range (13–16) of the school, and I cannot recall any class that has not found plea-sure in it. Indeed, I well remember, while reading the account of the death of Umslopogaas . . . to a class of 40 tough 15 year old boys, the anxiety of my Headmaster, who coming into my classroom, and finding them hushed and tearful, beseeched me in an agonised aside, to be more sparing with the cane!

And a headmistress observes: 'One school, from which girls come to this school, uses *King Solomon's Mines* as a class book. . . . We have had copies [of *King Solomon's Mines*], but these were discarded in July because they were worn out with use.'

What is more, schools often required students to read Haggard: *King Solomon's Mines* was one of the set books in English literature at the School Certificate examination of the Royal Society of Arts in 1958 and 1959. It was also set for study at the Society's examination in English, Stage I (Elementary). The Chief Education Inspector for the London County Council writes, moreover, that 'it is safe to say that every school library in London has copies of some of Rider Haggard's popular romances.' And a librarian in Kent has the impression 'that these books are read and enjoyed by children who . . . in most cases, come from bookish homes, where parents themselves read . . . [them] while young. If a child should acquire a liking for Rider Haggard, he usually reads as many as are available. [Furthermore,] quite a number of older men read these books for a second time, having enjoyed them in youth.'

Some facts of Haggard's continuing popularity in South Africa are available, and there too his works often appear as prescribed reading. The Senior Librarian of the Transvaal writes that '*King Solomon's Mines* has . . . been prescribed for school use. We do feel . . . that his books should be represented on the shelves of the 80 Transvaal Town libraries at present affiliated to this [rural] service . . . and to meet our needs we take 40 copies of each of the reprints as they appear.' Other librarians also indicate that Haggard's works are still widely read and are still in considerable demand.

But his popularity does not stop with the English-speaking peoples. Lin Shu, who has translated into Chinese the novels of Scott, Dickens, Doyle, Hugo, Stevenson, Tolstoi, Cervantes, and others, claims Haggard as his favourite Western writer. The *Index Translationum* gives a partial indication of Haggard's popularity among peoples speaking languages other than English. The *Index* has been tabulating a partial list of translations (there are innumerable pirated translations, and some countries do not even recognize the need to acknowledge translations or seek permission to translate) since 1932, when it began by listing translations in Germany, Spain, France, and Italy. Since then, it has expanded its coverage, and for 1957 it reports on fifty-one countries, though the East still remains largely uncharted. Between 1932 and 1955, for a period of twenty-four years beginning seven years after Haggard's death, the *Index* lists ninety-eight translations of Haggard's works, including a translation into Hungarian of his autobiography. For 1955 alone, already nine new translations have been reported, *Maiwa's Revenge* into Spanish (Argentina); two different translations of *Allan Quatermain* into Danish; *She* into Japanese; *Jess* into Norwegian; *Cleopatra* into Afrikaans; and *King Solomon's Mines* into Spanish (Spain), Japanese, and Norwegian.[51]

10

Serving the Empire

'ALL for England' was Haggard's fervent theme, and it motivated much of what he did. Love for his country had led him to
become an agricultural reformer, and in his last twenty years,
it caused him to perform other equally arduous tasks. Whenever his
duty stood out clearly to him, whenever he saw that he could do some
practical service for England, he gave freely of himself, subordinating
all his other responsibilities. In his declining years he was often called
upon to help his country.

During 1903, the year after *Rural England* appeared, when Haggard
spent much of his time writing letters on agriculture to influential
people and the Press and making innumerable short journeys to address
groups on the same subjects, he managed also, it seems, to write two
books. One is a historical romance suggested by his visit to the Holy
Land (*The Brethren*); and the other, *A Gardener's Year*, is a companion
to *A Farmer's Year*.

His desire to study English country life and his wish to advance his
agricultural cause precluded long holidays, and it was not until 1904
that he could leave England for any length of time. Then he went back
to Egypt for a second visit. With him went his eldest daughter, Angela,
and a type of hand camera that had recently come into use. Haggard
again explored the caves, tombs, temples, and relics of the ancient
Egyptians. He got the diversion he needed and additional material and
inspiration for more romances. He also wrote a series of articles on
Egyptian travels for the *Daily Mail*. On the return voyage, he and his
daughter stopped in Italy and then went on to Spain, which delighted
them immensely (and gave rise to Haggard's *Fair Margaret*).

In January 1905 Haggard received a letter from Alfred Lyttelton,
then Colonial Secretary, asking him to go to the United States as
'Commissioner' to inspect the Salvation Army Labour Colonies, a network of camps for rehabilitating indigents from U.S. cities. 'It is
thought,' Lyttelton wrote, 'that if on inquiry this system is found to be

financially sound and to be a real benefit to the poorer classes, it might prove a useful model for some analogous system of settlement from the United Kingdom to the Colonies.'[1] Lyttelton's letter reflected the growing concern for the urban poor towards the end of the century. Social movements, charity organizations, and religious missions had already arisen to combat more efficiently than the mid-Victorian 'do-gooders' the evil forces that accompanied city growth and social change.

Prominent among the new crusading philanthropies was the Salvation Army, led by William Booth, who had worked since 1865 in his Christian Mission at Whitechapel retrieving souls. Inspired by the belief that evil results from environment, he established a network of missions to help the destitute. To aid his cause he wrote *In Darkest England and the Way Out* (1890), a book that shocked the English-speaking world with the blatant facts of the unfortunate, forsaken English slum-dweller. He set up some rural training stations, where the Army taught men and women from the cities how to work the land, and then he helped them emigrate to the Colonies as farmers. Some observers thought this back-to-the-land movement could solve many urgent problems created by growing population, mechanized industries, a weakened empire, and a troubled national conscience. The missionary spirit of Booth and his pseudo-military organization spread swiftly and inspired thousands of Major Barbaras, not only in England but all over the world, in the Colonies (even India), in Japan, and perhaps most strikingly in the United States. Under Balfour's administration (1902–1905), Whitehall grew interested in the Salvation Army movement and its march upon the 'fortresses of sin,' and for a time seriously considered falling in behind 'General' Booth.

Haggard was delighted with this new request for his services; it was almost what he himself had been stumping for, a way to get people out of the cities and back on the land. He took the assignment, had a long interview with General Booth, looked over the Salvation Army Colony at Hadleigh, and on February 22, 1905, set out for the United States.

The inevitable interviews took place in New York. One, appearing in the Magazine Section of the *Herald*, gives us a particularly interesting picture of Rider Haggard, Commissioner. One of the sub-heads read: 'If he still has a She, he has put a Salvation Army bonnet on her.' Here, in part, is the newspaperman's report of his visit to Haggard at the Waldorf-Astoria:

Mr. Haggard puts formality at an end by a breezy, poseless, highly English manner. He is very tall and on his very broad shoulders his large enough head sits small in the manner of the 'Farnese

Hercules.' He lounges very low in his chair and puffs affectionately at a homely old pipe. . . . His answers are quick, blunt, brutally final: 'Oh, I don't want to talk about literature!' . . . 'I never had a penny from that book's [*She*'s] sale in America.' . . . 'Hey what?' came out like an explosion. It was fairly detonated. Mr. Haggard's speech is quite his own. Giant as he is and cultivated as he is, he has as much trouble with his 'th's' as a baby, a Frenchman or a Dutchman . . . and the effect is quaintly pleasant. . . . Mr. Haggard made hard interviewing as long as the talk clung to literature. He answered questions briefly and courteously in a dozen words, and then relaxed into his pipe and waited for the next query. It was only when he got to the practical side of life that he began to warm up and talk without prodding. He grew earnest, enthusiastic, cogent; but always without arrogance, without self-praise, or over-confidence. . . . He is thoroughly objective. He seemed to be actually bored by allusions to his books. He looked distressed when asked how he wrote his books. Did he read up much for *King Solomon's Mines*: 'Oh no. You see, I know my South Africa so well.' He is writing nothing at all just now. '. . . One can't do two things at once. My mind is all on this commission.' . . . The Rider Haggard of the new crusade is another man from the jaunty romancer of a decade ago.[2]

During the two months that Haggard spent in America, he carefully inspected the Salvation Army Colonies: Fort Romie, near San Francisco; Fort Amity, in Colorado; and Fort Herrick (for rehabilitating inebriates), in Ohio. He also visited Canada, spoke with Governor-General Earl Grey, and got an official commitment from the Canadian Government for 240,000 acres of land to be used in settling British immigrants. On March 9 Haggard went to see Theodore Roosevelt, then the newly elected President of the United States, at the White House. The two men got on famously from the start. They talked about South Africa (Haggard later wrote that Roosevelt 'expressed his hope that the Boers . . . with whom he had great sympathy, would settle down, learn English, and become a dominant factor in that country under British flag and rule'[3]). A few days after the initial interview, Roosevelt entertained Haggard and Angela at a White House luncheon ('to which we went straight from another luncheon, where we were also entertained by citizens of note in Washington'), and Haggard could later recall that Roosevelt was very amusing on that occasion, making light horseplay of diplomatic protocol. Haggard made a quick and firm friend of the President. The men had similar temperaments, and they had many interests in common. Having recorded a summary of his conversation with Roosevelt, Haggard could report it in his memoir six years later:

'It is an odd thing,' the President had said, 'that you and I, brought up
in different countries and following such different pursuits, should have
identical ideas and aims. I have been reading your book, "Rural
England," and I tell you that what you think, I think, and what you
want to do, I want to do. We are one man in the matter.'[4] It is not
surprising that the two men were drawn to each other and remained
friendly and in touch for many years to come.

As he travelled about the country, Haggard drafted reports on each
of the farm-labour camps. But all was not work, for he accepted invita-
tions and offers of hospitality from his American public and was entertained by literary clubs everywhere. He was taken on fishing trips in
the north-west, and on his return east he travelled in John Hays
Hammond's private railway car. (Later Haggard reported that he
suffered much from overheated sleeping-cars 'in which Americans
seem to prefer to be stewed alive.'[5]) Nor was the journey completely
without incident, for they 'had a great escape of being drowned in the
Colorado River,' and Angela developed influenza toward the end of
their stay.[6] Finally, however, they returned to Liverpool, arriving there
April 27, 1905.

Haggard worked diligently on his report during the voyage, and
soon after his return he submitted it, with the recommendations he had
been asked to make, to Lyttelton. It was of course published as a Blue
Book (in June 1905)[7] and later the same year appeared in popular form
as *The Poor and the Land*. Haggard reports thoroughly upon his investigations, and as usual supports his observations and conclusions with
photographs, transcripts of interviews, and statistical charts. He concludes that the Salvation Army is doing a remarkably fine job: 'I find
the settlers healthy, happy, hopeful, and, almost without exception,
doing well.' He is confident that similar projects would infinitely benefit
England and her depressed city population, and he presents a blueprint
for a scheme similar to the Salvation Army projects that he believes
England could profitably establish. His recommendations have a familiar ring; we have met them before, in somewhat modified form, in
Rural England. He seeks to 'combine a judicious use of the Public
Credit with that of what I have called the "waste forces of Benevolence"
and by means of these two levers to lift some of the mass of human
misery which demonstrates itself in the great cities of civilization to a
new level of plenty and contentment.' The unfortunates would be sent
off to the Colonies, where they would settle on allocated plots of land
in labour communities. The land would be their own, and they would
repay the value of it as they became self-sufficient. Supervising these
communities and all their affairs would be a benevolent institution, the
Salvation Army or something similar, to which men and women would

donate their administrative talents without remuneration in the cause of bettering their fellow-man.[8]

The report got an excellent Press. *The Times* notice appeared as its leading article, and virtually every newspaper and journal in Great Britain gave it serious attention. No one doubted that something had to be done about the conditions in English cities, and though a number of writers disagreed with some of Haggard's particular recommendations, only few of them disputed the essential worth of his scheme. *The Times*, the *Standard*, the *Morning Post*, the *Daily Telegraph*, and the *Daily News* all supported Haggard and his report, and the *Daily Express* said flatly that for 'so excellent an end the Imperial Government should have no difficulty in devising financial means.' The *Daily Mirror* wrote: 'The great thing is to get it started, and to realize that we are "laying great bases" for the future . . . the sooner we begin the better.'[9]

Haggard found no official enthusiasm for his report, however. There was no Roosevelt to welcome him and discuss the intricacies of the problems the nation faced. Lyttelton gave him half an hour of his time and told him that he wished the Prime Minister would take up the report. But *'Arthur won't read it – you know Arthur won't read it!'*[10] Balfour and his Conservative brethren still blanched at bills that called for 'State interference' and listened with a more attentive ear to the apostles of 'self-help.' Moreover, Haggard's proposal was based on the Salvation Army Colonies, and the Salvation Army, after all, had religious overtones. The opinion of the Press and the needs of the country were one thing; the opinion of the Government quite another. Though Victorian conservatism and complacency in politics were on their last legs, they still stood firmly enough to defend their worn-out principles. In June 1905, two months after Haggard returned from America, his report came up in both Houses of Parliament, where it was voted into Committee to die a lingering death. In the following year the Committee dealt it a final blow when it recommended that the Government take no steps to further Haggard's colonization scheme and that instead it entrust to other agencies, like the emigration information office, the job of stimulating and assisting emigration. People emigrating should be left to work out their own scheme of life in the Colonies, the Committee insisted, and should not be placed in prearranged communities. 'I never even received a letter of thanks from the Government,' Haggard later reflected, or for that matter 'a copy of the Report and Evidence of the Committee, which I had to buy like any other member of the public. All that I got was the privilege of paying the bill, for of course the small sum allowed . . . did not . . . meet the expenses of my tour in a high official position through that very expensive country, the United States.'

When, in 1906, Haggard read that the new Government (in December 1905 the Radicals under Campbell-Bannerman dislodged Balfour) was to form a Royal Commission on Coast Erosion, he wrote Lloyd George, then President of the Board of Trade, about his success in deterring erosion at his summer house in Kessingland with marram grass, and the inevitable followed. Haggard had barely recovered from an operation 'which the effects of my long journey [to the U.S.] made necessary,' when he was asked to serve on the Commission. He accepted and for five years was a member. For a time he was also Chairman of the Unemployed Labour and Reclamation Committee. Again he worked relentlessly: 'I do not suppose there is a groin or an eroded beach on the shores of the United Kingdom that I have not seen and thoughtfully considered,' he wrote. When the Commission had been meeting and inspecting coastlands for a year, it decided that coast erosion was not after all a pressing problem for Britain, but instead of voting itself out of existence, its Chairman (Lord Ashby St. Ledgers) and Haggard suggested to Lloyd George, 'one night at a dinner party,' that the Commission look into the question of afforestation. 'Afforestation' was tacked on to the Commission's title, a few more experts were added to its membership, and 'we investigated that great subject with much zeal,' concluding that England's forests were in danger of extinction. The Commission suggested that the nation undertake to reclaim and reforest its land systematically, a prospect that delighted Haggard particularly because it would give 'a great deal of employment on land which now uses but little labour.' But timber needs of future generations were less an issue than the Government's budget; any reforestation scheme would be costly indeed, and, while economical in the long run for the nation, of little immediate political value to the Radical Party. The Commission's recommendations were ignored, and not until post-World-War-I days did Britain move to save her forests.

During the years he spent on the Commission of Erosion and Afforestation (1906–11), Haggard kept the fires of his various interests dutifully fanned. His name constantly appeared before the public, in letters to editors, in interviews, in casual essays on current affairs, in reports of public appearances, in reviews of his fiction which he somehow continued to write, and as 'a leader of the "Back to the Land" movement,' as one journal called him.[11] When the Zimbabwe ruins were explored, he was happy to comment on them and their connection with his writing, and he periodically wrote critical and interpretative articles on political developments in South Africa. Sparrows, rats, psychical activities, intoxication, *The Letters of Queen Victoria*, the Transvaal Constitution, superstition, Dr. Barnardo's Homes, bird and tree schemes, the risk of invasion, the protection of children – all these and many more were subjects he dealt with either in public speeches or in articles and letters in the Press.

None of the early vitality seems to have left the greying Haggard; if anything, his early faculties and perceptions had sharpened through the years. Furthermore, at the peak of life, he seemed more genial, more sociable than before. He was the man who knew something about everything and could make the something he knew sound interesting, especially before an audience, which he rarely lacked.

Haggard's nephew gives us an interesting description of his uncle at about this time.

> He was long and loose-limbed, with sparkling, rather piercing blue eyes, a big nose over a sensitive mouth and a small beard which had turned grey. His hair was untidy. He wore his tie knotted through a gold ring (which once had graced the hand of a Pharaoh) and he avoided a crease to his trousers. . . . I think he had . . . [his clothes] made what is called 'easy fitting'. He looked like somebody and people, when I walked with him in London, turned round to stare at him, just as, about the Norfolk fields and lanes they would stop to speak to him, because he was a familiar figure.[12]

While Haggard was still working on the Erosion and Afforestation Commission, General Booth asked him to write an impartial history of the Salvation Army and offered an appropriate fee for his labours. Haggard refused initially, but his respect for Booth and the good work the Salvation Army had done for causes in which he himself believed strongly led him to reconsider, and he undertook the project. He may also have been swayed by an attack in John Manson's *The Salvation Army and the Public* that was published earlier in 1910, and which he probably believed called for an antidote. A letter from Arthur Conan Doyle* to Haggard warned him against writing the book:

> I think it is splendid of you to do it, but is it right or logical to take no notice of an indictment which is backed up by figures,

---

* Haggard and Doyle were friends over many years. They probably met in the mid-1890s and their common interests (Africa, religion, the supernatural, medicine, and writing) must have drawn them together. On November 25, 1898, Haggard wrote Doyle to say 'what an excellent vivid tale I thought "The Tragedy of the Korosko," especially to anyone who has been in Egypt.' On April 24 of the following year, Haggard, as Chairman of the Anglo-African Writers Club, invited Doyle to be the Club's Guest at a dinner to be held in May, and in 1902 Haggard asked Doyle to take over as the Club's Chairman. On September 22, 1900, and again on July 28, 1902, Haggard was Chairman and Doyle Guest of the Evening at dinners of the Authors Club. Their names occasionally appeared together on behalf of worthy causes, and when Haggard was principal speaker of the bicentenary celebration of the House of Longmans, Green & Co., at Stationers' Hall Court (November 5, 1924), Doyle was present. Scott, *Bibliography*, pp. 193, 195, 215; letters from H. Rider Haggard to Arthur Conan Doyle in the Sir Arthur Conan Doyle Estates Collection, reproduced in a letter (August 2, 1958) from Professor Pierre Weil-Nordon to the present author.

facts & most temperate reasoning? By lending your honoured name to it you are inducing very many people to support what if this book of Manson's is true, is in many ways (or has become) an evil organization so that the matter goes very far beyond yourself. Whereas if the heads of the Army found they were losing public support they would be forced to set their house in order & return to their pristine purity.[13]

Haggard's reply to Doyle has not survived, but it is not difficult to imagine it. Haggard refused to take the fee for writing the book (he did accept out-of-pocket expenses), and he turned the copyright over to the Salvation Army. Doing the job properly required him to spend three months on it, some of that time travelling about Great Britain to inspect various installations. The result, *Regeneration*, was published at the end of 1910.

Three years earlier, Shaw had given the English-speaking world a look at the life and love of a Salvation Army worker; *Regeneration* is something quite different. It is a record of Booth's crusade and the story of the Army's accomplishments against overwhelming odds. But the statistics and vivid pictures that Haggard produces also depict starkly and clinically the destitution, illness, depravity, and spiritual despair among many English people; it is, in fact, a sociological document. Haggard takes his readers into a London shelter where 462 men are accommodated, and he shows what the Army is doing for them; he describes a maternity home for unwed mothers and orphan homes for illegitimate children; he takes his readers to a free breakfast service for former criminals and on an expedition through London at midnight in search of the homeless. We go to slum settlements, an inebriates' home, and an anti-suicide bureau. The book, well interlarded with statistics, photographs, and charts, offers a clear picture of what it meant to be down-and-out in London or the provinces during the early years of the twentieth century. In spite of Lloyd George's famous budget of 1909 and other attempts to bridle *laissez faire*, Government had still not assumed much responsibility for alleviating economic and social distress. The reader emerges from the study with profound respect for Booth and his Army for undertaking to do alone what it takes today innumerable public agencies and vast sums of public money to accomplish.

Regeneration, also, was noticed in the leading article in *The Times* and received favourable reviews elsewhere in the English Press. In America, Theodore Roosevelt reviewed it in *Outlook*:

There are few men now writing English whose books on vital sociological questions are of such value as ... [Rider Haggard's, wrote the former President], and hardly one among this small number who has grasped the dangers that beset the future of the English-speaking people and the way these dangers can best be met. ... Few people who read this book can fail to be almost as much impressed as Mr. Haggard acknowledges himself to have been by what he witnesses. ... I wish it were in my power to convey to others the vivid impression which this book ... has made on me; and perhaps I may be allowed to add that my own limited experience with the Salvation Army has in every respect borne out what Mr. Haggard writes of it.[14]

Regeneration is one of those books which record for us the social awakening in England and America in the early years of the century; indeed it may have helped that awakening come about.

After Booth read the book, he wrote to Haggard: 'From my heart I thank you. ... May the blessing of the living God rest upon you.'[15] Within the year the old crusading General was dead. Haggard must have taken solace from the knowledge that he had given the militant Christian some satisfaction in his last days.

Haggard's concern for rural England never slackened, and soon he realized that he had been excessively optimistic over the Development Bill of 1909. The Bill's provisions were in effect too little and too late, and in the succeeding years the nation saw the rural exodus continue and the number of acres under cultivation decline. The spur to farming that the Bill provided was not enough to change a trend; more drastic measures were needed.

During his campaign for small holdings in England, Haggard admired the record of their use on the Continent, primarily in Denmark. He had read, talked and written about Danish accomplishments, but he had never seen for himself what the Danes had done. It occurred to him now that perhaps if he could inspect and report on Danish farming conditions on a somewhat smaller scale than he had done in England, he might help the cause of English farming considerably. He took the opportunity, while the Erosion and Afforestation Commission was in adjournment in September 1910, to go to Denmark, notebook in pocket, on another work-holiday. Accompanying him were his sister-in-law Agnes (*née* Barber, his former secretary) and his youngest daughter, Lilias, now seventeen years of age. From Harwich they sailed to Esbjerg, and then spent two months travelling through Denmark, Haggard gathering statistics, making official inquiries, and interviewing farmers (often with the help of an interpreter). They travelled north across the cold and barren terrain to see the landmarks of the Jutes. They visited the ancient seat of Aagard, whence, Haggard believed, his ancestors came. The old castle still stood, encircled by a double moat, gutted by fire, like the Burnt Njal he had visited in Iceland. Near-by stood the tumuli of the Vikings. From this castle, set afire in a peasant revolt in the fifteenth century, a nobleman fled, the legend told, and sailed across the sea to England. As Haggard stood among the burial monuments of the people who might have been his ancestors, he conceived the plot of another romance, what was later to be *The Wanderer's Necklace*.

Haggard and his companions went to visit Helsingör (Elsinore), though aware that Hamlet, 'if he ever existed at all, lived somewhere else about a thousand years before it was built,' and they saw Hamlet's reputed grave and the brook, 'a few inches deep,' in which ostensibly Ophelia was drowned. But more important, Haggard found in Denmark what he sought, 'the answer to the problem . . . [of] how agriculture could be made to pay in a Free Trade country with an indifferent climate.' The answer is 'medium or small holdings, for the most part owned and not rented, aided by universal co-operation, which will only flourish in the absence of too many large farmers, and by a system akin to that which is known as credit-banks.'[16] Denmark, he found, largely fed itself and exported agricultural produce worth over twenty million pounds a year, chiefly to the British Isles. These facts both elated and dejected him: certainly what Denmark could do England could also; but in order for England to do it, the Government would have to take new and courageous steps, and he did not expect courage in politics. Still Haggard was determined to do what he could, even in these days when the reins were held by Asquith, a legal-minded businessman content to carry on the government from day to day.

Haggard returned to England in early November, spread his Danish notes before him and wrote *Rural Denmark and Its Lessons*.[17] In his accustomed manner he presents the facts of Danish farming and rural life and education as he found them, and supports his statements with the familiar transcripts of interviews, statistical charts, photographs, and summaries of government legislation. In the last chapter, 'What Might Be and What Is,' he applies the information he collected to the facts of English rural life and farming, and he concludes that the lessons England has to learn from Denmark are essentially three: cooperative farming will solve many pressing problems; farmers will join cooperatives only when they are freeholders; and an economic and social structure that encourages the accumulation of estates, by passing them intact from generation to generation, does not permit small holdings to flourish. 'These are the main lessons,' Haggard avers, 'but there does not seem to be much prospect that they will be applied in Great Britain.' All parties, he knows, would oppose his solution. At least one would object because he advocates nationalizing land; all would oppose his demand for a law requiring lands to be divided when they passed from one generation to another. 'Whichever way we look,' he concludes, 'the road is barred.' Haggard grows fatalistic and detached:

> Thus things stand, and, after all, every community has a right to choose its own path to success or failure. So far as the land is concerned we seem to have chosen ours. . . . We might change . . . if we wished. The will is lacking, not the way. Perhaps, after all, this feudal system of landlords who do not farm their estates but let them out to others is that which suits us best. Perhaps, too, I am wrong in my conviction that it would be to the great benefit of the Country . . . that British land . . . should be popularized – like Consols.

> Only one consolation remains [he concludes] to such of us as may think our policy unwise. . . . Were we to take another course which would enable British farmers to adopt and grow rich on the Danish methods of ownership and co-operation, . . . that intelligent, industrious, and charming people might lose their best, if not their only market.[18]

This is a new Haggard, for in *Rural Denmark* there is a mellowness we have not seen earlier. Gone the impetuosity, the impatience, the self-conscious musing. In *Rural Denmark*, perhaps for the first time in his life, he faces the need to accept failure, and he realizes that hope and reality are things apart and sometimes irreconcilable. Haggard has come to terms with the world, and though he clings to his beliefs, his new wisdom tells him that his hopes will not be realized in his lifetime. Here Haggard takes his earlier programme of farm reform well along the road to socialization, and this time he does not apologize for the need of Government assistance and regulation. Government subsidy is the only answer, and he embraces it unconditionally, no longer insisting on 'indirect' assistance. But beyond that, Haggard asks for far more radical changes, particularly in the laws governing land ownership and inheritance. Haggard, in advocating compulsory surrender of land, moves completely out of the Conservative camp in which he was born. He is, whether he recognized it or not, a radical-socialist.

But there is still deeper significance in *Rural Denmark* for those who would understand the man. He was himself a gentleman farmer, born and bred by the squirearchy; he unquestionably had a strong sense of family, of 'blood,' and land. His dynastic sense fitted well with his strong sense of history. To Haggard Bradenham and Ditchingham were monuments to all his ancestors, and he believed that he and his brothers carried forth the tradition of a gentle, honourable breed. He desperately wanted that name and blood-line to continue. Yet Haggard loved Country, England and Empire, too – and Country and Family clashed within him. His concern for English agriculture, his surveys, and his work on commissions forced him personally to face a dilemma, and he asked his fellow-Englishmen to face it with him. Though they failed him, he did not fail himself. Somewhere during his crusade, in the lush Danish north perhaps, he must have realized that in order to support freeholds and cooperatives as a universal palliative for England's ills, he himself had to surrender his feudal inheritance, his hope for a secure Haggard dynasty. He could not hold to both the idea of a strong agrarian England and the picture of a feudal estate at the head of which sat one of his descendants. One had to give way to the other; they could not exist contemporaneously. 'The land,' Haggard wrote, '. . . can rarely return three clear living profits – one to the owner, one to the farmer, and one to the labourer. . . . The owner should be the farmer or the farmer the owner.'[19] In *Rural England* Haggard struggled against the inevitable surrender of one of his ideals; in *Rural Denmark* he has already surrendered – Haggard has given up Ditchingham and Braden-ham for England, and he is a better man for it. In arguing that it was futile to try to revive the dying feudalism, he alienated many who loved County more than Country. And later, the opposition that Haggard encountered rankled within him and conspired with the difficulties of an aging mind and weakened body to embitter him. Only here, at fifty-four, before the infirmities of age and the scars of political battles bend his frame, he walks with a strange new erectness, at peace with the world and his conscience. Haggard shows here a maturity not discernible in earlier days and often shaded by bitterness later. *

The Royal Commission on Coast Erosion and Afforestation filed its last report in 1911 and was honourably discharged. Haggard returned to Ditchingham, where, for the first time in many years, he faced a hiatus in the demands upon him from the outside world. He actually had time to spare – and it weighed heavy on his hands. 'I missed that Commission very much,' he wrote, 'since its sittings took me to London from time to time, and gave me a change of mental occupation and interests.' He had never been able to cope with inactivity, and he found the bleak autumn months unbearable. There was 'nothing to do except the daily grind of romance-writing, relieved only by Bench business,

---

* *Rural Denmark* was translated into Danish at an early date, appeared serially and in book form in Denmark, and is read in that country to this day. Haggard dedicated the book to 'The Farmers of Denmark, in token of the admiration of a foreign agriculturist for the wisdom and brotherly understanding that have enabled them to triumph over the difficulties of soil, climate, and low prices, and, by the practice of general cooperation, to achieve individual and national success.'

my farm affairs, . . . an afternoon walk through the mud . . . and a chat after church on Sunday upon the affairs of the nation with my fellow-churchwarden.'[20] His friends of South Africa days had all passed on, his children had all grown up, and his London acquaintances seemed to be disappearing too. Even at the Savile the old faces were gone: 'The last time that I visited the club there was not a soul in the place whom I knew. So feeling lonely and overoppressed by sundry memories, I sent in my resignation of membership [1908].' Everything worth thinking about seemed now to belong to the past; there was little to look forward to.

But his reminiscences could not have been entirely painful for him. He was after all a successful man. He had built a small fortune and made a huge name for himself. He had lived an honourable life, both in London and at Ditchingham, surrounded by a well-provided family and many good friends. He had overcome the stigma of 'penny-a-liner' and 'greengrocer' that his father had flung at him when he was young, and in spite of the spotty education he had received he had managed a greater success than any of his university educated brothers. He had even achieved a dignity in his middle years that earlier he would not have believed possible for a writer of romances; he had performed a considerable service to his country with his agricultural investigations and as a member of Royal Commissions. On the personal side, also, he had been more fortunate, for in recent years he had passed a number of happy milestones within the family circle. True, the memory of Jock had never left him, but he had enjoyed seeing the girls grow to woman-hood. Louisa was not, perhaps, a romantic wife, but she had been an agreeable companion, and their attachment for each other had deepened through the years. In August 1905, when he had been so involved with agriculture and other affairs, he went down to Kessingland for a short rest. When he awoke on the morning of the 11th, the twenty-fifth anniversary of his marriage, he wrote to Louisa before he arose.

> I shall get back to-morrow by the early train in case the Kiplings should turn up before they are expected. I do hope you are better this morning, my dear (I am writing this in bed in 'Nelson'). It is so unusual to see you unwell that it makes me quite uncomfort-able. I think, however, that we should be thankful that we have had our health during this past five and twenty years, also – notwith-standing our great sorrow – our share of happiness. It is a long time to look back upon, and in it one has made many mistakes, at least, I have, of judgment anyhow. I should perhaps have done better for you all, but it has been my best. Thank you, dearest, for all your

love and help during that period: I assure you that I appreciate them both and I hope that we may yet be spared to spend a good many years together.

... Best love, my dearest, from your old husband and lover – Rider[21]

Almost a year later Haggard celebrated his fiftieth year – or perhaps he did not, for those were the busy days on the Commission for Coast Erosion; and in addition to his Commission work, he appeared three days after his birthday as principal witness before the Select Committee considering the Housing of the Working Classes Bill. He had lived half a century, but there probably was not half an hour to spare on the anniversary.

In September 1907 Ditchingham was dressed for a wedding. The Haggards's eldest daughter, Angela, was married to her first cousin, Thomas Haggard, son of Bazett, Rider's elder brother,* a match that pleased Rider considerably and rekindled his hope for a male heir. It was a splendid wedding ('a very posh affair with half the county there,' a neighbour recalled), and the guests drank champagne on the lawn beneath a canopy. Rider toasted the young couple and announced that for the occasion he had retrieved from moth-balls the very same grey trousers he had been married in. With pride he proclaimed that they had to be let out only a very little.

But these happy memories were mingled with more than an equal number of regrets and sad thoughts. Perhaps the most ironic sorrow was his failure to achieve his initial fame in the service of his country. It was as though his success as a romance writer had come unasked-for, and that, although he grasped it gleefully when he was being jostled about by responsibilities and the difficulties of making a go at the law, he would have chucked it all gladly for a chance at a governorship in one of the Colonies or for a seat in the Commons. Then, when his agricultural activities had brought him to the attention of political leaders and he was called upon to make various public investigations, the reports he and his colleagues wrote were simply thrown onto a heap of blue-books and quickly forgotten. All in all, very little had come of his struggles on behalf of the English farmer, the destitute city dwellers, and England's vanishing forests. There had been no recognition, no success for those arduous years of labour in the service of his country. Ironically his only reward continued to come whence it had these many years, in payment of the few hours' labour he spent each

---

* Bazett had died in 1899. Bazett's widow, Julia, and the children had been estranged from the circle of Haggards for many years, a result of animosity that arose when Bazett and Julia separated.

day while pent up in his study, pacing back and forth, dictating to Ida
Hector.

Certainly he took no satisfaction from the ill fortune some of his
brothers had met with. It would have been very easy for him, as he
grew to manhood, to resent them and to cut himself and his family off
from them. But that he never did. Nor was it ever out of pride that he
let Ditchingham House become their second home, always open to and
constantly used by them until one relative suggested it be called 'The
Lost Dogs' Home.' The holidays usually brought his brothers' and
sisters' children to the square house for lengthy visits. And when his
own family was not occupying it – and sometimes even when it was –
Kessingland Grange was available to his relatives as well. But his
generosity went even beyond that. With traditional Haggard restlessness, his brothers shuffled from one pursuit to another, just as Rider
had tried to do; and this inability to take root precluded success for
most of them. Some ran into financial difficulty with monotonous
regularity, and Rider was the logical one to help. His assistance was
not always accepted gracefully, and we may even suspect that lack of
gentleness was not one-sided: a lecture probably accompanied the
loans. In any case, it was not like the Haggards to behave quietly, and
when an older brother had to succumb to the indignity of accepting a
loan or gift from Rider, somehow all the relatives got wind of it and
had strong opinions on the subject. Rider came in for much abuse at
the hands of his kin:

> [His] amazing family did and said the most outrageous and
> unforgivable things. They bit the hand that fed them with the
> utmost regularity, they were jealous of him, abused him, and even
> insulted him in their astonishing letters, having no control over
> their pens and little over their tongues. They landed their children
> on him to look after, then basely sheltered behind their wives'
> skirts when domestic differences of opinion arose over doctors,
> health, education and interfering grandmothers and mothers-in-law,
> or accused him of abusing their confidence.[22]

The case of his older brother Andrew is probably saddest of all. He
had been a handsome, promising young man, schooled at Winchester,
and he possessed a sharp critical sense. He had written a novel years
earlier, before Rider had tried to write fiction, and then had entered
the Army, where he distinguished himself as a soldier of unusual ability
and courage. Having achieved the rank of Captain, in 1891, after
eighteen years in uniform, he suddenly left the service, in hope of
finding greener fields. He found none, and when Rider went to the

United States to inspect Salvation Army camps in 1905, Andrew was in Maine, finding that a fortune was difficult to come by, even in the New World. The letter he wrote Rider before his ship sailed for England is astonishingly acrimonious.

> As to coming down to New York to see you sailing away home again after your rapid and triumphant progress – and leaving me behind, well, my dear Rider, it would be too absolutely distressing and I could not stand it. To be alone on the wharf in New York, with no friends, no glory, no excitement, no money, while seeing the smoke from your funnels disappearing. And then all the head-lines in the papers – 'Departure of Rider Haggard' – 'Distinguished Novelist Leaves for Europe.' . . . That sort of thing greeting me everywhere would be too much altogether – I know our positions are very different – and the cry is why did I ever leave the Army? Did I blame you for leaving Sir Henry Bulwer for Shepstone, Shepstone for the High Court, the High Court for Ostriches, Ostriches for the Bar and the Divorce Courts, the Bar for Litera-ture? I left the Army because I did not choose to serve in subordi-nate positions under Kitchener etc., who had served under me. Also I got two thousands pounds – gone now! Because *I* have been less fortunate than my rich and successful brother in my change of occupation, *I* must be reproached for leaving the Army.

It must have been difficult to read these words from his closest brother, 'whom I loved as he loved me.' But Andrew was bitter (his private life was particularly unhappy) and did not know how to hide it; later, Rider sent him some money, and Andrew replied more in the character of an affectionate brother:

> It has a great deal more significance than the actual gift, old fellow. It has taken me back to the days of my boyhood when we were all in all to each other. It has shown me that the love which still exists between us is the love that has always existed, that you want to help me, above all that you are not careless of my fate. The fact that it is done cheerfully, kindly, and with loving words has given me the most immense pleasure. There is a spiritual bond of union which will convey to you my affectionate and brotherly feelings better than any words.

Other troublesome memories came back to haunt Haggard during these quiet days, for with unmatched irony, the blue-eyed, curly headed beauty, the object of his first youthful love, came now to live in East

Anglia, a stone's throw away from Ditchingham House. She had met with grave misfortune and needed help; Haggard was her only recourse. Encouraged by Louisa, Rider provided a house and other means for the destitute woman and her sons. Louisa, dispassionate and efficient, took care of the details. 'As often as they could Rider and Louie went to see her – the ravaged shadow of the woman Rider had loved when they were both young, and whom, as Louie well knew, he still loved, with an affection which transcends all earthly passion.' In the spring of 1909 she died, and Haggard, 'almost in a dream,' walked through the churchyard behind the coffin to the grave.

To his sadness was added disappointment, for Angela's marriage to Tom Haggard, while in itself enduring, did not bring Rider's hopes to fruition; the only child born of that union was buried in St. Mary's Church within a year of its birth.

Haggard had stepped across the threshold of old age. When he looked in the glass, he saw that his beard was almost white and his face gaunt and deeply lined. Also, more and more, he suffered from bouts of bronchitis. The autumn months were grey and empty; to him 'it seemed as though everything had come to an end.'[23] The time had arrived for memorializing the past. Deep in his doldrums, he spread before him the documents, the letters, the scraps of paper, the memorabilia, the relics, the souvenirs he had collected all his life, and he set himself the task, in these latter months of 1911, at the age of fifty-five, to write another important story, the story of his life.

But Haggard was wrong. These sad, slow months he spent at Ditchingham in 1911 were not the beginning of the end; they were merely a lull in activity. Haggard would not pass from the world slowly. With the onset of the new year, things instantly changed. The Honours List contained Haggard's name – the King had awarded him a knighthood for service to his country. For Haggard it was 'recognition . . . after long years of . . . disinterested toil,' and he was particularly pleased to have his non-literary efforts, his public service, recognized.

Within a fortnight of this pleasant event, the post brought a letter from the Colonial Secretary, Lewis Vernon Harcourt, asking Haggard to accept the position of British Commissioner on a Royal Commission to visit the various Dominions and report upon them. This would be a gigantic undertaking, for the letter made it clear that the inquiry would probably take three years and require visits to Canada and Newfoundland, to South Africa, and to Australia and New Zealand. Later Harcourt personally urged Haggard to accept the post, 'and I trust,' he added, 'for the sake of the reading public that the Commission will not prevent you from pursuing a good deal of your usual avocations, and might even incidentally provide materials!' Haggard did not stop to consider the amount of work and travel that the mission would involve; the honour of being one of six men chosen for an Empire-wide inquiry was to him 'recognition – with a vengeance.' 'Now I saw that all my long years of toil in investigating and attempting to solve the grave problems which lie at the root of the welfare of our country had not been without effect upon the minds of its rulers.' Haggard took the post. Such extensive travel would mean long separation from his family, a partial shutting-down of Ditchingham House, and entrusting the management of his estate to others. But, more important, he had no idea how he could carry on his writing, his only source of income, since it would hardly be possible to take a secretary along on these official voyages. Haggard nevertheless decided with a flourish that 'such considerations should not be allowed to interfere with the execution of what I look upon as a high and honourable duty.' He could afford financially to go a while without writing, and, we may infer, he was only too happy to leave Ditchingham and his novels after the sad months of isolation that preceded for something more active – for 'service.'[24]

Before undertaking his duties as Commissioner, Haggard took time, early in 1912, to holiday in his southern paradise, Egypt, accompanied again by his daughter Angela. The climate helped restore his health, and the new excavations and mummy inspections revived his spirits. Returning from Egypt, he hastily completed his autobiography. On September 25 he wrote the last paragraph, locked the sealed manuscript in the safe of his publisher and friend, Charles Longman, and gave instructions that it not be opened until after his death.

The plan was adhered to; not until Haggard died did Longman break the seal on the manuscript. As editor and publisher, he issued it in 1927 in two handsome volumes called *The Days of My Life*. The autobiography is a lively, interesting work, but it is not one of Haggard's more distinguished literary efforts. Because he began to write it when he was in very low spirits, when disappointments and enforced idleness had set him musing on the past, sadness dominates much of it. It is, furthermore, too often a record of undeserved failure, defeat taken too hard; and the consequent acerbity does not lighten the text.

It is an honest story, to be sure, and the short-cuts Haggard takes and the excisions he makes from the documents he uses are only in the interest of brevity and speed and not to conceal or distort any facts. It is in the traditional sense an *apologia*, Haggard seeking to leave to posterity the picture of himself he wants the world to have. The record must be complete, and his official undertakings, his conversations and correspondence with political figures are reported in detail and usually supported by documents. But Haggard was not as selective as he should have been, and many pages are heavily laden with political minutiae of little enduring interest.

The autobiography has other faults as well. Haggard writes and organizes carelessly. He begins chronologically, but chronology very often yields to whim. Even when he is orderly, there is a charming chaos in his method. He writes among a sea of papers and documents, and he cannot always put his hand on the letter or scrap of paper he is writing about. Never mind; he tucks it into the text some hundred or so pages later, when he happens to come across it. The first volume is organized quite well, written as it was in those latter months of 1911, when Haggard was idle. But the second half of the work, set down after he became involved in the Royal Dominions Commission, shows impatience, haste, and considerable disorder. By his own admission, he could not bear to look at papers and letters from the last ten years. He had had his fill of the past, and he was eager to write *finis* to his memoir.

Too much sentiment and his proclivity for musing and moralizing also obtrude. For here, he decides to open his heart to the world for the first time, and he writes at length of his first love and its effect upon him, and of Jock. These are subjects Haggard could not be expected to write about in measured strokes, and he does not. Having decided to tell, he tells with a heavy hand. He reveals too much.

Perhaps one of Haggard's greatest faults was that he took himself too seriously. Humility and modesty were more conspicuous as words in his prose than as qualities in his character: 'In my own humble case ...' is invariably the cue for him to recite his accomplishments. Haggard never took credit for more than he deserved, but he would have been a greater man had he been willing to take less. In *The Days of My Life* he is too often a claimant. He suffers in his own hands.

But there are good things to be said about the autobiography as well. Few lives are in reality as interesting or exciting as was Haggard's, and in spite of the obstacles he places in his own way, the story of his life is readable. Although the tale moves along without much direction, there is an overall sturdiness to Haggard's outlook on life that gives the volumes coherence. His strong strain of common sense keeps his romantic inclinations and super-sensory wanderings in check. He is best, of course, not when explaining his spiritual ramblings, his agricultural struggles, or his devotion to Country and Truth, but when telling a good tale; and there are plenty of exciting moments when Haggard the story-teller is in command. Also the array of influential people whom Haggard knew adds interest, and the work itself gives us another valuable view of club society and County life around the turn of the century.

After Haggard locked the manuscript of his memoir in Longman's safe, he could forget the past and turn with renewed energies to the responsibilities that beckoned him. The Dominions Commission gave him a fresh interest in the future. In 1912 he was ready again for action.

On November 29, after some busy weeks putting his affairs in order, he sailed on his first journey for the Commission. New Zealand and Australia were his destinations, but before joining his colleagues he took the opportunity of visiting India. He had been interested in India from afar, and he was not the one to forgo lightly an opportunity of visiting a land with such a colourful culture and interesting past. But there was another reason: his second daughter, Dorothy, had married a military man, and she and her husband were then stationed in India. He spent the better part of January and some of February in India and Ceylon.* Ultimately Haggard joined his fellow-Commissioners in Melbourne.

The Commission was concerned with the well-being of the Dominions and their relationship to Mother England. Not only did it inquire into the state of imperial trade, but it looked into the general economic and social conditions in each of the Dominions and examined the way they used their natural resources. Haggard was a very active Commissioner, asking incisive questions everywhere, in the manner he had cultivated when surveying England and Denmark. He got to the bottom of the problem in each Dominion swiftly and perspicaciously.

The Commission itself attracted a fair amount of attention in the Press, and always Haggard's presence was particularly noted. He was often employed by the Commission as its mouthpiece; the members recognized that Rider Haggard, world-famous romancer and elder statesman, was pleasantly articulate, a charming toastmaster and after-dinner speaker, with a sharp manner, a clear and interesting style of speaking, and an awareness of the virtues of brevity. Haggard knew the importance of a witty phrase and a local reference, and he brought to each little speech a freshness, vigour, lightness, and whimsy, in the best tradition of English oratory. He, in turn, enjoyed the public attention and obliged newspapermen and audiences everywhere. Among the solid civil servants and businessmen who comprised the Commission, Haggard was a giant, a fact that seemed to please all. 'Every man loved Rider,' his daughter tells us, recounting her father's work on the Commission, 'from the Chairman down. . . . He was all things to all men – his sense of humour and love of change and travel lightened the most tiresome journeys, and his gentle chaff at their small

---

* 'I *am* glad you're seeing India, old man,' wrote Kipling from his holiday in Egypt. Letter dated March 3, 1913, Bambridge Collection.

fancies and peculiarities brought an almost boyish comradeship into the ill-sorted company.'[25] The Commission's work done in Australia and New Zealand, Haggard returned to England, and with the exception of an occasional journey up to London he spent the summer months at Ditchingham.

On January 24, 1914, he set out on the second stage of his Dominions inspection. But this was no ordinary lap of his tour: he was returning to South Africa for the first time since he left there as a young married man, thirty-two years earlier. South Africa had undoubtedly changed, as had he, and the reunion would be difficult. Perhaps to help him face the emotional crisis, and certainly because he longed for his family when he was away, he took Louisa and his youngest daughter, Lilias, with him on this tour. On the outward journey, the group stopped for a week or two at Madeira, and then they joined the other Commission members aboard the *Kinfauns Castle* for the journey south. After the long voyage they arrived at Cape Town at the end of February. Haggard watched Table Mountain aflame with sunshine in the distance as they approached the shore, and thinking back upon the last time he saw it, he wrote in his diary, 'I have passed from youth to age since then. . . . Much has changed, but the sunshine is the same.' The flood of reminiscences, recollected emotions, old scenes, and changed faces; the rush of activities, the receptions, the speeches, the interviews – all must have been exceedingly strenuous. But we know that Haggard preferred feverish activity that did not leave too much time for reflections and with Louisa and Lilias by his side, the return to the scenes of his youth must have been more bearable than they would have been had he come alone. Miss Haggard herself tells us that

[he was in a] strange mood . . . all the months he was in Africa; [the visit induced] a feeling as if he had come back from another life. Everything was so changed, towns unrecognizable, transport revolutionized by trains and motors where there had only been post carts and ox wagons; families who were household words forgotten, or but a tradition, for time moves fast in Africa and memory is short. Then on a sudden, he would find some place unaltered, untouched by the years, smiling in the sunshine as it smiled in those high-hearted days of his youth. Some man or woman who, by those magic words 'do you remember', recalled happy comradeship, dangers faced and shared, days of great adventure and endless promise, so that grey hairs and wrinkles were forgotten 'and to me it feels as though those three and thirty intervening years had vanished and once more I was back in Africa as she was in my youth.'[26]

There was indeed much to remind him of that youth. For one thing, his old Chief and companion, Judge Kotzé still lived at the Cape. The two men had a reunion and reminisced about their days together in the primitive Transvaal courts and of their treks across the veld. ' "Ah! Haggard," said the grey-headed man, looking at Rider with smiling affection, "how young we were, [I] the youngest Judge and [you] the youngest Master of the Court who had ever held office under the crown." ' In March the party travelled up country to Natal, where because Haggard's name was almost legendary, all newspapers sought to interview him, audiences urged him to muse aloud about the frontier days, and the local officials wined and dined him. From Newcastle, the Haggards drove over to Hilldrop, their South African honeymoon home, the 'last place on earth I ever expected to see again.' The ostrich kraal still stood, the gardens, and the orange trees were much the same. Where the old kiln had been, Haggard turned up some of his own discarded bricks when he prodded the ground. The house itself was the same, to the room where Jock had been born.

Miss Haggard notes that not all was thinking back, however, and that her father 'reverted to the ways of his youth' with ease. 'He rode the small veldt ponies with real enjoyment, smoked Boer tobacco, never bothering if his flannel shirt (a thing he was unknown to wear at home) went unchanged for a couple of weeks owing to perpetually lost luggage, and showed a regrettable lack of interest in a positive host of bugs in his bedroom.' In Maritzburg Haggard returned to Government House, where he had once worked and lived, and here too he met an old friend, one he had already immortalized in his tales of the Zulus. His former servant boy, Mazooku, came to see his master once again, and with the traditional formality of the Zulu, addressed his friend: ' "Chief from of old! Father! . . . Here am I returned to serve you." ' The papers seized the reunion of these two and ran a number of feature articles, one illustrated with a picture of Mazooku in European clothes, another telling the story of how Mazooku had years earlier saved Haggard's life when he had been lost on the veld.

Though Haggard was received in Pretoria with overwhelming hospitality from English and Dutch alike, he found the city too much altered; no longer was it the frontier town into which he had marched with Shepstone to annex the Boer territory. 'The whole aspect of the place had utterly changed,' he recorded in his diary. 'Who would know [Church Square] . . . for the same that I described in *The Witch's Head* where the Boers used to assemble in their wagons at Naachtmaal? . . . Oh I hate this grandeur – give me the Pretoria of the 'seventies – Rip van Winkle, Rip van Winkle – alas as well might I ask for my lost youth!' Also in Pretoria, the Administrator of the Transvaal, the Hon.

J. Rissik, reminded Haggard of the time he had read the proclamation annexing the Transvaal to the Crown aloud in the square. ' "At the moment," said Rissik, . . . "I would gladly have shot you!" ' Here Haggard also visited the Palatial, the house he and Cochrane built and lived in as wild, young bachelors, the house that had come to be known as Jess's Cottage.

From the Transvaal, he went on a special mission to Rhodesia to report to the Colonial Secretary on conditions in those two territories. But the journey did not take long, and in April he was back with his family and Commission. In Rhodesia, he visited the Zimbabwe excavations and saw the landmarks that had taken their names from his romances: two round hills called Sheba's Breasts, Allan Quatermain's Road, and others. The guide pointed out the residence of She and spoke of Kôr, her ancient city. The Curator, the explorer and archaeologist Richard Nicklin Hall, told Haggard in no uncertain terms that his romances were untrue to archaeology. 'He said I was responsible for various false ideas about Zimbabwe, and that at one time he made a practice of sitting upon the top of one of the great cones, reading my stories and noting their many errors! I had some difficulty in explaining a land where the ruins were built by the Fairies of Imagination!'

Back in Durban, Haggard exchanged farewells with Louisa and Lilias; they would precede him home, and he would stay on and return with the Commission. For the journey through Zululand, he took Mazooku along as his travelling companion. In Zululand he met the son of Cetywayo, heard the musical speech of the Zulu people again, and once more listened to their tales of old. Deep into the wild country he went, farther back into his youth – back to Chaka's kraal, back to Isandhlwana, roaming over the battlefields and graves of men and events he had written of in his romances. Haggard later reported his meeting with a gathering of Zulus in some detail:

I made a speech to them, which they received with a chorus of 'Inkoos! Inkoos y umcool! Inkoos y pagate!' which means 'Chief! Great Chief! Chief from of Old!' Then one of their headmen said that they wished to know by what name to remember me. They were told Sir Rider Haggard, at which they shook their heads, saying that their 'tongues could not go round those words.' Had I no other name? The answer was 'Yes'. In the land, years ago, in the time of their fathers, I had been called Lundanda, or, with my 'title of praise' Lundanda u 'dand Okalweni, which means 'The tall one who walks on the mountain-tops,' that possibly signifies, absent-mindedly, or dreaming of things above.

'Ah,' they cried with one voice, 'now we hear. Now we understand. Now we shall never forget.'

Nor will they. Fifty years hence they, if still living, or their sons,
would tell the inquirer how about this date a certain Lundanda,
'Sompseu's [Shepstone's] child,' one who wrote about their people
in books, had visited them and spoken kind words of comfort in
their ears.[27]

Finally, with a full heart and too heavy a collection of restored
memories, Haggard turned back. ' "At Maritzburg I said good-bye to
Masooku, whom I suppose I shall never see again. Poor Masooku!
his last salute to [me] 'Inkoos Baba' was given in a quavering voice
for the old man loved me. I felt very sad as I watched him disappear
with his bundle in the crowded station. . . . Whoever forgets me I am
sure Masooku never will, in whatever land memory remains to him." '
Haggard provided adequately for his old servant's remaining days
before leaving South Africa.

Haggard's special report to the Colonial Secretary on the Zulu
people reflects his keen knowledge of these people and his awareness
of their needs and abilities. His recommendations were, as usual, forthright, sensible, and progressive; and were, to be sure, ignored:

> In the case of the Zulus, [he wrote] civilization has one of the
> greatest opportunities, for certainly in them there is a spirit which
> can be led on to higher things. My earnest hope . . . is that this
> opportunity may not continue to be neglected in years to come. If
> so it seems to me that we shall incur a heavy responsibility towards
> a bewildered people, that we have broken and never tried to mend,
> and suffer evils to arise of which the effect will not be endured by
> them alone.

Haggard, facing facts, was again an unheeded seer.

> So ends my visit to South Africa [he wrote in the cabin of his
> ship as he sailed home] – on the whole it has been successful, if sad
> in ways. I am truly and deeply grateful for the extreme kindness
> with which I have been welcomed everywhere, in fact I have ex-
> perienced quite a little triumph. Affectionate as was my greeting I
> think really it was more to do with the fact that I am a sort of
> curiosity, a survival from a past generation, than to my own indivi-
> duality. . . . So to South Africa, farewell, which is the dominant
> word in my life. . . . My name will perhaps always be connected with
> Africa if it remains a white man's 'house' and even if it does not –
> perhaps. It is impossible for me to avoid contrasting the feelings

with which I bade good-bye to its shores in 1881 when I was young. Then life was before me, with its many failures and its few successes. [Later on the same journey, he added,] . . . In truth I grow weary of journeying by land and sea![28]

On June 6, 1914, Haggard's ship brought him back to Europe, but not for long, for he was off on the third leg of his mission in hardly more than five weeks, this time to Canada. While home, however, he was able to report on Rhodesia and Zululand to the Colonial Secretary and to sit (on July 1) as a member of the Royal Commission on Imperial Communications.*

The members of the Dominions Commission arrived in Canada on July 29 and within a week heard the report that the German army had invaded Belgium and that England had declared war on Germany. The news came as a terrible blow, of course, to men with families at home. But the Commission members decided to press on with their work until at least the Government clarified their position. The one concession they made to the emergency was to rule out public speech-making at the dinners and receptions given in their honour. This rule they adhered to, with one exception, for on August 12, at a dinner given them by the Mayor of St. John, a cry arose from the audience for a speech from Rider Haggard. So determined was the audience that Haggard had to speak, however disinclined he may have been to do so. He made a rousing appeal for imperial solidarity in a time of stress, and the response of the audience was overwhelming.

The Commission did not complete its task in Canada; it was recalled because of the national emergency. Haggard arrived in England on August 31 and went down to his family in Ditchingham. On September 4, he made a 'Call-to-Arms' recruiting speech in the Drill Hall at Bungay and later in the month had 10,000 copies of it reprinted at his own expense for distribution throughout the country.

The war was bound to bring changes to the Haggards and to Ditchingham. Very soon after his return from Canada, Haggard got word that his nephew Mark, Bazett's son, a young man he had grown fond of, had been killed in France. Then, as the days passed, it became evident that the Haggards would do well to leave Ditchingham. Haggard had to attend to Commission affairs in town, neither he nor Louisa wanted to spend the winter months in Ditchingham waiting impatiently for news, and there was not enough fuel in wartime to keep

---

* During the hearing, Haggard asked one of the witnesses, the manager of the Marconi Company, whether he expected a time would come 'when a subscriber can have a telephone in his house by which he can telephone all over the world?' The witness answered that he would not like to go so far as that in his claim. 'To Talk This Year Across Atlantic,' *New York Times*, LXIV (July 2, 1914), p. 1.

the House warm. Haggard could not keep his greenhouses heated either: the orchids and ferns he had collected were consequently war casualties. The Haggards moved into a London flat, but in January the old bronchitis-influenza returned, and he and Louisa were forced to remove to St. Leonards, where the sea air might help him recover.

Haggard's concern for the war and the Empire was genuine, and as soon after his influenza bout as he was able, he returned to give all his attention to the war effort. With his usual fervour, he pressed his ideas upon the public and the Government, unsparing of his own waning resources. He made speech after speech on war savings, recruiting, and the national food shortage. Also, he began to champion another project, which, characteristically, looked ahead. It was a back-to-the-land scheme for returning servicemen. He wanted to make it possible for ex-soldiers and ex-sailors to become rural dwellers and farmers, with the aid of the Government. But the Government again did not welcome his concern for the future. His daughter tells us that his letters were even 'censored out of *The Times*' and his offers to serve in any and every capacity were politely but firmly turned down, because (he was told by a friend) it was against the policy of the Government to suggest that any serious food shortage might occur from the submarine menace. Feeling the national emergency, his age, and his illness, he could no longer take frustration and defeat philosophically. 'It would appear,' he records in his diary, 'that men like myself who have lifelong experience and accumulated knowledge are of no value to the country. . . . The conclusion is, I think, wrong. Or perhaps it is right and nobody is of value now save those who can shoulder a rifle and wield a hammer. Yet foolishly enough perhaps I feel sore.'[29]

It was inevitable that the Government and public opinion would catch up with Haggard's ideas about food supply and land settlement for returning soldiers and sailors, and as a result he was kept very busy in 1916 and 1917.* He found backers for his scheme to get ex-servicemen onto the land: the Royal Colonial Institute not only listened attentively but undertook to send him as its representative to the various Dominions to determine whether Dominion lands could be used for resettling British soldiers and sailors. This was, in a sense, the same sort of plan Haggard had advanced for England's impoverished

* By 1917 Haggard was also in the thick of unofficial negotiations for the War Office. In a letter dated November 19, 1917, he writes Theodore Roosevelt that 'an eminent friend' on the General Staff has asked him to write the former President 'on crucial points vital to the interest of both countries.' The letter contains detailed questions about how many troops and planes the United States could send to Europe to assist the Allies. Can the United States send troops from San Francisco to Vladivostok, Moscow, etc.? Could the United States help to organize the Armenians? Could the United States give financial aid to Greece? The three-page letter was prompted by more than Haggard's patriotic concern, for it went to Roosevelt through the British Embassy in Washington, and Roosevelt was asked to reply through official Government channels. Huntington Collection.

city dwellers ten years earlier when he investigated Salvation Army
labour colonies; now he was doing it for men who had fought for
England. On February 1, 1916, the Institute gave a luncheon in
Haggard's honour at the Hotel Cecil; on February 3 Haggard was
guest of honour at a dinner of the Authors' Club, and on February 10
he said good-bye to his family at Paddington Station and left London
for South Africa, his first stop on his new mission. The war still raging,
the waters filled with submarines, Haggard, a tired man of sixty, set out
on a journey of 20,000 miles to twenty different lands. Nor was his
journey official or Government-inspired; he was going as an honorary
representative of the Institute. More than ever before he must have felt
aware that he might be embarking on just another useless survey; that
he would go, see, return, report – and then he and his report would be
ignored. But there was after all the mere chance that he might be useful
to the Empire, and that was enough for him. 'Here is my war offering,'
he wrote in his diary. And from the ship he wrote to Louisa:

> My Dearest, Dearest Wife, I feel parting from you and the
> children very much indeed. I am under no delusions as to the risks
> of this journey, but I felt it my duty to go, hoping and indeed
> believing that I shall emerge safe out of it at the end – so there is
> nothing more to be said. You know whatever comes I shall always
> be thinking of you my dear – also of them – the worst of it is that
> though I shall (all being well) be able to write to you frequently I
> cannot often expect to have letters from home, or anything but
> cables.[30]

The cables kept him in touch with his family, however, and from them
he learned that *Child of Storm*, the second part of his Zulu epic, had
gone on sale, and that a film of *King Solomon's Mines* was proving popular. Cape Town was Haggard's first stop, where he was again reunited
with Judge Kotzé and stayed with his other good friends, the 'Henry
Seton Merrimans.'[31] There was no need to travel about South Africa
this time, and so he pressed on with his queries within officialdom at
Cape Town and was soon ready to sail on to Australia. The voyage to
Australia was a long and cold one, with bad weather much of the way.
Haggard was much alone in his cabin.

> This kind of solitary confinement is not gay [he wrote home to
> Louisa]. All one's failures and failings rise before one in a melan-
> choly procession till one is sick of contemplating them. In short it
> is a lonesome job and there is another fortnight of it ahead. . . .
> However, it is supposed to be very healthy and one eats and sleeps

a lot, which with novel reading and reflections on one's latter end make up the day!

Today . . . wrapped in a multitude of garments I have been able to sit on deck. Here four or five people arrived to photograph me – a nice bundle I shall appear, will try to send you one if I can get it. On looking back I see I have been writing some melancholy stuff which I would not have set down to-night. The truth is, my dear, that I have as many moods as a woman – yes as She herself. I have half a mind to tear it up, but there – skip it and don't laugh at me, there's a good girl.

Haggard spent two months (April and May) in Australia and Tasmania, pouring out 'floods of the best eloquence I could muster in every direction,' winning officials and audiences over to his scheme, and getting promise after promise from one government official after another of land and provisions for settlers from England.

I never had such a reception . . . [he wrote home about a large meeting]. They cheered enough to lift the roof. I have been shouting all over the place until I am sick of the sound of my own voice and tired to my bones, and homesick for you all, for success has not been easy. With all modesty I think I may say it has been personal. For some reason or other I am popular in Australia, they think I am something of an orator which of course I am not, but at any rate I can always hold the attention of my audiences, and they like men who have made a success even if it is only writing romances. . . . They have given me a great civic and Official reception almost everywhere.

'My work in Australia has been successful beyond all my expectation,'[32] he told interviewers when he left, and in his diary he wrote, 'Well I have fired my shot and if it falls into the sea I cannot help it. . . . Oh, I am weary of these voyagings for which I grow old!'

New Zealand was more of the same, speeches, conferences with officials, continued weariness, but considerable success for his mission. Then in mid-June he sailed for Canada. On board the ship that brought him east, he passed his sixtieth birthday, a

very lonesome birthday among all this crowd of strangers [he wrote], and to-day I have entered upon old age, for at sixty a man is old, especially when he begins as young as I did. Of my early friends but two remain . . . for me the world is largely peopled with the dead; I walk among ghosts, especially at night. Well ere long I must join their company. Ten years more the Psalmist would give me, but with my weakened health I cannot expect as much. My work for the most part lies behind me, poor stuff it may be but I will say this, I have *worked*.

When he arrived at Victoria, British Columbia, at the end of the month, his brother Andrew was waiting at the dock to greet him, and that cheered him up. He continued, throughout Canada, to work for his scheme. Here too, he found, he was very popular, and in Calgary, before the largest gathering ever held in the city, he learned that a mountain peak and an adjacent glacier in the Rockies would be named Mount Sir Rider and Haggard Glacier in his honour. 'Here they give my name to a towering Alp,' he wrote in his diary; 'in Norfolk they would not bestow it upon the smallest "pightle." '[33] Across the plains he went, stopping to speak in each of the provinces, meeting with continued success. So wide were his travels and so determined his spirit that Francis Bell, the naturalist, later quipped that Haggard reminded him of a second Saint Paul 'engaged in converting the Dominions to the Gospel of Imperialism!'[34]

In late July Haggard was in New York, where he spent a day, with his old friend, Theodore Roosevelt, who had, earlier that same year, announced his retirement from politics.

He had grown older and stouter since last we met six years ago, and at times his burning manner of speech is nervous in its intensity – and Heaven, how we talked! Of all sorts of things; of the world and its affairs, of religion, of heaven and hell, of the fundamental truths, and the spirit of man; for when Roosevelt and myself meet – men who are in deep and almost mysterious sympathy with one another, there are many vital matters on which we need to know each other's mind.

Before the end of July Haggard was back in England after circling the globe. The remainder of the year he spent explaining his scheme and the assurances he had been given by Dominion Governments to Whitehall officials, to the Press, and the English Public, in spite of his physician's injunction that he was to live with ease. The picture his daughter gives us of the man at about this time is poignant.

On Christmas Day [1916] Rider and Louie had their three children at home, but the two sons-in-law, Tom Haggard and Reggie Cheyne, were in France, and for the first time in his daughters' remembrance their father had no heart for the usual drinking of healths after Christmas dinner. Usually, in the time-honoured

fashion, every absent member was mentioned by name, ending with
the phrase – 'Friends at home, Ships at sea – All round the hat,' with
a comprehensive wave of the glass of port over the candle-lit dinner.

In the spring of 1917 the family was in London, and Haggard kept
busy through the succeeding months on his various reports and commissions. In March he was elected Vice-President of the Royal Colonial
Institute, further recognition of his work in the Dominions. But
perhaps the greatest recognition came in April, when the Government,
under pressure from the Institute and influenced by Haggard's investigation and report, established an Empire Settlement Committee and
appointed Haggard one of its members.

Although prospects for victory improved in 1917, the final year of
the war was not personally a happy one for Haggard. In August 1918
Bradenham Hall was sold and its contents auctioned off. Rider's eldest
brother, William, could not hope to keep the old homestead any longer.
For Rider it was a sure sign that the end of an era was at hand. We learn
that 'from this year Rider commenced to set his affairs in order, as if he
felt that the time left to him was not very long.'[35] In September he
presented all but two of his manuscripts[36] and the notebooks of his
agricultural undertakings to the Norwich Castle Museum.[37] In the same
month he disposed of another piece of his world that was very dear to
him, his farming property. Knowing that he could not, at his age,
continue to give his energies to his farms, he put his pedigreed Shires
and shorthorn cattle up for sale. Looking back upon his life, he saw his
struggle as a gentleman farmer as unprofitable and difficult, and the
speech he made at the auction reflected his bitterness.

During the war Haggard's books continued to sell, but not with
the early intensity. He had trouble finding magazines to run them
serially (important tales like *Child of Storm* and *Finished* never did run),
and publishers were no longer scrambling after his work. When he sent
his manuscript of *Moon of Israel* to John Murray, he sent along a note
from Kipling praising the tale, and then, after Murray had agreed to
publish it, he wrote urging him to put the book on sale for six shillings
instead of five, 'and there would be a little more margin for everyone
concerned.'[38] The long notices in the Press were also a thing of the past;
now Haggard's books were reviewed, for the most part, in short
paragraphs, if at all. Writing to an anonymous reviewer who had given
The Holy Flower a favourable notice, Haggard revealed his attitude
toward his creative work at this time:

Personally I prefer to write fiction about old Egypt or historical
subjects. . . . But what happens? My name, as you remark, is

connected in the public idea with a certain stamp of African story and especially with one famous character. Therefore Editors and Publishers clamour for that kind of story reintroducing that famous character. If I write other things I am told they are 'not so good' though I well know them to be much better. At the bottom of all this are the fashion-following critics themselves who absolutely resent any new departure, although often enough they also blame the author for sticking in his old *cliché*.

... Oh, I grow weary of story telling and could it be managed, would devote the days that remain to me to the problems of the Land, that greatest of all Causes, and to the service of my Country. But few of us can do exactly what we wish.[39]

Haggard's waning popularity continued to discourage him, and on November 8, 1918, he wrote of himself as 'the deadest of dead letters.'[40]

When the war ended, Haggard sat down with his diary and looked into the future with his usual clarity. One might expect jubilation at such an hour; but Haggard sees nothing to be jubilant about.

So it comes about that our nation emerges from the struggle more potent, more splendid than ever she has shone before, laughing at all disloyalties, with mighty opportunities open to her grasp. How she will use them in the years to come, I shall never see. The Germans will neither forgive nor forget; neither money nor comfort will tell with them henceforth. They have been beaten by England and they will live and die to smash England – she will never have a more deadly enemy than the new Germany. My dread is that in future years the easy-going, self-centred English will forget that just across the sea there is a mighty, cold-hearted and remorseless people waiting to strike her through the heart. For strike they will one day, or so I believe.[41]

Haggard, in the years after the war, when travel was impossible, continued to spend the winters at St. Leonards, where he had bought North Lodge, an ornate old place that had been, like Chaucer's home at Aldgate, part of the original Toll Gate House. He used as a study the bright room atop the archway through which ran the road and from which he had a pleasant view. But by no means did he remain in retirement. The New Year, 1919, brought new recognition: Haggard was made a Knight of the British Empire for his service during the war on the Dominions Commission and the Empire Settlement Committee. In April he accepted an appointment to the British Rate Commission, on which he served for some time. He continued his public speaking, of course, and on May 14 appeared with George Bernard Shaw at Central Hall, Westminster, to oppose a Ministry of Fine Arts.

The condition of English agriculture was a continuing source of dismay to Haggard. In 1920 the farmers suffered another severe setback as a result of the fall in the general price level, and the entire rural picture again seemed hopeless. Haggard had to face the fact that England was no longer, and would not likely ever be again, a nation of prosperous farmlands, that the New Man felt bound to the city and the machine, not to nature and the land. 'I fear that no amount of reforming . . . will turn our farms into gardens of abundance,'[42] wrote Haggard to *The Times* in 1923. For two more years he looked on as England's power continued to decline, as her farmlands continued to deteriorate, as her villages became less and less populated.

But we cannot write an end to the tale of Haggard's agricultural efforts with his despair. A look at English farming today shows us that many of the reforms he fought for have been adopted: a cheapening of land transfer, a vastly improved network of agricultural postal services, and a revised code of rural education. The Government now points with pride to the '20,000 smallholdings provided by county councils . . . in England. . . . These smallholdings are let only to people with practical experience in agriculture, preferably agricultural workers, with the object of affording them an opportunity to become farmers on their own account. Loans may be made to the tenants up to 75 per cent of the working capital they require.' In 1931, furthermore, England finally faced the farmer's needs and undertook a programme of direct financial assistance to agriculture, including tariffs, subsidies, and quotas; and in 1947 the Agricultural Act finally provided the English farmer with guarantees which would ensure for the country 'a stable and efficient agricultural industry capable of producing such part of the nation's food as in the national interest it is desired to produce.'[43] The agricultural bureaux of the Government have multiplied and expanded, numerous investigations have been conducted (some of their recommendations have not been shelved), and many Government teams keep watchful eyes upon trends and conditions. There is an Agricultural Land Commission, an Agricultural Land Service, and Agricultural Advisory Service, an Agricultural Research Council, and many others – all devoted to one end: to keep English farming at the peak of efficiency and to keep the English farmer on his farm, content. English cooperative farming has widened also. In 1900 there were nineteen cooperative societies doing a gross business of £120,000. In 1951 there were more than two hundred societies and the business they did was £50,000,000.

Although we cannot credit Haggard directly with these advances, his diagnosis and prognosis were sound. If the government had listened to him, agricultural conditions would have improved enormously in his time. As it was, the collapse of English agriculture was one of the nation's catastrophes whose consequences would not become clear to cocksure politicians and complacent voters for many years. Haggard and his agricultural works did influence the ultimate reversal of policy and helped fix the tenor of the reforms in the years after the awareness dawned, in the 'thirties. It takes but a glance to see, for instance, that *Rural England* influenced more than the lad who 'ploughed through the two grim volumes . . . because the magic name was on the title page.'[44] An examination of some standard economic and agricultural histories and of the important Commission reports that lie behind the more recent reforms gives us a measure of Haggard's contributions. Lord Ernle, probably the nation's most respected agricultural historian of recent years, in his *English Farming Past and Present* (1932), calls *Rural England* 'a monument of physical energy and endurance. It is also a contemporary record of rural facts and conditions, to which time will add historical value,'[45] he writes, and he himself uses Haggard's work as a source book for his own study. Haggard's conclusions on coopera- tive farming at the close of *Rural Denmark* are cited verbatim by J. A. Vonn in his *Foundations of Agricultural Economics* (1923).[46] Both the *Report of the Land Enquiry Committee of 1909–12*[47] and the *Rural Report of the Liberal Land Committee of 1923–25*,[48] the latter often praised as the most far-sighted attempt to solve England's farm problems, lean on Haggard's writing and quote his statistics and opin- ions to support their recommendations. Innumerable writers on land problems, rural life, and economic history show that they have studied Haggard.[49]

That Haggard influenced the minds of men in responsible positions is also evident. W. E. Hartpole Lecky, the Irish rationalist, while struggling for educational reforms just after the turn of the century, wrote in a letter to an Australian historian, 'It is depressing to see how many good authorities are of the opinion that in the rural districts education is engendering an extreme distaste for rural life and labour and driving multitudes to wretched and debilitating existences in the great towns. I write rather under the impression of Rider Haggard's very interesting survey [*Rural England*] . . . a book which has much impressed me.'[50] Thomas Jones, the Welsh author and editor, indicated in his diary in what high esteem he held *Rural England* as a dependable source of information for contemporary rural problems as late as 1934. 'I ran into J. C. C. Davidson [he writes] back from his mission to study the unemployed in Cumberland. I could not but envy the original mind which had just discovered the land problem, schemes of co-operative agriculture, collective farming, etc. I suggested delicately that he might read two volumes on Rural England written 30 or 40 years ago by Rider Haggard.'[51]

Haggard also inspired men with strong ties to the land to follow in his footsteps. A. D. Hall's survey of English farmlands in 1910[52] owes at least its inspiration to Haggard. S. L. Bensusan, in his *Latter-Day Rural England*, 1927, takes more than his title from Haggard's opus. Bensusan admits that he had in mind the Preacher's words, 'What shall he do, that cometh after the King,' when he set out to emulate Haggard in his own limited survey of some English counties.

There are no legislative acts to which we can point and say that Haggard was responsible for this provision or that, nor is Haggard eulogized as the great father of rural reform. But he had an effect upon legislation, and he did much to change life in the country, and even in the city. For in the modern method of planning rural education and in the vastly improved rural post, we see Haggard proposals clearly at work; in the growth of farmer subsidies, cooperative societies, and small holdings, Haggard stands with other reformers in the shadowy background. In the cities, when the English housewife looks at the selection of meats in her butcher's window and tries to decide between the leg of lamb from New Zealand, the Australian joint, or the native-grown fowl – does she ever wonder about the origin of the law that requires her butcher to put the little markers on the meat showing the national origin of his products? It was not custom or law before Haggard wrote *Rural England*.

If we are content to call Haggard a 'minor reformer' of farm legislation, we miss the significance of his efforts and of his contribution to English life. He was a catalyst for reform more than a reformer, though certainly he would have preferred to be the latter. He opened the English people's eyes to the plight of the farmer, and he made the rural citizen front-page copy for the Press and a topic of discussion at the dinner-table and in the clubroom. His reform proposals stand between open markets and uncontrolled agricultural competition on the one hand and Protection, subsidies, and quotas on the other.

During the 'twenties the elderly, eloquent Haggard was still much in demand. Although he declined an offer to inspect a malaria-infested plain in Palestine to determine if it could be made habitable, reluctantly refused to go on another exploration in Mexico, and turned down a lecture tour of the United States, he continued to lend his name and energies to many causes and often performed the jovial duties of the elder statesman. Thus he was elected Vice-President of the Council of Public Morals, President of the Hastings and District Boy Scouts Association, President of the Vegetable, Fur and Feather Society; and many and frequent were his speeches at Rotary Clubs, the Home for Invalid Ladies, the London Society of East Anglians, the National Council for Promotion of Physical and Moral Race-Regeneration, at various grammar-school prize-giving ceremonies, at art-exhibit inaugurations, and before his favourite Delphian Coterie and Authors' Club. On one occasion, his willingness to help worthy causes led him into an embarrassing situation. On February 23, 1923, he appeared at the Gaiety Theatre in Hastings (he had got involved in local affairs at Hastings and vicinity because of his home at St. Leonards) to chair a meeting that would benefit the needy children of Europe. Before he knew it, someone rose and began reading aloud the minutes of a League of Nations Association meeting. Haggard interrupted the reader and asked what was the meaning of his performance. Someone sitting near Haggard then leaned over and reminded him that this was in fact a meeting of the Association. Haggard had never sympathized with the League, but he restrained his indignation and completed his task. On the way home he announced to his acquaintance, William Le Queux, that he would never again participate actively in charitable functions, a vow he seems to have kept.

Haggard's daughter tells us that the last five or six years of his life were happy.

Looking back on them it seemed to those who loved Rider that he, who had always been over anxious for the future, both personally and imperially; whose imaginative mind had so greatly feared old age, sickness, and death; and whose spirit was shadowed with a certain inescapable melancholy that at times touched all his family, had reached some haven of inner peace. As if the river of his life had passed the deep pools and troubled shallows of its earlier course and had spread out into quiet, sunlit waters, lipped on the horizon by the sea. Much of his zest for life, his ever present sense of fun, his pleasure in meeting people and in small things came back to him.[53]

Though his health gave him incessant trouble, he kept so busy that he could not dwell upon it. He enjoyed the summers at Ditchingham and became attached to his house at St. Leonards. Even into his sixty-fifth year he kept active. The tales kept pouring forth, and although he made fewer public appearances, he did not diminish his written appeals on behalf of worthy causes. His concern with current events continued, and he joined his voice to those speaking against the spread of Bolshevism. He carried forth to the end his campaign for revised land taxation, for adequate rural housing and education, for Dominions unity, for improved farm wages, for a better rural postal service, and for adequate education and rural housing.*

Having given up shooting,† he continued to find fishing congenial, and during the summer months of these last years he often went out on fishing trips with members of his family, Charles Longman, and with the only friend he had acquired in his later years, Sir Ronald Ross, the malaria expert and winner of the Nobel Prize for medicine.

Foreign travel became possible again, and the Haggards let North Lodge and sailed for Egypt in January 1924. This was largely a sea holiday, by slow boat southward, and Rider was accompanied by a daughter, a nephew, a niece, and some friends. It was a happy voyage indeed, as the boat took them to Egypt, up the Nile to Haggard's favourite tombs and temples and to excavations he had not yet inspected. They had planned to go on to Palestine, but Haggard decided instead to spend the time in his favourite city, Luxor, which he did with Lilias. By April, revivified and refreshed, he was back with his family at Ditchingham for the summer, and he came up to London, where he took his accustomed walks through the British Museum galleries and attended the Buckingham Palace Garden Party, the Prime Minister's Party at Hampton Court, and a meeting of the East Africa Committee, of which he had been appointed a member.

In November 1924, he made his last two public appearances, and, although he would have had it otherwise, they were both connected with his writing life – not with his life as gentleman farmer or commissioner. On November 5 he delivered the major address at a luncheon in Stationers' Hall celebrating the bicentenary of Longmans, Green and Company. It was no small honour for Haggard to be chosen as major speaker in the company that included the Dean of St. Paul's, Cardinal Bourne, G. M. Trevelyan, Mrs. Andrew Lang, Sir Arthur

---

* 'I think that electric power should be introduced into every parish so that it can be used for all household purposes; also there should be a bath-house where men coming in tired from work can have their clothes dried while they wash, with which a wash-house and perhaps a public kitchen might be combined,' he wrote to *The Times*. 'Population and Housing,' March 25, 1919, p. 6.

† Haggard's attachment to matters psychical was very strong indeed, and because of what he believed was a psychic experience, he gave up shooting, a favourite pastime and turned completely against blood sports. On July 9, 1904, Haggard dreamed that his daughter's black dog, Bob, lay dying in a bush. 'In my vision the dog was trying to speak to me in words,' Haggard wrote, 'and failing, transmitted to my mind in an undefined fashion the knowledge that it was dying.' The next morning at breakfast the family discussed Rider's nightmare, and on Thursday, the 14th, the body of the dog was found floating in the river; the animal had been killed by a passing train at about 10.25 p.m. Saturday, the evening before Rider's nightmare. For Haggard's detailed account of the above, references to his letter to *The Times*, and comment in the *Journal of the Society for Psychical Research* about the matter, see Haggard, *Days*, II, pp. 159–167. Still another dream he fashioned into a strange tale, *The Mahatma and the Hare*, that preaches against blood sports. For the last twenty years of his life, Haggard concentrated on fishing.

Conan Doyle, and Sir Edmund Gosse. But Haggard was Charles Longman's close friend and he proved an apt speaker on the occasion. This, in part, is *The Times'* report:

> He had often wondered, he said, when the [publishing] trade first began. There must have been authors before publishers. He supposed that Homer was his own publisher, and . . . collected his royalties in a hat. (Laughter.) Publishers and authors were supposed to be deadly enemies. It was not true. They would be uncommonly great fools if they were, because they were united in bonds of matrimony from which there was no possibility of divorce.[54]

On the way home he was stricken ill with 'a violent digestive upset, chill, and exertion.' By the 25th of the month, however, he was well enough to appear with his good friend Ross at a meeting of the Delphian Coterie. Both he and Ross addressed the group on 'The Good and the Bad of Imagination.' Haggard fell ill again after the dinner, and it became increasingly clear that he was suffering from an internal ailment. According to his daughter, he had grown gaunt and weak in the preceding months. 'He had changed . . . in some intangible fashion,' she remembered. 'His hands had grown oddly thin, so thin that the heavy Egyptian rings which he wore almost slipped off them. Also his face had settled into . . . [a] brooding sadness.'[55] Haggard remained bedridden in Ditchingham through December, attended by a nurse. In January, his oldest friend, Arthur Cochrane, died, and a few days later, Rider's youngest brother Arthur passed away.

Death and illness inaugurated the year, but Haggard did not surrender even to the ominous signs. All the evidence available points to an energetic Haggard, dictating to Miss Hector from bed and even writing himself on days when he felt improved. It must have been difficult for this quick-thinking, high-spirited man to lie bed-ridden, at sixty-eight, wondering whether he had reached the end of his life. The picture of these last days is not preserved in careful detail, but the broad strokes are visible – not in Haggard's words but in those of his friend, Rudyard Kipling, in a series of sixteen unpublished letters he sent to Ditchingham while Haggard lay ill.[56] They are long, intimate missives, and not written just from the comfortable study at Bateman's. Kipling and his wife were on a motor trip through France for the better part of that spring, but Kipling did not let the exigencies or diversions of travel interfere with his devotion to his friend. The letters came forth, every two or three days, long and full of chitchat about France and his experiences there, full of observations about life and nature, about body and spirit. These letters tell us a great deal about Kipling, but they also give us a mirrored image of Haggard's illness and of those last months at Ditchingham and in the nursing home, for Kipling often reflects here Haggard's mind and heart, shares his advances and reverses, his hopes and apprehensions.

They begin at Bateman's on February 15, 1925, after Kipling first hears of Haggard's illness:

> Dear old man,
>
> I heard, a day or two ago that you are under the weather at Ditchingham; and I write at once to send you mixed condolences and congratulations. In a hell-broth of a winter like this, bed's the best and soundest place there is; and anyhow, all England is one filthy ditch (full) at present. So lie up in peace: only send me a line when you feel like it. . . . [Turning to politics and Lloyd George, Kipling says,] He has just gone out – him and his sunsets and his mountains and his banners of dawn. You said he would. You said the mob threw him up and the mob would throw him down.

He asks what Haggard is writing or whether he is simply answering crank letters, and he asks him to recommend a film of one of his books he might see. Six days later he writes again, another chatty letter, in which he reports that he had met the 'Norweegee Minister who had just discovered Egypt. He went down there, this year, led, he says, by your works: and he was immensely full of it and of them.' At the end of the letter, he adds, 'I've been putting in a spare time of self-examination, rather envying your record.'[57] Exactly one week later, Kipling writes again, answering Haggard's heated reaction to a flippant remark Kipling had made about small holdings in one of his earlier letters: ' "Keep your hair on" as the boys used to say. I haven't your Isaiah-like gift of promiscuous fulmination,' and he assures him he is really on his side. He complains about his farm, and goes on to tell him how fond the Kipling children are of Haggard, adding,

> It must be nice to inspire affection at short notice. I haven't the gift. . . . My dear Rider you be glad you're in bed – even if those damnable nights are long and even Ecclesiasticus who is my refuge, doesn't help always. I've had a touch of it and done a deuce of a lot of thinking – the sum and substance of which is that I wish I had as straight and high a record as you have of work done. But I never took on commissions and now I rather regret it. . . . Dictate me another letter sometime.[58]

Two days later Haggard did, and this is one of the few letters of his to Kipling to survive. In part, he writes,

I am glad to say that I am somewhat better. I got up yesterday & sat in the old study next door for a little while, but of course my limbs are like sticks & the sight of *meat* is abhorrent to me. You would laugh to see me being fed by the nurse with milk pudding from a spoon just like a baby. Also my rings fall off my hands & there was the deuce of a hunt for one of them the other night – finally retrieved from the seat of my pyjamas.

By the way, I think I saw you had a birthday not long ago. Would you like a present of a ring to use as a seal, for it is too massive to wear, copper I think with a little gold in it, Egyptian 18th Dynasty, & very curious in its way, probably a memorial ring of Akhenaton, whose name has been perverted on it, perhaps because it was not lawful to use it after his death as it stood; just as the Zulus in my youth would not mention the names of their dead kings.

. . . . .

The truth is I fought against this illness too long; I ought to have gone to bed much earlier. But I kept at it sitting on that E. African Committee after the dark to suit Lord Southborough's convenience & so forth, & the thing grew & grew until it bowled me over.[59]

Within a week came another message in which Kipling thanks him for the seal: '(I'm sure he kept it in his Library) which you needn't tell *me* has no duplicate. . . . I don't care so much about Akhenaton's dealings with it (he probably countersigned a lot of tosh of the Social Progress nature before he was busted) but that it has been yours and that you've given it to me *does* mean a lot to this teacher of the alphabet.'[60] And a few days later, Kipling replied to a note from Haggard about the seal:

Yes I value old Akhenaton's thumb-piece but more than that I value your exceedingly cock-eyed p.c. [post card] (no I won't sell it for an autograph!) which shows 'evidences of design' – and improvement. *Did* you fabricate it [the message that accompanied the ring must have been in Haggard's own hand] lying on your belly, or did you do it from underneath – the thing held above you as I've done under like circumstance? . . . There's no news except that spring is here (with a hell of a N.W. wind) full of good intentions and on her way to Norfolk to make you whole again and exceedingly fractious, against my return. Don't let your attendants persuade you that you're getting better. Mine tried that trick on me, whereupon I would burst into tears. . . . [Kipling then suggests that Haggard read Doughty's *Arabia*.] It's styptic . . . in style and as Culpeper would say, 'helps mightily against the emerods.'[61]

Four days later, the Kiplings were off on a chauffeured auto holiday in France. But throughout that trip, there was a regular exchange between Kipling and Haggard. On March 12, Kipling writes a long letter from the R.M.S.S. *Normannia*, waiting to sail from Southampton. 'I wish you were along too. You'd cuss the cold – in spite of the lavish *and* odorous steam-heat – but you'd like the smell of the docks again.' From Chartres two days later another letter: 'I'll write anon. You can't tell me to stop because I haven't an address.'[62] Five days later came Kipling's remarkable tale of a visit to the château of the Princess of Monaco. Her Royal Highness had urged the Kiplings to stop even though she herself would be away, and they did. Although they found the château undergoing extensive repairs, Kipling and his party were regally. entertained by the household staff. After an *haute-cuisine* luncheon, they were shown the hen houses, 'brick villas,' with plumbing that would delight an English vicar's wife.[63] Six days later Kipling, now at Biarritz, acknowledges two of Haggard's letters:

> Your signature, Sir, is vastly improved and the fact that you can (whether vertical or horizontal) tell good tales is *most* gratifying. . . . Thank you *ever* so much for the tale of 'Her' adventures with the Huns [a German representative had probably called on Haggard about filming *She* in Germany]. It's exactly what they would do – energetically and shamelessly – as I've said: but it's also exactly like *you* that the hairy-chinned man should have stuck you for railway fares. Some folk are born to be benefactors: and you, old man, were long ago sealed of that tribe. But he'll pay you back; and I prophesy that 'She' will begin to pay you royalty – on a big scale. *Only* of course, I can't imagine how the tale could be adequately presented – even by all the means known to film-fakers. Can you tell me when there's a chance to have a look at it? . . . There are worse things in the world than to lie abed and read your books. I've done it. So I know. But it must give you peculiar satisfaction to run through 'em again: and to find out how big pieces of 'em you've utterly forgotten. Odd, though, that you don't mention 'Jess': whereof I mineself have something of an opinion. . . . If you habitually eat British Yorkshire pudding and gravy, it will end by depressing your morale and giving you what I have heard called 'tweezies in the trash bag'. England's all right to be ill in – owing to the sedative qualities of the air & the inhabitants – but it's no catch for a convalescent. When do you think they'll let you move out a little bit[?] You tell now of getting up in the afternoons. When will you arise in the morn, and stagger to a steamer – say even as far as Hull – and go 'foreign' for awhile?[64]

Six days later, still from Biarritz:

> You may be suffering from incurable diseases ... but you've still got a fine glow of moral wrath over the suffering of S. Africa. ... I don't quite accept your ideas of your travelling days being over: and the fact of calling a disease by a name as long as a probe don't make it any more obscene nor violent than it is. When they cut me open endways, I rejoiced in a lovely lot of names of disgusting import – but words beloved Rider, to men of *our* calling, do not kill. Put that in your Kaffir Calabash pipe and smoke it. ... I've written to a lunatic in Florida trying to make him understand that it is not my job to transplant him from that remote state to British India ... for which ... he is homesick unto death. Now *you* would have sent him a first class ticket by return post – which was practically what he demanded I should do. ... By some error, I find that I have gone on right up to the end of the 4th page, thinking it was the 3rd; so you'll have to stick it a little longer. ... Your letters always cheer me and make me laugh. Rummy! Seeing that *you* are the sick man, but it's all a question of temperament, (I come, I am persuaded, of a long line of bankrupt undertakers).[65]

On April 5, five days later:

> Dear old man: Nothing from you for the past few days, & as I've got to pull out of here in a day or two, I'm launching another yarn at you. ... The wife has bought her a new dress. You and I don't rake the first new town we come to for a pair of new trousers – why? Because, O Rider, we are Superior Animals. Here she cuts in and says we are by *no* means superior, because when the dress is worn, we enjoy looking at it. That *does* rather knock the bottom out of the argument.
>
> *Apr. 6 Palm Sunday*: And here comes yours of the 3rd (I was hoping it would) with the priceless tale of the drunkard & the leper (shall send it on to Elsie than whom you have no more fervent appreciator). ... I don't marvel that in your damnable weather you get setbacks. All nature is in conspiracy of course to chill you and gets in under the bedclothes for that purpose. But I note you've contributed two lines in your own fist – not so bad either – which greatly cheers me. ... *Do* write if you've time. Never mind what you say: all the letters are duly burned and so you can, if you feel like it, open the door at your pleasure. It's good for a man sometimes to say what is in his heart – even if he *is* running a temperature. Ever affectionately Rudyard.

From Paris, five days later:

> Dear old man – Just in from Tours, to find yours of the 8th with the *good* news that you've been trekking about in a Bath chair. Hurroo! It isn't quite the same as a Boer pony or even an ox-wagon; but 'twill serve for a start: and you've got the spring winds in your rear (on reflection this isn't a happy simile [*sic*]; but I'll let it stand). . . . Send us another line *here* to let me know how you are going out and getting on. Then I'll be home (In's hallah). Ever affectionately Rud.[66]

At this point in Haggard's illness, the doctors decided that he had best be taken up to London for a more thorough examination than was possible at Ditchingham House. The nurse dressed him, the ambulance came, and Haggard, daffodil in buttonhole, was driven up to London. Kipling gets the news of this development on April 20, while still in Paris. He replies instantly:

> Dear old man – Your last dictated letter catches me on the very edge of going off to Boulogne for this evening's boat. You don't tell me *when*, exactly, you go up for your exam: but I'm going to write to Ditchingham when I get back. One advantage of a committee of experts sitting on one is that (like Councils of War) they rarely recommend operations. It's the individual surgeon who does that.
>
> More likely 'twill be some kind of treatment – of infinite length & boredom. But you've got the year with you and the love of your friends round you – Bless you a thousand times. Ever with affection Rud.[67]

Two weeks later, from Bateman's, Kipling writes to Haggard in the nursing home:

> *Me voici* returned. . . . And I've got your note of yesterday; and this, you need not be told, comes to you with all-love (Bosch locution: but you know what it means) and sympathy not the less keen 'cause it has been shoved through the same mill.
>
> Don't know what happens to the Philistine in nursing homes and hospitals, but the man who lives by his imagination pays for his gift a thousand-fold in such places. The mere smell of 'em makes that terrible machine turn on its alleged owner and rend him to pieces. One pays in advance but – one never gets back the price of one's baseless apprehensions. And the grub matches the wallpaper; and the slow, sickening pully-haully of internal observations sinks one's soul into one's boots. So we are persuaded that our vitality is lowered, which, luckily, it isn't. Only we feel that way: so it is

deadly real. Can you, by any means, relax and let go altogether –
either in tears or lamentations[?] It's better they say, if one can – all
alone. I've tried but stuck half-way which was worse than not
beginning it at all. . . . But a council of surgeons, as a rule, is a heap
safer than one individual with a knife and a theory. They all ride
jealous on such occasions, I believe, and operate as limitedly as may
be. But there is this – and just this to be said – when the big Machine
of Fate is felt and realized to have us in its hold, one gets a blessed
incuriousness and content on the matter – on all matters: and the
odd feeling that somewhere at some time the self-same thing has
happened before and that, try as one may, one can't put a foot
wrong. I know that will come over you as you go up on the table
– if you've got to: and it beats any known anaesthetic.

And I've put in a long and wholly absorbed evening over your
young lady of the Dawn [*Queen of the Dawn*] – and – how the
dickens do you do it? How do you keep and outpour the vitality
and the conviction and *how* do you contrive to nail down and clinch
the *interest* that keeps a man lying along on one elbow till the whole
arm is tone-cramped? That's what I want to know. I don't pretend
(that 'ud be cheek) to judge the book in the least. I only know, in
my own person, that it held me as a drug might – but it was a good
drug. And here I am piddling and piffling with a tuppenny-ha'penny
short story that I can neither patch, punch or pot (try saying that
aloud!) into any satisfactory shape. You have the mastery of the
incommunicable gift of catching and holding – for the good reason
that you breathed your own good spirit into it. (And I ain't good)
Voila the little difference. Qua Stuff – I think the movement, flights
and fights before and during the Babylonian Army's battle are as
good as anything I've ever touched of yourn. That's no small thing
either, old man. And while I read, I was overcome by the ancient
marvel, as I lay, that a man's carcass should be such a disgusting,
ill-perfumed, vilely packed bag of tricks while his soul, at the same
moment, or almost, should sit cheerily trumpeting above it all! –
and therefore all my thanks and – for what they may be worth – my
abundant blessings.

. . . I'll be writing again in a day or two. Bless you and believe
in all the affection of your many many hundred thousand friends
the world about. And for me I am always lovingly Rud.[68]

Two days later:

Dear old man – Just a line . . . to acknowledge your note of the
6th. The Lord *is* treating you rough. It's the hanging about in-
definitely which makes the life unendurable indeed! I went to ask

after Milner . . . but (and this is a good omen, isn't it: he being 71–72) he is now making a most amazing recovery of it. So I went away much cheered – about *you*. I believe in these signs and significations. It's those d—d specialists who gather round a man and depress him. . . . By the way, has it occurred to you lately that your prophetic 'Doctor Thorne'[59] is in a fair way of coming true? Have you noticed how steadily smallpox is digging itself into certain crowded centres, and . . . is really getting ready to explode. I've been watching it for the last two years – but you foresaw it a good ten or twelve before that. And 'twill be d—d serious.[70]

The operation occurred during the second week of May, and there is one more letter from Kipling:

Dear Miss Hector:

I am tremendously in your debt for your notes about Sir Rider: and your bulletin of this morning made me feel a little easier.

Seeing that the operation was last Saturday morning and he is reported as reading & smoking on Tuesday, there seems to be a chance of the luck turning.

I'm off tonight for *Brussels* where I shall be staying at the *Hotel Astoria* till Sunday: in case there should be anything to tell me or wire in a hurry. I expect to be back in London on the 19th or 20th. I shan't trouble him with a letter unless you tell me. Very sincerely, Rudyard Kipling.[71]

The Kipling letters break off here. On the day this last letter was written, Haggard was in a coma. Louisa, their daughters, and other relatives spent the long, anxious hours either at his side or near by on call. One evening, Dorothy's husband, Major Cheyne, was alone with Haggard in his room in the nursing home. Suddenly strange shadows played on the walls, and Cheyne looked out the window to find a building ablaze in the distance. When he turned back, Haggard was sitting up in bed, his arm outstretched toward the flames, his drawn face and glassy eyes alive with the fire's reflection. 'My God!' murmured the stunned Cheyne, 'an old Pharaoh!'[72]

On the morrow, May 14, 1925, Rider Haggard was dead.

Ditchingham House has been for some years now a country hotel whose management offers its guests 'every home comfort and convenience, added to a first-class cuisine' on terms from seven guineas a week. Externally the House has lost much of the camouflage that Haggard added to break its abrupt squareness and has come once again to look very much like the Mustard Pot Hall of old. Many of the lawns and garden beds have gone to weed and pasture. Inside the contrast between past elegance and present utility is even more striking. The large dining-room is filled with separate tables at which the guests take dinner in silence. But although the expensive furnishings, the valuable relics, and the books have all gone the conventional road – each to the highest bidder – Haggard's influence is clearly seen everywhere. The oak fittings, the ebony and marble fireplaces, the mullioned windows remain. Here and there linger old Egyptian heads, African assegais, strange gongs, shields, and throwing knives. Some original drawings of illustrations for Haggard's stories line the main staircase, and in the vestibule still hangs a framed Margitson genealogy, with ink additions in Rider's hand. The huge study, with its expansive view of rich Norfolk fields and the winding river, is the master bedroom of the hotel. Here still hangs the Greiffenhagen portrait of Haggard with furrowed face, bony fingers, and deep, piercing eyes. Near the window stands the huge desk at which the story-teller worked.

If Haggard's hopes had been realized, Ditchingham House would today be in the National Trust, staffed with caretakers to tell anecdotes to sightseers; his letters and papers, carefully assembled and preserved throughout his life, would have been gathered under one roof and made available to scholars for study, instead of being scattered throughout the world; the twenty-odd volumes of his World War I journal would have been published and read, not merely lodged in the manuscript collection of the Norwich Library. For Haggard was, in his own words, 'determined to make a success in the world in one way or another, and that of a sort which would cause my name to be remembered long after I had departed therefrom.'[73] His thirst for fame had been whetted in the family battles on his father's hearth, and when he left Bradenham, he bore psychological scars of those encounters. He wanted to show everyone, and especially his father, that he could succeed.

But in his incessant struggle to re-establish the self-confidence his father had taken from him, he overemphasized the utilitarian. He sought the pot of gold, but he ignored the rainbow; he searched for success, not greatness. Though he found popularity and wealth, he never achieved the fame he desired, and at the end of his life he knew he never would. Writing to Kipling less than three months before he died, he complained that his life had been amorphous and full of frustration. Where he most wanted to succeed he had failed. He had done his best to serve his country, but he himself had had to create the opportunities.

> Some fifteen years solid of it I have put in as one of the great unpaid, . . . the effort *seems* to have been utterly wasted . . . [and my reports have been] chucked aside on the national rubbish heap

at Whitehall. . . . I have done the best I can single-handed, fighting against principalities and darksome, unknown powers in Government offices. . . . Lying in bed here day after day, one dissects oneself with thoroughness & alas – a somewhat miserable anatomy appears. Lack of sufficient principle . . . rashness, want of steady aim (except where the country was concerned . . .) & of character, liability to be swept away by primary impulse . . . all these bones & others equally unseemly, such as little secret jealousies, are very large & prominent.[74]

Haggard might have chronicled in this ten-page letter the many other tragedies that had occurred in his life – the poor education he had received, the loss of his first love, the death of Jock, the disappointments in politics and commerce – but he was incapable of recognizing the greatest tragedy of all: his failure to know himself. For he did not appreciate either his abilities or his limitations. At the end, he knew something had gone wrong, but he did not know what it was. He could never see that he had, in fact, followed false gods, that he had used his astonishing energy only to prove, not to perfect, himself and that all his life he had sought to achieve something he was not made to achieve and undervalued those gifts with which nature had endowed him.

Posterity would have responded to Haggard's accomplishments as he had hoped it would if they had been of a higher order, if Haggard himself had been half as sensitive to the demands of art as he was to what he conceived as the call to duty. But he did not afford a high place to creative endeavour. Unlike Stevenson, he never really tried to understand the gift of writing, nor did he honour it – never was he willing to put into his story-telling the effort he had put into *Rural England* and Government service. Even his friends could not induce him to accept the vast responsibilities of the artist. Time and again he refused to heed Jeaffreson, Henley, Lang, and Stevenson when they suggested that he take more care with his work. He was for ever concerned with dashing off, getting on with, or being through with a tale; he rarely bothered rewriting, redrafting, polishing, improving, or beginning again. His reach was too short, and, as Jeaffreson saw very early in his career, he made it with his left hand. His public mattered more to him than his critics; his purse more than his place in literature. He confessed that he never found writing an occupation 'altogether congenial, perhaps because at the bottom of my heart I share some of the British contempt for the craft of story writing.' And about his craft he believed strongly that

the story is the thing and every word in the book should be a brick to build its edifice. . . . Let the characters be definite, even at the cost of a little crudeness. . . . Tricks of 'style' and dark allusions may please the superior critic; they do not please the average reader, and ... a book is written to be read. The first duty of a story is to keep him who peruses it awake ... 'grip' is about everything.[75]

In public life, where Haggard wanted most to succeed, he was blocked by the exigencies of politics; in literature, where he might have triumphed without any outside assistance, he was blocked by his own narrow view. Although he was exceptionally enterprising, he vacillated between the world of affairs and the world of literature, never fully accepted in the one, never completely comfortable in the other. And because the public issues which commanded his attention have been so submerged in the greater cataclysms of the twentieth century, his name has not been written large in his country's history and men do not esteem him for his selflessness, for service to Country and Empire, for devotion to justice, agricultural reform, and social work, or for his schemes of colonial settlement.

Nevertheless, long after the public servant, the reformer, the commissioner, the agriculturist, have been forgotten, the story-teller still lives, and his writing today receives more critical attention than at any time since his death. Although he failed as an artist because he lacked the artist's temperament, his imagination has at least guaranteed him a reading public for many years. A man of action, he could write a tale of action with a robustness few could match; and many readers would agree with Graham Greene's judgement that 'these books live to-day with undiminished vitality,'[76] and with Arthur Ransome's opinion that they 'keep their magic still.'[77] There lingers in Haggard's tales more than hairbreadth escapes, an atmosphere of danger, fear, excitement, and a rapid flutter of nerves; there is, to paraphrase C. S. Lewis, the hushing spell, the truth of the thing. In spite of the imperfections in his style, Haggard's rough, simple, impetuous manner still carries the reader with him as in a flood.

There is little point in speculating about what Haggard might have accomplished had he been a more careful craftsman. Nor need we, like Henley, 'grudge him his genius, and wish (for art's sake) that he was only a man of talent.'[78] For there is ample talent in the world and there are too few men with Haggard's creative power. Haggard became a story-teller by accident, and he turned that accident to what he believed was good account: he made a fortune and a name with it. Because he set his sights too low, he failed to win for himself a high place among men of letters. But a modest place he has today and will have for a time to come. What is so astonishing is that he gained it not only with his left hand, but with half his mind and less heart.

NOTES

PREFACE

1. 'H. B.,' 'London Letter,' *Critic*, VII (February 12, 1887), p. 78.
2. *Something of Myself* (1937), p. 19.
3. H. Rider Haggard, *The Days of My Life*, C. J. Longman, ed. (1926), I, p. 249.
4. *Ibid.*
5. 'The Present State of the Novel,' *Fortnightly Review*, reprinted in *Eclectic Magazine*, XLVI (November 1887), p. 603.
6. 'Sir Henry Rider Haggard,' *Dictionary of National Biography* (1937), pp. 372–373.
7. Introduction to *She* (London: Collins, 1957), p. 15.
8. Review of L. Haggard, *The Cloak That I Left*, *New Statesman and Nation*, XLII (July 14, 1951), p. 45.
9. 'Of Stories,' *Essays Presented to Charles Williams* (1947), pp. 90–105; and 'High and Low Brows,' *Rehabilitations and Other Essays* (1939), pp. 95–116.

CHAPTER 1

1. G. A. Carthew, *A History, Topographical, Archaeological, Genealogical, and Biographical, of the Parishes of West and East Bradenham* (1883), p. 92.
2. Haggard, *Days*, I, pp. 17–21; and personal interviews.
3. See also Lilias Rider Haggard and Henry Williamson, *Norfolk Life* (1943), pp. 33–34.
4. Haggard, *Days*, I, p. 24.
5. H. Rider Haggard, 'Books Which Have Influenced Me,' *British Weekly Extra*, No. 1 (n.d.), pp. 65–68.
6. Haggard, *Days*, I, p. 5.
7. *Ibid.*, p. 8.
8. H. Rider Haggard, 'On Going Back,' *Longman's Magazine*, XI (November 1887), pp. 61–66; and Wilfred Partington, 'Champion of the British Farmer,' *Farmers Weekly*, September 11, 1936, p. 25.
9. Haggard, *Days*, I, p. 33.
10. *Ibid.*, p. 5.
11. Lilias Rider Haggard, *The Cloak That I Left* (1951), p. 31.
12. Haggard, *Days*, I, p. 5.

13. L. Haggard, *Cloak*, p. 28.
14. *Ibid.*, pp. 27–28.
15. Haggard, *Days*, I, pp. 28–33.
16. *See* Jean Burton, *Heyday of a Wizard* (1944); Horace Wyndham, *Mr. Sludge, the Medium* (1937); and Mme. Dunglas Home, *D. D. Home, His Life and Mission* (1888).
17. Haggard, *Days*, I, pp. 38–41.

CHAPTER 2

1. Haggard, *Days*, I, pp. 48–54.
2. Dated July 6. – *Ibid.*, p. 61.
3. A. P. Newton, E. A. Benians, and Eric A. Walker, eds., *The Cambridge History of the British Empire*, VIII (1936), p. 462.
4. Haggard, *Days*, I, p. 62.
5. Melmoth Osborn (1833–99) was to be Commissioner and Chief Magistrate of Zululand (1880–93). He is the original of Alston in Haggard's *The Witch's Head* (1885).
6. This spelling conforms to Haggard's; African scholars often prefer Keshwayo, and Cetewayo is another common spelling. Haggard later re-created the battle in *Child of Storm* (1913).
7. Haggard, *Days*, I, pp. 98–99.
8. Marshall Clarke (1841–1909) later served in the Transvaal Campaign (1880–81) and became Resident Commissioner of Basutoland (1884–93), Acting Administrator of Zululand (1893–98), and Resident Commissioner of Southern Rhodesia (1898–1905).
9. Haggard, *Days*, I, p. 90.
10. *Ibid.*, p. 104.
11. *Ibid.*, p. 105.
12. Annexation Proclamation, quoted in G. W. Eybers, *Selected Constitutional Documents Illustrating South African History, 1795–1910* (1918), p. 452.
13. Haggard, *Days*, I, p. 106.
14. John Kotzé, *Biographical Memoirs and Reminiscences* (n.d.), p. 451. I have found no early work of Haggard's in the *Cornhill*; Kotzé may have confused the *Cornhill* with *Macmillan's Magazine*.
15. Haggard, *Days*, I, pp. 101–103.
16. Kotzé, *Memoirs*, pp. 59, 465. Many of the cases the itinerant court heard are summarized in *Cases Decided in the High Court of the Transvaal Province, July 1877 to June 1881*, reported by J. G. Kotzé (1912).
17. Kotzé, *Memoirs*, p. 473.
18. L. Haggard, *Cloak*, p. 73.
19. Haggard, *Days*, I, p. 111.
20. C. W. De Kiewiet, *A History of South Africa* (1942), p. 105.

21. Haggard, *Days*, I, pp. 111–112.

22. *Ibid.*, p. 114.

23. Letter dated June 2, 1878. – *Ibid.*, p. 115.

24. Kotzé, *Memoirs*, p. 521.

25. Frederic Augustus Thesiger (1827–1905), later Lord Chelmsford; and Anthony William Durnford (1830–79). Durnford was killed in hand-to-hand fighting with the Zulus in this battle. Sir Henry Bulwer called him 'a soldier of soldiers . . . brave and utterly fearless.' – *Dictionary of National Biography*, XVI (1888), p. 265.

26. L. Haggard, *Cloak*, pp. 77–79.

27. *See* Kotzé, *Memoirs*, p. 560; and Gerald French, *Lord Chelmsford and the Zulu War* (1939), p. 138.

28. L. Haggard, *Cloak*, p. 68.

29. Haggard, *Days*, I, p. 21.

30. *Ibid.*, pp. 98–100.

31. *Ibid.*, p. 116.

32. *Ibid.*, p. 140.

33. L. Haggard, *Cloak*, p. 85.

34. Kotzé, *Memoirs*, p. 628.

35. L. Haggard, *Cloak*, p. 89.

36. *Ibid.*, p. 90.

37. *Ibid.*, p. 91.

38. *Ibid.*, p. 93.

39. *Ibid.*, p. 96.

40. Letter dated March 20, 1880, Clark Collection.

41. L. Haggard, *Cloak*, p. 94.

42. Letter dated January 2, 1881, Clark Collection.

43. L. Haggard, *Cloak*, p. 104.

44. Haggard, *Days*, I, 182; and L. Haggard, *Cloak*, pp. 105–106.

45. Letter from Louisa to Rider's mother dated May 4, 1881. – Haggard, *Days*, I, p. 189.

46. *Cambridge History*, VIII, p. 485.

47. John Martineau, *The Life and Correspondence of Sir Bartle Frere* (1895), II, p. 415.

48. L. Haggard, *Cloak*, pp. 108–109. Another version of this letter appears in Haggard, *Days*, I, p. 195.

49. L. Haggard, *Cloak*, p. 109.

50. Haggard, *Days*, I, p. 195.

51. *Ibid.*, p. 194.

52. For additional historical material on subjects dealt with in this chapter, see the following: James Bryce, *Impressions of South Africa* (1899); William Francis Butler, *An Autobiography* (1911); Frances E. Calenso and E. Durnford, *History of the Zulu War* (1881); R. C. K. Ensor, *England, 1870–1914* (1952); Jan H. Hofmeyer, *South Africa* (1921); Paul Knaplund, *The British Empire, 1815–1939* (1941); W. J. Leyds, *The First Annexation of the Transvaal* (1906); Leo Marquand, *The Peoples and the Policies of South Africa* (1952); Charles L. Norris-Newman, *In Zululand*

with the British Throughout the War of 1879 (1880); F. W. Reitz, *A Century of Wrong* (1900); G. M. Theal, *History of South Africa, 1873 to 1884,* I (1919); C. J. Uys, *In the Era of Shepstone* (1933); Eric A. Walker, *A History of South Africa* (1928); E. L. Woodward, *The Age of Reform, 1815–1870* (1954); G. M. Young, ed., *Early Victorian England, 1830–1865,* 2 vols. (1951).

CHAPTER 3

1. Haggard, *Days*, I, p. 173.
2. *Ibid.*, p. 61.
3. H.R.H., 'The Transvaal,' *Macmillan's Magazine*, XXXVI (May 1877), pp. 71–79.
4. Kotzé, *Memoirs*, p. 523.
5. Haggard, *Days*, I, p. 78.
6. *Ibid.*, p. 205.
7. H. Rider Haggard, *Cetywayo and His White Neighbours* (1896), pp. lxxiii–lxxvi.
8. *Ibid.*, p. 57.
9. 'Our Sable Visitor,' *Spectator*, LV (August 19, 1882), pp. 1089–1090.
10. Haggard, *Cetywayo*, pp. 91–99.
11. *Ibid.*, pp. 286–287.
12. *Ibid.*, p. lxxvi.
13. LXXVI (October 1882), pp. 460–461.
14. LV (August 19, 1882), pp. 1089–1090.
15. LIV (August 12, 1882), pp. 213–214.
16. XXVIII (July 29, 1882), p. 73.
17. Letter dated May 12, 1888, Columbia Collection.
18. Haggard, *Cetywayo*, pp. xlvii–lxxii.
19. LXV (April 7, 1888), p. 421.
20. CXXX (July 1888), pp. 100–101.
21. Haggard, *Days*, I, p. 209.
22. John Cordy Jeaffreson, *A Book of Recollections* (1894), II, p. 119.
23. Haggard, *Days*, I, pp. 211–212.
24. *Ibid.*, p. 213.
25. XXV (March 22, 1884), p. 200.
26. LXXXIII (March 22, 1884), p. 372.
27. XXXII (April 4, 1884), p. 27.
28. XXXI (April 12, 1884), p. 206.
29. *Academy*, XXVII (January 17, 1885), p. 41.
30. LXXXV (January 10, 1885), p. 49.
31. XXXI (February 14, 1885), p. 166.
32. XXXI (February 6, 1885), pp. 130–131.

33. XVI (May 2, 1885), p. 158.
34. LIX (January 17, 1885), pp. 84–85.
35. XXXIII (January 16, 1885), p. 29.
36. Haggard, *Days*, I, p. 221.
37. *Ibid.*, p. 219.

CHAPTER 4

1. The letter is dated merely 'Sunday,' but it was written between March and September 1885, Lockwood Collection.
2. Newman Flower, *Radio Times*, June 29, 1956, p. 6.
3. Max Pemberton, *Sixty Years Ago and After* (1936), p. 119.
4. J. C. Furnas, *Voyage to Windward: The Life of Robert Louis Stevenson* (1951), p. 197.
5. Haggard, *Days*, I, p. 242.
6. E. D. O'Brien, 'The Adventurous Life of a Great Storyteller [Review of L. Haggard, *The Cloak That I Left*],' *Illustrated London News*, CCXVIII (May 26, 1951), p. 857.
7. 'Modern Marvels,' LVIII (October 17, 1885), pp. 1365–1366.
8. LXXXVI (October 31, 1885), p. 568.
9. XXVIII (November 7, 1885), p. 304.
10. XXXVI (November 6, 1885), p. 271.
11. XXXVII (December 3, 1885), p. 13.
12. LXXVIII (November 7, 1885), p. 512.
13. LVIII (November 7, 1885), p. 1473.
14. XLVIII (October 30, 1885), p. 551.
15. LX (October 10, 1885), pp. 485–486.
16. R. R. Bowker, 'London As a Literary Centre,' *Harper's New Monthly Magazine*, LXXVII (June 1888), pp. 3–26.
17. Pemberton, p. 119.
18. Bowker, *Harper's New Monthly Magazine*, LXXVII, pp. 3–26.
19. II (December 1885), p. 324.
20. 'H.B.,' *Critic*, VI [N.S.] (April 3, 1886), p. 169.
21. Haggard, *Days*, I, p. 235.
22. *Private View* (1953), p. 64.
23. Claude Colleer Abbott, ed., *Letters of Gerard Manley Hopkins to Robert Bridges* (1935), pp. 236–237.
24. I (April 27, 1889), pp. 631–632.
25. Pemberton, p. 119.
26. Haggard, *Days*, I, p. 243.
27. *Ibid.*, p. 244.
28. *Ibid.*, pp. 245–246.
29. *Ibid.*, p. 251.

30. 'H.B.,' X (March 5, 1887), p. 126. Not that Henley approved of the book's popularity. See below for his opinion in detail.

31. 'A.M.F.R.,' 'A Letter from London,' XVIII (March 5, 1887), p. 72.

32. *Academy*, XXXI (January 15, 1887), pp. 35–36.

33. LXXIX (January 15, 1887), pp. 93–94.

34. LXIII (January 8, 1887), p. 44.

35. LX (January 15, 1887), pp. 78–79.

36. CXLI (February 1887), pp. 301–305.

37. XXXVII (January 22, 1887), p. 66.

38. XXXV (January 6, 1887), p. 28.

39. LXXXI (January 15, 1887), pp. 88–89.

40. LI (January 4, 1887), p. 38.

41. XXXV (January 7, 1887), pp. 3–4.

42. I (February 1887), p. 287.

43. X (February 12, 1887), p. 78.

44. 'The Book of 1906 Which Has Interested Me Most,' *Bookman* (London), XXXI (January 1907), p. 162.

45. H. Rider Haggard, *Nada the Lily* (7th ed., 1907), pp. xi–xv.

46. For an extensive study of the Lovedu, see E. Jensen and J. D. Krige, *The Realm of the Rain-Queen* (1947). For Haggard's comments on Mujaji, see 'The Death of "Majajie," ' *African Review*, VIII (September 19, 1896), p. 639.

47. *The Books in My Life*, p. 92.

48. In a letter to the *Yorkshire Weekly Post*, as quoted in *Critic*, XII (August 17, 1889), p. 79.

49. Carl G. Jung, *The Integration of the Personality* (1939), pp. 24, 78–80.

50. Nandor Fodor, *The Search for the Beloved* (1949), p. 392. See also Fodor's *New Approaches to Dream Interpretation* (1951).

51. Haggard, *Days*, I, p. 250.

52. Denis Mackail, *The Story of J.M.B.* (1941), p. 124.

53. Letter. See Lot 120, *Sotheby Catalogue, The Property of the Late J. E. Scott, Esq.* (1951), p. 18.

54. Letter dated October 29, 1906, Columbia Collection.

55. Letter dated July 12, 1886, Lockwood Collection.

56. *Rehabilitations*, p. 100.

57. Miller, p. 81.

58. 'Can Mr. Rider Haggard Write?' *Court and Society*, IV (March 30, 1887), p. 305.

59. *Critic*, X, p. 126.

60. Lisle March-Phillips and Bertram Christian, eds., *Some Harwarden Letters, 1878–1913* (1918), p. 225.

61. H. Rider Haggard, *She, A History of Adventure* (1887), p. 7.

62. *Ibid.*, p. 87.

63. *Ibid.*, p. 281.

64. CXLI (February 1887), pp. 301–305.

65. Samuel M. Clark, VIII (May 1887), pp. 5–7.

66. *Fortnightly Review*, reprinted in *Eclectic Magazine*, XLVI (N.S.) (November 1887), pp. 603–608.
67. Mrs. Lang, ed., *The Poetical Works of Andrew Lang* (1923), III, pp. 196–198.
68. 'Modern Men,' *Scots Observer*, I (April 27, 1889), p. 631.
69. 'Success in Fiction,' *Forum*, VII (May 1889), pp. 321–322.
70. 'The English Novel – 1892,' *The Collected Essays and Papers of George Saintsbury, 1875–1920*, III (1923), p. 133.
71. 'Sir Henry Rider Haggard,' *Dictionary of National Biography* (1937), pp. 372–373.
72. For additional information about the subjects treated in this chapter, see the following works, from which I have drawn material: Edith Batho and Bonamy Dobrée, *The Victorians and After (1830–1914)* (1938); A. T. Bryant, *The Zulu People* (1949); Leonard Cottrell, *Lost Cities* (1957); Amy Cruse, *The Victorians and Their Reading* (1935); B. H. Dicke, *The Bush Speaks* (1936); James Frazer, *The Golden Bough, A Study in Magic and Religion* (1950); Erich Fromm, *The Forgotten Language* (1951); B. Z. Goldberg, *The Sacred Fire* (1930); Elizabeth E. Goldsmith, *Life Symbols* (1928); Georgina A. Gollock, *Daughters of Africa* (1932); Louis Herbert Gray, ed., *The Mythology of All Races*, 13 vols. (1918); Lawrence G. Green, *Great African Mysteries* [1935]; James Hastings, ed., *Encyclopedia of Religion and Ethics*, 13 vols. (1951); Susanne Howe, *Novels of Empire* (1949); C. G. Jung, *Psychology of the Unconscious* (1952); Eileen Jensen Krige, *The Social System of the Zulus* (1936); Q. D. Leavis, *Fiction and the Reading Public* (1932); Donald A. Mackenzie, *Egyptian Myth and Legend* (n.d.); Erich Neumann, *The Great Mother, An Analysis of the Archetype* (1955); Geoffrey Parrinder, *West African Religion* (1949); Richard Ashley Rice, *Robert Louis Stevenson, How to Know Him* (1916); Herman and Georg Schreiber, *Vanished Cities* (1957); Edwin W. Smith, ed., *African Ideas of God* (1950); Charles Squire, *Celtic Myth & Legend, Poetry & Romance* (n.d.); C. J. Uys, 'Who Came First to South Africa?' *The South Africa-United Kingdom and Commonwealth Survey*, 1954, pp. 45–47; Wilson D. Wallis, *Religion in Primitive Society* (1939); Cornelius Weygandt, *A Century of the English Novel* (1925).

CHAPTER 5

1. ' "Squire" Rider Haggard at Home,' XIX (November 10, 1888), p. 393.
2. Letter dated October 4, 1887, Huntington Collection.
3. L. Haggard, *Cloak*, pp. 131–132.
4. Haggard, *Days*, I, p. 259.
5. L. Haggard, *Cloak*, p. 133.
6. *Critic*, X (December 15, 1888), pp. 302–303.

7. Colonel Eustace James Anthony Balfour (d. 1911), architect, antiquary, and military man, brother of the statesman, A. J. Balfour.

8. Reverend William J. Loftie (1839–1911), historian, author of numerous guidebooks, art critic, archaeologist, antiquary, and writer for the *Saturday Review* and *National Observer*.

9. Robert Alan Mowbray Stevenson (1847–1900), painter, art critic (for the *Saturday Review* in 1885), and university lecturer; cousin of Robert Louis Stevenson.

10. The two tales he later wrote were *Mr. Meeson's Will*, a story about the law and lawyers in which the villain is, with vengeance aforethought, a publisher, and *Allan's Wife*.

11. L. Haggard, *Cloak*, p. 148.

12. LI (February 1887), pp. 172–180. It was reprinted in *Living Age*, the *Critic*, and the *Eclectic Magazine*.

13. Somehow they all failed to accuse Haggard of lifting at least the name of his heroine and her city from a three-volume novel called *Ayesha, the Maid of Kars*, by James Morier, published in 1834. There is no similarity between Morier's and Haggard's tales.

14. IV (March 30, 1887), p. 305.

15. Quoted in J. M. Barrie's review of *Allan Quatermain*, *British Weekly*, II (August 5, 1887), p. 218.

16. XXV (January 1888), pp. 389–411; and reprinted in *Living Age*.

17. L (September 1, 1888), pp. 324–336.

18. See the *New Evening Sun*, October 1914, and the Dedication to Haggard's *When the World Shook*.

19. Haggard, *Days*, I, p. 264.

20. L. Haggard, *Cloak*, p. 130.

21. Haggard, *Days*, I, p. 273.

22. *Ibid.*, p. 274; and L. Haggard, *Cloak*, pp. 134–135.

23. Undated letter, Lockwood Collection.

24. Undated letter, Lockwood Collection.

25. Lockwood Collection.

26. Haggard, *Days*, I, pp. 286–187; and L. Haggard, *Cloak*, pp. 140–141.

27. Ralph Bergen Allen, *Old Icelandic Sources in the English Novel* (1933), p. 105.

28. Amy Cruse, *After the Victorians* (1938), p. 114.

29. Haggard, *Days*, II, p. 5.

30. *Ibid.*, p. 41.

31. 'Rider Haggard Here,' *New York Times*, XL (January 11, 1891), p. 8.

32. Haggard, *Days*, II, p. 68.

33. See also Mrs. John Gladwyn Jebb, *A Strange Career: Life and Adventures of John Gladwyn Jebb* (1895) for another account of the Jebb-Haggard pact to seek Montezuma's treasure.

34. Haggard, *Days*, II, p. 42.

35. H. Rider Haggard, *Allan Quatermain* (1887), Dedication and p. 1.

36. L. Haggard, *Cloak*, p. 156.

37. Haggard, *Days*, II, pp. 43–44.

38. L. Haggard, *Cloak*, p. 16.
39. Haggard, *Days*, II, p. 84.
40. L. Haggard, *Cloak*, p. 158.
41. Haggard, *Days*, II, pp. 28, 83–84; and L. Haggard, *Cloak*, p. 158.

CHAPTER 6

1. Haggard, *Days*, I, p. 264.
2. L. Haggard, *Norfolk Life*, p. 65.
3. Maurice Greiffenhagen, R.A. (1862–1931), portrait painter, art teacher, and decorator, had a robust sense of design. His early illustrations appeared in the *Daily Chronicle*, *Lady's Pictorial*, and *Punch*, but his most famous drawings are in some of Haggard's first editions.
4. 'Commissioner H. Rider Haggard,' *Review of Reviews*, XXII (July 1905), pp. 21–27; and H. Rider Haggard, 'An English Garden,' *Black and White*, XXXI (May 5, 1906), p. 614.
5. He is pictured beardless in the *Strand Magazine* for January 1892 and with a beard in *Black and White* for August 11, 1894.
6. L. Haggard, *Cloak*, pp. 196, 161.
7. *Ibid.*, p. 91; and Haggard, *Days*, I, pp. 165, 176.
8. L. Haggard, *Cloak*, pp. 91–92, 20–21.
9. Haggard, *Days*, I, p. 163.
10. L. Haggard, *Cloak*, pp. 18–19.
11. Harry How, 'Illustrated Interviews No. VII – Mr. H. Rider Haggard,' *Strand Magazine*, III (January 1892), pp. 3–17; 'A.D.,' 'An Interview with Mr. H. Rider Haggard,' *Christian Commonwealth*, November 1, 1906, pp. 75–76; Fred Dolman, *Young Man*, reprinted in 'How Mr. Rider Haggard Works,' *Review of Reviews* (London), IX (January 1894), p. 31; H. Rider Haggard, 'Authors at Work,' *Bookman* (London), XXXV (November 1908), p. 86; Haggard, *Days*, II, p. 92; and L. Haggard, *Cloak*, p. 159.
12. L. Haggard, *Cloak*, pp. 15–17, 196.
13. Harry How, *Strand Magazine*, p. 3.
14. Lilias Rider Haggard, *A Country Scrap-Book* (1950), p. 150.
15. Harry How, *Strand Magazine*, pp. 3–17.
16. *Unwritten History* (1924), p. 6.
17. 'A.D.,' *Christian Commonwealth*, p. 75.
18. Admiral Vernon H. Haggard, personal interview.
19. 'Sir H. Rider Haggard, His Life and Career,' May 25, 1925, p. 19.
20. Haggard, *Days*, I, p. 254.
21. The second letter is dated January 8, 1911, Maggs Brothers Collection.
22. See Horace G. Hutchinson, 'Sir Rider Haggard's Autobiography,' *Edinburgh Review*, CCLXIV (October 1926), pp. 343–355.

23. Haggard, *Days*, I, p. 255.
24. January 6, 1915, Huntington Collection.
25. 'Royal Commission on Emigration of Soldiers,' *New York Times*, LXVI (February 17, 1916), p. 3.
26. Haggard, *Days*, I, p. 256.
27. *Ibid.*, pp. 112–113.
28. Kotzé, *Memoirs*, pp. 487–488.
29. Haggard, *Days*, I, p. 143; II, p. 151.
30. L. Haggard, *A Country Scrap-Book*, p. 150; *Cloak*, p. 19.
31. L. Haggard, *A Norfolk Notebook*, pp. 83–84.
32. L. Haggard, *Cloak*, p. 17.
33. 'H. Rider Haggard Turned Colonizer,' *New York Herald*, March 19, 1905, p. 3.
34. L. Haggard, *Cloak*, pp. 17–18.
35. Lilias Rider Haggard, unpublished manuscript.

CHAPTER 7

1. L. Haggard, *Cloak*, p. 167.
2. 'Rider Haggard in Parliament,' quoted in the *New York Times*, XLIV (March 24, 1895), p. 23.
3. 'Mr. Rider Haggard as Politician,' LXXIX (March 23, 1895), pp. 372–373.
4. July 20, 1894. See J. E. Scott, *A Bibliography of the Works of Sir Henry Rider Haggard, 1856–1925* (1947), p. 356.
5. *Ibid.*, pp. 357–361. I am indebted to R. H. Mottram for a vivid account of the Battle of Stalham Bridge.
6. *Ibid.*, p. 362; and Haggard, *Days*, II, p. 115.
7. L. Haggard, *Cloak*, p. 167.
8. 'H.F.,' 'Tumble of Liberals,' XLIV (July 28, 1895), p. 1.
9. L. Haggard, *Cloak*, pp. 168–169.
10. *Ibid.*, p. 169.
11. *Ibid.*, p. 172; and Haggard, *Days*, II, p. 131.
12. See G. M. Young, 'Portrait of an Age,' *Early Victorian England*, II (1951), p. 485.
13. See J. H. Clapham, 'Work and Wages,' *Early Victorian England* (1951), I, p. 3; Bernard Darwin, 'Country Life and Sport,' *Early Victorian England* (1951), I, pp. 264–265; Ensor, p. 117; and George Macaulay Trevelyan, *British History in the Nineteenth Century, 1782–1901* (1922), pp. 145, 275n.
14. Ensor, pp. 54, 115.
15. H. Rider Haggard, *A Farmer's Year, Being His Commonplace Book for 1898* (1899), p. 1.
16. *Ibid.*, p. 2.
17. LI (January 6, 1900), p. 21.

18. LXI (March 23, 1900), pp. 273–274.
19. XVI (December 1899), p. 88.
20. 'Rider Haggard as a Farmer,' XLVII (August 19, 1899), p. 555.
21. See *Catalogue of the Library of Walter Theodore Watts-Dunton, Esq.*, Sotheby Auction (1917), Item number 388.
22. Haggard, *A Farmer's Year*, p. ix.
23. C. E. Carrington, *The Life of Rudyard Kipling* (1955), p. 332.
24. L. Haggard, *Norfolk Life*, p. 101. See also L. Haggard, *Cloak*, p. 193; *The Times*, November 18, 1928, p. 10; and 'A Chat with Mr. Rider Haggard,' *Graphic*, LXXII (July 29, 1905), pp. 124–125.
25. Haggard, *Days*, II, p. 136.
26. *Ibid.*, p. 137.
27. *Ibid.*, p. 138.
28. L. Haggard, *Cloak*, p. 182.
29. H. Rider Haggard, *Rural England, Being an Account of the Agricultural and Social Researches Carried out in the Years 1901 and 1902* (2nd ed., 1906), II, p. 536.
30. *Ibid.*, pp. 546–547.
31. *Ibid.*, p. 556.
32. *Ibid.*, p. 212.
33. CXCVII (April 1903), pp. 475–500.
34. LXXXIII (January 1903), pp. 143–145.
35. 'Mr. Rider Haggard's "Rural England," ' XC (February 14, 1903), pp. 260–261.
36. 'The Needs of Rural England,' CXCVII (April 1903), pp. 540–568.
37. Letter dated August 1, 1903, Columbia Collection.
38. *Far from the Madding Crowd* (1874), *The Return of the Native* (1878), *The Mayor of Casterbridge* (1886), *The Woodlanders* (1887), and *Tess of the D'Urbervilles* (1891). Haggard, too, wrote fiction about the decline of country life, and although his efforts are less distinguished than Hardy's, he succeeded best in *Colonel Quaritch, V.C.* (1888).
39. Though inaccurately. See Florence Emily Hardy, *The Later Years of Thomas Hardy, 1892–1928* (1930), pp. 93–96.
40. *Longman's Magazine*, II (July 1883), pp. 252–269. For more about Hardy and Haggard and the literature of rural England, see Douglas Brown, *Thomas Hardy* (1954).
41. Letter dated February 13, 1903, Weyman Collection.
42. 'Mr. H. Rider Haggard,' LXXII (March 15, 1906), pp. 121–122.
43. Thomas Adams, *Garden City and Agriculture* (1905), pp. 4–5.
44. Haggard, *Rural England*, I, p. vii.
45. XXXIII (January 1906), pp. 9–10.
46. H. Rider Haggard, 'The Government and the Land,' *The Times*, May 8, 1907, p. 10.
47. 'Mr. Rider Haggard and Small Holdings,' XCVIII (1907), pp. 968–969.
48. 'Cheerful about Agriculture, Mr. Rider Haggard at Bungay,' *The Times*, November 27, 1909, p. 13.

CHAPTER 8

1. March 28, 1885. Unless otherwise indicated all the letters from Lang to Haggard quoted in this chapter are from the Lockwood Collection and undated.
2. October 3 [1885].
3. *New Review*, VI (February 1892), pp. 243–251.
4. February 1, [1886].
5. July 22, 24, 25, [1886].
6. July 27, [1886].
7. April 23.
8. Haggard was finishing *Beatrice* and beginning *Mr. Meeson's Will*.
9. October 13.
10. [W. E. Henley,] 'Culture and Anarchy,' V (December 13, 1890), pp. 99–100.
11. IX (November 20, 1890), p. 54.
12. LXVI (February 14, 1891), p. 249.
13. XCVI (December 6, 1890), p. 773.
14. XLII (November 28, 1890), pp. 443–444.
15. Green, *Lang*, p. 134.
16. Haggard, *Days*, II, p. 77.
17. 'Mr. Lang as Poet,' *Bookman* (London), II (August 1895), pp. 24–26.
18. November 29, [1890].
19. August 7.
20. Thursday.
21. October 27.
22. October 4.
23. February 25, [1896].
24. August 14.
25. January 13.
26. July 18, [1897], Columbia Collection.
27. Undated, Eckman Collection.
28. June 7.
29. March 5.
30. 'The Dreadful Trade,' I (February 16, 1889), pp. 356–357.
31. December 30.
32. July 3, [1897].
33. July 2.
34. December 6.
35. December 30.
36. December 19.
37. July 2.
38. December 19.

39. March 26.
40. September 29.
41. November 28.
42. October 15.
43. September 7.
44. Monday.
45. Haggard, *Days*, II, p. 6.
46. January 13.
47. June 2.
48. January 1.
49. June 4.
50. September 7, [1887].
51. (1889), p. [ix].
52. June 29.
53. November 30.
54. October 12.
55. Haggard, *Days*, II, p. 75.
56. *Ibid.*, pp. 72, 80.
57. June 2, 1902.
58. 'To R. K.,' *Lapsus Calami* (1905), p. 3.
59. 'Her Little Responsibility' was first published on August 21, 1889, in *Civil and Military Gazette*. For the allusion to *Cleopatra*, see Rudyard Kipling, *Abaft the Funnel*, New York: Doubleday, Page & Company, 1909, p. 16.
60. See Carrington, p. 108. Thomas Anstey Guthrie (1856–1934), author of dialogues and novels, including *Vice Versa* (1882), wrote under the pseudonym of F. Anstey.
61. Horatio F. Brown, ed., *Letters and Papers of John Addington Symonds* (1923), p. 228.
62. March 21, 1890. Janet Adam Smith, ed., *Henry James and Robert Louis Stevenson* (1948), p. 184.
63. Kipling, *Something of Myself*, p. 85.
64. Rudyard Kipling's daughter, Mrs. George Bambridge, very kindly gave me access to the typescript copies she owns of forty-one unpublished letters written by her father to Rider Haggard. These letters cover a period of thirty-four years and are invaluable aids in charting the friendship between the two men. Unless otherwise indicated, the letters quoted below are from the Bambridge Collection and undated.
65. XV (May 21, 1898), pp. 311–313.
66. Kipling, *Something of Myself*, p. 193.
67. Undated, but date of receipt indicated as December 27, 1902.
68. January 7, 1916. The reference is to Elsie (*née* Kipling) Bambridge, the Kiplings' second child.
69. November 15, 1899.
70. December 22, 1902.
71. January 31, 1905.
72. The first letter in this group was received by Haggard on December 27,

1902. Kipling wrote the second letter from the Hotel Cattani, Engelberg, on January 28, 1909; and the third from Bateman's on December 14, 1909.

73. March 3, 1920, p. 12; and March 4, 1920, p. 16.

74. I have not been able to see the original of these verses ('G.G.,' 'Two Hearts that Beat as One,' *Daily Herald*, March 4, 1920), and the two reprints I have seen differ slightly. The version quoted is from L. Haggard, *Cloak*, p. 256. For the other, see Mrs. G. Broughton, 'R.K. and Rider Haggard,'*Kipling Journal*, XXIII (April 1956), pp. 8–10.

75. December 2, 1904.

76. Dated Saturday, but the letter's place of origin (Kessingland Grange) helps date it more specifically during the summer of 1914.

77. March 31, 1917.

78. September 1, 1917; November 6, 1918.

79. February 8, 1922.

80. November 26, 1920.

81. L. Haggard, *Cloak*, pp. 271–272.

82. Kipling, *Something of Myself*, p. 193.

83. Haggard, *Days*, II, p. 208.

84. J. E. Scott, 'Rudyard Kipling: Two Footnotes, II,' *New Colophon*, I (1948), pp. 335–365.

85. May 22, 1918. The Bambridge Collection contains some pertinent excerpts from Haggard's unpublished World War I diary. Unless otherwise indicated, these excerpts have been used in quoting from the diary.

86. November 15, 1918.

87. Miss Haggard tells us that her father read *Wisdom's Daughter* to Kipling in manuscript. *Cloak*, p. 271.

88. Haggard, *Days*, II, p.159.

89. A physician who had restored Haggard to health in the years following Jock's death. He was also one of the attending physicians at Haggard's operation.

90. Haggard, *Days*, II, pp. 207–208.

91. This and a number of items I quote from below are part of the James McGregor Stewart Kipling Collection, Dalhousie University, Halifax, Nova Scotia.

92. Scott,*New Colophon*, pp. 335–365. A letter from Kipling dated January 28, 1909, spurs Haggard on to finish the tale: 'Now let's have Murgh put in going order?'

93. L. Haggard, *Cloak*, p. 271.

94. Carrington, pp. 205–206.

95. July 10, 1897.

96. Kipling, *Something of Myself*, p. 113.

97. October 20, 1895.

98. September 30, 1911. Scott, *New Colophon*, pp. 335–365.

99. (1939), pp. 97–98.

100. This letter and those that follow between Haggard and Stevenson are quoted in Haggard, *Days*, I, pp. 235–241.

101. The references are to the Honorable Rupert Leigh (1856–1919) and Isobel Strong, *née* Osbourne, who in fact was Stevenson's step-daughter, and subsequently Mrs. Salisbury Field. Bazett's covering letter was dated July 17, 1893.
102. Haggard, *Days*, II, pp. 8–9.
103. One of the Haggards was a kind gift from Dr. Philip Gosse to the writer.
104. It is now in the Cambridge University Library.
105. See *A Catalogue of the Gosse Correspondence in the Brotherton Collection* (1950), p. xi.
106. April 10, 1894, April 8, 1887, and March 30, 1906.
107. VII (N.S.) (February 12, 1887), p. 78.
108. Unpublished letter in the Morgan Library, New York.
109. Haggard, *Days*, I, p. 277.
110. Lord Lothian offered it to him, but he declined on the grounds of ill health. John Connell, *W. E. Henley* (1949), p. 163.
111. *Ibid.*, pp. 13, 168.
112. '*Colonel Quaritch* must to the barber's with Polonius' beard. Mr. Rider Haggard has fallen into the fatal mistake of pandering to the lust after three volumes . . . and the result is a book that will not help . . . [him] to immortality. . . . It is a great deal better than half the novels that are published, but it is manifestly a pot-boiler; and, as the work of the author of *Jess*, it is unworthy of serious criticism.' [W. E. Henley,] *Scots Observer*, I (December 22, 1888), p. 137.
113. [W. E. Henley,] I (April 27, 1889), pp. 631–632.
114. July 20, 1889, Haggard, *Days*, I, p. 277.
115. Actually 'Romance and Farce,' it is the title of the review that appears below. Either Haggard misread Henley's letter or Longman Haggard's manuscript, for the error appears in Haggard's autobiography, the only source of the letter. The 'Farce' is a review of Stevenson and Osbourne's *The Wrong Box*.
116. Haggard, *Days*, II, p. 278.
117. [W. E. Henley,] 'Romance and Farce,' *Scots Observer*, II (July 27, 1889), pp. 275–276.
118. [W. E. Henley,] 'Culture and Anarchy,'V(December 13,1890), pp. 99–100.
119. December 17, [1890], Lockwood Collection.
120. Haggard, *Days*, I, p. 276. This chapter also draws upon Jerome Hamilton Buckley, *William Ernest Henley, A Study in the 'Counter-Decadence' of the 'Nineties* (1945).

CHAPTER 9

1. *Dr. Therne* (1898), dedicated to the Jenner Society and issued in the heat of the vaccination controversy of the time.
2. 'The Fall of Fiction,' *Fortnightly Review*, L (September 1888), pp. 324–336.

3. *Pall Mall Budget*, as quoted in 'Rider the Ripper,' *Critic*, XVIII (July 9, 1892), p. 23.
4. Letter dated November 10, 1912, Huntington Collection.
5. Besant's letter dated May 19, 1892, Huntington Collection; and letter from Ernest A. Ritter dated June 5, 1958.
6. Stuart Cloete, Introduction to *She* (1957), p. 11; *Times Literary Supplement*, April 11, 1958, p. xxii.
7. Roger Lancelyn Green, *A. E. W. Mason* (1952), p. 30.
8. Some were A. E. W. Mason (*The Three Gentlemen, Four Feathers, No Other Tiger*), Stanley Weyman (*A Gentleman of France, Under the Red Robe*), Anthony Hope Hawkins and Henry Seton Merriman. There were also Conan Doyle's adventure tales (*Micah Clarke, The White Company, The Lost World*), Maurice Hewlett's erudite romances, Winston Churchill's one Ruritanian romance (*Savrola*), and tales by Edgar Wallace.
9. Andrew Balfour's *The Golden Kingdom*, Reginald Hartley Thackeray's *Knights of the Wild*, Eden Phillpotts's *The Golden Fetish*, and Edgar Wallace's *Sanders of the River*.
10. John Buchan's *Prester John, Midwinter*, and *Witch Wood*; J. P. Fitzpatrick's *Jock of the Bushveld*; Arthur Armstrong's *Trader Horn*; Talbot Mundy's tales; Algernon Blackwood's stories of supernatural horror; and later James Hilton's *The Lost Horizon*, C. S. Forester's *The African Queen* and *The Sky and the Forest*, some of Joyce Cary's African tales, and Laurens van der Post's *Flamingo Feather*.
11. Advertisement, *New York Times*, March 19, 1950, p. 22.
12. *See* Hugh Kingsmill, *The Life of D. H. Lawrence* (1938); and Aldous Huxley, ed., *The Letters of D. H. Lawrence* (1932), p. 680.
13. Conversation with him.
14. See *Books in My Life*.
15. Introduction to *She* (1957), p. 11.
16. *The Lost Childhood and Other Essays* (1954), pp. 13–15.
17. H. Rider Haggard, 'The Real "King Solomon's Mines,"' *Cassell's Magazine*, XLIV (July 1907), pp.144–151.
18. 'New York Notes,' XVIII (1887), p. 136.
19. Scott, *Bibliography*, p. 35; 'Mr. H. Rider Haggard,' *Literary World* (London), LXII (March 15, 1906), pp. 121–122; Simon Nowell-Smith, *The House of Cassell, 1848–1958* (1958), p. 136.
20. April 11, 1958, p. xxii.
21. 'H. Rider Haggard,' *Book News*, VIII (June 1890), pp. 344–345.
22. 'Rider Haggard,' *Bookman* (London), LXXI (November 1926), pp. 108–110.
23. See Frederic Whyte, *The Life of W. T. Stead* (n.d.), I, p. 229.
24. Pp. 217–220.
25. Records of the House of John Murray, Publishers.
26. *British Weekly*, II (August 5, 1887), p. 218.
27. Haggard, *Days*, I, p. 280.
28. Dated December 26, Lockwood Collection.
29. See *Publisher's Weekly*, XXXV (January 26, 1889), p. 74.

30. Records of the House of John Murray, Publishers.
31. 'H. Rider Haggard,' *Book News*, VIII (June 1890), pp. 344–345.
32. L. Haggard, *Cloak*, p. 169.
33. Typewritten agreement, Huntington Collection.
34. 'H. Rider Haggard,' *New York Post*, May 14, 1925.
35. By E. B. Sargant and Bernhard Whishaw.
36. By W. Forbes Gray.
37. 'Simon Pure,' *Bookman* (London), LXI (July 1925), p. 560.
38. Undated letter, Lockwood Collection.
39. Maurice Baring, *The Puppet Show of Memory* (1922), pp. 105–107.
40. Peter Gamble, 'The Two Rider Haggards,' *John O'London's Weekly*, LIII (May 18, 1945), p. 63.
41. Letter from Professor A. C. Partridge, University of Witwatersrand, June 5, 1958.
42. Winfred Graham Cory (d. 1950), a minor novelist. Winfred Graham, *That Reminds Me* (n.d.), p. 159.
43. As quoted in *Literary News*, VIII (August 1887), pp. 232–233.
44. 'The Passing Throng,' *New York Daily Tribune*, LIX (February 21, 1900), p. 6.
45. Hamilton W. Mabie, 'The Most Popular Novels in America,' *Forum*, XVI (December 1893), pp. 508–516.
46. Augusta H. Leypoldt and George Iles, eds.
47. Vol. II: Fiction. By Edwin Diller Starbuck.
48. Frank Luther Mott, *Golden Multitudes* (1947), p. 177.
49. March 19, 1905, p. 3.
50. Quoted in Mott, p. 177.
51. Lin Shu, as reported in Pearl S. Buck, *My Several Worlds* (1954), p. 128; *Index Translationum* (1932–56 annually). The facts, figures, and statements relating to Haggard's current popularity in England and South Africa emerge from thirty-five letters written by librarians, school teachers, and Government officials, in response to queries. The present writer is extremely grateful for the co-operation these persons so kindly extended and regrets deeply that there is not space in this work to thank them individually.

CHAPTER 10

1. Haggard, *Days*, II, p. 173.
2. 'H. Rider Haggard Turned Colonizer,' *New York Herald*, March 19, 1905, p. 3.
3. Haggard, *Days*, II, pp. 177–178.
4. *Ibid.*, pp. 178–79.
5. 'Commissioner H. Rider Haggard,' *Review of Reviews*, XXXII (July 1905), pp. 21–27.
6. Haggard, *Days*, II, pp. 190–191.

7. Cd. 2562: *Report on the Salvation Army Colonies in the United States and at Hadleigh, England, with Scheme of National Land Settlement.*

8. H. Rider Haggard, *The Poor and the Land, Being a Report on the Salvation Army Colonies in the United States and at Hadleigh, England, with Scheme of National Land Settlement* (1905), pp. vii–ix.

9. See *ibid.*, pp. 146–147. Excerpts from seventy-three reviews were included in *The Poor and the Land*, and many others that appeared were not quoted.

10. The material in this and the succeeding paragraph is drawn from Haggard, *Days*, II, pp. 192–213.

11. *Cassell's Magazine*, XLVI (June 1908), pp. 478–481.

12. L. Haggard, *Cloak*, p. 19.

13. Taken from a copy of the letter (dated November 9, 1910) in Haggard's hand, marked: 'Copy, Confidential, HRH,' Huntington Collection.

14. 'Rider Haggard and the Salvation Army,' *Outlook*, XCVIII (July 1, 1911), pp. 476–477.

15. Haggard, *Days*, II, p. 218.

16. *Ibid.*, p. 220.

17. Four articles from *Rural Denmark* appeared in *The Times* in February and March 1911, before the book was published.

18. H. Rider Haggard, *Rural Denmark and Its Lessons* (1913), pp. 274–276.

19. *Ibid.*, pp. 263–264.

20. Haggard, *Days*, II, p. 226.

21. L. Haggard, *Cloak*, p. 194.

22. This and the following four quotations are drawn from L. Haggard, *Cloak*, pp. 188–190, 202–203, 274.

23. Haggard, *Days*, II, 226.

24. *Ibid.*, pp. 227–228.

25. L. Haggard, *Cloak*, p. 215.

26. *Ibid.*, pp. 219–220. For Haggard's return to South Africa I have drawn from L. Haggard, *Cloak*, pp. 221–243, from which the quotations below are taken.

27. H. Rider Haggard, 'A Journey through Zululand,' *Windsor Magazine*, XLV (December 1916), pp. 85–90.

28. L. Haggard, *Cloak*, pp. 242–243.

29. *Ibid.*, p. 247.

30. This and the following quotations are drawn from L. Haggard, *Cloak*, pp. 248–250.

31. 'Henry Seton Merriman' was the pseudonym of Hugh Stowell Scott (1862–1903).

32. 'Farewell Message to Australia,' *The Times*, June 15, 1916, p. 7.

33. This and the two preceding quotations are drawn from L. Haggard, *Cloak*, pp. 250–253. *Pightle* is a localism of obsolete origin meaning 'a small field or enclosure; a close or croft.' *New English Dictionary on Historical Principles* (1909), VII, p. 848.

34. This and the following two quotations are drawn from L. Haggard, *Cloak*, pp. 251–254.

35. *Ibid.*, p. 258.

36. He gave *Allan Quatermain* to Charles Longman and *Mr. Meeson's Will* to A. P. Watt.
37. They have since been moved to the Norwich Public Library.
38. Letter dated June 1918, owned by the House of John Murray, Publishers.
39. Letter dated May 5, 1915, Berg Collection.
40. Bambridge Collection.
41. L. Haggard, *Cloak*, p. 264.
42. 'Liberalism and Land Reform,' May 1, 1923, p. 15.
43. *Agriculture in Britain* (1955), pp. 2, 8.
44. Peter Gamble, 'The Two Rider Haggards,' *John O'London's Weekly*, LIII (May 18, 1945), p. 63.
45. P. 382.
46. Pp. 54, 292.
47. *The Land, The Report of the Land Enquiry Committee, 1909–1912* (3rd ed., 1913).
48. *The Land and the Nation, A Rural Report of the Liberal Land Committee, 1923–1925* (n.d.).
49. Some are George Cadbury, Jun., and Tom Bryan, *The Land and the Landless* (1908); Hermann Levy, *Large and Small Holdings* (1911); J. A. R. Marriott, *The English Land System* (1914); G. E. and K. R. Fussell, *The English Countryman* (1955); Viscount Astor and Keith A. H. Murray, *Land and Life* (1932); Montague Fordham, *Mother Earth* (1908); C. S. Orwin, *History of English Farming* (1949); and the agricultural writings of H. J. Massingham.
50. Mrs. William Edward Lecky, *Memoir of the Right Honourable William Edward Lecky* (1909), p. 406.
51. *A Diary with Letters* (1954), p. 130.
52. *A Pilgrimage of British Farming* (1913).
53. L. Haggard, *Cloak*, p. 267.
54. November 6, 1924, p. 17.
55. L. Haggard, *Cloak*, pp. 277, 278.
56. Unless otherwise indicated, the letters quoted below are from the Bambridge Collection.
57. February 21, 1925.
58. February 28, 1925.
59. March 2, 1925.
60. March 6, 1925.
61. March 8, 1925.
62. March 14, 1925.
63. March 19, 1925.
64. March 25, 1925.
65. March 31, 1925.
66. April 11, 1925.
67. April 20, 1925.
68. May 5, 1925.
69. Kipling, it seems, inadvertently confused Trollope's and Haggard's doctors. Haggard's is *Dr. Therne*.

70. May 7, 1925.
71. May 13, 1925.
72. L. Haggard, *Cloak*, p. 21.
73. Haggard, *Days*, I, p. 221.
74. March 2, 1925.
75. Haggard, *Days*, II, p. 92.
76. *New Statesman and Nation*, XLII (July 14, 1951), pp. 45–46.
77. Review of L. Haggard, *The Cloak That I Left*, *Spectator*, LXXVI (June 15, 1951), pp. 789–790.
78. *Critic*, VII (February 12, 1887), p. 76.

BIBLIOGRAPHY

This list contains all works cited and some other useful references. For additional writings by and about Haggard, see J. E. Scott, *Bibliography*.

Unpublished Material

Bambridge Collection. Letters and other holograph material owned by Mrs. George Bambridge.

Blum, Bruce. 'Sir H. Rider Haggard, Agricultural Reformer.' Unpublished Master's Essay, Columbia University, 1955.

The Book of Gosse. A record of the guests entertained by the Edmund Gosses. Cambridge University Library.

Clark Collection. Letters and other holograph material owned by Mr. C. O. Clark.

Columbia Collection. A collection of miscellaneous Haggard correspondence in the Columbia University Library.

Eckman Collection. Letters and other holograph material owned by S. Eckman, Jr.

Huntington Collection. Letters and other holograph material in the Henry E. Huntington Library and Art Gallery, San Marino, California.

Hyde, William James. 'The English Peasantry in Contemporary Novels.' Unpublished Ph.D. Thesis, University of Wisconsin, 1953.

Letters from H. Rider Haggard to Arthur Conan Doyle in the Sir Arthur Conan Doyle Estates Collection, as reproduced in a letter (August 2, 1958) from Professor Pierre Weil-Nordon.

Letter from H. Rider Haggard to Stanley Weyman, dated February 13, 1903, owned by the Weyman family.

Letter from W. E. Henley to H. Rider Haggard, dated June 9, 1888, in the Morgan Library, New York.

Lockwood Collection. Autograph letters from Andrew Lang, Thomas Hardy and W. B. Yeats to H. Rider Haggard in the Lockwood Memorial Library, University of Buffalo.

MacDonald, Jane. 'The Boer War in English Fiction.' Unpublished Master's Essay, Columbia University, 1940.

Maggs Brothers Collection. Letters and other holograph material owned by Maggs Brothers, London.

John Murray Collection. Letters and other holograph material owned by the House of John Murray, Publishers.

Stewart Kipling Collection. Kipling holographs in the James McGregor
Stewart Kipling Collection, Dalhousie University, Halifax, Nova Scotia.
Terblanche, J. D. V. 'H. Rider Haggard: A Critical Study of His Prose
Fiction.' Unpublished Master's Thesis, University of Witwatersrand, 1955.

Writings by H. Rider Haggard:

Articles and Letters to Periodicals

'About Fiction,' *Contemporary Review*, LI (February 1887), pp. 172–180.
'Authors at Work,' *Bookman* (London), XXXV (November 1908), p. 86.
'The Book of 1906 Which Has Interested Me Most,' *Bookman* (London),
XXXI (January 1907), p. 162.
'Books Which Have Influenced Me,' *British Weekly Extra*, No. 1. London:
British Weeklies Office, n.d.
'An English Garden,' *Black and White*, XXXI (May 5, 1906), p. 614.
'The Government and the Land,' *The Times*, May 8, 1907, p. 10.
'Hydrophobia,' *The Times*, November 3, 1885, p. 10.
'A Journey Through Zululand,' *Windsor Magazine*, XLV (December 1916),
pp. 85–90.
'The Land Question,' *The Times*, April 28, 1886, p. 4.
'Liberalism and Land Reform,' *The Times*, May 1, 1923, p. 15.
'An Olive Branch from America,' *Nineteenth Century*, XXII (November 1887),
pp. 601–624.
'On Going Back,' *Longman's Magazine*, XI (November 1887), pp. 61–66.
'Our Position in Cyprus,' *Contemporary Review*, LI (June 1887), pp. 878–886.
'Population and Housing,' *The Times*, March 25, 1919, p. 6.
'The Real "King Solomon's Mines," ' *Cassell's Magazine*, XLIV (July 1907),
pp. 144–151.
'The Transvaal,' *Macmillan's Magazine*, XXXVI (May 1877), pp. 71–79.
'A Visit to the Chief Secocoeni,' *Gentleman's Magazine*, CCXLIII (September
1877), pp. 302–318.
'A Zulu War Dance,' *Gentleman's Magazine*, CCXLIII (July 1877), pp. 94 ff.

Books – Fiction

Allan Quatermain. London: Longmans, Green & Co., 1877.
Allan's Wife and Other Tales. London: Spencer, Blackett, 1889.
The Ancient Allan. London: Cassell & Co. Ltd., 1920.
Ayesha, the Return of She. London: Ward, Lock & Co. Ltd., 1905.
The Brethren. London: Cassell & Co. Ltd., 1904.
Child of Storm. London: Cassell & Co. Ltd., 1913.
*Cleopatra, Being an Account of the Fall and Vengeance of Harmachis, the Royal
Egyptian, as Set Forth by His Own Hand*. London: Longmans, Green &
Co., 1889.

Colonel Quaritch, V.C., a Tale of Country Life. London: Longmans, Green & Co., 1889.

Dawn. New York: Harper & Brothers, 1887.

Doctor Therne. London: Longmans, Green & Co., 1898.

Eric Brighteyes. London: Longmans, Green & Co., 1891.

Fair Margaret. London: Hutchinson & Co., 1907.

Heart of the World. London: Longmans, Green & Co., 1896.

The Holy Flower. London: Ward, Lock & Co. Ltd, 1915.

The Ivory Child. London: Cassell & Co. Ltd., 1916.

Jess. London: Smith, Elder & Co., 1887.

King Solomon's Mines. London: Collins Classics, 1955.

Lysbeth. London: Longmans, Green & Co., 1951.

The Mahatma and the Hare, a Dream Story. London: Longmans, Green & Co., 1888.

Maiwa's Revenge; or, The War of the Little Hand. London: Longmans, Green & Co., 1888.

Marie. London: Cassell & Co. Ltd., 1912.

Mr. Meeson's Will. London: Longmans, Green & Co., 1894.

Montezuma's Daughter. London: Longmans, Green & Co., 1893.

Nada the Lily. 7th ed. London: Longmans, Green & Co., 1907.

Queen of the Dawn, a Tale of Old Egypt. London: Hutchinson & Co., [1925].

Queen Sheba's Ring. London: Eveleigh Nash, 1910.

Red Eve. London: Hodder & Stoughton, [1911].

'She, A History of Adventure,' *The Graphic*, XXXIV–XXXV (October 2, 1886 – January 8, 1887), Nos. 879–893.

She, A History of Adventure. London: Longmans, Green & Co., 1887.

She, A History of Adventure. London: Longmans, Green & Co., 1921.

She and Allan. London: Hutchinson & Co., 1921.

The Way of the Spirit. London: Hutchinson & Co., 1906.

When the World Shook, Being an Account of the Great Adventure of Bastin, Bickley, and Arbuthnot. London: Cassell & Co. Ltd., 1919.

Wisdom's Daughter, The Life and Love Story of She-Who-Must-Be-Obeyed. London: Hutchinson & Co., 1923.

The Witch's Head. New York: P. F. Collier & Son, n.d.

With Andrew Lang. *The World's Desire*. London: Longmans, Green & Co., 1890.

Books – Non-Fiction

Cetywayo and His White Neighbours; or, Remarks on Recent Events in Zululand, Natal, and the Transvaal. London: Kegan Paul, Trench, Trübner & Co. Ltd., 1896.

The Days of My Life. Edited by C. J. Longman. 2 vols. London: Longmans, Green & Co., 1926.

A Farmer's Year, Being His Commonplace Book for 1898. London: Longmans, Green & Co., 1899.

A Gardener's Year. London: Longmans, Green & Co., 1905.

The Poor and the Land, Being a Report on the Salvation Army Colonies in the United States and at Hadleigh, England, with Scheme of National Land Settlement. London: Longmans, Green & Co., 1905.

Regeneration, Being an Account of the Social Work of the Salvation Army in Great Britain. London: Longmans, Green & Co., 1910.

Rural Denmark and Its Lessons. London: Longmans, Green & Co., 1913.

Rural England, Being an Account of the Agricultural and Social Researches Carried out in the Years 1901 & 1902. 2 vols. 2nd ed. London: Longmans, Green & Co., 1906.

Reviews of Haggard's Writings

Allan Quatermain
    'Gavin Ogilvy.' [J. M. Barrie] *British Weekly*, II (August 5, 1887), p. 218.

Cetywayo
    British Quarterly Review, LXXVI (October 1882), pp. 460–461.
    Literary World (London), XXXVIII (July 27, 1888), pp. 76–78.
    Saturday Review, LIV (August 12, 1882), pp. 213–214.
    Spectator, LV (August 19, 1882), pp. 1089–1090.
    Vanity Fair, XXVIII (July 29, 1882), p. 73.
    Westminster Review, CXXX (July 1888), pp. 100–101.

Child of Storm (*Mameema:* dramatization)
    Athenaeum, CXLIV (October 10, 1914), p. 364.

Cleopatra
    [Henley, W. E.] 'Romance and Farce,' *Scots Observer*, II (July 27, 1889), pp. 275–276.

Colonel Quaritch, V.C.
    [Henley, W. E.] *Scots Observer*, I (December 22, 1888), p. 137.

Dawn
    Athenaeum, LXXXIII (March 22, 1884), p. 372.
    Pall Mall Budget, XXXII (April 4, 1884), p. 27.
    Saintsbury, George. *Academy*, XXV (March 22, 1884), p. 200.
    Vanity Fair, XXXI (April 12, 1884), p. 206.

The Days of My Life
    Collins, J. P. 'Rider Haggard,' *Bookman* (London), LXXI (November 1926), pp. 108–110.
    Hutchinson, Horace G. 'Sir Rider Haggard's Autobiography,' *Edinburgh Review*, CCXLIV (October 1926), pp. 343–355.

Devil Caresfoot (dramatization of *Dawn*)
    'C.H.' *Theatre* (London), X (August 1, 1887), pp. 100–101.

A Farmer's Year

    Athenaeum, LI (January 6, 1900), p. 21.

    Literary World (London), LXI (March 23, 1900), pp. 273–274.

    'Pegasus at the Plow,' *Bookman* (London), XVI (December 1899), p. 88.

    'Rider Haggard as a Farmer,' *New York Times*, XLVIII (August 19, 1899), p. 555.

King Solomon's Mines

    Academy, XXVIII (November 7, 1885), p. 305.

    Athenaeum, LXXXVI (October 31, 1885), p. 568.

    Independent, XXXVII (December 3, 1885), p. 13.

    [Lang, Andrew] *Saturday Review*, LX (October 10, 1885), pp. 485–486.

    Public Opinion, XLVIII (October 30, 1885), p. 551.

    Queen, LXXVIII (November 7, 1885), p. 512.

    Spectator, LVIII (November 7, 1885), p. 1473.

    Times Literary Supplement, April 11, 1958, p. xxii.

    Vanity Fair, XXXVI (November 6, 1885), p. 271.

    'The Wheat and the Chaff,' *Times Literary Supplement*, April 11, 1958, p. xxii.

Regeneration

    Roosevelt, Theodore. 'Rider Haggard and the Salvation Army,' *Outlook*, XCVIII (July 1, 1911), pp. 476–477.

Rural England

    Contemporary Review, LXXXIII (January 1903), pp. 143–145.

    Edinburgh Review, CXCVII (April 1903), pp. 475–500.

    'Mr. Rider Haggard's "Rural England," ' *Spectator*, XC (February 14, 1903), pp. 540–568.

    'The Needs of Rural England,' *Quarterly Review*, CXCVII (April 1903), pp. 540–568.

She

    Athenaeum, LXXXIX (January 15, 1887), pp. 93–94.

    Blackwood's Edinburgh Magazine, CXLI (February 1887), pp. 301–305.

    'H.B.' [Henley, W. E.]. 'London Letter,' *Critic*, VII [N.S.] (February 12, 1887), p. 78.

    Lang, Andrew. *Academy*, XXXI (January 15, 1887), pp. 35–36.

    Literary World (London), XXXV (January 7, 1887), pp. 3–4.

    Murray's Magazine, I (February 1887), p. 287.

    Pall Mall Budget, XXXV (January 6, 1887), p. 28.

    Public Opinion, LI (January 4, 1887), p. 38.

    Queen, LXXXI (January 15, 1887), pp. 88–89.

    Saturday Review, LXIII (January 8, 1887), p. 44.

    Spectator, LX (January 15, 1887), pp. 78–79.

    Vanity Fair, XXXVII (January 22, 1887), p. 66.

She (dramatization)
  Athenaeum, reprinted in *Critic*, X (September 29, 1888), p. 157.
  Illustrated London News, XCIII (September 15, 1888), p. 306.

The Witch's Head
  Athenaeum, LXXXV (January 10, 1885), p. 49.
  Graphic, XXXI (February 14, 1885), p. 166.
  Literary World (Boston), XVI (May 2, 1885), p. 150.
  Literary World (London), XXXI (February 6, 1885), pp. 130–131.
  Pall Mall Budget, XXXIII (January 16, 1885), p. 29.
  Saintsbury, George. *Academy*, XXVII (January 17, 1885), p. 41.
  Saturday Review, LIX (January 17, 1885), pp. 84–85.

The World's Desire (with Andrew Lang)
  Athenaeum, XCVI (December 6, 1890), p. 773.
  Barrie, James. *British Weekly*, IX (November 20, 1890), p. 54.
  [Henley, W. E.] 'Culture and Anarchy,' *National Observer*, V (December 13, 1890), pp. 99–100.
  Literary World (London), XLII (November 28, 1890), pp. 443–444.
  Spectator, LXVI (February 14, 1891), p. 249.

Writings about H. Rider Haggard

'A.D.' 'An Interview with Mr. H. Rider Haggard,' *Christian Commonwealth*, November 1, 1906, pp. 75–76.
'A.M.F.R.' 'A Letter from London,' *Literary World* (Boston), XVIII (March 5, 1887), p. 72.
Besant, Walter. Speech Before the Authors' Club. 'Chronicle and Comment,' *Bookman* (New York), II (November 1895), pp. 179–180.
'Boers Are Loyal, Says Rider Haggard,' *New York Times*, LXIV (October 18, 1914), p. 4.
Books from the Libraries of Sir H. Rider Haggard and Harry and Maurice Buxton Forman. Takeley: Elkin Mathews Ltd., Catalogue 102, May 1940.
Broughton, Mrs. G. 'R.K. and Rider Haggard,' *Kipling Journal*, XXIII (April 1956), pp. 8–10.
'A Chat with Mr. Rider Haggard,' *Graphic*, LXXII (July 29, 1905), pp. 124–125.
'Cheerful about Agriculture. Mr. Rider Haggard at Bungay,' *The Times*, November 27, 1909, p. 13.
Clark, Samuel M. 'Mr. Haggard's Romances,' *Dial*, VIII (May 1887), pp. 5–7.
Cloete, Stuart. Introduction to *She*. London: Collins, 1957, pp. 11–16.
Commissioner H. Rider Haggard,' *Review of Reviews*, XXXII (July 1905), pp. 21–27.
'The Culture of the Horrible: Mr. Rider Haggard's Stories,' *Church Quarterly Review*, XXV (January 1888), pp. 389–411.
Dolman, Fred. *Young Man*, reprinted in 'How Mr. Rider Haggard Works,' *Review of Reviews* (London), IX (January 1894), p. 31.

'The Fall of Fiction,' *Fortnightly Review*, L (September 1, 1888), pp. 324–336.

'Farewell Message to Australia,' *The Times*, June 15, 1916, p. 7.

Flower, Newman. 'The Most Amazing Book Ever Written,' *Radio Times*, June 29, 1956, p. 6.

Gamble, Peter. 'The Two Rider Haggards,' *John O'London's Weekly*, LIII (May 18, 1945), p. 63.

Greene, Graham. Review of L. Haggard, *The Cloak That I Left*. *New States-man and Nation*, XLII (July 14, 1951), p. 45.

'H.B.' [Henley, W. E.] 'London Letter,' *Critic*, VI [N.S.] (April 3, 1886), p. 169.

'H. Rider Haggard,' *Book News*, VIII (June 1890), pp. 344–345.

'H. Rider Haggard,' *New York Post*, May 14, 1925.

'H. Rider Haggard Turned Colonizer,' *New York Herald*, March 19, 1905, p. 3.

Haggard, Lilias Rider. *The Cloak That I Left*. London: Hodder & Stoughton, 1951.

[Henley, W. E.] 'Modern Men: H. Rider Haggard,' *Scots Observer*, I (April 27, 1889), pp. 631–632. See also 'H.B.'

How, Harry. 'Illustrated Interviews. No. VII, Mr. H. Rider Haggard,' *Strand Magazine*, III (January 1892), pp. 3–17.

Michael, Leo. *She, an Allegory of the Church*. New York: Frank F. Lovell & Co., 1889.

'Mr. H. Rider Haggard,' *Literary World* (London), LXXII (March 15, 1906), pp. 121–122.

'Mr. Rider Haggard as Politician,' *Saturday Review*, LXXIX (March 24, 1895), p. 23.

'Mr. Rider Haggard on Small Holdings,' *Spectator*, XCVIII (1907), pp. 968–969.

'Modern Marvels,' *Spectator*, LVIII (October 17, 1885), pp. 1365–1366.

Moore, Augustus M. 'Rider Haggard and "The New School of Romance," ' *Time*, XVI (May 1887), pp. 513–524.

Moore, George. 'Can Mr. Rider Haggard Write?' *Court and Society*, IV (March 30, 1887), p. 305.

O'Brien, E. D. 'The Adventurous Life of a Great Storyteller [Review of L. Haggard, *The Cloak That I Left*],' *Illustrated London News*, CCXVIII (May 26, 1951), p. 857.

Partington, Wilfred. 'Champion of the British Farmer,' *Farmers Weekly*, September 11, 1936, p. 25.

'The Passing Throng,' *New York Daily Tribune*, LIX (February 21, 1900), p. 6.

Prescott, Orville. Introduction to *She and King Solomon's Mines*. New York: Modern Library, 1957, pp. v–ix.

Property of the Late J. E. Scott, Esq. (Sotheby Auction). London: Sotheby & Co., 1951.

Ransome, Arthur. Review of L. Haggard, *The Cloak That I Left*. *Spectator*, LXXXVI (June 15, 1951), pp. 789–790.

'Rider Haggard Here,' *New York Times*, XL (January 11, 1891), p. 8.

'Rider Haggard in Parliament,' *Pall Mall Gazette*, quoted in *New York Times*, XLIV (March 24, 1895), p. 23.

'Rider the Ripper,' *Critic*, XVIII (July 9, 1892), p. 23. Quoted from *Pall Mall Gazette*.

Runciman, James. 'King Plagiarism and His Court,' *Fortnightly Review*, XLVII [N.S.] (March 1890), pp. 421–439.

'Sale of Kessingland Grange,' *The Times*, November 18, 1928, p. 10.

Scott, J. E. *A Bibliography of the Works of Sir Henry Rider Haggard, 1856–1925*. Takeley: Elkin Mathews Ltd., 1947.

Scott, J. E. 'Rudyard Kipling: Two Footnotes, II,' *New Colophon*, I (1948), pp. 335–365.

Scott, J. E. See also *Property of* . . . .

'Sir H. Rider Haggard, His Life and Career,' *The Times*, May 25, 1925, p. 19.

' "Squire" Rider Haggard at Home,' *Literary World* (Boston), XIX (November 10, 1888), p. 393.

'Theophilus.' 'To the Author of "She," ' *Month*, September 1888.

Walpole, Hugh. 'Sir Henry Rider Haggard,' *Dictionary of National Biography*. Edited by J. R. H. Weaver. London: Oxford University Press, 1937, pp. 372–373.

'Where Is Mr. Haggard?' *Review of Reviews*, XXXIII (January 1906), pp. 9–10.

Literary and Historical Background

Adams, Thomas. *Garden City and Agriculture*. London: Simpkin, Marshall, Hamilton, Kent & Co., 1905.

Advertisement, *New York Times Book Review*, LVI (March 19, 1950), p. 22.

'Agriculture,' *Encyclopaedia Britannica*, Vol. I (14th ed., Chicago: Encyclopaedia Britannica, Inc., 1956), p. 360.

Agriculture in Britain. London: Central Office of Information, 1955.

Allen, Ralph Bergen. *Old Icelandic Sources in the English Novel*. Philadelphia: University of Pennsylvania Press, 1933.

Altick, Richard D. *The English Common Reader*. Chicago: University of Chicago Press, 1957.

Asche, Oscar. *Oscar Asche, His Life*. London: Hurst & Blackett, n.d.

Astor, Viscount, and Murray, Keith A. H. *Land and Life*. London: Victor Gollancz Ltd., 1932.

Baker, Ernest A. *Guide to the Best Fiction in English*. New York: Macmillan Co., 1913, 1932.

Baker, Ernest A. *History of the English Novel*. 10 vols. London: H. F. & G. Witherby, 1938.

Baring, Maurice. *The Puppet Show of Memory*. Boston: Little Brown & Co., 1922.

Batho, Edith, and Dobrée, Bonamy. *The Victorians and After*. London: The Crescent Press, 1938.

Bensusan, S. L. *Latter-Day Rural England, 1927*. London: Ernest Benn Ltd., 1928.

Bertram, March, Lisle, and Christian, eds. *Some Harwarden Letters, 1878–1913*. New York: Dodd, Mead, 1918.

Blathwayt, Raymond. *Looking Down the Years*. London: George Allen & Unwin Ltd., 1935.

Bowker, R. R. 'London as a Literary Centre,' *Harper's New Monthly Magazine*, LXXVII (June 1888), pp. 3–26.

Bremont, Comtesse de. *Sonnets and Love Poems*. New York: J. J. Little & Co., 1892.

Brown, Douglas. *Thomas Hardy*. London: Longmans, Green & Co., 1954.

Brown, Horatio F., ed. *Letters and Papers of John Addington Symonds*. London: John Murray, 1923.

Bryant, A. T. *The Zulu People*. Pietermaritzburg: Shuter & Shooter, 1949.

Bryce, James. *Impressions of South Africa*. London: Macmillan & Co., 1899.

Buck, Pearl S. *My Several Worlds*. New York: John Day Co., 1954.

Buckley, Jerome Hamilton. *William Ernest Henley, A Study in 'Counter-Decadence' of the 'Nineties*. Princeton: Princeton University Press, 1945.

Burnham, Mary, ed. *United States Catalogue*. New York: H. W. Wilson Co., 1928.

Burton, Jean. *Heyday of a Wizard*. New York: Alfred A. Knopf, 1944.

Butler, William Francis. *An Autobiography*. New York: Scribner's Sons, 1911.

Cadbury, George, Jun., and Bryan, Tom. *The Land and the Landless*. London: Headley Brothers, 1908.

Calenso, Frances E., and Durnford, E. *History of the Zulu War*. London: Chapman & Hall, 1881.

Cambridge History of the British Empire. See Newton, A. P.

Canton, William. 'Mr. Lang as Poet,' *Bookman* (London), II (August 1895), pp. 24–26.

Carrington, C. E. *The Life of Rudyard Kipling*. New York: Doubleday & Co. Inc., 1955.

Carthew, G. A. *A History, Topographical, Archaeological, Genealogical, and Biographical, of the Parishes of West and East Bradenham*. Norwich: Agas H. Hoose & Co., 1883.

Catalogue of the Gosse Correspondence in the Brotherton Collection. Leeds: The Brotherton Library, 1950.

Catalogue of the Library of Walter Theodore Watts-Dunton, Esq. (Sotheby Auction). London: Dryden Press, 1917.

Catalogue 337. London: Myers & Co., Autumn 1953.

Catalogue 386. London: Myers & Co., Spring 1956.

Cazamian, Madeleine L. *Le Roman et les Idées en Angleterre*. Vol. III. Strasbourg: Librairie Istra, 1955.

Chevalley, Abel. *The Modern English Novel*. New York: Alfred A. Knopf, 1925.

Chew, Samuel C. 'The Nineteenth Century and After (1789–1939),' *A Literary History of England*. Edited by Albert C. Baugh. New York: Appleton-Century-Crofts Inc., 1948.

Child-Villiers, Margaret Elizabeth. *See* Jersey, Dowager Countess of.

Clapham, J. H. *Economic History of Modern Britain*. Vol. III. Cambridge: Cambridge University Press, 1938.

Colvin, Sidney, ed. *The Letters of Robert Louis Stevenson*. 4 vols. New York: Charles Scribner's Sons, 1911.

Connell, John. *W. E. Henley*. London: Constable, 1949.

Conway, William Martin. *Episodes in a Varied Life*. London: Country Life Ltd., 1932.

Cottrell, Leonard. *Lost Cities*. New York: Rinehart & Co., 1957.

Cross, Wilbur L. *The Development of the English Novel*. New York: Macmillan Co., 1923.

Cruse, Amy. *After the Victorians*. London: George Allen & Unwin Ltd., 1938.

Cruse, Amy. *The Victorians and Their Reading*. New York: Houghton Mifflin Co., 1935.

Cumulative Book Index. See Thompson, Nina. R.

Daiches, David. *Stevenson and the Art of Fiction*. New York: Privately printed, 1951.

Darton, F. J. Harvey. *Children's Books in England*. Cambridge: The University Press, 1932.

Darwin, Bernard. 'Country Life and Sport,' *Early Victorian England*. Edited by G. M. Young. Vol. I. London: Oxford University Press, 1951.

De Kiewiet, C. W. *A History of South Africa*. London: Oxford University Press, 1942.

De La Mare, Walter, *Private View*. London: Faber & Faber Ltd., 1953.

De La Mare, Walter, ed. *The Eighteen-Eighties*. Cambridge: The University Press, 1930.

'The Deserted Village,' *The Times*, August 24, 1905, p. 57.

Dicke, B. H. *The Bush Speaks*. Pietermaritzburg: Shuter & Shooter, 1936.

Dickson, Asa Don. *World's Best Books*. New York: H. W. Wilson Co., 1953.

Dictionary of National Biography. See Stephen, Leslie.

Elwin, Malcolm. *Old Gods Falling*. New York: The Macmillan Co., 1939.

Ensor, R. C. K. *England, 1870–1914*. London: Oxford University Press, 1952.

Ernle, Lord. *English Farming Past and Present*. London: Longmans, Green & Co., 1932.

Eybers, G. W., ed. *Select Constitutional Documents Illustrating South African History, 1795–1910*. London: George Routledge & Sons Ltd., 1918.

Five Thousand Books, an Easy Guide to the Best Books. Philadelphia: Curtis Publishing Co., 1895.

Flower, Newman. *Just As It Happened*. New York: William Morrow & Co., 1950.

Fodor, Nandor. *New Approaches to Dream Interpretation*. New York: The Citadel Press, 1951.

Fodor, Nandor. *The Search for the Beloved*. New York: Hermitage Press, 1949.

Fordham, Montague. *Mother Earth*. London: Open Road Publishing Co., 1908.

Foster, Joseph. *Men-at-the-Bar*. 2nd ed. London: Hazell, Watson & Viney Ltd., 1885.

Frazer, James. *The Golden Bough: A Study in Magic and Religion*. Abridged Ed., London: Macmillan & Co. Ltd., 1950.

French, Gerald. *Lord Chelmsford and the Zulu War*. London: John Lane, 1939.

Frierson, William Coleman. *The English Novel in Transition*. Norman: University of Oklahoma Press, 1942.

Fromm, Erich. *The Forgotten Language*. New York: Rinehart & Co. Inc.' 1951.

Fuller, Thomas. *The History of the Worthies of England*. 3 vols. London: Thomas Tegg, 1840.

Furnas, J. C. *Voyage to Windward, The Life of Robert Louis Stevenson*. New York: William Sloane Associates, 1951.

Fussell, G. E. and K. R. *The English Countryman*. London: Andrew Melrose, 1955.

Gerould, Gordon Hall. *The Patterns of English and American Fiction*. Boston: Little, Brown & Co., 1942.

Gissing, Algernon and Ellen, eds. *Letters of George Gissing*. London: Constable & Co., 1937.

Goldberg, B. Z. *The Sacred Fire*. New York: Horace Liveright, 1930.

Goldsmith, Elizabeth E. *Life Symbols*. New York: G.P. Putnam's Sons, 1928.

Gollock, Georgina A. *Daughters of Africa*. London: Longmans, Green & Co., 1932.

Gordon-Brown, Alfred, ed. *The Yearbook and Guide to Southern Africa*. New York: H. W. Wilson, 1952.

Gosse, Edmund. *Critical Kit-Kats*. New York: Dodd, Mead & Co., 1900.

Gosse, Edmund. See *Catalogue of the Gosse Correspondence*.

Graham, Winifred. *That Reminds Me*. London: Skeffington & Sons Ltd., n.d.

Gray, Louis Herbert, ed. *The Mythology of All Races*. 13 vols. Boston: Marshall Jones Co., 1918.

Gray, W. Forbes. *Books That Count, a Dictionary of Standard Books*. London: Adam & Charles Black, 1912.

Green, Lawrence G. *Great African Mysteries*. London: Stanley Paul & Co., [1935].

Green, Roger Lancelyn. *A. E. W. Mason*. London: Max Parrish, 1952.

Green, Roger Lancelyn. *Andrew Lang, A Critical Biography*. Leicester: Edmund Ward, 1946.

Greene, Graham. *The Lost Childhood and Other Essays*. London: Eyre & Spottiswoode, 1954.

'H.F.' 'Tumble of Liberals,' *New York Times*, XLIV (July 28, 1895), p. 1.

Hackett, Alice Payne, *Sixty Years of Best Sellers, 1895–1955*. New York: R. R. Bowker Co., 1956.

Haggard, Lilias Rider. *A Country Scrap-Book*. London: Faber & Faber, 1950.

Haggard, Lilias Rider. *Norfolk Life*. London: Faber & Faber Ltd., 1943.

Hall, A. D. *A Pilgrimage of British Farming*. London: John Murray, 1913.

Hamilton, Cosmo. *Unwritten History*. Boston: Little, Brown & Co., 1924.

Hansen, Agnes Camilla. *Twentieth Century Forces in European Fiction*. Chicago: American Library Association, 1934.

Hardy, Florence Emily. *The Later Years of Thomas Hardy, 1892–1928*. London: Macmillan & Co., 1930.

Hardy, Thomas. 'The Dorsetshire Labourer,' *Longman's Magazine*, II (July 1883), pp. 252–269.

Hastings, James, ed. *Encyclopaedia of Religion and Ethics*. 13 vols. New York: Charles Scribner's Sons, 1951.

Hill, Winifred. *The Overseas Empire in Fiction*. London: Oxford University Press, 1930.

Hobman, D. L. *Olive Schreiner, Her Friends and Time*. London: Watts & Co., 1955.

Hofmeyer, Jan H. *South Africa*. London: Ernest Benn, 1921.

Holliday, Carl. *English Fiction*. New York: The Century Co., 1912.

Home, Mme. Dunglas. *D. D. Home, His Life and Mission*. London: Trübner & Co., 1888.

Hopkins, Gerard Manley. *Letters of Gerard Manley Hopkins to Robert Bridges*. Edited by Claude Colleer Abbott. London: Oxford University Press, 1935.

Houghton, Walter E. *Victorian Frame of Mind, 1830–1870*. New Haven: Yale University Press, 1957.

Howe, Susanne. *Novels of Empire*. New York: Columbia University Press, 1949.

Index Translationum. Paris: International Institute of Intellectual Cooperation and UNESCO, 1932–58. Annual.

James, Henry. *Notes on Novelists*. New York: Charles Scribner's Sons, 1914.

Jeaffreson, John Cordy. *A Book of Recollections*. 2 vols. London: Hurst & Blackett Ltd., 1894.

Jebb, Mrs. John Gladwyn. *A Strange Career: Life and Adventures of John Gladwyn Jebb*. London: William Blackwood & Sons, 1895.

Jersey, Dowager Countess of [Margaret Elizabeth Child-Villiers]. *Fifty-one Years of Victorian Life*. London: John Murray, 1922.

Jones, L. E., *A Victorian Boyhood*. London: Macmillan & Co., 1955.

Jones, Thomas. *A Diary with Letters*. London: Oxford University Press, 1954.

Jung, Carl G. *The Integration of the Personality*. New York: Farrar & Rinehart Inc., 1939.

Jung, Carl G. *Psychology of the Unconscious*. New York: Dodd, Mead & Co., 1952.

Kellner, Leon. *Die Englische Literatur der Neuesten Zeit (von Dickens bis Shaw)*. Leipzig: Verlag von Bernhard Tauchnitz, 1921.

Kingsmill, Hugh. *The Life of D. H. Lawrence*. New York: Dodge Publishing Co., 1938.

Kipling, Rudyard. *Abaft the Funnel*. New York: Doubleday, Page & Co., 1909.

Kipling, Rudyard. *Something of Myself*. London: Macmillan & Co. Ltd., 1937.

Knaplund, Paul. *The British Empire, 1815–1939*. New York: Harper & Brothers, 1941.

Knight, Grant C. *The Novel in English*. New York: Richard R. Smith Inc., 1931.

Kotzé, John. *Biographical Memoirs and Reminiscences*. Cape Town: Maskew Miller Ltd., n.d.

Kotzé, John. *Cases Decided in the High Court of the Transvaal Province, July 1877 to 1881*. London: Stevens & Haynes, 1912.

Krige, E., and Krige, J. D. *The Realm of the Rain-Queen*. London: Oxford University Press, 1947.

Krige, Eileen Jensen. *The Social System of the Zulus*. London: Longmans, Green & Co., 1936.

Land Enquiry Committee. *The Land, The Report of the Land Enquiry Committee, 1909–1912*. 3rd ed. London: Hodder & Stoughton, 1913.

Lang, Andrew. 'The Dreadful Trade,' *Scots Observer*, I (February 16, 1889), pp. 356–357.

Lang, Andrew. *In the Wrong Paradise and Other Stories*. New York: Harper & Bros., 1887.

Lang, Andrew. *A Monk of Fife*. London: Longmans, Green & Co., 1896.

Lang, Andrew. *A Monk of Fife*. New York: Longmans, Green & Co., 1895.

Lang, Andrew. 'A Monk of Fife,' *Monthly Packet*, XC (December 1895), pp. 621–647.

Lang, Andrew. *Prince Prigio*. London: J. W. Arrowsmith, 1889.

Lang, Andrew. *The Poetical Works of Andrew Lang*. Edited by Mrs. Lang. 4 vols. London: Longmans, Green & Co., 1923.

Lang, Andrew. Review of *Tess of the D'Urbervilles*. *New Review*, VI (February 1892), pp. 243–251.

Lawrence, D. H. *The Letters of D. H. Lawrence*. Edited by Aldous Huxley. New York: Viking Press, 1932.

Leavis, Q. D. *Fiction and the Reading Public*. London: Chatto & Windus, 1932.

Lecky, Mrs. William Edward. *Memoir of the Right Honourable William Edward Lecky*. London: Thomas Nelson & Son, 1949.

Leslie, David. *Among the Zulus and Amatongas*. Glasgow: Privately printed, 1875.

Letters Addressed to A. P. Watt. London: A. P. Watt & Son, 1894.

Levy, Hermann. *Large and Small Holdings*. Cambridge: Cambridge University Press, 1911.

Lewis, C. S. 'Of Stories,' *Essays Presented to Charles Williams*. London: Oxford University Press, 1947, pp. 90–105.

Lewis, C. S. *Rehabilitations and Other Essays*. London: Oxford University Press, 1939.

Leyds, W. J. *The First Annexation of the Transvaal*. London: T. Fisher Unwin, 1906.

Leypoldt, Augusta, and Iles, George, eds. *List of Books for Girls and Women and Their Clubs*. Boston: Library Bureau, 1895.

Liberal Land Committee. *The Land and the Nation, A Rural Report of the Liberal Land Committee, 1923–1925*. London: Hodder & Stoughton, n.d.

Lines, Kathleen M. *Four to Fourteen, a Library of Books for Children*. Cambridge: Cambridge University Press, 1950.

Longman, Charles James. *The House of Longman (1724–1800)*. Edited by John E. Chandler. London: Longmans, Green & Co., 1936.

Mabie, Hamilton W. 'The Most Popular Novels in America,' *Forum*, XVI (December 1893), pp. 508–516.

Mackail, Denis. *The Story of J.M.B.* London: Peter Davies, 1941.

Mackenzie, Donald A. *Egyptian Myth and Legend.* London: Gresham Publishing Co., n.d.

Manson, John. *The Salvation Army and the Public.* London: G. Routledge & Sons Ltd., 1910.

Marriott, J. A. R. *The English Land System.* London: John Murray, 1914.

Martineau, John. *The Life and Correspondence of Sir Bartle Frere.* 2 vols. London: John Murray, 1895.

Miller, Henry. *The Books in My Life.* London: Peter Owen Ltd., 1952.

Mott, Frank Luther. *Golden Multitudes.* New York: Macmillan Co., 1947.

Moulton, Richard G., ed. *The Modern Reader's Bible.* New York: Macmillan Co., 1939.

Murray, James A. H., ed. *New English Dictionary on Historical Principles.* Vol. VII. New York: Macmillan Co., 1909.

Nash, Eveleigh. *I Liked the Life I Lived.* London: John Murray, 1941.

Nathan, Manfred. *Paul Kruger: His Life and Times.* Durban. Knox Publishing Co. [1942].

Nathan, Manfred. *South African Literature.* Cape Town: Juta & Co. Ltd., 1925.

Neumann, Erich. *The Great Mother, an Analysis of the Archetype.* New York: Pantheon Books, 1955.

Newton, A. P., Benians, E. A., and Walker, Eric A., eds. *The Cambridge History of the British Empire.* Vol. VIII. Cambridge: Cambridge University Press, 1936.

Norris-Newman, Charles L. *In Zululand with the British Throughout the War of 1879.* London: W. H. Allen & Co., 1880.

Nowell-Smith, Simon. *The House of Cassell, 1848–1958.* London: Cassell & Co. Ltd., 1958.

Oliphant, M. O. W. 'Success in Fiction,' *Forum,* VII (May 1889), pp. 321–322.

Orwell, George. *Inside the Whale.* London: Victor Gollancz Ltd., 1940.

Orwin, C. S. *History of English Farming.* London: Thomas Nelson & Son, 1949.

Parrinder, Geoffrey. *West African Religion.* London: The Epworth Press, 1949.

Pemberton, Max. *Sixty Years Ago and After.* London: Hutchinson & Co., 1936.

Praz, Mario. *The Romantic Agony.* 2nd ed. London: Oxford University Press, 1951.

'Reality and Romance,' *Spectator,* LXI (April 28, 1888), pp. 569–571.

Reference Catalogue of Current Literature. 2 vols. London: J. Whitaker & Sons Ltd., 1951, 1957.

Reitz, F. W. *A Century of Wrong.* London: Review of Reviews, 1900.

Rice, Richard Ashley. *Robert Louis Stevenson, How to Know Him.* Indianapolis: The Bobbs-Merrill Co., 1918.

'Royal Commission on Emigration of Soldiers,' *New York Times,* LXVI (February 17, 1916), p. 3.

'The Ruins in South Africa,' *Chambers's Journal*, reprinted in *Living Age*, CXC (July 4, 1891), pp. 62–64.

Saintsbury, George. *The Collected Essays and Papers of George Saintsbury, 1875–1920.* Vol. III. London: J. M. Dent & Sons Ltd., 1923.

Saintsbury, George. 'The Present State of the Novel,' *Fortnightly Review*, reprinted in *Eclectic Magazine* [N.S.] XLVI (November 1887), pp. 603–608.

Sargent, E. B., and Whishaw, Bernhard. *A Guide Book to Books.* London: Henry Frowde, 1891.

Scarbrough, Dorothy. *The Supernatural in Modern English Fiction.* New York: G. P. Putnam's Sons, 1917.

Schreiber, Hermann and Georg. *Vanished Cities.* New York: Alfred A. Knopf, 1957.

Schreiner, Olive. *The Letters of Olive Schreiner, 1876–1920.* Edited by S. C. Cronwright-Schreiner. London: T. Fisher Unwin Ltd., 1924.

'Simon Pure' [Frank Swinnerton]. *Bookman* (London), LXI (July 1925), p. 560.

Smith, Edwin W., ed. *African Ideas of God.* London: Edinburgh House Press, 1950.

Smith, Janet Adam, ed. *Henry James and Robert Louis Stevenson, A Record of Friendship and Criticism.* London: Rupert Hart-Davis, 1948.

Sonnenschein, William S. *The Best Books.* London: George Routledge & Sons, 1935.

Standard Catalogue for High School Libraries. New York: H. W. Wilson Co., 1952.

Starbuck, Edwin Diller. *A Guide to Books for Character.* Vol II: Fiction. New York: Macmillan Co., 1930.

Stephen, James Kenneth. 'To R.K.,' *Lapsus Calami.* Cambridge: Macmillan and Bowes, 1905.

Stephen, Leslie, ed. *Dictionary of National Biography.* Vol. XVI. London: Smith, Elder & Co., 1888.

Stevenson, Fanny and Robert Louis. *Our Samoan Adventure.* Edited by Charles Neider. New York: Harper & Bros., 1955.

Stevenson, Robert Louis. *Essays of Travel and in the Art of Writing.* New York: Charles Scribner's Sons, 1919.

Stevenson, Robert Louis. *Treasure Island.* New York: Charles Scribner's Sons, 1898.

Stevenson, Robert Louis. See also Colvin.

[Stevenson, Robert Louis, *et al.*] *An Object of Pity; or The Man Haggard.* Amsterdam: Privately printed, n.d.

Squire, Charles. *Celtic Myth & Legend, Poetry & Romance.* London: Gresham Publishing Co., n.d.

Swinnerton, Frank. See 'Simon Pure'.

Theal, G. M. *History of South Africa, 1873 to 1884.* Vol. I. London: George Allen & Unwin Ltd., 1919.

Thompson, Nina R. ed. *Cumulative Book Index.* New York: H. W. Wilson Co., 1957.

Tindall, William York. *Forces in Modern British Literature, 1885–1946.* New York: Alfred A. Knopf, 1947.

'To Talk This Year Across Atlantic,' *New York Times*, LXIV (July 2, 1914), p. 1.

Trevelyan, George Macaulay. *British History in the Nineteenth Century (1782 1901)*. London: Longmans, Green & Co., 1922.

'Two Centuries of Publishing,' *The Times*, November 6, 1924, p. 17.

Uhlendorf, B. A., ed. *Books in Print*. New York: R. R. Bowker Co., 1950, 1957.

United States Catalogue. See Burnham, Mary, ed.

Uys, C. J. *In the Era of Shepstone*. Lovedale: Lovedale Press, 1933.

Uys, C. J. 'Who Came First to South Africa?' *The South Africa-United Kingdom and Commonwealth Survey*. Johannesburg, 1954, pp. 45–47.

Venn, J. A. *Foundations of Agricultural Economics*. Cambridge: Cambridge University Press, 1923.

Walker, Eric A. *A History of South Africa*. London: Longmans, Green & Co., 1928.

Wallis, Wilson D. *Religion in Primitive Society*. New York: F. S. Crofts & Co., 1939.

Wameling, Grete. *Geisterhaftes und Okkultistisches in der Englischen Erzählungs- kunst von 1880 bis 1890*. Ensdetten: Heinr. & J. Lechte, 1931.

Watt, A. P. See *Letters Addressed to . . . .*

Watts-Dunton, Walter Theodore. See *Catalogue of the Library of . . . .*

Weygandt, Anna M. *Kipling's Reading*. Philadelphia: University of Penn- sylvania Press, 1939.

Weygandt, Cornelius. *A Century of the English Novel*. New York: The Century Co., 1925.

Whyte, Frederic. *The Life of W. T. Stead*. 2 vols. London: Jonathan Cape Ltd., n.d.

Woodward, E. L. *The Age of Reform, 1815–1870*. London: Oxford Univer- sity Press, 1952.

Wyndham, Horace. *Mr. Sludge, the Medium*. London: Geoffrey Bles, 1937.

Young, G. M., ed. *Early Victorian England, 1830–1956*. 2 vols. London: Oxford University Press, 1951.

'Zimbabwe,' *Encyclopaedia Britannica*, Vol. XXIII. 14th ed. Chicago: Encyclo- paedia Britannica, Inc., 1956, p. 950.

Index